CAREER DEVELOPMENT AND SYSTEMS THEORY
A New Relationship

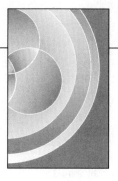

CAREER DEVELOPMENT AND SYSTEMS THEORY
A New Relationship

WENDY PATTON
MARY McMAHON

Queensland University of Technology

Brooks/Cole Publishing Company

I(T)P® An International Thomson Publishing Company

Pacific Grove • Albany • Belmont • Bonn • Boston • Cincinnati • Detroit • Johannesburg
London • Madrid • Melbourne • Mexico City • New York • Paris • Singapore
Tokyo • Toronto • Washington

Sponsoring Editor: *Eileen Murphy*
Marketing Team: *Michael Campbell, Jean Thompson, and Deanne Brown*
Editorial Assistants: *Susan C. Carlson and Julie Lehmann*
Production Editor: *Mary Anne Shahidi*
Manuscript Editor: *Elisabeth Magnus*

Permissions Editor: *Connie Dowcett*
Interior and Cover Design: *Sharon Kinghan*
Interior Illustration: *Suffolk Technical Illustrators*
Art Editor: *Lisa Torri*
Typesetting: *CompuKing*
Printing and Binding: *Webcom*

For more information, contact:

BROOKS/COLE PUBLISHING COMPANY
511 Forest Lodge Road
Pacific Grove, CA 93950
USA

International Thomson Publishing Europe
Berkshire House 168-173
High Holborn
London WC1V 7AA
England

Thomas Nelson Australia
102 Dodds Street
South Melbourne, 3205
Victoria, Australia

Nelson Canada
1120 Birchmount Road
Scarborough, Ontario
Canada M1K 5G4

International Thomson Editores
Seneca 53
Col. Polanco
11560 México, D. F., México

International Thomson Publishing GmbH
Königswinterer Strasse 418
53227 Bonn
Germany

International Thomson Publishing Asia
60 Albert Street
#15-01 Albert Complex
Singapore 189969

International Thomson Publishing Japan
Hirakawacho Kyowa Building, 3F
2-2-1 Hirakawacho
Chiyoda-ku, Tokyo 102
Japan

Printed in Canada

10   9   8   7   6   5   4   3   2   1

Library of Congress Cataloging-in-Publication Data
Patton, Wendy [date]
    Career development and systems theory : a new relationship / Wendy Patton, Mary McMahon.
        p.   cm.
    Includes bibliographical references and index.
    ISBN 0-534-34813-0 (pbk.   :   alk. paper)
    1. Career development.   2. Vocational guidance.   I. McMahon, Mary, [date]   II. Title.
HF65381.P295   1998
331.7'02—dc21

97-52264
CIP

Credits continue on page 287

ABOUT THE AUTHORS

WENDY PATTON has worked in the area of career education and career counseling for 20 years. She was the writer for the Queensland Education Department curriculum materials in career education developed during the early 1980s and worked as a secondary school counselor for several years. After completing her Ph.D. research in youth unemployment, she commenced lecturing at the Queensland University of Technology, where she is a senior lecturer. She coordinates and teaches career theory and other career units in the Master of Education program at Queensland University of Technology. She has an extensive publishing background in writing curriculum documents, research reports and articles, book chapters, and textbook material. She currently edits the *Australian Journal of Career Development*.

MARY MCMAHON has been a secondary guidance officer for seven years and has been involved in training secondary guidance officers in Queensland for the past four years. Her master's degree research involved conducting a cross-sectional study from preschool to twelfth grade to test the applicability of the systems theory framework. She recently earned a Ph.D. at Queensland University of Technology, where she also lectures in educational and career counseling. She has extensive experience in writing professional materials for school counselors and has published in professional journals. In addition, currently she is in constant demand to present workshops to counselors throughout Australia on the practical application of systems theory in career counseling.

C O N T E N T S

C H A P T E R 3
THEORIES FOCUSING ON PROCESS   36

C H A P T E R 4
THEORIES FOCUSING ON CONTENT AND PROCESS   58

C H A P T E R 5
COMPARISON OF THE MAJOR THEORIES   78

C H A P T E R 8
SYSTEMS THEORY   134

C H A P T E R 9
A SYSTEMS THEORY FRAMEWORK OF CAREER DEVELOPMENT   154

P A R T III
SYSTEMS THEORY AND CAREER PRACTICE   179

C H A P T E R 10
LIFELONG CAREER DEVELOPMENT LEARNING   180

C H A P T E R 11
CAREER DEVELOPMENT LEARNING SYSTEMS   192

C H A P T E R 12
CAREER DEVELOPMENT LEARNING IN SCHOOL SYSTEMS 207

C H A P T E R 13
THERAPEUTIC SYSTEMS 225

CHAPTER 14
LIFELONG LEARNING IN SUPERVISORY SYSTEMS   244

T A B L E S

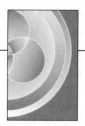

FIGURES

PREFACE

There is little disagreement within the career theory field that, while there are a number of theoretical propositions and models accounting for career behavior, the field remains segmented, incomplete, and lacking in comprehensiveness and coherence. Each theory or model offers explanations about differing parts of the process of career development. Such a theoretical base, however, presents difficulties for instructors attempting to provide students with an integrated theoretical base on which to prepare for career practice.

The issue of whether career theories need integration or convergence has been debated, and texts have been written on this issue. A related debate within the career field is the relationship between theory and practice, with authors suggesting that practitioners either disregard theory because of its irrelevance or adhere rigidly to one theory only because of the confusion engendered by trying to come to terms with many theories.

It is against this background that we have developed a metatheoretical framework for the integration of career theories using systems theory and have presented it in this text. We also propose the value of the systems theory framework in developing a relationship between theory and practice centered on the individual. For these reasons, the present text is a valuable addition to the field.

The principles of systems theory emphasize the self-organizing nature of open systems. In portraying the field of career theory as a system, open to changes and developments from within itself and through constantly interrelating with other systems, this book adds to the pattern of knowledge and relationships between knowledge within the career field. The contents of this book will be incorporated into the field as representative of a shift in understanding existing relationships within theories. In the same way, each reader will integrate the contents of the book with his or her existing views about the current state of career theory and with his or her current theory-practice relationship.

OUTLINE OF THE BOOK

The book is divided into three parts. Part One, consisting of six chapters, presents a comprehensive review of the existing theoretical literature. While a number of comprehensive reviews of the literature exist (D. Brown & Brooks, 1990b; 1996b; Hackett & Lent, 1992; Hackett, Lent, & Greenhaus, 1991; Osipow & Fitzgerald, 1996), the present review traces the progress of career theory from content and process, approaches to those that reflect both content and process and illustrates its movement toward theory integration and convergence.

Chapter 1 presents an overview of the field and discusses the overall content and structure of the existing state of career theory. Chapter 2 introduces theories focusing on content. It therefore traces the field from the work of Parsons to trait-and-factor theories and the more recent person-environment fit theories. It includes the work of Holland, Bordin, D. Brown, Dawis and Lofquist, and the recent "Big Five" personality theory work of McRae and John. Chapter 3 presents theories that focus on the process of career development, including the work of Ginzberg and his colleagues; Super; Tiedeman and O'Hara and Miller-Tiedeman; and Tiedeman; and L. S. Gottfredson. Theories that focus on content (of the individual and the context) *and* process are reviewed in Chapter 4; these include the work of L. K. Mitchell and Krumboltz; the work of Roe; the social cognitive approach of Lent and his colleagues; the developmental-contextual approach of Vondracek, Lerner, and Schulenberg; and the action approach of Young, Valach, and Collin. A table illustrating the theories reviewed, their major themes, and the diversity and commonality between and across them is presented at the end of each of Chapters 2 through 4. Chapter 5 presents an overview of these main theories, including a discussion of their similarities and differences. Finally, Chapter 6 focuses on some of the areas that have been insufficiently dealt with in existing theories. It therefore reviews theories proposed to account for the career development of women, racial and ethnic minorities, lesbians and gay men, and socioeconomic groups.

Part Two of the book consists of three chapters. It represents the theoretical core of the book and links Parts One and Two. Part Two explores the traditional philosophical underpinnings of career theory and practice and traces some of the more recent philosophical directions driving change. Chapter 7 describes philosophical underpinnings of the field and recent changes and presents the history of previous integrative frameworks. Finally, it outlines the recent moves toward integration and convergence in the career theory literature. Chapter 8 describes the development of systems theory and presents its important elements. The relationship between these elements and aspects of career theory and practice is included. Chapter 9 outlines our systems theory framework of career development that has been developed over a number of years. The discussion in this chapter emphasizes the relationship of the framework with existing theories.

Part Three of the book consists of five chapters that address the integration of theory and practice through the concept of lifelong learning systems. In particular, Chapter 10 advances the concept of lifelong career development learning, emphasizing the notion of career as being defined within the individual as learner. Chapter 11 examines the issue of learning from a systems theory perspective through the theme of learning systems and presents a specific example of the learning systems necessary for the training and preparation of career development facilitators. Chapters 12, 13, and 14 apply the concept of learning systems to traditional career development learning settings. In particular, Chapter 12 discusses career development learning in school settings, and Chapter 13 describes career counseling as a process of learning from a systems theory perspective. Finally, Chapter 14 examines supervision as a learning system that facilitates the lifelong learning of career development facilitators.

The present book is the first to offer an encompassing framework for career theory convergence using a metatheoretical approach. In addition, the framework is presented in an unfolding series of graphic illustrations. These illustrations are also included as representations of learning systems in Part Three, which includes specific examples of the use of systems theory elements in teaching and learning and in counseling. Another unique feature of the book is the presentation of tables that illustrate similarities and differences between theories.

While each of the chapters of the book can be read separately according to the learning needs of the individual learner, within systems theory thinking, each of the chapters contributes to a whole and has been written as such. The whole story of the book will be less meaningful without attention to each of the parts, and the following themes are present throughout the book:

• development and change within career theories
• the trend toward integration and convergence of career theories
• the role of systems theory and the systems theory framework
• the embeddedness of systems theory in career practice
• the embeddedness of lifelong learning in career development

To encourage your exploration of the whole book, we have made frequent references to related chapters or parts where we believe that this will help you develop your own sense of patterns and relationships within the book and your existing knowledge.

ACKNOWLEDGMENTS

The production of this book is an example of systems theory at work. The book evolved over a number of years, and our revisions have been related to our interactions with each other and with members of our interconnected systems. Thus it has evolved through ongoing learning, coconstruction of ideas, and developments of new meaning. The book represents our understanding at this point in time.

We would like to thank the following reviewers for their helpful insights and suggestions: Paul Blisard, Southwest Missouri State University; LeeAnn Eschbach, University of Scranton; Lynda Mitchell, California State University–Los Angeles; Margaret Pinder, Amber Univesity; Ann Puryear, Southeast

Missouri State University; and Sandra Tomlinson-Clarke, Rutgers, The State University of New Jersey.

Many people have been invaluable parts of our system in this process. We acknowledge and thank them in the following graphic of our system.

Wendy Patton
Mary McMahon

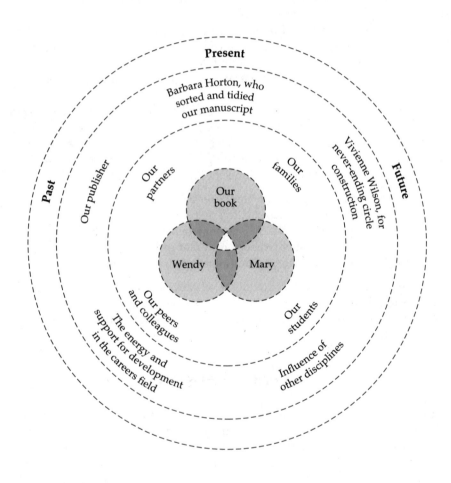

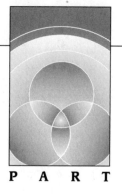

I

REVIEW OF
EXISTING THEORIES

1

RATIONALE FOR A
SYSTEMS THEORY PERSPECTIVE

Career development theory has had a relatively short history. Reflecting on this, Isaacson and Brown (1993) commented that "the behavioural sciences," of which career development theory is a part, "are still in a developmental stage" (p. 20). This is not surprising, since vocational guidance, the precursor to career development counseling, did not begin until the early 1900s. Parsons (1909) is credited with being the founder of vocational guidance. He identified three elements of career selection: self-knowledge, knowledge of the world of work, and "true reasoning on the relations of these two groups of facts" (Parsons, 1909, p. 5). In terms of today's thinking about career development, Parson's view of career selection was simplistic. However, much of the current work in career counseling and career education for career choice remains structured around these three elements.

Out of these beginnings, trait and factor theories that focused on the content of career choice, such as characteristics of the individual and of the workplace, evolved. Developmental theories, which placed more emphasis on the stages and process of career development, followed later. More recently, theorists have focused on both content and process, including the interaction between these and the role of cognition in the process. However, the broadening of the concept of career development has far outpaced the evolution of theory to account for career development. In addition, the unprecedented and ongoing rapid changes occurring within the workplace and in individual careers demand flexible and adaptive career theory. Thus, the present state of career development theory has been the subject of considerable criticism (e.g., Brown

& Brooks, 1990b). Before exploring the field, however, it is important to discuss present definitions of career and career development.

DEFINITIONS

THE MEANING OF "CAREER"

It is clear that the term *career* is still variously understood. This lack of conceptual clarity maintains ambiguity and continues to prevent the development of a common ground of thinking in this area. From the time of Parsons (1909), the terms *career, vocation,* and *occupation* have often been used synonymously (McDaniels & Gysbers, 1992). Traditional definitions restricted *career* to a professional work life that included advancement, and several researchers have proposed broadening this conceptual definition (e.g., Byrne & Beavers, 1991). For example, the Department of Education and Science (1989) defined *career* as "the variety of occupational roles which individuals will undertake throughout life. It includes: paid and self employment; the different occupations which a person may have over the years and periods of unemployment; and unpaid occupations such as that of student, voluntary worker or parent" (p. 2).

The concept of career has expanded to include prevocational and postvocational activities, as in the definition proposed by Super in 1976: "the sequence of major positions occupied by a person throughout his preoccupational, occupational and postoccupational life; includes work related roles such as those of student, employee, and pensioner, together with complementary vocational, familial and civil roles" (p. 20). A more concise definition, that of Arthur, Hall, and Lawrence (1989), described career as "the evolving sequence of a person's work experiences over time" (p. 8), again emphasizing the centrality of the themes of work and time.

A number of writers have gone further and have proposed alternative terms to describe career, such as *working life* (Thomas, 1989) and *work history* (Nicholson & West, 1989). These latter authors "recommend use of the more neutral term 'work histories' to denote sequences of job experiences and reserve the term 'career' for the sense people make of them" (p. 181). However, Arthur et al. (1989) maintained that career "better captures the focal relationship between work and time" and were emphatic that "everyone who works has a career" (p. 9), indicating that the term *career* can be a neutral descriptive term applied to all occupations. Richardson (1993, 1996) suggested that career is a limited and irrelevant concept and subject to a middle-class bias in perception. She proposed that theoreticians and practitioners focus on how people create their own definitions of work in their lives and suggested that we use the terms *work, jobs,* and *career* in our discussion of work and career. For example, work that involves community welfare and social activity—"caring work"—is often included in people's definitions of their career-related or work activity.

Expounding on this theme, Miller-Tiedeman (1988) and Miller-Tiedeman and Tiedeman (1990) discussed the concept of "lifecareer," which expresses the integration of career and other aspects of an individual's life. Similarly, Collin and Watts (1996) discussed the need to focus on career as a subjective construction of the individual rather than something that is objective, and Herr (1992) emphasized that careers do not exist as jobs or occupations do but rather are created by individuals. We concur with these more recent constructions of career, perceiving that people develop a career on the basis of their perceptions of, and attitudes toward, career.

CAREER DEVELOPMENT

These broader definitions of career draw attention to the concept of career development, which Brown and Brooks (1990b) described as being "for most people a lifelong process of getting ready to choose, choosing, and typically continuing to make choices from among the many occupations available in our society" (p. xvii). The concept of career development was first advanced by Ginzberg, Ginsburg, Axelrad, and Herma (1951), who proposed that occupational choice is a developmental process that occurs over a number of years. Their original theory, which assumed that the process was completed in early adulthood, was later revised to recognize occupational choice as a lifelong process of decision making (Ginzberg, 1972, 1984). More recently, Pryor (1985b) described career development as a series of continuous decisions about career choice. The importance of acknowledging career development over the life span is incorporated in the following definition: "Career development is the total constellation of psychological, sociological, educational, physical, economic and chance factors that combine to shape the career of an individual over the life span" (Sears, 1982, p. 139). Similarly, for Wolfe and Kolb (1980),

> Career development involves one's whole life, not just occupation. As such, it concerns the whole person. . . . More than that, it concerns him or her in the ever-changing contexts of his or her life. The environmental pressures and constraints, the bonds that tie him or her to significant others, responsibilities to children and aging parents, the total structure of one's circumstances are also factors that must be understood and reckoned with. In these terms, career development and personal development converge. Self and circumstances—evolving, changing, unfolding in mutual interaction—constitute the focus and the drama of career development.

We favor this dynamic definition, which encompasses the individual, the environment, interaction, and change as the key elements of a definition of career development.

PRESENT STATUS OF CAREER DEVELOPMENT THEORY

A number of authors have pointed out that career development theory is still in its infancy (Brown, 1990; Hackett & Lent, 1992; Isaacson & Brown, 1993). While theoretical propositions and models have proliferated during the previous four decades, conclusions within the literature generally agree that it remains inadequate and incomplete (Brown, 1990; Warnath, 1975) and lacking in comprehensiveness and coherence (Brown, 1990; Gallos, 1989), particularly in its failure to account for diversity within the population. In addition, it has been criticized for focusing on intraindividual issues to the detriment of contextual issues (Collin & Young, 1986) and for being hampered by an overlap in conceptualization of many elements (Borgen, 1991; Osipow, 1990).

Further, career theory has been criticized for its tendency, both within individual theoretical models (Super, 1990) and within the disciplinary field (Arthur et al., 1989; Hackett, Lent, & Greenhaus, 1991), to be formed by the accretion of discrete segments. For example, Super (1990) acknowledged that his theoretical formulation was segmental and represented an effort to bring together concepts from various branches of psychology. In reflecting on the growth of career development theory, Osipow (1983) commented that "vocational psychology seems to be moving towards a collection of miniature theories, each dealing with circumscribed, explicit segments of vocational behavior" (p. 323). This seems to have been an accurate prediction: in 1996, Osipow and Fitzgerald maintained that little had changed.

Despite this dismal picture, Osipow (1983) acknowledged that career development theory was only beginning and assured researchers and practitioners that an incomplete theory is better than no theory. In addition, several authors (e.g., Gottfredson, 1983) have commented on the importance of the contributions made by the existing theories to our overall understanding of career behavior. The field of career theory has experienced considerable growth in recent years, and while some theoretical formulations have been accorded less significance (e.g., Ginzberg, 1984; Roe & Lunneborg, 1990), others have been expanded and refined (e.g., Holland, 1985a, 1992; Super, 1990, 1992), and still others have been and continue to be created (e.g., Brown, 1996a; Lent, Brown, & Hackett, 1994).

More recently, theorists, noting the disparity of the numerous existing theories and the need to use more than one theory to describe the complexity of career development, have acknowledged the value to be gained from attempting to provide a more integrative theoretical picture of career development. Thus, the concept of integration or convergence within career development theory has emerged (Borgen, 1991; Osipow, 1990) and promises to be the issue of the 21st century in this field. Osipow (1990) noted that current theoretical approaches are evolving toward similarities, although they still differ in the stress placed on the constituent elements and themes. Other authors have called for the integration of career theory through the development of an overarching theory or framework of career development (Dawis, 1994; Hackett et al., 1991).

Convergence in career development theory was the specific focus of a 1992 conference, papers from which were published in Savickas and Lent (1994). This conference illustrated the importance of the trend toward integration of career theories, despite varying views of the definition of convergence, its value, and the form it might take. Brown and Brooks (1996b) remained skeptical about the likelihood of convergence among theories and the emergence of an integrated theory. We believe that convergence is occurring and that systems theory can provide an overarching framework within which commonalities and relationships in existing career development theory can be identified. The issue of integration and convergence will be expanded in Chapter 7, and the systems theory framework will be outlined in Chapter 9 following an explanation of systems theory in Chapter 8.

THE STRUCTURE OF CAREER DEVELOPMENT THEORY

This section provides an overview of the structure of career theory and presents the framework within which the theories will be discussed in more detail later in Part 1. The segmental nature of career development theory discussed previously is reflected in attempts to categorize and group the theories. Herr and Cramer (1992) identified eight different groupings that had been offered by a number of authors, including those of Crites (1969), who distinguished psychological and nonpsychological theories, and Osipow (1968), who classified theories as trait-and-factor approaches, sociology and career choice, self-concept theory, and vocational choice and personality theories. Herr and Cramer (1992) grouped the theories as trait and factor, actuarial or matching, decision, situational or sociological, psychological, and developmental. While acknowledging the arbitrariness of their categorization, Osipow and Fitzgerald (1996) grouped the theories as trait-factor, society and career choice, developmental/ self-conceptions, vocational choice and personality, and behavioral approaches, and Osipow (1990) grouped them as developmental, trait oriented, reinforcement based, and personality focused. In reflecting on the different groupings, Herr and Cramer (1992) commented that "the categories depicted are not mutually exclusive or independent, but they attempt to explain differential career behavior and choice from somewhat different vantage points" (p. 156).

Hackett et al. (1991) noted that "these theories generally highlight the content and/or process of decision making" (p. 4). In this book, we have chosen content and process as the dimensions on which to categorize career development theories, a tactic also adopted by Minor (1992). *Content* refers to the influences on career development, such as interests and values, and *process* refers to accounts of change over time and decision-making processes. Historically, career development theory focused on either content or process. Major theories focusing on the content of career development include the psychological approaches of trait and factor theory (Holland, 1973, 1985a, 1992; Parsons, 1909), Bordin's psychodynamic theory (1990), Brown's (1996a) values-based theory, the work adjustment person-environment correspondence theory (Dawis, 1996; Dawis & Lofquist, 1984), and the personality-based five-factor theory (McCrae & John, 1992). The developmental theories of Ginzberg et al. (1951), Ginzberg (1972, 1984), and Super (1953, 1957, 1980, 1990, 1992, 1994) have attempted to account for the process of career development. While Gottfredson (1981, 1996) specifically attempted to include both content and process variables into her model, this book has categorized her with the process theorists, since she focused on developmental stages. This categorization of her work as developmental has also been made by others (Brown, 1996b; Osipow & Fitzgerald, 1996). The work of Miller-Tiedeman and Tiedeman (1990) also focused on stages and is included in the process category.

More recently, the need for theory to take into account both content (characteristics of the individual and the context) and process (their development and the interaction between them) has been recognized. Theoretical models based on social learning theory, recently conceptualized as the social cognitive theory of Bandura (1986), include the learning theory of Mitchell and Krumboltz (1990, 1996), the social cognitive perspective (Lent, Brown, & Hackett, 1996), and the cognitive information-processing approach (Peterson, Sampson, Reardon, & Lenz, 1996). Context-based approaches include Vondracek, Lerner, and Schulenberg's (1986) developmental-contextual approach and the contextual approach to career (Young, Valach, & Collin, 1996). In addition, we include the work of Roe (Roe, 1957; Roe & Lunneborg, 1990) in this category, since her work considered characteristics of the individual and of the context.

Much of existing theory has been criticized for not adequately taking into account issues of socioeconomic status, women and racial and ethnic groups, and other minority groups such as lesbians and gay men. Thus, a body of theory has been developed to attempt to explain the career development issues of individuals in these groups. In particular, Astin (1984), Hackett and Betz (1981), Farmer (1985), and Betz and Fitzgerald (1987) have presented theoretical explanations for the career development of women. While sociological or situational approaches can be categorized in terms of content and process, we have discussed them in Chapter 6 of this book, which focuses on issues that have received too little attention. In particular, we discuss the work of Roberts (1977), Blau and Duncan (1967), Miller (1983), and Hotchkiss and Borow (1996).

Theorizing about career development of racial and ethnic groups is at a particularly early stage of development (Arbona, 1996; Hackett et al., 1991; Smith, 1983). While broader theories have attempted to acknowledge the effects of race (e.g., Gottfredson, 1981; Super, 1990), these perspectives generally have not been integrated within their theoretical models. Gottfredson's (1986) concept of "at-risk" factors in career choice, originally proposed as a framework for assessment and intervention in career counseling, is especially useful in considering such potential barriers to career choice as gender, sexual orientation, racial/ethnic minority, disability, and socioeconomic status.

Another "major individual difference category" (p. 112) identified by Fitzgerald and Betz (1994) is that of sexual orientation. Morgan and Brown (1991) discussed three theories of women's career development (Astin, 1984; Farmer, 1985; Gottfredson, 1981) and identified propositions from which practitioners can extract relevant elements in working with lesbians and gay men. The authors stressed, however, that existing theories in general are inapplicable to the career development concerns of lesbians and gay men.

Some theoretical models are less easily categorized into one group. For example, Gottfredson's (1981, 1996) circumscription and compromise theory proposes a stage model of the development of the self-concept but also includes contextual variables. The model proposed by Miller-Tiedeman and Tiedeman (1990) also focuses on context but proposes a stage approach to an individual's career choice and implementation. Both of these theories have been categorized as developmental theories in this text.

The work of Vondracek et al. (1986) drew heavily on the principles of developmental psychology, but we have grouped it with the context approaches. Because it stresses the importance of environmental variables, the work of Gottfredson has also been classified under social systems perspectives by other authors. In addition, its contribution to theories of career development of women and racial and ethnic groups has been noted.

Just as there is no agreement in the literature on the grouping of career development theories, there is no agreement on which theories remain the most influential. The review by Osipow (1990) focused on the work of Holland, Super, Dawis and Lofquist, and Krumboltz. Watkins (1994a) referred to "the real Big Five"—the theoretical models of Bordin, Dawis and Lofquist, Holland, Krumboltz, and Super—as those that continue to be strongly influential. The third edition of Brown and Brooks (1996a) restricted theories to those that are "currently influencing either research or practice" (p. ix) and included the work of Holland, Dawis, Super, Gottfredson, and Krumboltz, as well as sociological approaches. Theoretical perspectives characterized by Brown and Brooks as emerging included Brown's values-based model, social cognitive (Lent et al., 1996) and cognitive information-processing (Peterson et al., 1996) approaches, and the contextual approach of Young et al. (1996).

In tracing the progress of career development theory away from either content or process thinking and toward a more integrated perspective, Chapters 2 through 6 of this book provide as comprehensive a review as possible. Further, like Osipow and Fitzgerald (1996), we take a broad view of what is important and influential in career development theory. We include a large number of theories, with the aim of focusing on the role that each has played in the evolution of career development theory. In particular, we focus on how each theory has developed in response to others, and the theories' similarities and differences. We believe that all theories have a place in our understanding of career behavior.

RELATIONSHIP WITH OTHER FIELDS

Our perspective on the potential of systems theory to provide an overarching framework for career theories comes out of counseling theory. Both career development and counseling and psychotherapy are characterized by a diverse range of theoretical views. In counseling and psychotherapy, this diversity has been addressed by the concept of eclecticism.

In reflecting on the move toward eclecticism in counseling, Corey (1991) commented that "one reason for the trend towards eclectic and integrative perspectives is the recognition that no single theory is comprehensive enough to account for the complexities of human behavior, especially when the range of client types and their specific problems are taken into consideration" (p. 427). Corey further claimed that "eclecticism should instead be thought of as a way to harmoniously blend theoretical concepts and methods into a congruent framework" (p. 426). It offers the opportunity to integrate existing perspectives and transcend individual models.

It is instructive to examine the implications of these comments in relation to career theory. First, given the diverse and complex range of influences and theoretical perspectives on career development, it is probable that no single theory can be comprehensive enough (Super, 1992). Second, it is unlikely that one theory could adequately account for the career development of all individuals in all epochs. Third, acceptance of one comprehensive theory raises doubts about the future of the more "'narrow' schools" (Corey, 1991, p. 426). Thus, the question is raised whether the career development literature needs, or indeed can provide, one comprehensive theory that synthesizes and incorporates all others or whether it needs a "congruent framework" that is able to "harmoniously blend theoretical concepts and methods" (Corey, 1991, p. 426).

DEVELOPMENT OF THE SYSTEMS THEORY APPROACH

The perspective presented in this book therefore draws on counseling theory and systems theory (Plas, 1992; von Bertalanffy, 1968). Systems theory is well established in other fields, such as family therapy, but it is relatively new to career development theory. While its potential was acknowledged as early as 1983 (Osipow, 1983), and while theorists and researchers have commented on its applicability at various levels (e.g., Collin, 1985; Krumboltz & Nichols, 1990; see Chapter 8 of this book), its potential as an overarching framework has not been explored. Systems theory is broadly based and is able to take into account the diversity and complexity of the influences on career development and thus of career development itself. Its elements are present in a number of perspectives being discussed in relation to careers and career development. For example, L. S. Hansen (1997) developed her integrative life planning perspective on principles of interconnectedness, relatedness, and wholeness, emphasizing that all parts must work together to maintain the whole. Hall (1996) similarly asserted that we need a relational approach to career that features mutuality and interdependence.

Each of these concepts is derived to some degree from systems theory. While this theory will be described in considerably more detail in Chapter 8, key aspects are outlined here. They include:

- an emphasis on wholeness and the interrelationship of parts within a whole
- view of the whole as greater than the sum of its parts
- the inclusion of elements from a variety of fields (e.g., while developmental psychology refers to the importance of a stage approach to career development and sociology raises the importance of socioeconomic status, both are relevant in varying ways to individuals' systems)
- an emphasis on mutuality of action and interaction—that is, the dynamic and recursive impact of the individual and the context on each other

The emphasis in systems theory is on the recursiveness, or ongoing relationship, between elements or subsystems of the system and the changes that occur over time as a result of these continual interactions. The application of systems theory to career development allows the disparate concepts addressed in the literature to be drawn together in one theoretical framework. This does not make the existing theories redundant or devalued; rather, each can be viewed in the context of all available theory.

Thus, the present book uses a systems theory framework to explore career development. This framework was first presented as a contextual model for understanding adolescent career decision making (McMahon, 1992). It has been further developed and broadened on the basis of two premises: (1) context is an integral part of systems theory, and (2) decision making is an integral part of career development (McMahon & Patton, 1995). Broadening the original model to develop a systems theory framework provided the following advantages (discussion of these will be expanded in Chapter 9):

1. The important contribution of all career theories can be recognized.
2. Similarities, differences, and interconnections between theories can be demonstrated.
3. The contribution to career development theory and practice of other fields, such as family therapy, can be recognized.
4. Systems theory brings to career development a congruence between theory and practice and new approaches for use in career practice.
5. The emphasis is placed on the individual and not on theory. Therefore, systems theory can be applicable at a macro level of theory analysis, as well as at a micro level of individual analysis.
6. A systems theory perspective enables practitioners to choose the theory that is most relevant to the needs and situation of each individual, thus drawing on key constructs of all theories.
7. Systems theory offers a perspective that underlies the philosophy reflected in the move from positivist approaches to constructivist approaches.

While not preempting a fuller discussion of the systems theory framework that we have developed (which will be discussed in Chapter 9), it is necessary here to outline the variables (termed *influences*) that are included in the framework, since they will form the basis of the comparison tables in Chapters 2 through 4. These influences have been derived from the career theory literature. Systems theory is used to illustrate their interrelationships in the context of individual career development. Systems theory provides the framework for a macro-level analysis of theory and also facilitates a micro-level analysis of an individual's career development.

The systems theory framework is composed of several key interrelated systems, including the intrapersonal system of the individual, the social system, and the environmental/societal system. The processes between these systems are explained via the recursive nature of interaction within and between these systems, change over time, and chance. The *individual system* is composed of several intrapersonal content influences, including gender, age, self-concept, health, ability, disability, physical attributes, beliefs, personality, interests, values, aptitudes, skills, world of work knowledge, sexual orientation, and ethnicity. Influences representing the content of the *social system* include peers, family, media, community groups, the workplace, and education institutions. *Environmental/societal system* influences include political decisions, historical trends, globalization, socioeconomic status, the employment market, and geographical location. Process influences include chance, change over time, and recursiveness.

CONCLUSION

This book presents a review of the existing theoretical literature from its early development through recent attempts to account for the complexity of career development more comprehensively. Moves toward integration and convergence of the theory literature are examined, and the development of a systems theory framework designed to provide conceptual unity to the field of career development theory is described. We believe that such a framework can forge a new pattern of relationships between existing theories and between theory and practice.

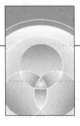

2

THEORIES FOCUSING ON CONTENT

A study of theories focusing on content historically takes us to the origins of career development theory and the work of Frank Parsons at the turn of the 20th century. In essence, theories of content "predict career choices from individual characteristics" (Minor, 1992, p. 14). Parsons' (1909) work gave rise to what is now known as trait-and-factor theory. Despite criticism, discussed later in this chapter, trait-and-factor models based in the early theorizing of Parsons continue to dominate practice and cannot be disregarded. A study of theories focusing on content is important for two reasons: It introduces many of the key concepts essential to an understanding of career development, and it provides a historical overview of the evolution of this field of study.

This chapter will trace the historical development of career theory, particularly theories focusing on content. The dominant theoretical approaches of trait-and-factor theory and, more recently, person-environment fit theory will be discussed. The work of Parsons (1909) and the five-factor model or Big Five (McCrae & John, 1992; Pryor, 1993) will be examined as examples of trait-and-factor theory, and the work of Holland (1966, 1973, 1985a, 1987, 1992), Dawis and Lofquist (1976, 1984), and Dawis (1992, 1994, 1996) will be examined as examples of person-environment fit theory. In addition, the work of D. Brown (1996a) and Bordin (1990) will be discussed as examples of theories focusing on content. Similarities and differences between these theories will be examined.

THE WORK OF FRANK PARSONS

Frank Parsons is seen by many as the founder of modern career guidance, since his "work has had a lasting influence" on the field (McDaniels & Watts, 1994,

p. 263). Possibly his best known contribution is his identification of three key elements of career selection:

- First, a clear understanding of yourself, aptitudes, abilities, interests, resources, limitations, and other qualities.
- Second, a knowledge of the requirements and conditions of success, advantages and disadvantages, compensation, opportunities, and prospects in different lines of work.
- Third, true reasoning on the relations of these two groups of facts. (Parsons, 1909, p. 5)

Each of these three elements represents a major contribution to career theory and practice, both of which "formed a seamless amalgam to Parsons" (Spokane & Glickman, 1994, p. 299)—a point that is in itself significant, given recent debate on the links between theory and practice (Savickas & Walsh, 1996a).

Parsons' approach to the first element, self-knowledge, "is strikingly consistent with the contemporary practice of career assessment" (Zytowski & Swanson, 1994, p. 305). His format for career counseling interviews was designed to gather comprehensive information from individuals through a course of questioning, by the end of which the counselor was "able, as a rule, to classify the applicant with a reasonable degree of accuracy" (Parsons, 1909, p. 19). In so doing, Parsons acknowledged that individuals differ in terms of their interests, abilities, values, personality, and skills. Parsons suggested that this process would take 15 minutes, a length of time that by today's counseling standards seems remarkably short. He also developed the first self-assessment form, a comprehensive questionnaire of over 100 questions that clients completed before their career counseling interview. His assessment and interview process "established the format for career counseling" (Holland, 1987, p. 29). Thus, while Parsons introduced the concept of career assessment, it was not until the development of the psychometrics movement (discussed later in this chapter) that the tools needed to efficiently enhance self-knowledge and provide links to the world of work were provided.

Parsons' second element was knowledge about the world of work, which he considered vital to comprehensive career planning and development. Parallels can be drawn between the information sources advocated for use by Parsons with those used by modern-day career counselors, including lists and classifications of industries, information on training and courses, and general industry information. Thus, the development of career information delivery systems so essential to modern career guidance also has its origins in the work of Parsons.

Parsons' concept of "true reasoning" is, in the opinion of Herr and Cramer (1992), his "most enduring contribution" (p. 5). While "true reasoning" was never fully explained, it seems that he saw cognitive processes and analytical skills as fundamental to career selection. This reflects the visionary nature of his work and again emphasizes its relevance to modern career guidance.

These three much-cited concepts are those for which Parsons is best remembered. Less attention has been given to some aspects of his "personal record and self-analysis questionnaire" (Parsons, 1909, p. 27). As well as gathering information on abilities and interests, he invited the applicant to reflect on contextual influences such as family, health, resources (including financial situation), relatives and friends, lifestyle, and mobility. While he did not explain how this information was used, he did at least include it in the assessment process, a point that seems to have been overlooked in the development of the trait-and-factor theories.

Parsons' (1909) work represents the "first conceptual framework for career decision making and became the first guide for career counselors" (D. Brown & Brooks, 1996b, p. 1). It was Parsons' hope that individuals who engaged in such a process would be more satisfied with their work, and to this end, he emphasized maximizing the fit between individuals and occupations. This concept is as relevant today as it was in the days of Parsons. As testament to the longevity and influence of the work of Parsons, Spokane and Glickman (1994) noted that the counselor-directed approach to career counseling outlined by Parsons "would dominate the field for 70 or more years, as would the individual differences approach to assessment" (p. 302).

Differential Psychology

While Parsons understood the importance of self-knowledge in career selection, he had to rely to a large extent on self-study by clients due to a lack of appropriate assessment instruments. However, during the early part of the 1900s, there was also growth in the differential psychology movement, with its emphases on individual differences and the use of psychometric assessment. Thus, the psychology of individual differences provided counseling psychology with a technology for client assessment based on the psychological test (Dawis, 1992). The influence of the movement toward individual differences "shifted the emphasis in vocational guidance to the assessment of individuals' abilities, interests, and personality traits in relation to occupational requirements and occupational adjustment" (Dawis, 1992, p. 10), a process that gained considerable momentum with the advent of each of the world wars.

Trait-and-Factor Theory

The technology provided by the psychology of individual differences, such as inventories and psychological tests, paved the way for the development of what is the oldest and most widely used of the career development theories (Sharf, 1992), the trait-and-factor approach. Betz (1992) claimed that the advent of trait-and-factor approaches can be attributed to the combination of matching models such as that of Parsons (1909) with the concepts and technology of individual differences. Trait-and-factor theory is founded on the notion that individuals are different and that their different capacities can be measured and related to occupations.

The psychometric movement that emerged in the early 1900s developed two main thrusts: the measurement of individual differences and the identification of the traits needed by individuals for successful job performance. The development of tests of abilities and aptitudes and inventories of interests, which were increasingly used in the counseling process, complemented and broadened the work of Parsons in particular and vocational guidance generally (McDaniels & Gysbers, 1992).

According to trait-and-factor theory, choosing an occupation involves trying to match an individual to a job so that his or her needs will be met and his or her job performance will be satisfactory (D. Brown, 1990). "The terms *trait* and *factor* refer to the assessment of characteristics of the person and the job" (Sharf, 1992, p. 17). Traits are individual characteristics that can be measured through testing, and factors are characteristics required for successful job performance. Traits were originally viewed as being biologically based and therefore unchanging and were later viewed as learned and subject to change. The term *trait and factor* implies a matching between individuals and jobs: Career selection is seen to occur as a result of understanding the relationship between knowledge about self and knowledge about occupations (Chartrand, 1991). This process clearly reflects Parsons' (1909) concept of vocational guidance and in doing so establishes his place as the founder of what is now known as trait-and-factor theory.

D. Brown (1987) identified five characteristics of trait-and-factor theory that reflect its origins in differential psychology. The first is that traits are not independent of each other and that there is interaction between them that leads to behavior patterns. However, the links remain unclear. In line with differential psychology, Brown commented on the value of quantification of data to trait-and-factor theorists and the objective use of inventories, tests, and other measures. Related to this is external validation, in which individuals are compared with reference groups in particular work environments. Brown also commented on the interactive nature of trait-and-factor theory, which focuses on the influence of the environment on the personalities of individuals and in turn their influence on the environment as they attempt to satisfy their needs. This has been emphasized more with the evolution from the trait-and-factor approach to the person-environment fit approach. The final assumption discussed by Brown is that the "average or typical individual has the innate ability to make adequate decisions if both personal and environmental data are available to him or her" (D. Brown, 1987, p. 14), in the process described by Parsons as true reasoning.

Such thinking portrayed career decision making as a cognitive process in which decisions were made on the basis of objective data. There was little, if any, consideration given to subjective processes or contextual influences. The theory presumed that choice was available for everyone. In addition, career choice was viewed as a single, static, point-in-time event for which there was a single right answer.

Theorists and practitioners of trait-and-factor theory have developed and used a number of assessment instruments to identify objectively the profile of traits possessed by an individual. In particular, interests, aptitudes, values, personality, and achievement can be measured by inventories and psychological tests. Occupations can also be considered by the "amounts" of individual traits that they require. When the profile of a person is matched with the profile of an occupation, the degree of fit between the person and the occupation can be seen. "This theory greatly influenced the study of job descriptions and job requirements in an attempt to predict future job success from the measurement of traits that are job related" (Zunker, 1994, p. 26). In fact, the major contribution of trait-and-factor theory to career counseling has been in the development of many assessment instruments and techniques and occupational information (Isaacson & D. Brown, 1993).

Until the 1950s, trait-and-factor theory was the preeminent approach in vocational psychology. However, its shortcomings were gradually realized (Super, 1992). At the same time, challenges to it emerged "as Rogerian psychotherapy permeated the counseling field, and developmental (Super, 1957) and social learning approaches (Krumboltz, Mitchell, & Jones, 1976) to career counseling matured" (Chartrand, 1991, p. 519). Thus, as different conceptualizations of career development and the counseling process emerged, awareness of the limitations of the trait-and-factor approach was also heightened.

LIMITATIONS AND CRITICISMS OF TRAIT-AND-FACTOR THEORY

It is useful to examine some of the limitations and criticisms of the trait-and-factor approach, since such examination paves the way for discussing the evolution of the person-environment model. Criticism has generally been directed toward the approach as a theory of career development and toward the counseling process derived from it. Both will be discussed here.

The assumptions previously discussed invite criticism. For example, it has been questioned whether people actually use reasoning in all career choices and whether all people actually have a reasoned choice in relation to career (Roberts, 1977; see also Chapter 6). It can also be questioned whether occupational choice is a single event, whether single types of people are found in each type of job, or whether there is a single right goal for each career decision maker. Isaacson and Brown (1993) claimed that trait-and-factor theory does not account for the broad range of individual differences in every occupational group. In addition, it has been acknowledged that people make several career choices in a lifetime.

Criticism has also been leveled at trait-and-factor theory for failing to "adequately consider and define the universe of variables that impinge on the occupational choice-making process and define causal relationships among traits and variables (such as socioeconomic status)" (D. Brown, 1990, p. 346). Zunker (1994) was critical of the failure to account for growth and change in traits such as interests, values, aptitudes, achievements, and personality characteristics.

Criticisms have also been leveled at counseling practices based solely on this model. Sharf (1992) described the three-step process as "deceptively simple" (p. 41) and expressed concern that the reliance on tests by career counselors that seems to result in an authoritative position for the counselor occurs at the expense of the development of a counseling relationship. Crites (1981) described the trait-and-factor approach as a "test and tell" approach that occurs as "three interviews and a cloud of dust" (p. 49). However, despite these criticisms, it must be remembered that "trait-and-factor theory, as it is understood today, continues to undergird counseling for career development" (McDaniels & Gysbers, 1992, p. 32). It seems that the simplicity of the approach is appealing to practitioners, if not to theorists (an issue discussed in Part 3 of this book).

D. Brown (1996b) claimed that "in its current state, trait and factor theory cannot stand alone as an explanatory system for occupational choice making and has even less validity as an explanatory system for the career development process" (p. 347). By way of explanation, Sharf (1992) noted that

> there is little research supporting or refuting trait and factor theory itself as a viable theory of career development. Rather, the research that has been done, of which there is a large amount, has related traits and factors to one another or has established the validity and reliability of measurements of traits and factors. (p. 18)

Thus, it would be fair to say that trait-and-factor theory is not a theory of career development but rather a collection of theories based on influences that contribute to career development. Typical of these theories are the five-factor model (McCrae & John, 1992; Pryor, 1993), which will be discussed here, and the early work of Holland (1966, 1973, 1985a, 1987). However, Holland's original work has been refined to the point of being more reflective of the person-environment fit theory and will be discussed as an example of that theory later in this chapter.

FIVE-FACTOR MODEL OF PERSONALITY

Since the growth of the differential psychology movement and its emphasis on assessment, personality has been one of the traits that has attracted the most attention, and the development of the five-factor model corresponds with this. "In the personality field, a consensus seems to be developing among trait theorists that there are five overarching factors termed the Big 5" (Walsh & Chartrand, 1994, p. 193), a hierarchical organization of personality traits in terms of five basic dimensions: extraversion, agreeableness, conscientiousness, neuroticism, and openness to experience (McCrae & John, 1992, p. 175). These are best explained by drawing on the "lexical tradition" through the use of adjective descriptors (see Table 2.1). Significantly, while these five terms are widely used, consensus has not been reached about either the names (McCrae & John, 1992; Pryor, 1993) or the number of factors (Pryor, 1993), a topic discussed at length by McCrae and John. For example, Pryor (1993) suggested that researchers are moving away from *neuroticism* toward *emotionality* or *emotional stability*. Each dimension represents groups of traits, and five-factor theorists claim that these can be found in almost all personality instruments. However, McCrae and John (1992, pp. 194–195) raise the question: "Precisely which traits define each factor, and which are central and which are peripheral?"

Because of the comprehensiveness of the model, there is no overarching theory; rather, there are a number of complementary theories, each accounting for various sections of the model. The debate in five-factor theory about the titles of the factors mentioned previously stems out of two predominant traditions in five-factor theory—the "lexical tradition" and the "questionnaire tradition" (McCrae & John, 1992). The lexical tradition holds that throughout the

T A B L E 2.1 AN ILLUSTRATIVE ADJECTIVE
SUMMARY OF THE FIVE-FACTOR MODEL (FROM PRYOR, 1993)

FACTOR	ADJECTIVES
Extroversion	Active, assertive, energetic, enthusiastic, outgoing
Agreeableness	Appreciative, forgiving, generous, kind, sympathetic, trusting
Conscientiousness	Efficient, organized, planful, reliable, responsible, thorough
Neuroticism	Anxious, self-pitying, tense, touchy, unstable, worrying
Openness	Artistic, curious, imaginative, insightful, original, wide interests

Note: From "Returning from the wilderness: Personality in career decision making," by R. G. L. Pryor, 1993, *Australian Journal of Career Development, 2*(3), p. 15. Copyright 1993 by the Australian Council for Educational Research. Reprinted with permission.

development of a language, all traits will have been observed by the speakers of that language and encoded. Thus, by decoding the language, researchers can "discover the basic dimensions of personality" (p. 184). However, questionnaires have been used as the basis for most personality research. While there has been "considerable redundancy in what they measure" (McCrae & John, 1992, p. 185), the major contribution of the questionnaire tradition is in fact a body of theory.

McCrae and John (1992) claimed that the five-factor model has appeal on three levels. First, it has the ability to integrate a wide variety of personality constructs and as such provides a ground on which researchers of different orientations can communicate. Second, it is comprehensive, and its measurement of all five factors keeps relevant personality traits from being neglected in studies and career counseling practice. Third, it is efficient in providing "at least a global description of personality with as few as five scores" (p. 206). In addition, the model has cross-cultural replication. For example, it has been studied with samples of German, Japanese, Chinese, and Dutch people. In light of recent criticism of the cross-cultural applicability of career theory, this is a considerable point in its favor.

Pryor (1993) observed that "the five factor model is becoming in personality what the Holland hexagon has been in vocational interest measurement—the preeminent theoretical framework for practice in the field" (p. 15). In keeping with the psychology of individual differences, Digman (1990) noted that "at a minimum, research on the five factor model has given us a useful set of broad dimensions that characterize individual differences" and that they "provide a good answer to the question of personality structure" (p. 436). Despite limitations, which include limited consensus on the nature of the factors and limited prediction and explanation capabilities, Pryor (1993) maintained that the five-factor model of personality has much to offer the understanding of the construct of personality in career development theory. For example, it has relevance for organizational, industrial, and educational psychologists and in any field where "personality assessment has been employed" because it "provides a set of tools which can be used" (McCrae & John, 1992, p. 206). Due to its developmental infancy and its origins in personality psychology, the five-factor model has not had wide application in the field of career theory. However, it clearly has application in career guidance and counseling, where the measurement of personality has been a focus of the trait theories.

The five-factor model typifies the trait-and-factor models. It is static, relies on the measurement of individual differences, and does not describe the process of development. But like Parsons (1909), McCrae and John (1992) acknowledged the "richness of human individuality" (p. 207) and life contexts and history. Unlike Parsons, they did not explain how they would gather these data. Thus, while trait-and-factor theorists acknowledge contextual variables, in their applications they rely heavily on the measurement of individual traits and matching processes.

PERSON-ENVIRONMENT FIT

Clearly evidenced in the five-factor model is the static nature of the trait-and-factor theories and their lack of emphasis on development. As the notion of development was embraced by career theorists, proponents of trait-and-factor theory could no longer ignore criticism of its static approach. Consequently, over time there has been an evolution from the static approach of trait-and-factor theory, in which a person is matched with an occupation, to the more dynamic approach of person-environment fit. Chartrand (1991) identified three assumptions that have transferred to the person-environment approach from trait-and-factor theory:

1. "People are viewed as capable of making rational decisions" (p. 520).
2. "People and work environments differ in reliable, meaningful, and consistent ways" (p. 520).
3. "The greater the congruence between personal characteristics and job requirements, the greater the likelihood of success" (p. 520).

Although the assumption of congruence between personal characteristics and job requirements as a predictor of job satisfaction is central to both approaches, the concept of dynamic reciprocity is a feature of the person-environment fit approach (Rounds & Tracey, 1990). This concept indicates an ongoing process of adjustment as environments are influenced by individuals and individuals are influenced by environments. "The P × E fit perspective explicitly assumes that people and environments change continually in ongoing adjustment" (Chartrand, 1991, p. 521) and that individuals seek out congruent environments, thus reflecting a shift from the trait-and-factor approach. This significant concept addresses some of the criticism that has been leveled at trait-and-factor theory, including Crites' (1969) criticism that trait-and-factor theory focuses only on content and does not account for the process of career development and D. Brown's (1990) criticism that trait-and-factor theory does not have "validity as an explanatory system for the career development process" (p. 347).

Chartrand (1991) suggested that two questions guide the person-environment fit approach: "(a) what kinds of personal and environmental factors are salient in predicting vocational choice and adjustment, and (b) how is the process of person and environment interaction best characterized" (p. 520). The first question is typical of the purely descriptive, static matching model of trait-and-factor theory, whereas the second reflects the move to a more dynamic, process-oriented person-environment fit approach and is illustrative of the acceptance of career development as a lifelong developmental process (discussed further in Chapter 3). Two theories will be presented to illustrate the person-environment fit approach: Holland's theory of vocational choice and Dawis and Lofquist's theory of work adjustment.

HOLLAND'S THEORY OF VOCATIONAL CHOICE

Originally proposed in 1959, Holland's theory was conceptualized as a trait-and-factor theory and "remains in the tradition of differential psychology" (Weinrach & Srebalus, 1990, p. 47). In complimenting the significance of Holland's work, Weinrach and Srebalus (1990) claimed that it was the "most popular career theory of the last decade" (p. 47). Holland set out to write a theory that was simple and practical, and its success can be attributed to the achievement of these goals. The basic concept of the theory is uncomplicated, and many assessment instruments based on it have been produced to assist practitioners. Hackett et al. (1991) described Holland's theory as "simple and eminently practical" and praised Holland for "his continual revision and refinements" (p. 9).

In his typological theory of vocational choice, Holland (1966, 1973, 1985a) illustrates a person-environment perspective and remains a major proponent of the person-environment fit approach. This is reflected in three questions explained in Holland (1992):

1. What personal and environmental characteristics lead to satisfying career decisions, involvement, and achievement, and what characteristics lead to indecision, dissatisfying decisions, or lack of accomplishment?
2. What personal and environmental characteristics lead to stability or change in the kind of level and work a person performs over a lifetime?
3. What are the most effective methods for providing assistance for people with career problems? (p. 1)

Underlying Holland's theory is the assumption that vocational interests are one aspect of personality and therefore that a "description of an individual's vocational interests is also a description of the individual's personality" (Weinrach & Srebalus, 1990, p. 39). Weinrach and Srebalus (1990) described Holland's theory as "structural-interactive" because of the links it provides between personality and job types. Holland (1992) described his typology as the structure for organizing information about jobs and people, whereas his assumptions about people and environments acting on each other are the inter-active component of his theory. In this regard, he claimed that "jobs change people, and people change jobs" (Holland, 1992, p. 11).

Holland's theory described the career decision maker in terms of six personality/interest types. These six types are "theoretical organizers for understanding how individuals differ in their personality, interests and behaviors" (Spokane, 1996, p. 40), or "models against which we can measure the real person" (Holland, 1992, p. 2). Holland (1992) explained that individuals develop preferences for certain activities as a result of their interaction with "cultural and personal forces including peers, biological heredity, parents, social class, culture, and the physical environment" (p. 2) and that these preferences become interests in which individuals develop competencies. As a result of his or her interests and competencies, an individual develops a "personal disposition that leads him or her to think, perceive, and act in special ways" (p. 2). Personality types are therefore indicated by choice of school subjects, hobbies, leisure activities, and work, and vocational interests and choices are reflected by personality. In choosing or avoiding certain environments or activities, types are seen to be active rather than passive (Holland, 1992).

As mentioned previously, Holland's (1985a, 1992) typology categorized people into one of six broad types of personality: realistic (R), investigative (I), artistic (A), social (S), enterprising (E), or conventional (C). As a result, Holland's type theory is commonly referred to as the RIASEC model (Holland, 1985a) and is represented diagrammatically by a hexagon showing the relationships between the personality or occupational types (see Figure 2.1).

Holland proposed that these personality types are related to needs and that an individual's type is indicative of his or her major needs. In addition, the nature of the work environments can be classified in a similar way. Holland claimed that individuals seek out work environments that are compatible with their attitudes and values and that allow them to use their skills and abilities— a corollary of which is that people in similar jobs will have similar personali-

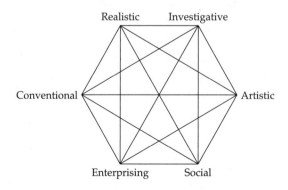

F I G U R E   2.1 HEXAGONAL MODEL FOR DEFINING THE RELATIONS AMONG HOLLAND'S PERSONALITY TYPES AND ENVIRONMENTS AND THEIR INTERACTIONS (FROM LOKAN & TAYLOR, 1986)

ties. Behavior is determined by interaction between the individual and the environment and determines factors such as job satisfaction, stability and achievement, educational choice, and personal competence and susceptibility to influence. These outcomes all can be predicted from a knowledge of personality types and environmental models (Holland, 1992). While matching is still central to Holland's approach, it is his attention to interaction, a feature of recent refinements, that places him with the person-environment fit theorists rather than the trait-and-factor theorists.

In keeping with its origins in differential psychology, many assessment instruments have been developed in conjunction with Holland's theory. One such instrument is the Self-Directed Search (SDS), developed to measure Holland's six personality types. Individuals who complete the SDS receive a score on each of the six types; typically, an individual's profile contains characteristics of each of the six types. However, subtypes are ascribed using a three-letter code representing the three most prevalent types in a profile. The types can best be described using both descriptors and examples of occupations that would match each type, as illustrated in Table 2.2.

Several "secondary assumptions" (Holland, 1992, p. 4) are fundamental to the work of Holland. They are calculus, consistency, congruence, differentiation, and identity. Holland uses the hexagon as a diagnostic system, indicating that relationships within and between types and environments can be ordered

T A B L E   2.2 TYPES, DESCRIPTORS,
AND OCCUPATIONS ACCORDING TO HOLLAND'S TYPOLOGY

TYPE	DESCRIPTORS	OCCUPATIONS
Realistic	Has practical abilities and would prefer to work with machines or tools rather than people	Mechanic; farmer; builder; surveyor; pilot
Investigative	Analytical and precise; good with detail; prefers to work with ideas; enjoys problem solving and research	Chemist; geologist; biologist; researcher
Artistic	Artistic or creative ability; uses intuition and imagination for problem solving	Musician; artist; interior decorator; writer; industrial designer
Social	Good social skills; friendly and enjoys involvement with people and working in teams	Nurse; teacher; social worker; psychologist; counselor
Enterprising	Leadership, speaking, and negotiating abilities; likes leading others toward the achievement of a goal	Salesperson; television producer; manager; administrative assistant; lawyer
Conventional	Systematic and practical worker; good at following plans and attending to detail	Banker; secretary; accountant

according to the hexagonal model. This concept he calls *calculus,* for reasons that become more evident as the other concepts are explained. *Consistency* means that some types have more in common than others; it is best illustrated using the first two letters of the three-letter code. Diagrammatically, types that are adjacent on the hexagon (e.g., SA) have more in common than types that are opposite (e.g., SR). Therefore, individuals demonstrate high consistency when the first two letters of their three-letter code adjoin on the hexagon, as in the case of a realistic investigative (RI) profile; medium consistency when the first two letters of their code are separated by a letter on the hexagon, as in the case of a realistic artistic (RA) profile; and low consistency when two letters on the hexagon separate the first two letters of their code, as in the case of a realistic social (RS) profile. Types that are seen as being inconsistent—that is, nonadjacent or opposite on the hexagon—may have difficulty finding employment that accommodates all aspects of their personality.

Differentiation relates to individual profiles. An individual who has a clearly defined type is regarded as well differentiated, whereas an individual who fits several types is regarded as undifferentiated, a quality that when taken to extreme would be represented by a "flat profile with identical scores on all six types" (Spokane, 1996, p. 45). *Differentiation* refers to how well crystallized an individual's interests are. *Identity,* a more recent addition to Holland's (1992) theory, refers to the degree of clarity and stability an individual has about his or her goals, interests, and talents. An individual who has many goals would be referred to as having low identity. *Congruence,* the last of Holland's concepts, refers to the degree of fit between the individual's personality and work environment. This would be represented by a similar three-letter code for the personality and the work environment, as in the case of an artistic type working in an artistic environment.

Holland's influence in career theory and practice has been significant (D. Brown, 1990; Spokane, 1996). This is demonstrated by its application to a wide range of career materials, such as interest inventories, occupational information, books, and computer programs. Several instruments have been developed to specifically measure personality according to Holland's theory. These include the Strong Vocational Interest Blank (Strong & Campbell, 1981), the Self-Directed Search (Holland, 1985b), and the Vocational Preference Inventory (Holland, 1985c). Further, Holland has applied his RIASEC typology to occupations (G. D. Gottfredson, Holland, & Ogawa, 1982) so that occupations can be coded in the same way as personality. Thus, in applying Holland's theory, the degree of fit, or congruence, between personality type and occupational type is also used to indicate the level of job satisfaction and stability.

More recently, refinements in Holland's theory have emphasized that an individual's heredity and interactions with his or her environment contribute to the development of type and that vocational predictions for a person based on his theory work better when contextual variables such as age, gender, and socioeconomic status are taken into account (Holland, 1992). He has also conceded that chance can play a role in vocational choice (Holland, 1985a). This addresses the criticism of Holland's approach as being simplistic and as underestimating the need for career counseling (Weinrach & Srebalus, 1990). It is also reflective of recent trends in career counseling and the need to place career assessment within a framework of a dynamic interaction of multiple contextual factors. L. S. Gottfredson (1981) supported this notion and indicated that there is value in the career assessment devices but that they need to be viewed in the light of the career decision maker's situation—that is, context. Thus, the onus is on users of specific career assessment devices such as Holland's Self-Directed Search and the Strong Interest Inventory not to use them in isolation but to address the contextual issues relevant to the individual.

Since his 1973 theory revision (Holland, 1973), Holland has more adequately reflected the life span perspective of career development, thus addressing the notion of development over the life span. In terms of the process of career development, Holland (1992) claimed that "the reciprocal interactions of persons and successive jobs usually leads to a series of success and satisfaction cycles" (p. 54). This is in line with Super's (1980) notion that career decision making is a developmental process. In particular, Holland discussed the relationship between the individual and the environment in terms of congruence, satisfaction, and reinforcement and suggested that incongruence is resolved by changing jobs, changing behavior, or changing perceptions. However, Holland's theory remains "primarily descriptive, with little emphasis on explaining the causes and timing of the development of hierarchies of the personal modal styles. He concentrated on the factors that influence career choice rather than on the developmental process that leads to career choice" (Zunker, 1994, p. 49).

Holland's theory has also been criticized for not adequately addressing the career development needs of women and of racial, ethnic, and other groups. In fact, he cautioned that "age, gender, social class, physical assets or liabilities, educational level attained, intelligence, and influence" (Holland, 1992, p. 12) may affect the successful application of his theory. This issue is discussed in more detail in Chapter 6.

While Holland's contribution to career development theory is unquestioned, his theory provides only a partial, though detailed, account of career development. Thus, D. Brown (1987) has expressed concern about the usefulness of Holland's model to recent approaches to life career counseling. His concern arises out of Holland's lack of attention to other life roles and the relationships between them. Possibly reflecting Brown's sentiments, L. S. Hansen (1997) made no reference to the work of Holland in her approach to integrative life planning.

THEORY OF WORK ADJUSTMENT

Like Holland's theory, Dawis and Lofquist's theory of work adjustment reflects a long history of research and strong links to the psychology of individual differences, with its emphasis on measurement and quantification of data. The theory of work adjustment "provides a model for conceptualizing the interaction between individuals and work environments" (Dawis & Lofquist, 1976, p. 55) and is "founded on four basic psychological concepts: ability, reinforcement value, satisfaction, and person-environment correspondence" (Dawis, 1994, p. 34). In essence, an individual exists in a dynamic relationship with his or her work environment, in which he or she seeks to develop a satisfactory relationship by making continual adjustments. However, the theory of work adjustment places greater emphasis on adjustment over time than Holland's theory, and in so doing, it more clearly establishes itself as a person-environment fit theory. It also reflects a move away from point-in-time career choice to adjustment over the life span, another difference between trait-and-factor theory and person-environment fit theory, and a point on which Holland's theory is less clear.

According to this theory, an individual has requirements or needs of a work environment, and a work environment in turn has needs or requirements of a worker. For example, a worker may need money or good working conditions, and a work environment may need certain work skills. A situation "where the interaction is mutually satisfying" (Dawis, 1996, p. 81)—that is, in which the needs of both the individual and the environment are met—is described as *correspondence*. "Correspondence—when person and environment are co-responsive to each other's requirements—is the ideal state" (Dawis, 1996, p. 85). "Whatever satisfies needs are called reinforcers because they can maintain or increase the rate of behavior" (Dawis, 1996, p. 80). Examples of reinforcers include achievement, advancement, coworkers, activity, security, social service, social status, and variety. Individuals and environments behave in order to have their needs met. When correspondence occurs, both parties express satisfaction. However, in this theory, the term *satisfaction* is reserved for the individual's experience of the environment, and the term *satisfactoriness* is reserved for the environment's experience of the individual—that is, whether the individual is meeting the expectations of the environment. Thus, correspondence occurs when "the worker is both satisfied and satisfactory" (Dawis, 1996, p. 82). Correspondence can lead to stability and tenure. The concept of tenure, which is based on satisfaction and satisfactoriness, is fundamental to career planning with this model.

Application of the theory of work adjustment to the career counseling process draws heavily on the psychology of individual differences. Specifically, the matching process first articulated by Parsons and the quantification of data—that is, assessment—are important components. Both ability and values are measured as part of the assessment process. It is assumed that if a person can be described in certain terms and if environments can be similarly described, as in Holland's theory, then matching can occur. The theory of work adjustment considers work skills and work needs. While it is acknowledged that all individuals have a range of skills, it is also acknowledged that they have abilities—that is, "the potential to acquire the skills required by a task and—by extension—a job or occupation" (Dawis, 1996, p. 83). Dawis (1994) described skills and needs as *surface traits* and abilities and values as *source traits*. Source traits provide the structure of personality and generally remain stable over time, whereas surface traits may change with time or in response to situations. This is clearly acknowledgment of the individual's capacity to change over time and indicates recognition of a process variable in career development. The measurement of abilities enables matching of a much wider range of occupations than does skills. Underlying work needs are the reinforcers or values. Thus, a dynamic interaction occurs between the needs of the individual and the needs of the work environment. The individual's behavior is reinforced when needs are met, and reinforcement generally occurs when the values of the individual and the work environment correspond. "Thus, personality structure for TWA [the theory of work adjustment] is constructed from abilities and values" (Dawis, 1996, p. 84).

The theory of work adjustment not only includes descriptions of the characteristics of personality but also pays attention to the identification and labeling of process variables. The terms used to describe work behavior include "celerity, to denote the quickness with which the worker initiates interaction with the work environment; pace, to denote the level of effort expended in the interaction; rhythm, to denote the pattern of pace in the interaction, whether steady, cyclical, or erratic; and endurance, to denote how long the worker remains in the interaction" (Dawis, 1996, p. 85). Over time, an individual will develop unique behavioral tendencies, which in this theory are equated with personality style. The process variables described above can also be used to describe the environment.

However, the needs of the work environment and the needs of the worker are not static. Change in either may lead to dissatisfaction. Work adjustment, therefore, is a dynamic and ongoing process between the individual and the environment, both of which are continually trying to satisfy and be satisfied. Discorrespondence occurs when correspondence is not reached. The degree to which an individual can tolerate discorrespondence depends on his or her flexibility. During these times, the individual and the environment may make adjustments to improve satisfaction or satisfactoriness. Individuals who are more flexible can "tolerate greater degrees of discorrespondence and are less easily dissatisfied" (Dawis, 1996, p. 86). During times of discorrespondence, individuals may adjust in one of two ways: They may try to change the environment (active mode), or they may try to change themselves (reactive mode). For example, an individual who prefers to work on his or her own may move to another room (active mode) or may rationalize that his or her concentration will not be disturbed by the presence of others (reactive mode). When adjustment fails, the worker may leave the work environment. "The duration of this persistence in adjustment behavior defines the worker's level of perseverance" (Dawis, 1996, p. 87). Thus, an individual's adjustment style is determined by his or her flexibility, activeness, reactiveness, and perseverance and is also related to their personality style discussed earlier.

The emphasis on ability and values in the theory or work adjustment establishes it as a theory of content, while the dynamic interaction described delineates it as a person-environment fit theory.

BORDIN'S PSYCHODYNAMIC MODEL OF CAREER CHOICE

Bordin's (1990) psychodynamic model of career choice synthesized previous applications of psychodynamic theory to career choice. In line with the psychodynamic perspective, Bordin turned to development in early childhood to account for work motivation and in particular focused on the development of personality.

His emphasis is on the development of personality in relation to the role of work and play in an individual's life. However, research has yet to provide a strong empirical base for Bordin's hypotheses on work and play. A basic tenet of the theory is that individuals seek enjoyment in work as in other areas of their lives. Bordin proposed that play is intrinsically satisfying and that the satisfaction of simply engaging in an activity distinguishes play from work. Individuals express their need for play in work as in other areas of their lives by looking for something they will enjoy doing.

Bordin claimed that in young children play and work are fused and that through the process of development and socialization, play and work become demarcated. He accounted for this demarcation in terms of "spontaneity, which is used to refer to elements of self-expression and self-realization in our responses to situations" (Bordin, 1990, p. 105). In essence, this means that the activities of young children are intrinsically satisfying. However, as children mature, their play becomes more complex, and they become aware of the effort needed to achieve mastery as well as the external pressures exerted by others, such as parents and caregivers, to achieve mastery, sometimes perceived in terms of rewards and punishments. A process of socialization and "external pressures from parents and caretakers" (p. 107) affects how an individual distinguishes play from work. In particular, Bordin (1990) claimed that "overemphasis on analysis, activation of self-consciousness, and overambition may be intimately tied to failures to fuse work and play" (p. 108). Extreme effort converts spontaneity into compulsion; that is, activities are performed out of a need or compulsion to do them rather than out of an intrinsic desire to do them because they are enjoyable. In adults, this process is reflected in the reality of needing to earn a living and the desire for personal meaning and creative expression.

It is also during these early years that individuals build a unique identity, drawing to some extent on the influences of their parents. This point illustrates the developmental and contextual themes of Bordin's (1990) theory related in particular to identity development. Bordin acknowledged the influence of biologically and culturally determined sex roles in identity development, as well as the level of parental support and nurturance and the need to be unique from but connected to others. However, he claimed that development is largely an unconscious process in which the individual draws on aspects of both parents as well as the extended family. While his theory was "directed towards the participation of personality in career development and the series of choices that comprise it" (p. 104), he also acknowledged the interaction of a number of influences, including economic, cultural, geographic, biological, and accidental factors, and in turn their influence on personality.

In terms of career choice and satisfaction, Bordin described the evolution of personality as the mechanism that guides cognitive processes at times of career choice, whether those choices have presented themselves for external or internal reasons. External reasons include particular stages of the education system, and internal reasons include the desire for increased work satisfaction.

In making choices, the individual conducts a self-assessment and gauges the probabilities of success based on intrinsic satisfaction, which may include "curiosity, precision, power, expressiveness, and concern with right and wrong and justice, as well as ... nurturance" (Bordin, 1990, p. 114).

While Bordin's theory has been discussed as a theory of content, it is clearly much more broadly based than traditional theories in this area, such as the work of Holland. Bordin questions traditional career guidance practices and their emphasis on the realities of work, such as monetary reward, rather than on self-realization through work. His emphasis in career counseling is focused much more on the individual striving for inner meaning. He advocates the use of guided fantasy, dreams, examination of life histories, and imaginative approaches. He also advocates examining clients' feelings. His approach is clearly a significant move away from the tradition of matching approaches, with their emphasis on objectivity. The breadth of Bordin's approach is also reflected in the work of Brown, who focuses on a particular trait but places the counseling process in a much broader context.

BROWN'S VALUES-BASED, HOLISTIC MODEL

Values are central to Brown's theory; thus, it is placed in this chapter as a theory of content. However, his theory, described by D. Brown and Brooks (1996a) as an emerging theory, reflects the current state of career development theory and the move toward holistic approaches. Thus, while it emphasizes the importance of a particular trait, values, it also acknowledges the concept of development and the broader context in which individuals exist. Thus, Brown's theory is indicative of the significant shift that has taken place in theorizing about career development. D. Brown (1996a) has presented his theory in two discrete sections. The first focus of his theory is his emphasis on values and the role they play in career choice, and the second focus is on career counseling. These will be discussed separately.

Brown's thinking about values has been influenced by the work of Rokeach (1973). He has claimed that individuals judge their own performance and that of others against a core set of beliefs or values (D. Brown, 1995), which are important not only in the selection of life roles but also in the satisfaction derived from life roles (D. Brown & Crace, 1996). D. Brown (1996a) claimed that expected outcomes are the most important source of motivation in decision making and that values are the basis on which individuals decide which outcomes are more important than others; that is, "values form the basis for attributing worth to situations and objects" (D. Brown & Crace, 1996, p. 212). However, he also claimed that "values have been the overlooked dimension in the counseling process as well as in the research that has been conducted on career development" (D. Brown, 1996a, p. 368). Therefore, in his theory, he has attempted to draw attention to the function of values in decision making and career counseling, as well as to set values in the broader context of life roles and life space.

D. Brown and Crace (1996) advanced seven propositions about the function of values in decision making, whereas D. Brown (1996a) advanced six, possibly a reflection of the developmental stage of this theory. However, the concepts proposed are similar and will now be discussed. Fundamental to the model is the concept that each person develops a relatively small number of values, which "dictate cognitive, affective, and behavioral patterns" (D. Brown, 1996a, p. 341). Individuals are exposed to value-laden messages throughout their lives from a variety of sources, including family, friends, and the media. Values therefore "develop as a result of the interaction between inherited characteristics and experience" (D. Brown, 1996a, p. 340). Cultural background, gender, and socioeconomic status influence opportunities and social interaction; thus, there is variation in values both within and between subgroups of society. Acknowledgment of such issues reflects the recency of this theory's development and the trends toward contextualism that are discussed in Chapter 4.

As values are formed, they become crystallized in the mind of the individual and prioritized, and the extent to which this occurs relates to cognitive clarity (D. Brown, 1996a). Values are said to be crystallized when they can be labeled and articulated by an individual. Crystallization of values enables people to judge their own behavior and compare themselves with others (D. Brown, 1995). Once values are crystallized, they can be prioritized. D. Brown and Crace (1996) claimed that individuals who are described as "high functioning people" (p. 219) have values that are well crystallized and prioritized.

To make decisions, it is desirable that individuals have their values crystallized and prioritized. D. Brown and Crace (1996) claimed that "values with high priorities are the most important determinants of choices made, providing that the individuals have more than one alternative available that will satisfy their values" (p. 212). Thus, individuals are most likely to be satisfied when their choices are compatible with their values. Clearly, then, they also need information about their options to determine whether their values will be satisfied by a decision. In the case of career decision making, this reflects the trait-and-factor principle of matching self-knowledge with world-of-work knowledge. But unlike trait-and-factor theorists, and possibly reflecting the development of this theory in the 1990s rather than earlier, Brown acknowledged life roles other than worker and the interaction of these roles and included them as an integral part of his theory. In particular, he acknowledged that different roles may satisfy different values. "The result of role interaction is life satisfaction, which differs from the sum of the marital, job, leisure, and other roles satisfaction indices taken separately" (D. Brown & Crace, 1996, p. 217). However, a combination of factors, not only satisfaction of values, determines success in a role. While it is yet to be studied, D. Brown (1996a) has hypothesized that "a combination of role-related skills and aptitudes and values congruence between the individual and the principal person(s) in the environment will be the best predictor of success in a role" (p. 355). In this respect, Brown's theory differs from both the theory of work adjustment and Holland's theory, since neither of the latter makes predictions about success.

The second focus of Brown's theory is its contribution to career counseling. He outlined five assumptions underlying his "values-based approach to career counseling" that deviate considerably from the predominantly matching process of trait-and-factor theory and person-environment fit theory. His first assumption stressed the importance of considering career decisions in relation to other life roles rather than as isolated events. D. Brown (1996a) claimed that "a central premise of the theory is that, because people function holistically, career counseling should only be conducted in the context of the entire life space and other life roles" (p. 368). This is in line with more recent thinking about the importance of context and the place of work in people's lives (Richardson, 1996) and is in contrast with Holland's career counseling process, which has been criticized as being simplistic. Therefore, just as values should be considered not in isolation but rather in the context of all life roles, so the work or job role needs to be considered in relation to other life roles. Life "roles may function synergistically, may be in conflict, or may be compensatory" (D. Brown, 1995, p. 8) in relation to the satisfaction of values. Brown discussed inter-role and intrarole conflict, both of which result in a lack of satisfaction and may lead to transitions. Intrarole conflict occurs when the values of the individual are not reinforced in the workplace, as when a worker has different values than his or her supervisor (D. Brown & Crace, 1996). Inter-role conflict occurs when the current job is in conflict with another role, as when a less satisfying role (work) takes time away from a more satisfying role, parenting (D. Brown & Crace, 1996). These conflicts may be compared with the theory of work adjustment's concept of change that brings about the need for adjustment.

The concept of role conflict leads into the second of Brown's assumptions, the need for the counselor to assess the degree of crystallization and prioritization of values and role relationship problems. In addition, counselors need to be able to assess mood problems such as anxiety or depression, according to the third of Brown's assumptions. Dealing with such issues in career counseling draws attention to the links between career and personal counseling. In this regard, D. Brown (1996a) has emphasized the importance of the counseling relationship, which he has regarded as essential for success. Such thinking distances Brown from traditional exponents of trait-and-factor career counseling.

In the fourth of his assumptions, Brown acknowledged the importance of other variables such as career interests in the career counseling process and advocated that counselors be able to "translate various types of psychological data into values-based terms" (D. Brown, 1996a, p. 357). Following from this is his fifth assumption, that "if clients understand their values and have values-based information, they will be able to make effective decisions" (D. Brown, 1996a, p. 357)—a matching concept that aligns him with the trait-and-factor theorists.

D. Brown's (1996a) contribution to career development is twofold. First, he has drawn attention to an important concept in career development, that of values, which previously received little in-depth attention. Second, he has forged important links between the positivist approach of trait-and-factor theory and more recent approaches to career counseling and to some extent has demonstrated how they can coexist. He has done this in the counseling process by combining a focus on a trait, values, with the concept of interconnected life roles. Brown's theory draws attention to the developmental status of career theory and highlights some of the similarities and differences between the theories of content.

SIMILARITIES AND DIFFERENCES
BETWEEN THEORIES OF CONTENT

In this chapter and in Chapters 3 and 4, a table will be presented to illustrate the similarities and differences between the theories discussed in the chapter. Shown on the X axis are the influences on career development discussed in Chapter 1 and presented in the systems theory framework in Chapter 9. On the Y axis are shown the theories discussed in the chapters. Shading on the table illustrates the degree of emphasis placed on particular influences by each theory. The tables compare the emphasis of theories within chapters and may also be used to compare across chapters.

The theories of content have played a useful role in elaborating influences on career development. As illustrated in Table 2.3, individual influences such as abilities, interests, personality, and values have been focused on more than the contextual or process influences. As mentioned previously, in the main, these theories do not account for development, either development of the focus variable of the theory or the broader issue of career development. Similarly, while most of the theorists discussed in this chapter acknowledge the influence of contextual variables on career development, they do not do so in any systematic way, and this has not been the focus of their work. They also acknowledge the interaction of different traits, yet they do not expound on the links between them. These acknowledgments could be seen as recognition of the issue of rapprochement and convergence, although this is not stated. The following discussion will be structured around the three main elements of this theory group: the content variables of self-knowledge and work environment and the process variable of matching, which constitutes the major approach to career decision making in this group of theories. In addition, the process variable of person-environment fit will be discussed.

SELF-KNOWLEDGE

Each of the theories discussed emphasizes the importance of self-knowledge in the decision-making process. Self-knowledge covers a broad array of information. However, most theories emphasize knowledge about one trait at the expense of other self-knowledge. For example, Holland focuses on a typology of interest/personality, Bordin on personality, and Dawis and Lofquist and Brown on values.

Clearly, then, theorists can address the same traits, but conceptualize them differently. For example, "Bordin, unlike Holland, does not posit that personality is static" (D. Brown, 1990, p. 353) and claims that as a result of the changing personality, different career needs emerge. Thus, Bordin's conceptualization of personality is more dynamic than Holland's. Dawis and Lofquist and Brown both focus on values, but Brown places greater emphasis on the importance of values in career choice. However, in both theories, work satisfaction is connected to values' being met in the workplace. According to Dawis (1996), reinforcers or values such as achievement, social service, or status can satisfy needs. These are similar to Holland's concepts of satisfaction, stability, and achievement when congruence is achieved.

T A B L E   2.3 INFLUENCES ON
CAREER DEVELOPMENT: THEORIES OF CONTENT

CONTENT INFLUENCES	PARSONS	FIVE-FACTOR MODEL	HOLLAND	DAWIS & LOFQUIST	BORDIN	BROWN
Intrapersonal system						
Ability						
Aptitudes						
Interests						
Gender						
Age						
Skills						
Ethnicity						
Sexual orientation						
Beliefs						
Health						
Disability						
Values						
World-of-work knowledge						
Personality						
Self-concept						
Physical attributes						
Social System						
Family						
Peers						
Community groups						
Education institutions						
Media						
Workplace						
Environmental/Societal System						
Political decisions						
Historical trends						
Employment market						
Geographical location						
Socioeconomic status						
Globalization						

PROCESS INFLUENCES						
Recursiveness						
Change over time						
Chance						

☐ No acknowledgment   ☐ Acknowledgment   ■ Significant emphasis

In line with differential psychology, the self-knowledge described by all of the theories is quantifiable. It is only Bordin who deviates from this by drawing attention to the importance of subjective self-knowledge. D. Brown (1996a) also deviates away from the objective by drawing attention to the affective components of anxiety and depression, but in line with the quantifiable nature of self-knowledge in these theories, he has suggested that these should be assessed.

WORK ENVIRONMENT

Parsons and Holland have made the most significant contribution in terms of knowledge about the world of work; Parsons through what he termed the industrial investigation, and Holland through his classification of occupations and work environments. Parsons developed a classification of industry groups and aligned this with what he described as "the conditions of efficiency and success" (p. 47). These were "fundamentals" (p. 27), such as health, enthusiasm, reliability, and interest, and knowledge pertinent to a particular industry, such as "ability to draw and work by drawings" for the "mechanical trades, manufacturing and construction, transportation, etc." industries (p. 51). This information clearly paved the way toward a matching process in career decision making between self-knowledge and work knowledge, the process of "true reasoning" previously discussed. Holland's theory also typifies this approach. He emphasized the characterization of work environments by the people who occupy them. Work environments can be classified by type in the same way as individuals because their chief characteristics reflect the personalities of the individuals who work in them. This is a point of considerable variation from the theory of work adjustment, in which the work environment is viewed independently of the characteristics of the workers. Holland's theory implies that matching self-knowledge with knowledge about the type of individuals who characterize particular occupations or work environments will lead to person-environment congruence.

PERSON-ENVIRONMENT FIT

Much of the criticism that has centered on these theories concerns their perceived static nature. However, Rounds and Tracey (1990) disputed this critique, claiming that person-environment fit theorists have never assumed that individuals are incapable of change and that in fact, dynamic interplay is evident in the descriptions of most of the theories.

Since the days of Parsons, the essence of these theories has remained the same—that is, a matching process between self-knowledge and world-of-work knowledge that leads to career choice. Little has changed in the decision-making processes advocated by these approaches since the days of Parsons, and there is still a heavy reliance on methodical, rational, cognitive processes that are assumed to result in a choice of best fit for the individual (Phillips, 1994).

The exception to this is again found in the work of Bordin, who allows for subjectivity to enter into the decision-making process. Bordin's allowance for the subjective experience of the individual distinguishes him from the other content theorists and is more reflective of the constructivist approaches, such as that of Young et al. (1996), discussed in Chapter 4. An exception is also found in the work of Brown, who takes into account mood problems such as anxiety and depression.

With the move from trait-and-factor origins to person-environment fit approaches discussed previously in this chapter, there has been a shift in the theories of content away from matching for an initial career choice, as in the days of Parsons, to adjustment throughout the life span. This is evident in the work of Holland, Dawis and Lofquist, and Brown. However, it is addressed more explicitly and comprehensively by Dawis and Lofquist than by the other theorists.

Parsons' attempt to maximize the fit between individuals and jobs reflects the visionary nature of his work, and this goal has more recently been termed *congruence* by theorists such as Holland. Holland (1994) claimed that Parsons' concept of congruence was the same as the concept of correspondence proposed by Dawis and Lofquist to explain the fit between the individual and his or her environment. Dawis (1996) extended knowledge of the adjustment process further by actually labeling the process variables of celerity, pace, rhythm, and endurance, which describe interaction between the individual and the work environment or work behavior.

Parsons believed that congruence not only had benefits for both employees and employers but also served as a motivator. This is reflective of the theory of work adjustment's concepts of satisfaction and satisfactoriness, which describe a situation in which the needs of both the work environment and the individual are met. Significantly, Parsons viewed congruence not as static but rather as a fluid construct responding to individuals' development and adaptation—a concept in keeping with person-environment fit theory, particularly the theory of work adjustment (Dawis, 1994). In this regard, Dawis and Lofquist also introduced the notion of discorrespondence, the situation in which the needs of one or both parties are not being met, resulting in a period of adjustment and possibly followed by the individual's changing jobs (an outcome described by Holland, 1996, as resulting from "incongruent interactions" [p. 50]). D. Brown (1996a) also addressed discorrespondence or incongruent interactions by discussing intrarole conflict, or conflicts in the workplace that lead to a lack of satisfaction and the need for adjustment. However, as the most recent theorist, Brown extended the concept of congruence further by setting work in the context of life and discussing conflicts that occur between the work role and other life roles.

CONCLUSION

In this discussion of the similarities and differences between the theories of content, it can be seen that "today's person-environment congruence model is a direct descendant of Parsons' formula" (Zytowski & Swanson, 1994, p. 309) and that his formula provides a conceptual consistency throughout this group of theories. The development of the theories presented in this chapter spans the period from the early 1950s to the middle of the 1990s and as such reflects trends in conceptualizations of career theory. For example, early theories such as those of Parsons and the early work of Holland are less dynamic in that they pay less attention to process and, while not ignoring contextual influences, do not adequately address them. Refinements of Holland's work and theories proposed later, as in the work of Dawis and Lofquist, reflect acceptance by the early 1970s of the concept of development. However, unlike Holland's theory, in which the inclusion of process is a refinement of the theory, Dawis and Lofquist's work includes process in the form of adjustment as an integral part. In fact, the process variable of adjustment is much more integrated into the theory of work adjustment than it is in the work of Holland and indicates how this group of theories can be viewed as dynamic. The most recent theory discussed in this chapter reflects yet another trend in the development of career theory, that of the acceptance of contextual influences. This is evident in Brown's consideration of work roles in relation to other life roles. Thus, there is a clear historical trend in this chapter that reflects a broadening of the base of career development theory.

However, it is clear from this discussion of the theories of content that they tell only part of the story of career development. Significantly, the process of career development is to a large extent overlooked in these theories. This is reflected in criticisms, discussed previously, that the theories are static and not dynamic. These theories have attempted to address such criticism by moving toward a person-environment fit approach and acceptance of the concept of career adjustment in addition to career choice. But despite these efforts, the theories of content do not provide extensive or satisfactory explanations of the process of career development, and this omission has paved the way for the promotion of theories that address the issues of process in career development. The theories of process will be discussed in Chapter 3.

C H A P T E R

3

THEORIES FOCUSING ON PROCESS

The previous chapter discussed the early history of career development theory and its origins in the "matching" models steeped in the tradition of differential psychology. In addition, it discussed more recent work on content variables and the shift toward person-environment fit approaches. As previously discussed, the 1950s was a time of change in the history of career theory. Some of this change can be attributed to the release of developmental theories, which viewed career choice as part of a developmental process rather than as a matching exercise. The developmental theories do not compete with the matching theories discussed in Chapter 2; rather, the two groups of theory complement each other. As Super (1992) has stated, it is not valid to ask which group of theories is better, since neither is "sufficient without the other" (p. 59).

The developmental approaches take into account that career choice is not just a single static decision but rather a dynamic developmental process involving a series of decisions made over time. This idea was alluded to in the theories discussed in Chapter 2 but was not addressed in any depth by any theory, except perhaps the theory of work adjustment. Acceptance of the concept of career development was firmly established by 1971 (Hackett et al., 1991). Career development does not imply vertical progression but rather the emergence or shaping of a career over time. In fact, career decisions are made throughout life; thus, the developmental theories are referred to as *life span approaches*. Four theories will be discussed here to illustrate the developmental approaches: the work of Ginzberg and his colleagues (Ginzberg, 1972, 1984; Ginzberg et al., 1951); Super (1953, 1957, 1980, 1990, 1992, 1994); Tiedeman and O'Hara (1963) and Miller-Tiedeman and Tiedeman (1990); and L. S. Gottfredson (1981, 1996).

THE WORK OF GINZBERG

The work of Ginzberg et al. (1951) is historically significant in that it represents one of the earliest deviations from the existing static trait-and-factor theories and as such is a vital contribution to developmental theory. Ginzberg et al.'s theory is generally considered to be the first to have focused on occupational choice from a developmental standpoint. Ginzberg and his colleagues gave rise to the notion that career choice is a developmental process and proposed that career development begins in early childhood and progresses through three broad stages that conclude with career choice in early adulthood. During this time, many career decisions are made as the individual deals with the tasks of preadolescence and adolescence. The three stages through which the individual passes are the fantasy, tentative, and realistic stages. The tentative stage has the substages of interest, capacity, value, and transition, and the realistic period is divided into substages of exploration, crystallization, and specification. The theory proposed that individuals move through these stages by their late teens or early 20s.

In the *fantasy* stage, the occupational preferences expressed by individuals generally reflect identification with the role of an adult they know and a lack of realism rather than a mature career decision. The *tentative* stage involves a maturational process during which individuals at first base their career choice on their interests and abilities (*interest* substage) and later begin to weigh these against their capacities (*capacity* substage). In the *value* substage, there is also a growing awareness of their work values and the need to order them (Ginzberg, 1984). The final substage of the tentative stage, transition, leads into the first phase of the realistic stage, exploration. It is during the *transition* substage that occupational choice becomes less of a subjective process based on interests, capacities, and values, and more of an exploratory process based on realistic consideration of opportunities and limitations such as the amount of study required and anticipated income (Ginzberg, 1984). During the third and final stage of this model, the *realistic* stage, individuals have "reached the point of integrating likes and dislikes with capabilities and tempering these two variables with society's and personal values" (Osipow & Fitzgerald, 1996, p. 29). They begin to implement their tentative occupational choices and evaluate feedback on their vocational behavior. Eventually *crystallization* occurs when the young person "makes a definitive occupational commitment" (Ginzberg, 1972, p. 169). The process of career development is completed with the substage of *specification*, during which individuals make decisions about implementing their occupational choice. For example, they may choose between public and private sector employment or decide on the type of organization in which they will work (Ginzberg, 1984).

The original theory comprised the three key elements of process, irreversibility, and compromise (Ginzberg, 1972). *Process* referred to the career decision making that occurred from prepuberty until the late teens or early 20s, when individuals were believed to make an occupational commitment. This commitment to or choice of an occupation was seen as being irreversible, basically the concept of a job for life. Irreversibility was based on the notion that previous education and training had channeled the individual down a path that, once set, provided little opportunity to change direction. In addition, choice of an occupation was seen as a compromise as individuals attempted to "find an optimal fit" (Ginzberg, 1972, p. 169) between factors such as their interests and abilities and the reality of the world of work. Thus, while Ginzberg et al.'s theory is developmental, the choice process closely resembles that of the matching models discussed in Chapter 2. This possibly reflects its place as the first developmental theory and its proposal at a time when the matching approaches were firmly established as the theory base.

Career choice was thought to depend on four variables. The first, reality, took into account the constraints of the world of work and the pressures of the environment. The second, the educational process, was considered a significant influence on career choice because the nature of the education an individual received could restrict or enhance opportunities. The third, emotional factors, comprised the interaction between individuals and their environment and the work satisfaction they received. The fourth was personal values and the need to satisfy them in a career choice. These factors are evidenced in the previous description of the stages.

While the theory is predominantly developmental, there are similarities to the matching models as previously discussed and also to the contextual models to be discussed in Chapter 4. For example, Ginzberg and his colleagues took into account contextual influences such as education, socioeconomic status, and the realities of the world of work. Consideration of development in context, particularly during the 1950s, is commendable. However, the original theory was based on studies of young men from upper income homes; thus, it did not attend to the career development needs of women or minority or disadvantaged groups, points on which it has been criticized.

While this theory was visionary in its time, it quickly dated with the acceptance of the concept of lifelong career development, which resulted in Ginzberg's (1972, 1984) subsequent revision of the original theory. Probably the most significant change that Ginzberg conceded was that career development does not conclude in early adulthood but rather is a lifelong process in which individuals continue to seek satisfaction from career decisions by improving "the fit between their changing career goals and the realities of the world of work" (Ginzberg, 1984, p. 180), a comment reflective of the person-environment fit approach discussed in Chapter 2.

Ginzberg (1972) described the reformulated theory as sociopsychological rather than developmental because he took into account what he referred to as "reality factors," locating the individual at the center of the decision-making process as the "prime mover" or "principal actor" (Ginzberg, 1972, p. 175). Thus, Ginzberg (1972, 1984) brought together person-environment fit theories, developmental theories, and contextual theories. In his exploration of contextual elements, he drew attention to the familial and environmental circumstances of the individual. In particular, he acknowledged changes in personal and family circumstances and the career development needs of women and minority and disadvantaged groups. He also acknowledged what he termed "constraints on occupational choice" (Ginzberg, 1972, p. 173), including low socioeconomic status, parental education and values, prejudice and discrimination, educational inadequacies, linkages among institutions, and access to guidance information. Thus, Ginzberg and his colleagues were among the first to acknowledge that factors outside the individual may affect career development. Little, if any, attention had previously been paid to such issues, a trend that has continued in the career development literature. Although Ginzberg did not explain how to address these issues, raising awareness of them in the career development field was significant.

Once reformulated, the essence of the theory was restated in 1972: "Occupational choice is a lifelong process of decision making in which the individual constantly seeks to find the optimal fit between career goals and the realities of the world of work" (Ginzberg, 1984, p. 179). It was restated again in 1984: "Occupational choice is a lifelong process of decision making for those who seek major satisfactions from their work. This leads them to reassess repeatedly how they can improve the fit between their changing career goals and the realities of the world of work" (Ginzberg, 1984, p. 180).

These restatements portray career development as a lifelong process in which individuals attempt to derive satisfaction from their work by making adjustments and choices. Their reference to "those who seek major satisfactions from their work" also hints at life roles other than work that may provide satisfaction in life. In addition, they reflect a change from a static to a dynamic theory with the shift from the concept of compromise to that of optimization (Ginzberg, 1972), which portrays individuals as actively trying to seek satisfaction from their work and making career moves accordingly. In addition, the revised theory places less emphasis on irreversibility. The three elements of the revised theory are stated as follows:

- Occupational choice is a process that remains open as long as one makes and expects to make decisions about his work and career. In many instances it is coterminous with his working life.
- While the successive decisions that a young person makes during the preparatory period will have a shaping influence on his later career, so will the continuing changes that he undergoes in work and life.
- People make decisions about jobs and careers with an aim of optimizing their satisfactions by finding the best possible fit between their priority needs and desires and the opportunities and constraints that they confront in the world of work. (Ginzberg, 1972, p. 172)

Clearly, the concept of person-environment fit is evident in these statements in that the process of choice has now become dynamic rather than static with the ideas of lifelong career choice, seeking of work satisfaction, and making adjustments to meet personal needs.

The work of Ginzberg and his colleagues is significant as the first developmental theory, and Ginzberg's (1972, 1984) revisions are significant for their ability to respond to changes in thinking about career development. Despite the revisions, the theory has declined in importance; Osipow and Fitzgerald (1996) cite it as an example of how theories may become time bound. However, it has served as a major stimulus in the development of career theory, and the notion of development that it proposed is still of undeniable importance in the field.

SUPER'S LIFE SPAN, LIFE SPACE APPROACH

Although the work of Ginzberg and his colleagues was a forerunner in the field of developmental career theory, it has been overshadowed by the extensive and significant work of Super. Super's work and that of Holland, discussed in Chapter 2, secure them positions as the most influential writers in the field of career development. While Holland's early work, steeped in the tradition of differential psychology, is narrowly focused on vocational type and career choice, Super's work encompasses the broader perspective of life span career development. Thus, Super advanced the previous thinking on career development by suggesting that it did not conclude in young adulthood but rather continued throughout the life span of an individual. Not only did Super (1953, 1957, 1980, 1990, 1992, 1994) shift the focus of career development away from approaches based on differential psychology, but he also changed "the focus of vocational psychology from occupations to careers" (Savickas, 1994, p. 22) and provided "the main impetus to expand vocational guidance to encompass career counseling" (Savickas, 1994, p. 4). Super, therefore, has made a major contribution to the field of career development at both a theoretical and a practical level.

The work of Super and Ginzberg and their colleagues changed the focus of career choice from that of a static point-in-time event to that of a dynamic process. Despite widespread acceptance of this concept, there is still a tendency for career choice and career development to be viewed as static events (Hackett et al., 1991) and for career interventions to be based on the matching approaches.

Developmental psychology was a major influence on Super's early work, which emphasized life stages and vocational tasks. The other major influence was self-concept theory, referred to as the "keystone" (Super, 1990, p. 221) of his theory. Super believed that the development of vocational self-concept is a part of life stage development and that occupational choice is an attempt to implement self-concept. These have remained central features of Super's work throughout his long career. More recently, Super (1990) has regretted that he did not adopt the term *personal construct* (Kelly, 1955) rather than *self-concept*, since it is more reflective of "personal perception and construction of the environment" (p. 223). A construct is a point of view "internally generated" by the individual on the basis of his or her interaction with and experiences of the world (Law, 1996a, p. 55), whereas concepts are previously known and may be learned from others. Thus, an individual could be seen to be more "active" in relation to constructs, which have the capacity to change over time, and more "passive" in relation to concepts, which are more established.

While Super's work is most often associated with the developmental theorists, his more recent work (Super, 1980, 1990, 1992) is actually far more comprehensive and "brings together life-stage psychology and social role theory to convey a comprehensive picture of multiple-role careers, together with their determinants and interactions" (Super, Savickas, & Super, 1996, p. 126). Super's most lasting contribution has been his life span, life space approach to career development, in which he not only presented a stage model of career development but also "constructed an overarching framework within which to explore career development" (Savickas, 1994, p. 22). The following description of Super's work will begin with the propositions that outline his key concepts and will be followed by a discussion of self, which is central to his theory, and then of his life span, life space approach to career development.

PROPOSITIONS

The essence of Super's theory is contained in his list of propositions. Originally, he listed 10 propositions, but the list has been expanded to 14 with subsequent refinements of his theory. The propositions, reprinted from Super (1990), are as follows:

1. People differ in their abilities and personalities, needs, values, interests, traits, and self-concepts.
2. People are qualified, by virtue of these characteristics, each for a number of occupations.
3. Each occupation requires a characteristic pattern of abilities and personality traits, with tolerances wide enough to allow both some variety of occupations for each individual and some variety of individuals in each occupation.
4. Vocational preferences and competencies, the situations in which people live and work, and, hence, their self-concepts change with time and experience, although self-concepts, as products of social learning, are increasingly stable from late adolescence until late maturity, providing some continuity in choice and adjustment.
5. This process of change may be summed up in a series of life stages (a "maxicycle") characterized as a sequence of growth, exploration, establishment, maintenance, and decline, and these stages may in turn be divided into (a) the fantasy, tentative, and realistic phases of the exploratory stage and (b) the trial and stable phases of the establishment stage. A small (mini) cycle takes place in transitions from one stage to the next or each time an individual is destabilized by a reduction in force, changes in type of manpower needs, illness or injury, or other socioeconomic or personal event. Such unstable or multiple-trial careers involve new growth, reexploration, and reestablishment (recycling).
6. The nature of the career pattern—that is, the occupational level attained and the sequence, frequency, and duration of trial and stable jobs—is determined by the individual's parental socioeconomic level, mental ability, education, skills, personality characteristics (needs, values, interests, traits, and self-concepts), and career maturity and by the opportunities to which he or she is exposed.
7. Success in coping with the demands of the environment and of the organism in that context at any given life-career stage depends on the readiness of the individual to cope with these demands (that is, on his or her career

maturity). *Career maturity* is a constellation of physical, psychological, and social characteristics; psychologically, it is both cognitive and affective. It includes the degree of success in coping with the demands of earlier stages and sub-stages of career development, and especially with the most recent.

8. Career maturity is a hypothetical construct. Its operational definition is perhaps as difficult to formulate as that of intelligence, but its history is much briefer and its achievement even less definitive. Contrary to the impressions created by some writers, it does not increase monotonically, and it is not a unitary trait.

9. Development through the life stages can be guided, partly by facilitating the maturing of abilities and interests and partly by aiding in reality testing and in the development of self-concepts.

10. The process of career development is essentially that of developing and implementing occupational self-concepts. It is a synthesizing and compromising process in which the self-concept is a product of the interaction of inherited aptitudes, physical makeup, opportunity to observe and play various roles, and evaluations of the extent to which the results of role playing meet with the approval of superiors and fellows (interactive learning).

11. The process of synthesis of or compromise between individual and social factors, between self-concepts and reality, is one of role playing and of learning from feedback, whether the role is played in fantasy, in the counseling interview, or in such real-life activities as classes, clubs, part-time work, and entry jobs.

12. Work satisfactions and life satisfactions depend on the extent to which the individual finds adequate outlets for abilities, needs, values, interests, personality traits, and self-concepts. They depend on establishment in a type of work, a work situation, and a way of life in which one can play the kind of role that growth and exploratory experiences have led one to consider congenial and appropriate.

13. The degree of satisfaction people attain from work is proportional to the degree to which they have been able to implement self-concepts.

14. Work and occupation provide a focus for personality organization for most men and women, although for some persons this focus is peripheral, incidental, or even non-existent. Then other foci, such as leisure activities and homemaking, may be central. (Social traditions, such as sex-role stereotyping and modeling, racial and ethnic biases, and the opportunity structure, as well as individual differences, are important determinants of preferences for roles such as worker, student, leisurite, homemaker, and citizen.) (pp. 206–208)

Super's 14 propositions clearly illustrate the breadth of his theory and demonstrate that it is much more than a pure developmental theory. As reflected in his propositions, Super's approach draws on aspects of career development "taken from developmental, differential, social, personality, and phenomenological psychology and held together by self-concept and learning theory" (Super, 1990, p. 199). Significantly, this description is reflective of the move away from complete reliance on differential psychology toward the integration of concepts from a number of fields. In line with differential psychology are Super's Propositions 1, 2, 3, 9, 12, and 13. Propositions 4, 5, 8, and 10 are linked to developmental psychology. Social learning principles are reflected in Propositions 4, 6, 11, and 14, and phenomenology is reflected in Propositions 1, 7, and 10. This illustrates that a reliance on only one field is not adequate to explain the complex process of career development, and it reinforces the importance of Super's work in highlighting the need for integration.

SELF

As reflected in these propositions, the concept of self is a major focus of Super's theory because it is in self that the processing of the life span, life space information occurs. Super (1990) referred to the individual as the "socialized organizer of his or her experience" (p. 221). "The *Self* (the person) and his or her Role Self-Concepts are the culminating products of the interaction of the person and the environment" (Super, 1992, pp. 41–42). Super et al. (1996) described the importance of conceptions of self in relation to career choice and adjustment. Conceptions of self may be objective (vocational identity) or subjective (occupational self-concept). The acknowledgment of subjective processes in the career development process was a significant deviation away from the trait-and-factor traditions of objective and quantifiable data.

Vocational identity, sometimes described as *occupational identity*, refers to the combinations of traits that apply to an individual and that may be observed by self or others and assessed through instruments such as interest inventories (Super et al., 1996). Descriptions generated by these means provide a point of comparison with others in an objective way.

While vocational identity is an objective concept, *occupational self-concept* refers to the personal meaning that individuals ascribe to their traits—for example, how particular traits have developed. Occupational self-concept develops over time as a result of interaction between a number of factors, such as aptitudes and the opportunity to see or perform certain roles. The fourth of Super's propositions describes the process whereby self-concept changes over time through social learning as a result of an individual's experience.

Self-concept implementation describes the process of choosing an occupation that matches one's image of oneself. The satisfaction that people derive from work is related to the extent to which they are able to implement their self-concepts. More recently, Super has commented on the way that careers evolve over time and has used the term *emergent career decision making* (Freeman, 1993, p. 261) to refer to the process in which successive career decisions by people are sharper and finer and may be different at different times in their lives.

The terms *career* and *vocational maturity*, used interchangeably (Super, 1990, p. 209), are defined by Super (1990) as

> the individual's readiness to cope with the developmental tasks with which he or she is confronted because of his or her biological and social developments and because of society's expectations of people who have reached that stage of development. This readiness is both affective and cognitive. (p. 213)

Career maturity contributes to the career pattern followed by an individual. In brief, Super described it as "readiness to make career decisions" (Freeman, 1993, p. 261). Super suggested that the attitudes of individuals and their knowledge of the world of work and of life stages may be used as measures of career maturity. Attitudes constitute the affective domain of career maturity and include "career planning, or planfulness; and career exploration, or curiosity" (Super, 1990, p. 213). The cognitive characteristics of career maturity include knowledge and application of career decision making, knowledge of the world of work, and occupational preference. Realism may also be used to judge career maturity (Super, 1990) by comparing occupational self-concept and vocational identity with the reality of the occupational preference. It was Super's reference to time and subjective processes that set him apart from his predecessors in the career field.

LIFE SPAN AND LIFE SPACE

Super's conceptualizations of self previously discussed are essential to his life span, life space approach to career development, in which the self is set in a broad context. The terms *life span* and *life space* basically represent the content and process of career development. *Life span* represents the process of career development throughout life and relates Super's stages of vocational development to recognized life stages. *Life space* represents the roles individuals play during their lives and takes into account the context of their lives. Super (1980, 1990) depicted his life span, life space approach using diagrams of a "life-career rainbow" and an "archway model," both of which will be discussed. In reviewing Super's work, it is useful to examine his concepts of life span and life space in more detail.

LIFE SPAN. Super (1980, 1990, 1992) depicted the concept of life span using the diagram of a rainbow, termed the "life-career rainbow" (see Figure 3.1). The outside of the rainbow illustrates ages and stages of life. As depicted on the diagram, his five vocational development stages, termed *growth, exploration, establishment, maintenance,* and *decline,* correspond with the life stages of childhood, adolescence, adulthood, middle adulthood, and old age and their approximate ages. Each life stage is named to reflect "the nature of its principal life-stage task" (Super et al., 1996, p. 131). More recently, the term *disengagement* has been favored over the term *decline* (Super, 1992; Super et al., 1996).

The *growth* stage is characterized by the exploration by children of the world around them. During the growth stage, individuals attend school, develop work habits, gain more control over their lives, and become future oriented (Super et al., 1996). As a result, they may identify with role models and begin to develop interests and an awareness of their abilities. Fantasy and play help them to develop concepts of themselves in adult roles.

The *exploratory* stage is the time when career choices are narrowed and individuals frequently have selected and embarked on training or education to prepare them for their chosen vocation. It is during this stage that a vocational identity develops. This stage involves three career development tasks. The first

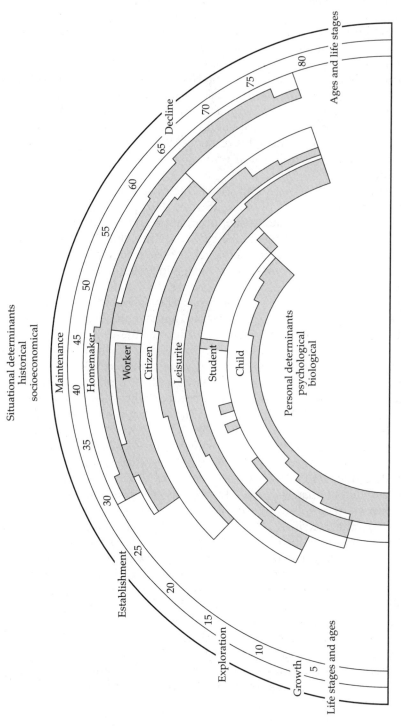

Situational determinants
historical
socioeconomical

Maintenance

Homemaker

Worker

Citizen

Leisurite

Student

Child

Personal determinants
psychological
biological

Ages and life stages

Decline

Establishment

Exploration

Growth

Life stages and ages

F I G U R E 3.1 The Life-Career Rainbow: Six Life Roles in Schematic Life Space (from *Guided Career Exploration*, 1979) task during this stage is *crystallization*, the cognitive process of forming a vocational goal on the basis of vocational information and awareness of traits such as interests and values. The next task, *specification*, involves the actual selection of a specific career. Finally, *implementation* involves training for one's selected vocation and beginning employment.

This is followed by the stage of *establishment*, during which time the individual gains employment. The first task is to stabilize one's position in the organization through becoming familiar with its culture and performing satisfactorily (Super et al., 1996). Once stabilized in an occupation, the next task for the individual is to consolidate his or her position. Some individuals may also choose the task of advancement or promotion and seeking higher levels of responsibility.

Maintenance, the fourth stage, is characterized by "preserving the place one has made in the world of work" (Super, 1992, p. 44). Before entering this stage, individuals may evaluate their occupation and decide to change organizations or occupations. If this is the case, they recycle through the stages of exploration and establishment, a minicycle. Those who do not change enter the stage of maintenance. The tasks of this stage include holding on, keeping up, and innovating.

The final stage, *decline* or *disengagement*, is associated with planning for retirement, possible reduction of workload, and eventual retirement. As mentioned in Super's Proposition 5, progression through these broad stages is termed a *maxicycle*. It is important to remember that Super sees the ages of transitions between stages as flexible and that individuals may recycle through stages, referred to as *minicycles* (Super, 1990) as a result of a planned or unplanned change. For example, individuals can expect to change jobs several times during their working life and thus can also expect to recycle through the stages several times. The concept of recycling through stages is a refinement of Super's earlier work on stages that enhances its relevance to today's world.

The "life-career rainbow" (Super, 1980) also features personal and situational determinants of career development, an aspect of the model later described as a deficit because it "merely suggests" the determinants (Super, 1994, p. 67). Super attempted to remedy this in his later work by presenting more detail in what he described as a "second attempt" at the model (Super, 1992, p. 38). This attempt took the form of a "segmental model of career development" (Super, 1990, p. 200), also referred to as the "archway model" (Super, 1990, p. 201), in which he set out to specifically acknowledge the multifaceted nature of career development and the contributions of many theorists. This model, depicted in Figure 3.2 and described later in this chapter, provides greater detail about the determinants by representing them individually as the stones of an arch. In a later publication, Super (1992) referred to it as "the Arch of Career Determinants" (p. 39) and the "determinant/choice model (the Arch)" (p. 41). These changes are illustrative of the refinements that Super has made to his theory over time to keep it as relevant in the 1990s as it was in the 1950s when it was first proposed.

LIFE SPACE.   While the concept of life span provides the process dimension of Super's model, the concept of life space "provides the contextual dimension in the theory, denoting the constellation of social positions and roles enacted by an individual" (Super et al., 1996, p. 128). Super originally identified nine life roles: child, student, "leisurite," citizen, worker, spouse, homemaker, parent, and pensioner, and four main contexts, or "theaters" in which these roles were most commonly enacted, specifically the home, community, school (college and university), and workplace.

Significantly, Super acknowledged that the work role may be only one of a number of roles that an individual may hold at any one time, and this is illus-

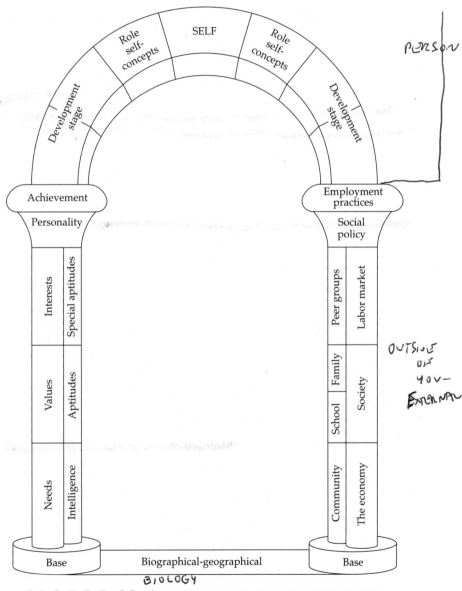

F I G U R E   3.2   A SEGMENTAL MODEL OF CAREER DEVELOPMENT
(FROM D. BROWN & BROOKS, 1990A)

trated on the life-career rainbow. Roles interact with each other and provide each individual's life with a focus. Acknowledgment of multiple roles constituted an advance in conceptualizing career development. Thus, Super played an instrumental role in setting vocational roles in the broader context of an individual's life and in doing so emphasized the importance of role salience, a concept he (1990) described as "the constellation of positions occupied and roles played by a person" (p. 218). The life-career rainbow (Figure 3.1) can be used to "focus on the concept and measurement of role salience" (p. 218) and to demonstrate the importance of the major life roles to an individual as well as the relationship between the work role and other life roles. Life role salience became the "pivotal construct" (Savickas, 1997, p. 251) in that it allowed for roles other than the work role to be central in an individual's life.

Interaction occurs between roles. For example, conflict between roles could occur when a less satisfying role takes time away from a more satisfying role, or alternatively, roles may compensate in that satisfaction not found in one role is provided in another. Super et al. (1996) reminded us that "to understand an individual's career, it is important to know and appreciate the web of life roles that embeds that individual and her or his career concerns" (p. 129). More recently, Richardson (1993, 1996) has discussed the importance of understanding the place of work in people's lives in relation to understanding the meaning of career. It is also significant in light of much recent debate about the link between personal and career counseling, which is discussed in more detail in Part 3.

In the archway model (Figure 3.2), Super (1990) introduced the concepts of "personal determinants" and "situational determinants," which are the range of factors that could have an impact on career decision making. The personal determinants, represented on the left column of the archway, include personal factors such as interests, values, needs, intelligence, special aptitudes, and aptitudes. The situational determinants, represented on the right column of the archway, include contextual factors such as peer group, school, family, community, society, the labor market, and the economy. Developmental stages and role self-concepts are also included on the arch on each side of the keystone. As previously mentioned, the keystone of the arch is the person, "self," in whom all of the variables are brought together. Super more recently explained the need to understand the interaction between the segments of the model rather than which segment is most important (Freeman, 1993). Thus, the emphasis is not on one or other of the segments but rather on the interactions between all of them.

Super (1990) noted the "dynamic interaction of individual and society" (p. 203). In his later work, he proposed that "learning theory" was the "cement" that held the segments of the archway together (p. 204). He claimed that individuals learn through interaction with the environment or social learning (interpersonal learning or learning from others) and termed this *experiential* or *interactive learning*. Learning theory is reflective of the interactive nature of the model in that the information is brought together in and processed by the individual, resulting in the shaping of his or her self-concept and occupational concept. However, the static nature of the model does not reflect this. Super himself suggested that lines representing interaction could be drawn on his model.

Thus, while his model reflects the variety of factors that influence career development, it does not adequately reflect the complexity of the interaction between the influences over time.

In his archway model, Super (1990) acknowledged the work of other theorists and included many factors that influence career development. This also supports his description of his work as a "segmental theory" (as discussed previously) and his claims that "there is no 'Super's theory'; there is just an assemblage of theories" (p. 199) that he has attempted to synthesize. His constant revisions and open-mindedness on the breadth of career development have made a lasting contribution to the field, and his work has stimulated thinking and further research long after his death (Blustein, 1997; Herr, 1997; Nevill, 1997; Phillips, 1997; Savickas, 1997).

INDIVIDUALISTIC APPROACH

Just as self is central to the work of Super, so too is it central to the work of Miller-Tiedeman and Tiedeman (1990). The original work in this area was undertaken by Tiedeman and O'Hara (1963) and has been developed more recently by Miller-Tiedeman (1988) and Miller-Tiedeman and Tiedeman (1990). The work of Tiedeman and O'Hara (1963) will be discussed first, followed by the work of Miller-Tiedeman (1988) and Miller-Tiedeman and Tiedeman (1990).

Tiedeman and O'Hara (1963) viewed career development as an ongoing process of differentiating ego identity. This reflected their choice of Erikson's (1959) psychosocial theory of ego identity as a basis for their career decision-making model (Miller-Tiedeman & Tiedeman, 1990). Like Super (1953), they proposed a developmental model of stages through which individuals pass during their lifetime. Unlike Super, they placed greater emphasis on the personal development of the individual. Critical to this development of the self are biological, social, and situational factors. "Their decision making model is an attempt to help individuals bring to conscious awareness all of the factors inherent in making decisions so that they will be able to make choices based on full knowledge of themselves and appropriate external information" (McDaniels & Gysbers, 1992, p. 56). Basically, the model assists the individual to understand the "organization of self and environment" (Miller-Tiedeman & Tiedeman, 1990, p. 316).

Miller-Tiedeman and Tiedeman proposed a model in two phases: anticipation and implementation. They also described the processes that underlay progression through the stages of the model. The essence of their model is that events are experienced by the individual, who in turn derives meaning from them. In brief, an individual develops an ego identity by interacting with and collecting observations about the environment and processing the collected information into a meaningful whole. These processes are termed *differentiation* and *reintegration* (also termed *integration* by Miller-Tiedeman & Tiedeman, 1990). "It is a period of collecting observations about the interaction (differentiation) and incorporating that information into the ego identity (integration)" (Minor, 1992, p. 26). Influences may be internally or externally generated. "Differentiating is a matter of separating experiences; integrating is a matter of structuring them into a more comprehensive whole" (Miller-Tiedeman & Tiedeman, 1990, p. 312). Integration involves processing new information, combining it with existing information, and integrating it into the ego identity. Thus, an individual is "the whole of all earlier decisions" (Miller-Tiedeman & Tiedeman, 1990, p. 314).

This approach has its base in decision-making theory, which posits that within the continuous process of career development, there will be points at which individuals are faced with decisions, such as job entry, educational choice, and career change. The anticipation of career decisions comprises four stages: exploration, crystallization, choice, and clarification. *Exploration* describes a period of interaction with and feedback from the environment. During the next stage, individuals begin to synthesize and order the information they have gathered, and *crystallization* is said to occur when they are able to recognize patterns "in the form of alternatives and consequences" (Miller-Tiedeman & Tiedeman, 1990, p. 313). Once crystallization has occurred, *choice* follows, and the individual begins to act upon it and prepare to enter an occupation, a process called *clarification*.

Once the four preparatory stages have been completed, the second phase of the career decision-making process, *implementation*, occurs. This phase involves three stages: induction, reformation, and reintegration. *Induction* occurs when choice has been implemented and the individual is settling into the new workplace. During this stage, the behavior of individuals is mainly responsive as they learn what is expected of them in their new position. The next stage is that of *reformation*, which occurs after individuals have gained their confidence and credibility in the organization and can begin to assert themselves more. Finally, the stage of *integration* occurs when a balance has been achieved between the organization and the individual. This could be compared with Dawis and Lofquist's (1976) concepts of satisfaction and satisfactoriness.

While Tiedeman and O'Hara (1963) proposed seven stages, they did not propose that the stages were instantaneous or irreversible (Miller-Tiedeman & Tiedeman, 1990) or that an individual's progress could not deviate from the path set by their model. However, they contended that "a person's career normally moves forward in comprehensivity, toward unity" (Miller-Tiedeman & Tiedeman, 1990, p. 314). A significant feature of their model was their belief that the tasks of each stage invoke a different range of emotions and subjective processes.

More recently, Miller-Tiedeman and Tiedeman (1990) have contended that "how one advances one's career can be seen in the language one uses; . . . the language people use about their career mirrors the self, as both a reactor and an actor, and discloses personal assumptions about the career" (p. 320). In essence, they claimed that the language people use to describe their careers can be used as a measure of how far advanced they are in their career. In particular, they focused on defining "reality" and identified two perspectives from which individuals describe their careers—personal reality and common reality.

"Common reality is a notion similar to societal, parental, or other external expectations" (Minor, 1992, p. 27), or what "they" say you should do (Miller-Tiedeman & Tiedeman, 1990). Miller-Tiedeman and Tiedeman (1979) described attempts to predict what is right for another as "common reality." They posited that if individuals are to advance in their career, they "need to become conscious of the difference between the two realities. Such consciousness gives individuals a choice of realities to follow" (Miller-Tiedeman & Tiedeman, 1990, p. 320). As people become aware of the difference between the two realities, they can become more proactive. Miller-Tiedeman and Tiedeman's theory held as a premise individuals' capacity to process information and arrive at their own "personal reality" (Miller-Tiedeman & Tiedeman, 1979)—that is, a decision that is right for them. Personal reality is recognized when an individual understands that the "life process is guided by inner knowledge" (Miller-Tiedeman, 1988, p. 7). In applications of this theory, a goal is for individuals to be empowered enough to act on the basis of their personal reality. That reality will feel "right" or good to the individual, irrespective of the expectations of others, and may be represented as an act, thought, behavior, or direction. Arriving at a personal reality is a subjective and evolutionary process because individuals continuously perceive and react to contextual information; their decision cannot necessarily be predicted by others and may in fact be different from what others say they should do (Miller-Tiedeman & Tiedeman, 1979). The concept of personal reality is based on the authors' belief that people are open, self-organizing systems capable of career development and career decision making in their response to environmental input. This concept challenges both traditional models of career decision making based on logical, cognitive processes and traditional approaches to career guidance, in which the practitioner has taken a role of "expert adviser."

The work of Tiedeman and O'Hara has formed the basis for Miller-Tiedeman and Tiedeman's (1990) more recent theoretical position of "life is career" (p. 331), described by D. Brown (1990) as a "holistic theory" (p. 359) and by Miller-Tiedeman (1988) as a "process theory" (p. 5). This is a considerable deviation from traditional career theory in that it embraces process only; the content is supplied by the individual (Miller-Tiedeman, 1988). Miller-Tiedeman's (1988) "lifecareer" theory presented a challenge to career theorists by proposing that individuals should write their own career theory and that the career practitioner should not impose someone else's theory on them. Miller-Tiedeman claimed that existing theories attempt "intellectual explanations of why things occur as they do in career" (p. 3) and that none deal with the "lived-in-the-moment life process" (p. 3) experienced by the individual. She was critical of the failure of existing theories to "personalize to the client's perspective" (p. 4), claiming that they fail to empower clients because they stem from the differential psychology tradition of a hierarchical counselor-client relationship.

Drawing on literature outside the career development field (described in more depth in Chapter 8), lifecareer theory is based on quantum mechanics, self-organizing systems theory, universe process theory, and decision-making theory and as such is distinctly different from most other career theories. Although this theory accommodates very recent thinking in career development, decision making, and counseling, it is curious that it was not included in the recent edition of D. Brown and Brooks (1996) as either an established theory or an emerging theory.

GOTTFREDSON'S THEORY
OF CIRCUMSCRIPTION AND COMPROMISE

L. S. Gottfredson's (1981, 1996) theory is "concerned with both the content of career aspirations and their course of development" (L. S. Gottfredson, 1996, p. 181). In common with other theories are the assumptions that "career choice is a developmental process beginning in childhood; occupational aspirations reflect people's efforts to implement their self-concepts; and satisfaction with career choice depends on how well that choice fits the self-concept" (L. S. Gottfredson, 1996, p. 181). While the theory is developmental, there is a similarity with the person-environment fit theories and the concept that "people seek jobs compatible with their images of themselves" (L. S. Gottfredson, 1981, p. 546). Gottfredson also attended to the influence of social class and gender on career development, which will be discussed in Chapter 6.

Gottfredson (1981) presented a developmental model of four stages beginning in early childhood and ending in late adolescence. During these stages, individuals become more self-aware and narrow their occupational options by eliminating those that are no longer acceptable in a process termed *circumscription*. The stages reflect levels of mental development and the degree of self-knowledge integrated by the individual. The process and stages of circumscription will be discussed first and will be followed by a discussion of compromise.

CIRCUMSCRIPTION

The process of circumscription can be described by five principles. The first principle contends that individuals move from a stage of concrete thought to more abstract thinking as they get older and that they move through this process at different rates. The second principle holds that the development of self-concept and the development of occupational preferences are closely linked. The third principle is that, as individuals develop, information is absorbed according to complexity. Less complex information is absorbed at a younger age, followed by more abstract information as the individual grows older. Often, while information is being absorbed, the individual is becoming aware of the existence of more complex information. The fourth principle describes the process whereby self-concepts become more clearly delineated and complex as the young person incorporates more abstract information such as that on gender and social class. Thus, while the development of self-concept progresses, a narrowing of options occurs as the young person irreversibly eliminates certain occupations from his or her considerations—for example, on the basis of social class or gender. The fifth principle claims that the development of self-concept is so subtle and gradual that individuals are not aware of it until their awareness is heightened by an external source. This is reflected when individuals can express occupational preferences but not verbalize why they hold these preferences.

STAGES OF CIRCUMSCRIPTION.   The first stage in this process is orientation to size and power, which occurs from approximately age 3 to age 5. During this stage, young people become aware of the adult world—that is, "big people" compared with them, "little people"—and become aware that work is a part of what "big people" do. Thus, developing an awareness that occupations are a part of being an adult is the main task during this stage.

The second stage is orientation to sex roles, which occurs from approximately ages 6 to 8. During this stage, individuals develop an awareness of sex roles and what is appropriate for their sex—for example, clothing. This is also reflected in vocational choice, in which young people actively reject occupations they see as belonging to the opposite sex. During this stage, they also become aware of social class, and this is the beginning of distinguishing between jobs on that basis.

Stage 3 is orientation to social valuation, which occurs from approximately ages 9 to 13. During this time, they become more aware of the more abstract concepts, such as social class and its trappings, and more concerned about the opinions of others. They become more aware of high-status and low-status jobs and begin to reject occupations that they perceive as low status. During this stage, they become aware of the link between education, occupation, and income, as well as the occupational expectations of their parents. They also become aware of their ability. Thus, their self-concept is shaped during this stage by the addition of information on social class and ability. Again, circumscription occurs as young people eliminate from their occupational options those occupations they see as low prestige or too difficult for them to achieve in light of their ability.

Stage 4 is orientation to the internal, unique self, which occurs from approximately age 14 on and is often referred to as the "adolescent identity crisis" (L. S. Gottfredson, 1981, p. 549). Unlike the first three stages, in which the individual focused on eliminating unacceptable alternatives, this stage is concerned with weighing up the acceptable alternatives in terms of personal preference and accessibility. Individuals also begin to view these alternatives in light of an anticipated future lifestyle. During this stage, they begin to implement their career decisions and become increasingly aware of the availability of training and education and job vacancies.

Progression through these stages is critical to the development of self-concept, a fundamental aspect of Gottfredson's model. Self-concept comprises many elements, including those that are vocationally relevant, such as "gender, social class background, intelligence, and vocational interests, competencies and values" (L. S. Gottfredson, 1981, p. 548). A significant aspect of this theory is Gottfredson's acknowledgment of the influence of gender and social class.

COMPROMISE

Unlike circumscription, compromise is a process of vetting the preferred alternatives on the basis of "external reality" (L. S. Gottfredson, 1996, p. 195) or accessibility. This refers to "obstacles or opportunities in the social or economic environment that affect one's chance of getting into a particular occupation" (L. S. Gottfredson, 1981, p. 548). For example, socioeconomic circumstances, family contacts, or geographic location may affect an individual's occupational opportunities.

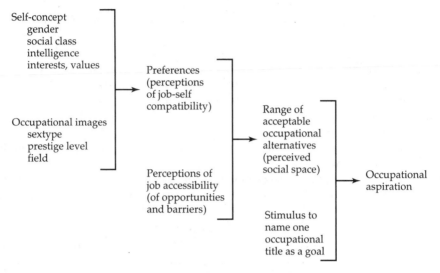

F I G U R E 3.3 RELATIONS AMONG
THEORETICAL CONSTRUCTS (FROM L. S. GOTTFREDSON, 1981)

Gottfredson represented the relations among her theoretical constructs diagrammatically, as shown in Figure 3.3. This clearly illustrates the relationship between her theory and the matching models. On the basis of compatibility between the two primary sources of information in her theory, self-concept (self-knowledge) and occupational images (a concept bearing some resemblance to work knowledge), the individual forms preferences for occupations. These are later offset against perceptions of accessibility of opportunities and barriers, causing the range of acceptable occupational outcomes to be narrowed.

SIMILARITIES AND DIFFERENCES
BETWEEN THEORIES OF PROCESS

While the theories presented in this chapter are classified as developmental theories and as such exhibit similarities and differences, they also exhibit similarities and differences with the theories discussed in Chapters 2 and 4. The discussion in this chapter will focus on similarities and differences between the theories contained in this chapter; similarities and differences with other theory groups will be discussed in Chapter 5. As mentioned in Chapter 2, the discussion on similarities and differences will be illustrated by a table (Table 3.1).

Whereas the theories in Chapter 2 had their origins in differential psychology, the theories presented in this chapter have their origins in developmental psychology. As a result, these theories tend to be "more inclusive, more concerned with longitudinal expressions of behavior, and more inclined to highlight the importance of self-concept. They tend to be process-oriented in their conceptions of how career behavior develops and changes over time" (Herr & Cramer, 1992, p. 207). Interestingly, these theories, particularly that of Super (1990), also take into account contextual influences, a trend that could reflect

T A B L E   3.1 INFLUENCES ON CAREER DEVELOPMENT: THEORIES OF PROCESS

CONTENT INFLUENCES	GINZBERG	SUPER	GOTT-FREDSON	MILLER-TIEDEMAN & TIEDEMAN
Intrapersonal system				
Ability				
Aptitudes				
Interests				
Gender				
Age				
Skills				
Ethnicity				
Sexual orientation				
Beliefs				
Health				
Disability				
Values				
World-of-work knowledge				
Personality				
Self-concept				
Physical attributes				
Social System				
Family				
Peers				
Community groups				
Education institutions				
Media				
Workplace				
Environmental/Societal System				
Political decisions				
Historical trends				
Employment market				
Geographical location				
Socioeconomic status				
Globalization				

PROCESS INFLUENCES				
Recursiveness				
Change over time				
Chance				

☐ No acknowledgment   ☐ Acknowledgment   ☐ Significant emphasis their later development in the history of career theory. While this discussion will examine similarities and differences related to the content influences (of the individual and the context) and the process influences, it will not do so in discrete sections, since the two are entwined in these theories.

The most significant content influence in this group of theories is that of self-concept. Self-concept is closely linked with the process influences because the process of career development concerns the implementation of self-concept (Betz, 1994b). All theorists describe the self-concept as influenced by a range of variables, with the largest range of influences being acknowledged by Super (1990) in his segmental model. However, none of the theories adequately account for the nature of the influence on career development. A significant feature of the work of Super is that he is the only theorist of this group to address the issues of life roles and role salience.

The process orientation of these theories is reflected in the stage models of development that they present. While there is no agreement between the theories on the number of stages, each theory presented in this chapter addresses the issue of change over time. Historically, the most significant advance in the stage models is acknowledgment that career development covers the life span, an advance that led to the demise of the theory of Ginzberg and his colleagues. However, Gottfredson's stages also span only the period from early childhood to late adolescence.

Associated with the stages are vocational development tasks that individuals master as they mature. Basically, the tasks describe the process of making finer decisions about occupations by ruling some out on the basis of new self-knowledge or occupational knowledge. Super described this in his Propositions 10 and 11 as a narrowing of options. However, Gottfredson described the process in much more detail. Using the terms *circumscription* and *compromise*, she outlined a process of circumscription in which, as young people grow older, they rule out some occupations as possible options on the basis of factors such as gender and social class. She also described the process of compromise, in which individuals consider their possible options on the basis of the external reality—that is, the employment realities of their social or economic environment. Compromise on the basis of the individual's reality was also a feature of Ginzberg's theory, in which the process variable of compromise was closely tied to the content variables of the world of work, education, and personal values. These factors, termed *external reality* by Gottfredson, resemble Super's "situational determinants" and to some extent Miller-Tiedeman and Tiedeman's "common reality."

None of the theories claim that progress through their stages is only a forward movement. For example, Super introduced the concept of "minicycles" to indicate recycling through stages. Inherent in each of the theories is a forward momentum and what could be described as personal growth. This is reflected in Miller-Tiedeman and Tiedeman's concept of "personal reality," in which individuals reach the point of being able to make their own decisions, free of the influence of others, and Super's concept of "career maturity," explained in his seventh and eighth propositions as an ability to cope with life stage demands.

A significant feature of the work of Super, and of Miller-Tiedeman and Tiedeman, is the attention they draw to subjective processes and the affective domain of development. This is emphasized to a greater extent by Miller-Tiedeman (1988) and is significant in its capacity to empower the individual in the career counseling process. As previously discussed, it challenges the traditional ways in which career counselors have worked with their clients. It also challenges traditional views of decision making proposed in Chapter 2 in the discussion of the matching models.

As evidenced in this discussion on similarities and differences, there is considerable overlap between the theories. The main contribution of this group of theories has been their concept of life span career development. While development has been the focus of these theories, they also acknowledge the context in which career development takes place. However, they do not sufficiently account for the influence of the contextual elements on career development. Chapter 4 will examine a group of theories that place more emphasis on contextual influences.

4

THEORIES FOCUSING
ON CONTENT AND PROCESS

Acknowledgments such as those by Holland (1985a) of the developmental nature of career and the influence of contextual influences and by Super (1990) of "personal determinants" and "situational determinants" influencing the developmental process of career decision making represent a significant change in thinking about career development and career decision making. These views reflect what Savickas (1995) has described as rapprochement in career development theory, in which theorists are sharing new ideas in refinements of their theories. It means that the matching theories and the developmental theories can no longer stand alone as explanations of career development and suggests that the key concepts of these theories are parts of a complex interaction that cannot be viewed as objectively as those of earlier theories. More recently, theories have focused on the content of both the individual and the context and the nature of the interactions within and between these variables. In addition, the more subtle cognitive processes that are part of career decision making have received considerable attention.

Just as responses to these criticisms are reflected in the refinements of the earlier theories of Holland and Super, so they are reflected in more recent models and approaches to career development, such as the social learning theory of career choice (Krumboltz, 1979, 1994; L. K. Mitchell & Krumboltz, 1990, 1996), a social cognitive theory–based model (Lent & Brown, 1996; Lent, Brown, & Hackett, 1994, 1996; Lent & Hackett, 1994), and cognitive information-processing models (Peterson, Sampson, & Reardon, 1991; Peterson et al., 1996). Two additional theoretical models include the developmental-contextual approach of Vondracek et al. (1986) and the more recently conceptualized contextual approach (Young et al., 1996). The work of Roe (Roe, 1956; Roe & Lunneborg, 1990) is also included in this chapter, since she focused on individual and context variables. All of these theoretical approaches have taken into account the complex society in which we live and the many influences on career decision makers, as well as changes from place to place and time to time. They are representative of attempts to address the complexity of context. Although the work of L. S. Gottfredson (1981, 1996) is acknowledged as the first and perhaps still the only (D. Brown, 1996b) theory to discuss contextual factors systematically, it also includes developmental processes. It has therefore been discussed in Chapter 3.

KRUMBOLTZ'S LEARNING THEORY OF CAREER DECISION MAKING

Krumboltz and his colleagues formulated the first adaptation of Bandura's (1977) social learning theory to the career field. The theory was first formulated in 1976 (Krumboltz, Mitchell, & Jones, 1976), and a significant restatement was published in 1979 (Krumboltz, 1979). This theory was also one of the first to address both the content and process of career decision making, although Hesketh and Rounds (1995) have commented that the theory has a stronger emphasis on process than content.

The social learning theory of career decision making aims to explain how people become employed in the wide variety of available occupations. It extends trait-and-factor theory in its attempt to explain the process of person-job congruence. Holland (quoted in Minor & Burtnett, 1983) commented that this theory "fills in the cracks in my typology." The theory, which is based on learning principles, suggests that individuals learn about themselves, their preferences, and the world of work through direct and indirect experiences. They then take action based on these knowledge- and skill-based learnings.

Four categories of factors influence an individual's career decision-making process: genetic endowment and special abilities, environmental conditions and events, learning experiences, and task approach skills (L. K. Mitchell & Krumboltz, 1990). The first category, an individual's genetic endowment and special abilities, includes gender, ethnicity, appearance, and ability or disability. Krumboltz makes clear that certain talents, such as musical ability and muscular coordination, may be developed only if the exposure to environmental events is favorable. For example, a young girl with musical ability raised in a low-income family may not be able to develop her ability because of the prohibitive costs of the musical instrument and related tuition.

Thus, the second factor of influence raised in the theory is environmental conditions and events. Krumboltz (1979) listed 12 such conditions and events that may be planned or unplanned and attributable to human action or nature. These factors are most often outside the individual's control. They include

(1) number and nature of job opportunities, (2) number and nature of training opportunities, (3) social policies and procedures for selecting trainees and work-

ers (for example, requirement of a high school diploma), (4) monetary and social rewards of various occupations, (5) labor laws and union rules, (6) natural disasters, (7) availability of and demand for natural resources, (8) technological developments, (9) changes in social organization (for example, welfare), (10) family training experiences and social and financial resources, (11) the educational system, and (12) neighborhood and community influences. (L. K. Mitchell & Krumboltz, 1996, p. 238)

Learning experiences are the third category of influence. Each person is assumed to have a unique pattern of learning experiences that result in a career (and life) path. These learning experiences are divided into two types, instrumental and associative. Instrumental, or direct, learning experiences are those in which the individual acts on the environment to produce a positive response (based on operant conditioning). Thus, Krumboltz (1979; L. K. Mitchell & Krumboltz, 1996) discussed a process whereby antecedents—that is, the special characteristics and genetic endowments, the environmental conditions, and the characteristics of a particular task—interact in an overt or covert way with the individual, who responds and receives consequences (positive or negative) from the environment. For example, individuals learn from an early age that they are physically nimble or clumsy or have a sense of humor. These personal characteristics are responded to positively or negatively. Through experiences over time with relevant personal characteristics, individuals learn skills relevant to decision making about careers that they view as appropriate to them.

The term *associative learning experiences*, based on a classical conditioning model, refers to the development of positive and negative attitudes and beliefs about occupations through a broad array of external stimuli. For example, children may learn positive messages about sporting heroes and negative messages about politicians. The association of these messages with occupation produces a positive or negative response in the individual that will be relevant in career decision making.

Finally, the fourth influence, task approach skills, results from an interaction of the first three influences. These skills include performance standards, work habits, perceptual and cognitive processes, mental sets, and emotional responses. As a result of the interaction of the four influences, four outcomes can be described, with the second of these representing a recent addition to the theory (L. K. Mitchell & Krumboltz, 1996). The first outcome is self-observation generalizations, or beliefs about the self, used to describe an individual's own reality. These are the generalizations that individuals make about themselves as a result of feedback over time. For example, an individual may state that he or she is good at making people laugh but may not remember all the specific incidents that led him or her to this conclusion.

A second outcome is worldview generalizations, in which people observe the environment and trends and draw conclusions about how things are and how they might be in the future. These observations may be accurate or inaccurate and, like self-observation generalizations, may have derived from positive or negative learning experiences.

A third outcome, also discussed previously as an influence, is task approach skills. L. K. Mitchell and Krumboltz (1996) defined outcome task approach skills as "cognitive and performance abilities and emotional predispositions for coping with the environment, interpreting it in relation to self-observation generalizations, and making covert and overt predictions about future events" (p. 246). Individuals examine their generalizations about themselves and the world of work and formulate specific skills to use in relation to career decision making. Finally, the fourth outcome is action. These behaviors include engaging in activities that lead to career entry, such as enrolling in an appropriate training program and actively applying for jobs.

A number of testable hypotheses have been proffered by Krumboltz and his colleagues. These include that people will prefer an occupation (a) if they have succeeded at tasks that they believe are similar to those relevant to certain occupations; (b) if they have observed an important model being reinforced for tasks similar to those performed by members of that occupation; and (c) if they have experienced positive associations with the occupation through direct or indirect messages (Krumboltz, 1994).

Social learning theory is significant to the development of career theory because it recognizes the importance of a wide range of influences on career choice rather than focusing on a single influence. L. K. Mitchell and Krumboltz (1990) acknowledged the importance of context in the social learning approach to career decision making: "The social learning theory of career decision making suggests that maximum career development of all individuals requires each individual to have the opportunity to be exposed to the widest array of learning experiences, regardless of race, gender or ethnic origin" (pp. 167–168). Thus, they acknowledged the influence on career choice of the interaction between many contextual elements. The third outcome, task approach skills, is also suggestive of an interaction between the individual and the environment, although the nature and process of this interaction are not fully explained.

The most recent development of the social learning theory of career decision making is that of Krumboltz and Nichols (1990), who attempted to integrate principles of the living systems framework (Ford, 1987) with learning theory. This development is described further in Chapter 7. A number of authors (e.g., Krumboltz, 1994; Savickas, 1995) have discussed the potential of social learning theory as a framework for the convergence of career theories. This development is also discussed further in Chapter 7.

SOCIAL COGNITIVE CAREER THEORY

The development of cognitive models of vocational psychology reflects what Borgen (1991) has termed "the cognitive revolution" (p. 279). The cognitive revolution has been instrumental in strengthening the view of individuals as possessing personal agency and being active shapers of their own development. This view is in contrast to the determinism of psychoanalytic perspectives and the view of humans as malleable proposed by behaviorist approaches. At the same time, we cannot ignore that there are internal and external factors that are barriers to positive change and growth. For example, Krumboltz spoke of genetic endowments that may be negative or positive factors in an individual's career planning. Similarly, changing social and economic conditions can have a marked effect on career development. "In short, a complex array of factors—such as culture, gender, genetic endowment, sociostructural considerations, and disability/health status—operate in tandem with people's cognitions, affecting the nature and range of their career possibilities" (Lent et al., 1996, p. 374). Hackett (1995) asserted that the role of sociocognitive mechanisms, especially self-efficacy, in career choice and development is strongly supported in the research literature. In addition to its role in career choice and career decision making, self-efficacy has a role in the development of interests, values, and goals.

In response to this cognitive revolution, and as an attempt to contribute to the trend toward theoretical convergence in career psychology, the social cognitive career theory (SCCT) was developed (Lent & S. D. Brown, 1996; Lent et al., 1994, 1996; Lent & Hackett, 1994). The theory developers have characterized their work as emergent and evolving. As a strategy to pursue convergence, its aim is to develop constructs and concepts to bridge differences and incomplete conceptualizations in existing theory. This aim was declared following a major review of the current state of career development theory (Hackett & Lent, 1992), when the authors commented that

> the time may be ripe for beginning to construct integrative theories that (a) bring together conceptually related constructs (e.g., self-concept, self-efficacy); (b) more fully explain outcomes that are common to a number of career theories (e.g., satisfaction, stability); and (c) account for the relations among seemingly diverse constructs (e.g., self-efficacy, interests, abilities, needs). (p. 443)

Chapter 7 discusses the contribution of SCCT to convergence; aspects of the theory itself are presented in this chapter.

The SCCT was derived primarily from Bandura's (1986) revised social cognitive theory. It has also been informed by the self-efficacy theory of Hackett and Betz (1981; see Chapter 6) and the learning theory of Krumboltz discussed previously. It aims to update each of these theoretical formulations with changes derived from the revised general social cognitive theory (Bandura, 1986). For example, the developers of SCCT acknowledged the importance of learning experiences and the influence of genetic factors and environmental conditions on career decisions. However, they emphasized that social cognitive theory extends beyond the narrow behavioral bases of the learning theory principles of learning and conditioning. SCCT focuses more on the specific cognitive mediators that influence learning experiences in career decision-making behavior. In addition, the theory focuses on how interests, abilities, and other relevant variables interrelate and how personal and environmental factors influence career decisions. SCCT also emphasizes that the individual is an active agent in these processes.

SCCT focuses on three interlocking segmental processes: how career and academic interests develop, how career choices are made and enacted, and how performance outcomes are achieved. It seeks to explain a bidirectional relationship between variables using Bandura's (1986) triadic reciprocal model of causality. Using this model, Lent, S. D. Brown, and Hackett described how three intricately related social cognitive variables (self-efficacy beliefs, outcome expectations, and personal goals) interact with aspects of the individual such as gender and ethnicity, relevant environmental issues, and learning experiences. Importantly, the individual is central to the three interlocking processes.

According to Bandura (1986), *self-efficacy* refers to individuals' beliefs about their capacity to "organize and execute courses of action required to attain designated types of performances" (p. 391). Social cognitive theory suggests that self-efficacy is not a static unitary trait but rather a constantly changing set of self-beliefs that are peculiar to given performance areas and that interact with other personal, behavioral, and environmental factors (Hackett & Lent, 1992). *Outcome expectations* refers to beliefs about the probable consequences of a particular course of action. Like self-efficacy beliefs, they are derived through various learning experiences. The final social cognitive variable, *personal goals*, refers to the determination to undertake a certain activity to produce a particular outcome. By establishing goals, individuals are able to coordinate, direct, and maintain their own behavior and thereby to have agency in their behavior. Lent and Hackett (1994) suggested that these three social cognitive variables (self-efficacy, outcome expectations, and personal goals) interact in a dynamically reciprocal way in the self-regulation and maintenance of an individual's behavior. In particular, they focused on the development of interests, career choice, and career-related performance.

INTERESTS

In relation to interests, SCCT suggests that self-efficacy and outcome expectations regarding activities and tasks influence career interests. That is, individuals form an enduring interest in an activity when they believe that they are good at it and that performing it will produce an outcome that is valued. In turn, ongoing interest and positive self-efficacy and outcome expectations will promote goals that encourage an individual to continue to engage in the activity. An ongoing positive feedback loop will be maintained by positive experiences or revised with failures. The theory developers posited that "this process repeats itself continuously throughout the lifespan, although it is perhaps most fluid up until late adolescence or early adulthood, at which point interests tend to stabilize" (Lent & S. D. Brown, 1996, p. 314). These authors acknowledged, however, that new experiences and factors such as new technology will continue to stimulate interests.

Lent et al. (1994) suggested that although aptitudes (abilities) and values are important in the development of interests, they are mediated by self-efficacy and outcome expectations. For example, an individual may be good at public speaking, but he or she must believe that he or she is and believe that it is worthwhile for public speaking to be developed as an interest. SCCT conceptualizes work values within outcome expectations—that is, as related to preferences for particular work conditions and perceived reward (e.g., status or money) and the extent to which it is believed that these are part of particular occupations.

Importantly, this theory emphasizes the relevance of other person and contextual variables such as gender, race and ethnicity, genetic endowment, and socioeconomic status. SCCT views gender and race as socially constructed and emphasizes their relevance to how they are viewed in the sociocultural environment and their relationship to opportunity structure.

> Framing gender and ethnicity as socially constructed aspects of experience leads naturally to a consideration of sociostructural conditions and processes that mould the learning opportunities to which particular individuals are exposed, the characteristic reactions they receive for performing different activities, and the future outcomes they anticipate. (Lent & S. D. Brown, 1996, p. 315)

Thus, the effect of gender and ethnicity on career interests, choice, and performance is also posited to operate through self-efficacy and outcome expectations.

CAREER CHOICE

SCCT proposes that career choice is a function of interests orienting people toward activities that support them. This equation requires a supportive environmental background. However, the literature on job satisfaction suggests that individuals' career choices do not always reflect interests and that environmental conditions are not always supportive (see Chapter 5, particularly the discussion of the null hypothesis; Betz, 1989). In attempting to be an integrative model, SCCT highlights a range of factors that mediate between interests and career choice. These include self-efficacy and outcome expectations as discussed, in addition to a large array of contextual influences. Although contextual influences can be positive or negative, SCCT emphasizes that an individual's formulated goals afford a measure of personal agency. SCCT (Lent et al., 1994, 1996) draws on the conceptualizations of the environmental context of Astin (1984) and Vondracek et al. (1986), opportunity structure (discussed further in Chapter 6), and contextual affordance (discussed later in this chapter), respectively. SCCT further develops these constructs, which are influential in an individual's career development, by dividing them into two types:

> (1) more distal influences (such as opportunities for skill development, culture and gender-role socialization processes, one's range of potential academic/career role models) that help shape social cognitions and interests; and (2) proximal influences (for instance, emotional and financial support for selecting a particular option, job availability in one's preferred field, sociostructural barriers) that come into play at critical choice junctures. (Lent et al., 1996, p. 393)

Each of these constructs refers to the differential way in which the environment supports or fails to support an individual's career development processes; thus, as discussed, each can be viewed as positive or negative.

CAREER-RELATED PERFORMANCE

SCCT is also concerned with work task performance and perseverance at a work activity or career (job stability). Again, an interaction between ability and the social cognitive variables of self-efficacy, outcome expectations, and goals is crucial. Consistent with the triadic-reciprocal approach, which emphasizes bi-

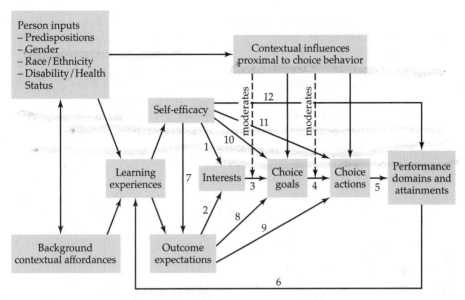

F I G U R E   4.1   PERSON, CONTEXTUAL, AND
EXPERIENTIAL FACTORS AFFECTING CAREER-RELATED CHOICE BEHAVIOR
(FROM LENT, BROWN, & HACKETT, 1993)

directional interaction between influences, a feedback loop between performance attainment and further behavior is posited. Therefore, mastery of a certain task or tasks will further develop abilities and, in turn, self-efficacy and outcome expectations. The development and revision of personal goals is a further element in this loop. Figure 4.1 presents the diagrammatic framework of this theoretical approach.

While SCCT is a particularly new development, the 12 hypotheses (Lent et al., 1994) formulated and the rich theoretical and empirical base on which it has been developed make it a valuable additional theoretical model designed to explain individual variability in career interests, choice, and performance. It is particularly important because it embraces a constructivist view of the individual as an active shaper of his or her life within the constraints of personal and environmental or contextual factors. Further, the social cognitive variables offer key explanatory mechanisms that are missing from other theoretical models.

COGNITIVE INFORMATION-PROCESSING MODEL

The cognitive information-processing approach (Peterson et al., 1991, 1996) aims to present a guide for career problem-solving and decision-making skills. It too is an emerging theory, based on cognitive processing theory, and reflects the importance of cognition processes in developing career theories. Cognitive information-processing theory emphasizes the thought and memory processes involved in career problem solving and career decision making.

The Peterson et al. (1991, 1996) model is based on the three key factors in making career choices identified by Parsons (1909), which are viewed as three distinct lines of inquiry in the model. These are self-knowledge, occupational knowledge, and career decision making. The aim of the model is to assist individuals to become better problem solvers and decision makers; therefore, it has a strong practice orientation, a notion reiterated by D. Brown (1996b).

Peterson et al. (1996) conceptualized the model as "ever broadening concentric circles from the smallest inner circle, which is the career problem, to the largest encompassing outer circle, which is lifestyle, with each succeeding concept encompassing the previous concept" (p. 427). Within these two inner and outer circles, a number of definitions key to this paradigm are described. These include career problem solving, career decision making, and career development. The capability that underpins career and lifestyle adjustment is the ability to recognize a problem, define it, solve it, and act on it.

In describing career problems and career problem solving, Peterson et al. (1996) emphasized that they are not always structured and that problem solving involves cognitive as well as emotional processes. The availability of cognitive operations is crucial, as is the recognition that self-knowledge and occupational knowledge involve continual change over time. The authors also emphasized the need for information-processing skills, which they view as being employed in a cycle known by the acronym *CASVE*. These skills, which come into play in response to internal or external problem signals, are communication (identifying a gap), analysis (relating problem components), synthesis (creating alternatives), valuing (prioritizing these alternatives), and execution (forming strategies). Peterson et al. (1996) suggested that these skills are generic—that is, relevant to a range of life problems in addition to career problems.

Finally, these authors posited the importance of higher order cognitive functions, or metacognitions. These metacognitions serve to "monitor, guide, and regulate lower order functions . . . /, namely the acquisition, storage, and retrieval of information, as well as the execution of cognitive strategies to solve a problem" (Peterson et al., 1996, p. 437). The principal metacognitions include self-talk, self-awareness, and monitoring and control.

In formulating these concepts for practical application, Sampson, Peterson, Lenz, and Reardon (1992) developed a guide to good decision making (see Figure 4.2). They further described the need to determine a client's decision readiness before determining where in the CASVE cycle an intervention needs to be carried out. For example, an undecided individual may need to experience an intervention that incorporates all phases of the cycle, whereas an individual who is decided and ready to focus on implementation may need to focus only on the execution phase of the cycle.

Peterson et al. maintained that their framework can integrate existing theories, but many issues, such as interaction between person and environment, are not explained. While the model describes the relevant variables in career problem solving and decision making, a description of how the factors of self-knowledge, occupational knowledge, generic information-processing skills, and metacognitions interact within the individual has not been adequately provided.

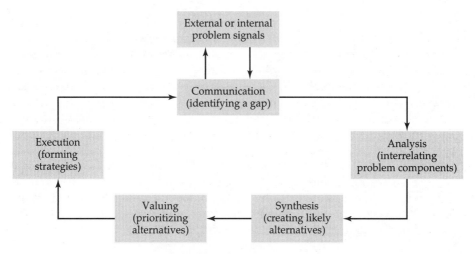

F I G U R E 4.2 THE FIVE STAGES OF THE CASVE CYCLE
OF INFORMATION-PROCESSING SKILLS USED IN CAREER DECISION MAKING
(FROM PETERSON, SAMPSON, & REARDON, 1991)

Similarly, the theory does not adequately relate to ages of development of some of these skills, particularly the higher order skills. Finally, the universality of these skills and the impact of contextual issues on these processes are remaining questions. Acknowledged strengths of the model (Peterson et al., 1991, 1996) include its derivation from an existing theoretical base, its relationship to existing theoretical constructs, and its ready translation to counseling and programmatic interventions.

DEVELOPMENTAL-CONTEXTUAL APPROACH

Vondracek et al. (1986) were also critical of the adherence of theorists to stage explanations of career development and the assumptions that these stages are ubiquitous, linear, invariant, and universal. They asserted that attempting to interpret contemporary career development through a normative framework is out of step with new understandings of the complexity of the process of development and change. Their developmental-contextual approach proffers instead the notion of probabilistic epigenesis, which emphasizes variability at both the individual and the contextual level. As a result, traditional normative prescriptions of career development are viewed as futile. One of the basic tenets of the developmental-contextual view is that "people, by interacting with their changing context, provide a basis of their own development" (p. 77); that is, individual development needs to be the key element in discussion of career development. Individuals' construction of career *is* their career.

On the basis of the work of Lerner (1979), Vondracek et al. (1986) also attempted to address some of the concerns about the failure of career theory to take into account the dynamic nature of the interaction between individuals and their ever-changing contexts. These authors merged the developmental organic perspective with the environmental perspective to produce developmental-contextualism. They suggested that there has been an overemphasis on within-person factors, such as values, abilities, and interests in career choice, at the expense of contextual issues, such as family-of-origin issues, labor market changes, and organizational constraints. The developmental-contextual framework attempts to account for the manner in which the environment differentially inhibits or encourages an individual's capacities to capitalize on personal characteristics and translate them into career futures, a concept referred to as *contextual affordance*. In addition, Vondracek et al. (1986) asserted that traditional career theories fail to consider the active, purposeful interaction of individuals with their changing contexts. Their "developmental life-span view leads to the idea that people, by interacting with their changing context, provide a basis of their own development" (p. 77), thereby emphasizing the personal agency of individuals.

The developmental-contextual model was designed as a general conceptual framework, a metamodel, not a specific career development theory. It is therefore not specific in delineating processes or hypotheses, although it has been useful in guiding a broader understanding of factors relevant to career development. The dynamic interaction model of career development proposes an outer circle of eight contextual variables (e.g., social policy, education, organizational/institutional context) and four inner circles that illustrate the interactive roles of family of origin and family of procreation and the adult and child extrafamilial networks. These networks (or sites for them) include peers, part-time work, school for children and adolescents, and work and interpersonal relations for adults. The model illustrates the interaction within the inner networks and between these and the outer contexts. This model has been reproduced in Figure 4.3.

Vondracek, Lerner, and Schulenberg (1983) identified the three key elements in career development as the individual, the context, and the relationship between the two. Thus, career decisions need to be viewed in light of the interaction of these factors. Basically, this approach means that as the individual changes and as the contextual influences change, so too will the decision. This approach highlights the dynamic nature of career development—that is, how decisions change over time as the interaction of the contextual elements changes. Consequently, time and the evolutionary nature of career development are important components of the process. It is particularly important to understand in this discussion the notion of dynamic interaction, in which the individual is seen as an active organism operating in and acting on a constantly changing environment. While the environment engenders change in the individual, so too the context is facilitated or constrained by the individual's unique characteristics. The continuous interplay of person and context is the basis of the development of an individual's unique career path.

In addition to dynamic interaction, an important concept crucial to the developmental-contextual model is embeddedness. Derived from life span developmental psychology, embeddedness emphasizes that life exists at multiple levels (e.g., biological, psychological, social, dyadic, community, cultural) and

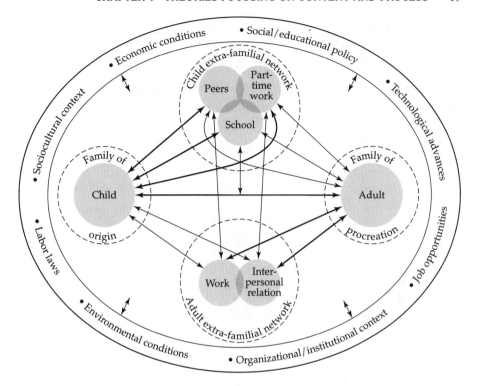

F I G U R E 4.3 A DYNAMIC INTERACTIONAL MODEL OF CAREER DEVELOPMENT (ADAPTED FROM LERNER, 1984)

that at any one time, variables from any one, any combination, or all of these levels can be operating in an individual's functioning. According to this principle, change in any level can engender change in another level. This assumption has implications for intervention; that is, intervening at one level of analysis can produce a change at another level. For example, a change in an aspect of biology (e.g., ill health) may contribute to a change at the psychological level (e.g., reduced self-efficacy). Additional changes in other levels will inevitably follow.

Finally, the developmental-contextual perspective involves a temporal component in that features of the individual and of the environment change over time. The emphasis of this change is related not to normative stages but to individual change and individual responses to contextual change.

In line with other theorists who have conducted refinements of their work, Vondracek and Kawasaki (1995) recently attempted to address the limitations of the initial developmental-contextual model, particularly the lack of detail about the underlying processes in career behavior. To expand on this earlier theoretical formulation, they proposed a framework that "not only incorporates the defining features of developmental-contextualism but also guides scientists toward understanding the processes underlying career decisions and pathways, the how and why of the behaviors that determine the work lives of individuals" (p. 118). They drew on the recent theoretical advances of developmental systems theory (D. Ford & Lerner, 1992) and motivational systems theory (M. Ford, 1992), which in turn are based on the living systems framework developed by M. Ford and Ford (1987). Vondracek and Kawasaki (1995) suggested that the living systems framework will add to developmental-contextualism by providing explicit details about "the specific nature of individuals and the processes by which they function and change" (p. 118).

Following the living systems framework, developmental systems theory posits the following account for the organized dynamics of human development: "1. the unitary functioning of the whole person-in-context; 2. the functioning of the component parts of the person; and 3. stability and change in the functioning of the component parts of the person and the person-as-a-whole" (M. Ford, 1992, p. 20). Therefore, the approach integrates nomothetic knowledge (e.g., knowledge about stages of career development) with idiographic knowledge (e.g., information about the unique characteristics of each individual).

In combining developmental systems theory and motivational systems theory with developmental contextualism, Vondracek and Kawasaki (1995) integrated aspects of individuals with processes of human functioning and with motivation or "effective person-in-context functioning" (M. Ford, 1992, p. 66), with a particular focus on adult career development. They also focused on appropriate interventions, specifically drawing on 17 principles for motivating humans derived from motivating systems theory.

The developmental-contextual model was one of the first approaches to effectively integrate person and context factors in career development theory. It is also important because it firmly placed career development within the field of human development (Vondracek & Fouad, 1994), thereby encouraging the use of a multidisciplinary approach. While it has not generated specific research, this was not to be expected from a conceptual framework that did not develop specific hypotheses.

While the developmental-contextual approach is derived directly from the field of human development, it does not focus directly on groups that traditionally have been neglected in the literature. Vondracek and Fouad (1994) maintained that because the developmental-contextual model can account for changing socioeconomic and cultural influences on career development, it eliminates the need for different theories for different groups. This view is disputed by many authors (see Chapter 6).

It is clear, however, that the ongoing interaction of person and context over the life span is an important development in career theory. By the agreement of the framework's developers (Vondracek & Kawasaki, 1995), the developmental-contextual approach remains incomplete, although its comprehensiveness and life span focus do provide important constructs for theory integration. It must be noted, however, that the key constructs of embeddedness and dynamic interaction and the life span orientation of the model suggest important possibilities for interventions and thus reflect the potential for integration between theory and practice. Developmental-contextualism was also proposed as one of six potential unifying frameworks for career theories (Savickas, 1995). This aspect of the framework will be discussed further in Chapter 7.

ROE'S THEORY OF PERSONALITY
DEVELOPMENT AND CAREER CHOICE

Although it is not traditionally viewed as a process and content theory, we have classified the work of Roe (Roe, 1956; Roe & Lunneborg, 1990) in this category because it focuses on the interaction of person (needs) and context (the family) variables. While Roe has always been outside the mainstream of counseling psychology (Roe & Lunneborg, 1990, p. 101), her ideas have stimulated discussion and research in career theory. Her work is also noteworthy because it was first developed within the era of trait-and-factor theory, yet it clearly included a focus on contextual variables.

Much of her work focused on possible relationships between occupational behavior and personality (Roe & Lunneborg, 1990). One of her major achievements was the development of an occupational classification system based on the intensity and nature of the interpersonal relationships in occupations. She identified eight occupational groups: service, business contact, organization, technology, outdoor, science, general culture, and arts and entertainment. Within these groups, she identified six levels of responsibilities: professional and managerial (Level 1), professional and managerial (Level 2), semiprofessional and small business, skilled, semiskilled, and unskilled.

Another important focus of her work was on the development of interests and needs, for which she advanced five propositions (Roe & Lunneborg, 1990). She proposed that genetic inheritance influences the development of personal characteristics but that it influences some characteristics more than others. In addition to genetics, the individual's life experience, in terms of such factors as cultural background, socioeconomic situation, and gender, also affects the development of personal characteristics.

Roe particularly focused on the relationship between parent and child and how the child's needs are met. She claimed that the modes and degrees of need satisfaction determine which needs will become the strongest motivators. Thus, types of childhood environments are predictors of person- or nonperson-oriented occupations. For example, needs that have been only minimally satisfied may become dominant motivators. In reviewing research into her propositions, Roe acknowledged the lack of a "direct link between parent-child relations and occupational choice" (Roe & Lunneborg, 1990, p. 81), although there was some evidence that in very narrow fields of interest, the primary work activities chosen by individuals did relate to experiences of early childhood. However, she emphasized that the negative direct relationship did not invalidate the relevance of propositions that related specifically to needs and interests and parent-child relations. Indeed, Roe and Lunneborg (1990) cited a number of studies in which these propositions have influenced research in parent-child relations and considerations of practitioners in relation to familial determinants of vocational choice.

Another valuable contribution from Roe was her formula for occupational choice, which assesed the relative importance of many variables and how their interactions may change with time. In particular, she considered gender, the state of the economy, family background, learning and education, special acquired skills, physical attributes and impairments, chance, friends and peer group, marital situation, cognitive abilities, temperament and personality, and interests and values. Roe distinguished between these variables according to the degree of control that the individual has over them. She also attempted to acknowledge the nature of interactions between some of the variables. She assigned weights to the variables and used her formula to show "probable age-related differences" (Roe & Lunneborg, 1990, p. 90) within the categories of Super's stages, thereby contributing to a developmental understanding of career choice. What is significant about this aspect of her theory is her acknowledgment of many contextual variables in career development and the changes in their relative importance over time. While her work has little empirical support, such thinking placed her ahead of her time and challenged the research and thinking of others.

Roe and Lunneborg (1990) commented that the theory is inadequate in accounting for the career development of women and minorities, but the constructs are considered in the formula discussed above. These authors also emphasized the contribution of the work of Roe to interest assessment, career counseling practice, and career development.

A Contextualist Action Theory Explanation of Career

Young et al. (1996) formulated a contextualist approach to career, with action theory used as a means of integrating aspects of contextualism. This is an emerging approach, with most of the work used to support it coming from the field of counseling practice (Valach, 1990; Young & Valach, 1996; Young, Valach, Dillabough, Dover, & Matthes, 1994). These authors acknowledged the various ways that context is understood, as in the work of Vondracek et al. (1986) discussed previously.

Young et al. (1996) asserted that the term *action* reflects the importance of purposive intentional human behavior as well as the dynamic transformational processes occurring in career choice and development. In addition to individual intentionality, contextual or situational factors are seen as important and as inextricably entwined with the individual. Consequently, action or goal-directed behavior can be interpreted and understood only when viewed in context, and contextual or environmental issues are salient only when viewed within the framework of individual volition (Valach, 1990).

Action theory is based on the notion of goal-directed action, which in turn is viewed as a function of self-active systems, characterized as "higher living systems." Young et al. (1996) described what they referred to as the contextual characteristics of action and depicted them in a complexly conceptualized cube. These characteristics of action are shown on three axes:

1. perspectives on action (manifest behavior, conscious cognitions, and social meaning)

2. action systems (individual action, joint action, project, and career)
3. levels of action organization (elements, functional steps, and goals)

Each cell of "action" can then be described through processes of interpretation and narrative. We will describe each of these in turn.

Goal-directed action can be interpreted from three perspectives; manifest behavior, conscious cognitions (or internal processes), and social meaning (Cranach, 1982). Manifest behavior involves overt observable behavior, such as completing an application for a job. *Conscious cognitions* refers to intrapersonal cognitive and emotional processes that occur, such as thinking strategically about how to word a job application letter or feeling anxious about compiling the letter. Young and Valach (1996) suggested that emotion, which is related to needs, desires, purposes, and goals and can be an outcome or a motivation, has been inadequately addressed in the career theory literature. However, each of the three social learning, social cognitive, and cognitive information-processing theories discussed earlier in this chapter also discusses the relevance of emotion. Social meaning, the third perspective, represents the meaning of the action to the self and to others; for example, the successful completion of the application may lead to a positive job outcome that has social rewards. Each of these perspectives pertains equally to goal-directed action and to career behavior. Young and Valach (1996) emphasized that "the uniqueness of the action theoretical approach is its efforts to link and make explicit the three perspectives of action" (p. 366). The other advantage of the three perspectives is that they can be applied to the process of career counseling, thereby effectively integrating theory and practice.

There are three action systems, a hierarchically organized grouping of constructs that extend the notion of action and that further distinguish joint action from individual action. At the lowest level is joint action, whereby career work is done not individually but in collaboration with others. For example, individuals discuss career issues with family and friends, and perhaps with counselors. Concepts such as interests, values, and career identity are viewed as being constructed not intrapersonally but socially and therefore are products of joint action. Such a perspective provides a new dimension to the interrelationship between individual and context.

At the next level in the action systems hierarchy is the notion of project. A project allows individuals to develop linkages between actions, often involves action over time, and includes individual and joint actions, as well as the three perspectives of manifest behavior, internal processes, and social meaning. Young et al. (1996) described the example of a project of a couple who are trying to develop egalitarian career, education, and family plans for their lives. Their project will need to be defined and redefined over time, and the example represents an ongoing purposive synthesis of a series of individual and joint actions.

The superordinate construct, career, provides the opportunity for social meaning in an individual's actions. Career also involves the interconnection between all the actions and all the processes of action operating in both feedforward and feedback ways (Young & Valach, 1996). Young et al. (1996) acknowledged that the term that people use to refer to career may vary, but it is relevant that a career provides meaning over a long period of time (longer than project) at the societal level.

The final aspect of action theory described by Young et al. (1996) is the organization of action, including elements, functional steps, and goals. At their most basic level, actions can be organized by their elements, which include verbal and nonverbal behaviors such as words, phrases, sentences, and gestures. These elements cannot be separated from their context, and interpretation of their meaning needs to be contextualized. For example, Young et al. (1996) described how the statement "I don't feel like working any longer" will be interpreted differently by someone who has been working for a long period at a challenging task and by someone who has been unemployed for a long period.

Functional steps are described as behaviors that give meaning to elements. For example, one partner in a relationship may say to the other, "Leave work now." This statement may refer to the partner's coming home from work or resigning or retiring from work. The step embodied within this statement can have different meanings. Finally, these elements and steps are contextualized by the individual's goals—that is, the intention of the individual. Therefore, in the previous example, the statement is contextualized according to the goal of the partner making the statement. If the statement was about coming home, it would be about a joint action or project. However, if it was about a major life career decision, it would be about a career. Thus, to return to the cube developed by Young et al., each cell of career-related behavior can be described according to these aspects of action theory.

The action theory explanation of career posited by Young et al. (1996) adds to our understanding of the processes of goal-directed behavior. It therefore extends our understanding of action proposed in the models of Krumboltz and Lent and his colleagues. However, since it is based on contextualism (as discussed in Chapter 7) and the present event, and since it shuns causality, it does not provide any assistance in understanding notions of development and process (although these are explained in part through discussions of the social construction of relevant constructs). Its perspective that concepts such as interests are socially constructed illustrates a new understanding of the relationship between individual and context.

However, this discussion of social construction led Young et al. (1996) to suggest that their theory accounts for cultural and gender factors in career theory. They maintained that the individual "interacts with these factors in a dynamic way to construct the self and the potential for action and career" (p. 494). While they acknowledged the inhibiting possibilities of these factors, they emphasized that an action explanation accounts for the context in which an action occurs, including culture and gender. We believe that this approach denies the value of theory's identifying specific factors of influence in relation to culture and gender (see Chapter 6). In addition, it does not adequately explain the process of influence and the relationships between factors of influence.

D. Brown (1996b) raised a number of other concerns about the viability of this theoretical approach as the basis of a theory of career choice and development. However, a strength noted by Brown, one that we support, is the application of the concepts in action theory to career counseling.

SIMILARITIES AND DIFFERENCES BETWEEN THEORIES OF CONTENT AND PROCESS

As in Chapters 2 and 3, this summary will focus on the main elements within this group of theories.

INDIVIDUAL CONTENT INFLUENCES

Each of the theories discussed in this chapter has been included because of its focus on both content and process variables. Comparison of Table 4.1 with the equivalent tables in Chapters 2 and 3 illustrates the greater acknowledgment of and significant emphasis on context variables in these theories. In terms of intrapersonal or content influences, all theories have been categorized as acknowledging or giving significant emphasis to most previously identified variables. The theories or approaches that give significant emphasis to most variables include the social learning theory of career decision making, social cognitive career theory, and the developmental-contextual approach. The individual content variables that have received the least attention include gender, ethnicity, sexual orientation, beliefs, health, and disability.

The cognitive information-processing approach places most attention on the structure and processes of self-knowledge acquisition. Thus, much discussion of content of individual self-knowledge is implied. A minor comment on knowledge in this theory is its focus on occupations as opposed to a broad world-of-work knowledge. Similarly, the action theory focuses more on process, on action and interpretation. Although there is little specific mention of individual and contextual factors, they are implied. As discussed, this approach accounts for the specific context in which action occurs, including gender and culture, and the theory developers believe that there is no need to spell them out specifically. It is important also to point out the conceptual overlap inherent in the literature and therefore in some of these variables. For example, self-concept, self-observation generalizations, and self-efficacy are similar and where relevant to a particular theory are noted in Table 4.1 under self-concept. However, it is clear that each of these also incorporates beliefs. While some theories (e.g., social learning theory and social cognitive career theory) have acknowledged aptitudes as a separate influence, others may well subsume aptitudes under abilities.

CONTEXT INFLUENCES

If we compare Table 4.1 with similar tables in Chapters 2 and 3, it is clear that context influences are given more attention in the theoretical approaches discussed in this chapter. The three theories that have not paid as much attention are the work of Roe, the action theory approach, and the cognitive information-processing approach. The latter two have been discussed in the previous section, and the work of Roe was included in this chapter even though its main focus was not context. Social influences, particularly family, peers, community, education institutions, and the workplace, are given considerable attention. An influence that is consistently underrated is that of the media.

T A B L E 4.1 INFLUENCES ON CAREER DEVELOPMENT:
THEORIES OF CONTENT AND PROCESS

CONTENT INFLUENCES	KRUM-BOLTZ	LENT, BROWN, & HACKETT	PETERSON ET AL.	VONDRACEK	ROE	YOUNG, VALACH, & COLLIN
Intrapersonal system						
Ability						
Aptitudes						
Interests						
Gender						
Age						
Skills						
Ethnicity						
Sexual orientation						
Beliefs						
Health						
Disability						
Values						
World-of-work knowledge						
Personality						
Self-concept						
Physical attributes						
Social System						
Family						
Peers						
Community groups						
Education institutions						
Media						
Workplace						
Environmental/Societal System						
Political decisions						
Historical trends						
Employment market						
Geographical location						
Socioeconomic status						
Globalization						

PROCESS INFLUENCES						
Recursiveness						
Change over time						
Chance						

☐ No acknowledgment   ☐ Acknowledgment   ■ Significant emphasis

Within the environmental/societal influence section, all influences identified are given considerable emphasis, with only one influence, that of geographical location, being afforded no emphasis.

PROCESS INFLUENCES

The importance of interaction between relevant influences and change over time is again acknowledged by all theoretical approaches in this chapter. The only influence that is not acknowledged by all approaches and that we think is important enough to be included on its own in these tables is chance. This has been acknowledged as relevant in career behavior only in the work of Krumboltz and Roe.

CONCLUSION

This chapter has discussed six theories that have focused on content and process variables in career development: Krumboltz's social learning theory, Lent et al.'s social cognitive theory, cognitive processing theory (Petersen et al.), action theory (Young et al.), the developmental-contextual approach (Vondracek et al.), and Roe's theory. These approaches have been compared in terms of their attention to important influences that have been derived from the existing literature.

Chapter 5 will explore these theories both in relation to each other and in relation to the theories that were included in Chapters 2 and 3. Chapter 6 will then discuss four main areas that have received very little attention: career theory in relation to women, racial and ethnic groups, lesbians and gay men, and socioeconomic issues.

CHAPTER

5

COMPARISON OF
THE MAJOR THEORIES

In Chapters 2, 3, and 4, the similarities and differences of the theories presented have been reviewed. The purpose of this chapter is twofold. First, it will review trends that have emerged during the historical development of career theory, since these will guide the development of themes that will be used as the basis of comparison. Second, it will examine themes that cross the chapter and theory boundaries.

As the previous chapters have illustrated, the field of career theory has developed over time, with each new theoretical formulation focusing on a different element of career behavior, refining and advancing an original theoretical notion, introducing into the careers field relevant conceptualizations from other disciplines or from related branches of psychology. The early work of Parsons in 1909, based on a matching between a knowledge of self and a knowledge of aspects of the world of work, remained the primary focus of theory and practice until the 1950s. Out of these beginnings, trait-and-factor approaches characterized by the earlier work of Holland (1973, 1985a) emerged. With the work of Ginzberg and his colleagues (Ginzberg et al., 1951) and Super (1953, 1957, 1980, 1990), the emphasis moved from trait-and-factor approaches, with their focus on the content of career choice, to developmental approaches that emphasized the process of career development and decision making. Refinement of trait-and-factor approaches (e.g., Holland, 1992), known as person-environment fit approaches, included a greater focus on the interaction between the individual and the work environment. Since then, a number of theorists have contributed to our understanding of career choice and development (e.g., Bordin, 1990; D. Brown, 1996a; Dawis, 1996; Dawis & Lofquist, 1984; Roe, 1956;

Roe & Lunneborg, 1990). These theorists have variously focused on content of the individual, content of the context, or process. Other recent theories have attempted to include both content (of individual and context) and process variables in their explanations of career behavior (L. S. Gottfredson, 1981, 1996; Krumboltz, 1994; L. K. Mitchell & Krumboltz, 1990, 1996; Vondracek et al., 1986). More recently, the development of constructivism in cognitive science has led to the development of additional approaches that emphasize the individual as an active agent in his or her own career development. These new and emerging theories include the work of Lent et al. (1996) and Young et al. (1996).

These developments in career theory have raised a number of themes relevant for comparison. The concept of reviewing the literature by themes is not new, and several examples can be found, including the work of Hackett et al. (1991) and Savickas and Lent (1994). Hackett et al. (1991) reviewed career development theory from a number of perspectives, including the cognitive perspective, the cultural diversity perspective, the multiple-role perspective, and the developmental perspective. More recently, Savickas and Lent (1994) identified themes that became the focus of chapters in their book, such as the "cognitive revolution" (p. 75); the cultural context, including gender, race, class, and sexual orientation; person-environment fit; identity; and decision making.

Some of these themes have earned their place in these reviews as areas that have traditionally been neglected in the extant literature, while others are areas of emphasis or commonality in the literature. This chapter will review themes that have received emphasis, and Chapter 6 will focus on areas that traditionally have received little attention in the career development literature. Of the themes mentioned in the previous reviews, gender, sexual orientation, culture, race, and class have generally not been emphasized and for that reason will be the focus of the next chapter. The present chapter will focus on the themes that have received the attention of many theorists, specifically the content themes of the individual and the context of career development, and the process themes of development; decision making, including cognitive processes; interaction; and chance. In addition, the chapter will address philosophical underpinnings. Tables 2.3, 3.1, and 4.1 will be used as points of comparison between the groups of theory where possible.

THE INDIVIDUAL

The need for individuals to understand themselves in order to implement career decisions has been a central feature of career theory since its genesis in the work of Parsons (1909), with its proposal that understanding of self is one of his three elements of career selection. In fact, an attempt to quantify personal traits in order to help individuals understand themselves was central to the differential psychology movement, which has been so influential in vocational psychology. In turn, a body of occupational information was also developed so that individuals could match their self-understanding against their knowledge about the world of work, a process exemplified in the work of Holland.

The individual is central to all theories, yet this concept has been dealt with differently. For example, some theories emphasize the importance of particular individual traits such as values, personality, or interests, and much attention has been focused on the concept of self as an organizing concept for theories. The major theories have used a number of terms to discuss the individual, such as *self* (Bordin, 1990; Miller-Tiedeman & Tiedeman, 1990), *self-concept* (L. S. Gottfredson, 1981; Super, 1953, 1957, 1990), *vocational identity* (Holland, 1985a), and *self-observation generalization* (L. K. Mitchell & Krumboltz, 1990). In addition, Miller-Tiedeman and Tiedeman (1990) drew on Erikson's (1959) concept of ego identity. Whatever the term used, Super (1992) describes concepts of the self as "fundamental and central" (p. 47) to career development theory.

While the focus for much of the extant career theory has been the quantification of objective data on the individual, there has increasingly been a move toward the validation of the subjective processes of the individual. This is reflected in Super's use of the terms *vocational identity* and *occupational self-concept* to depict objective and subjective perceptions of self. Miller-Tiedeman and Tiedeman's (1990) work is also an example of this trend. This has been a significant shift in the career development literature and is associated with an increasing focus on personal agency. Associated with this is a necessary corresponding shift in the nature of career guidance and counseling practices, which are discussed in Part 3.

THE CONTEXT OF CAREER DEVELOPMENT

What has become apparent in career theory is an increasing emphasis on the person and context as coexisting and jointly defining each other (see Chapter 4). Blustein (1994) described this as "one of the more exciting trends in the identity development literature" (p. 142) and claimed that the importance of relationships has traditionally received little attention in psychology. This trend has emerged as a result of the work of theorists in other areas, including family systems and feminist thought, and their work "has underscored the fundamental significance of human connectedness or relatedness as an important antecedent to adaptive development" (Blustein, 1994, p. 143). It is also clearly evidenced in the theories presented in Chapter 4 and in the work of L. S. Gottfredson (1981, 1996) and has been addressed in refinements of other theories, such as those of Holland (1992) and Super (1957, 1980, 1990, 1992).

The influence of family on career development has been discussed by theorists since the time of Parsons (1909) and is probably the contextual influence that has drawn most attention. In fact, Parsons (1909) and Super (1990, 1992) drew attention to two themes related to family that have persisted in the career literature to the present time, those of biological or genetic influences and relational or interactive influences. Specifically, Parsons inquired after clients' health ("hereditary diseases"; Parsons, 1909, p. 17) and the occupations of their fathers and male relatives as a possible indicator of aptitude or opportunity. Since that time, discussions of family as an influence can be traced throughout the history of career theory, with major attention being given to the influence of childhood family experiences in the work of Roe, Bordin's psychoanalytic theory, and refinements of Holland's theory. Roe and Lunneborg (1990) discussed the link between need satisfaction in childhood and motivation. The degree to which a need is satisfied will determine how strong it becomes as a motivator. For example, needs that are regularly satisfied will constitute low-level motivators, whereas needs that are rarely satisfied become dominant motivators.

Bordin (1990) likewise made links between occupational choice and satisfaction and childhood experiences. He claimed that individuals learn to cope with external pressures from others, particularly parents as they grow up, and that these are internalized as "conscience, duty, expectations, and other concepts of modes of behavior required by society before one can be rewarded by a livelihood" (p. 107). He distinguished between intrinsic motives (those linked to enjoyment, self-satisfaction, and self-realization) and extrinsic motives (such as money, prestige, security). The distinction between intrinsic and extrinsic motives is linked to the separation of play and work in childhood that is discussed in Chapter 2. In terms of occupational choice or career decisions, the individual is often faced with competing motives, the development of which can be traced back to his or her childhood experiences.

In a refinement of his theory, Holland (1992) claimed that emotional stability is influenced by an individual's childhood experiences and accounted for this in terms of his typology. For example, individuals are more likely to be stable if they have "parents whose individual personality patterns are consistent in themselves and are congruent with the other parent's personality pattern" (Holland, 1992, p. 56). If this is not the case, the individual may develop inconsistent values, interests, and competencies and have little self-confidence. The need for Holland to refine his theory to include the influence of family reflects increasing recognition of family as a significant influence on individual career development, particularly in relation to the development of personality, motivation, and work satisfaction.

The inclusion of context as relevant to career development has led to the identification of a large number of relevant variables. The breadth of context was identified by Blustein (1994), who noted that contextual variables occur at two levels, social context and societal context. The work of Krumboltz, Lent et al., Vondracek et al., and Roe and Lunneborg has particularly been instrumental in identifying contextual variables (see Table 4.1). These variables include the influence of genetic endowments, special abilities, aspects of the work world and the political world, socioeconomic status, and other environmental conditions.

DEVELOPMENT

The concept of development entered into the career theory literature with the work of Ginzberg et al. (1951). They presented a linear stage model of career development ending in early adult life. While their theory and subsequent theories of Super and Gottfredson depicted career development as a series of stages, other theories, such as those of Dawis and Lofquist and Holland, depicted career development more as change over time in terms of adjustment. Brooks (1990) criticized the stage theories for neglecting adult development, a comment that is particularly pertinent given the demise of the theory of Ginzberg and his colleagues, despite Ginzberg's later revisions. Of the stage theories, Super's is the most comprehensive, taking into account the life span, whereas the theories of Ginzberg and his colleagues and of Gottfredson finish in late adolescence.

The process of development of career theory includes an expansion in theoretical scope. Whereas these earlier theories (save for Dawis and Lofquist's work adjustment theory) were restricted to the topic of career decision making and the period of pre- or early adulthood, more recent theories extend beyond career entry. The most notable was social cognitive career theory (Lent et al.), which included the interrelated processes of interest development, career choice, and career-related performance once the decision has been made. In addition, the work of Vondracek and Kawasaki (1995) attempted to extend the developmental-contextual approach to adult career development.

Another recent trend in relation to the concept of development is that of cycles. This is evidenced in the work of Super, who, in revisions of his work, made allowance for recycling through stages. Thus, he used the term *maxicycle* for progression through all of his stages and *minicycle* for the recycling process. In line with this change, Super (1992) asserted that the stages have "no rigid boundaries of age or of concern, and that people recycle through some of them throughout the life course" (p. 60). Holland (1992), whose theory is primarily content focused, also acknowledged that careers tend to be a series of "success and satisfaction cycles" (p. 54).

Significantly, what this trend toward a more cyclical view has done is forge closer links between the stage development theories, the theories portraying adjustment, and the content theories. Thus, theories tend to adopt "a more or less implicit or explicit person-environment or trait oriented approach to career choice and implementation" (Osipow, 1990, p. 128). This is reflected in Super's concept of self-concept implementation in work, correspondence in Dawis and Lofquist's theory of work adjustment, congruence in Holland's theory, and circumscription and compromise in Gottfredson's theory. Adjustment and recycling occur as a result of dissatisfaction or a lack of fit between the individual and his or her environment. Similarly, in the theory of work adjustment, discorrespondence between the individual and the environment brings about adjustment until satisfaction is reached or the individual changes to another occupation or company (Dawis & Lofquist, 1976). Thus, development is increasingly being portrayed as an incremental process that does not necessarily follow a prescribed plan.

Bordin (1990) drew attention to the fact that development, while ongoing, is "not a smooth, continual process" (p. 117). He also warned against simplifying or trivializing the process of development of ego identity by "assuming that it is solely a rational decision process" (p. 117) and claimed that the process is "largely silent and unconscious" (p. 117). Similarly, Super (1992) commented that career development does not follow a path but rather evolves or emerges.

Miller-Tiedeman and Tiedeman (1990) and Miller-Tiedeman (1988) concurred; in their "lifecareer" framework, they proposed two kinds of reality, personal reality and common reality (discussed in Chapter 3). If individuals are guided by their personal reality rather than common reality, they will do what feels right for them rather than what others expect. This evolving of reality reflects the process of change.

PHILOSOPHICAL UNDERPINNINGS

Such philosophies as those espoused by Miller-Tiedeman and Tiedeman (1990) clearly pose challenges to the objective views of career development proposed in earlier theories. Awareness and acceptance of the subjective process of career development increasingly makes the individual, rather than theory, the driver of his or her career development. This move toward a subjective perspective is reflected in theory development. For example, the social learning theory of Krumboltz (1979) includes social and cognitive influences and focuses on personal agency and the construction of meaning. However, these variables are seen to relate to each other causally. A clear description of the individual's personal action in the process is not provided. However, the social cognitive career theory (Lent et al., 1994, 1996), developed from the revised work on social cognition, reflects a more constructivist approach in its emphasis on personal agency in that it describes individual action as well as reaction. It focuses on feedforward mechanisms in which individuals actively construct meaning from their interaction with environmental conditions rather than relying on responses to external forces, or feedback, only. Although the inclusion of elements of the living systems framework may serve to highlight the self-regulatory aspect of humans in their functioning in social learning theory (see Chapter 4), this remains in an early stage of development. Philosophical underpinnings of career theory will be discussed further in Chapter 7.

RELATIONSHIP BETWEEN VARIABLES

The process of interaction between individual and work-related variables was for a long period centered on the notion of matching. This process was variously termed *congruence* (Holland, 1985a), *correspondence* (Dawis & Lofquist, 1984), or *self-concept implementation* (Super, 1980). The process assumed a conscious search by the individual for a good fit between the self and an occupation or job. This process also inevitably involved compromise (L. S. Gottfredson, 1981).

The integration of social learning theory (L. K. Mitchell & Krumboltz, 1990), self-efficacy (Hackett & Betz, 1981), and social cognitive theory (Lent et al., 1994, 1996) into career theory created a greater understanding of the process of development of variables and of the relation between them. Dawis (1994) commented that social learning theory, in offering a fine-grained analysis of learning processes, complements the more coarse-grained concepts in theories such as those of Holland and Super. Learning theory extended the work of Holland and Super in its description of how people learn about their interests and abilities in relation to existing occupations and in describing how different interests and skills develop from learning experiences, aspects of understanding not detailed by these authors. Similarly, the social learning theory of career decision making emphasizes the role of learning theory in explaining how individuals develop the combination of interest orientations depicted in Holland's hexagon model. Finally, the social learning theory of career decision making builds on Holland's theory in acknowledging the importance of environmental influences mediating the link between interests and goals and action behavior. That is, environmental support is crucial if career interests and goals are to translate into career entry actions.

Social learning theory and, more recently, social cognitive theory also attempt to describe how learnings are acquired. Again, "each theory focuses on different aspects of the process" (Krumboltz, 1994). In combination, these theories illustrate how people refine aspects of self and their environments over time. An individual's learning experiences lead to the formulation of a group of occupational aspirations that may or may not come to fruition according to a set of socioeconomic and cultural conditions that is unique to that individual.

The degree of importance of cognitive processes illustrates the development of the theories and their recent close links to cognitive psychology. Social cognitive career theory emphasizes cognitive processes far more than Krumboltz's social learning theory, particularly the three social cognitive variables of self-efficacy, outcome expectations, and goals. For example, social learning theory views self-efficacy as an outcome of learning experiences, whereas social cognitive career theory further describes self-efficacy in a role as an important mediator of interests, career choice, and performance. Self-efficacy therefore is used as a more detailed explanatory construct in social cognitive career theory. Social cognitive career theory also describes the mediation process of social cognitive variables such as self-efficacy in the development of interests and the related effect of environmental variables through the constructs of opportunity structure and contextual affordance.

The theory of work adjustment (Dawis, 1996; Dawis & Lofquist, 1984) offers some points of relationship with social cognitive career theory. Work adjustment theory emphasizes the relationship between an individual's abilities and work tasks and outcomes such as promotion and tenure. However, the process of this relationship is not clarified. Social cognitive career theory would focus on the relationship of self-efficacy as a mediating factor in successful completion of work tasks. That is, individuals with strong self-efficacy beliefs about their work abilities may maximize their performance and therefore their work outcomes.

It can be noted that the cognitive information-processing theory (Peterson et al., 1991, 1996) extends the work of social cognitive career theory in the depth of its consideration of cognitive processes. This theory explores in considerable detail what it terms the "executive processing domain" (Peterson et al., 1996, p. 437), or higher order cognitive functions. These higher order skills, or metacognitions, include self-talk, self-awareness, and monitoring and control.

The construct of action, the central core of the contextualist explanation of career (Young et al., 1996), also extends the social cognitive theory somewhat. It offers further explanation of the cognitive processes inherent in career choice and in career-related performance, particularly in its depth description of action as "cognitively and socially steered and controlled" (p. 483).

DECISION MAKING

Since the days of Parsons (1909) and his concept of "true reasoning," career development, career choice, and career decision making have been portrayed as rational, logical processes based on objective information. The maintenance and longevity of this concept in career theory is probably a legacy of the influence of differential psychology. However, while practice still seems to be driven by cognitive, rational, and objective processes (see Part 3), theorists are increasingly drawing attention to influences other than logical thought processes that contribute to career development, choice, and decision making. For example, Lent and Hackett (1994) posited that "it is well known that people's career trajectories are not just the result of their cognitive activity" (p. 77). They cited emotional reactions, achievement histories, social and economic conditions, culture, gender, genetic endowment, social context, and unexpected life events as influences that "may interact with or supersede the effects of career-related cognitions" (p. 78). Similarly, Young et al. (1996) suggested that emotion has received too little attention in the career theory literature and that we need to focus on its role in interaction both with cognition and with other processes in career decision making.

INTERACTION PROCESS

The concept of development clearly implies the unfolding of a process in which the individual is the central player. It must also be remembered that all of the variables in the multifaceted picture of career development change and interact with each other. Super (1992) claimed that the individual and his or her role self-concepts are "the culminating products of the interaction of the person and the environment" (p. 41). Our understanding of this process of interaction has expanded considerably in recent times. Vondracek et al. (1986) emphasized the embeddedness of relevant variables and the way in which a change in one level of a variable can bring change to another variable. Similarly, increasing focus on the agency of the individual (Lent et al., 1994, 1996; Vondracek et al., 1986; Young et al., 1996) has drawn our attention to the mutuality of influence—that is, how an individual acts on an environment in addition to the environment's acting on the individual.

CHANCE

Chance has been acknowledged by a number of theorists, clearly influenced by the work of Bandura (1982) and sociological theories. Krumboltz's work explores how place and era of birth, socioeconomic status of family of birth, and genetic endowments at birth can all be seen as aspects of chance in an individual's career development. A number of theorists (Krumboltz, Lent et al., Roe) include these aspects of chance in their discussion of relevant influences.

CONCLUSION

What is clearly evident in this review of the literature is the breadth of the career development field. Lent and Hackett (1994) commented that "any truly comprehensive approach to career development should account for the complex connections between the person and his or her context, between intrapsychic and interpersonal mechanisms, and between volitional and nonvolitional influences on the career development process" (p. 78). This trend is clearly emerging in the career development literature and is reflected in terms of how theories are grouped in recent reviews and books. It is also reflected in the development of more comprehensive emerging theories and the refinement of existing theories to a new level of complexity.

It is interesting that this review of the theories in Chapters 2 through 4 and the comparisons in relation to each other described in this chapter still leave us with a picture of a group of theories moving toward some theory perfection. There is little doubt that theory development is also one of growth, ongoing refinement, and continuing attempts at integration. Recent developments, such as social cognitive career theory, are drawing from existing work, integrating old and new constructs and processes, and thereby providing an expanded explanation of content variables and process variables relevant to career behavior.

Each theorist acknowledges strengths of other theories and points of rapprochement of his or her theory with existing theories. There also appears to be little, if any, disagreement among the theorists, possibly a reflection of the historic tendency in the field to focus on discrete facets of career development. For example, Krumboltz (1994) acknowledged that each theory focuses on a different aspect of the overall map of career behavior.

However, theorists also continue to comment on differences between theories and propose suggestions for improvement in other theories. For example, Lent and Hackett (1994) suggested that "a more adequate and faithful incorporation of social cognitive mechanisms within Super's theory may prove valuable" (p. 96), and regarding the attempt to integrate social learning theory with the living systems framework, they commented that the "move toward greater emphasis on cognitive and self-regulatory capacities within SLT (social learning theory) signals the potential for reconciling some of its assumptive differences with the current social cognitive career perspective" (p. 96). Similarly, after reviewing several major theories, Minor (1992) commented that with the addition of some of the developmental concepts of Super and perhaps of Gottfredson, as well as some propositions regarding work adjustment detailed by Dawis and Lofquist, Krumboltz's theory, which now stops at career entry, could be a more comprehensive theory.

Rather than merely continuing to refine existing theories and/or develop new individual theories, we believe that a focus on an overarching pantheoretic framework, as suggested by Lent and Hackett (1994), is also needed. *Pantheoretic* is prefaced by the prefix *pan-*, which is defined as "combining form—all or every . . . including or relating to all parts or members" (Hanks, 1980, p. 1059). This definition is reflective of the key principles of systems theory and the aim of the systems theory framework as detailed in Part 2 of this book. This framework aims to incorporate each of the constructs and process explanations in existing theories into a frame of reference, thereby acknowledging what each has to offer. The central focus is the individual and what is relevant to his or her career development.

This focus on the individual reflects a recurring theme in the career theory literature—that is, the importance of recognizing the heterogeneity of individuals whose career behavior the theories are attempting to explain and predict. In commenting on the gains in our knowledge into men's career behavior that have come from our study of women's career behavior, Fitzgerald, Fassinger, and Betts (1995) noted that "as we go into our separateness, our individuality, into that which makes us different, we will learn more about our commonalities as well" (p. 102). Cook (1994) called on the legacy of Super, commenting that "I would expect that Super would once again remind us that diversity of human experience is the rule rather than the exception, and would encourage us to look for universals that help our clients understand the particulars of their lives" (p. 93). A unifying framework of career theory, paying attention to the universals as they are relevant to each individual, would seem to be a worthwhile and useful addition to the theory literature as well as the practice literature. The framework proposed in Chapter 9 is such a framework.

But despite the breadth of career development theory, there are still areas that are significantly underdeveloped. This has resulted in the career development of some groups of individuals being more adequately accounted for than that of others. The career development of these neglected groups—namely, women, racial and ethnic groups, and lesbians and gay men—and the issue of socioeconomic status and its relationship to career development will be discussed in Chapter 6.

CHAPTER

6

THEORIES OF CAREER DEVELOPMENT: WIDER EXPLANATIONS

It is generally agreed in the career development literature of the 1990s that too little attention has been paid in both the theoretical and the practical literature to groups other than White, Western, able-bodied, middle-class males. D. Brown (1996b) commented that none of the theories included in the theory text *Career Choice and Development* (D. Brown & Brooks, 1996a) deal sufficiently with gender, ethnicity, and socioeconomic status.

A growing number of theoretical and empirical reports, in addition to theoretical texts, attest to the attention now being paid to the career development of women and racial and ethnic groups. Sociological perspectives have paid attention chiefly to socioeconomic issues. A growing body of work is also focusing on the career development of lesbians and gay men. Fitzgerald and Betz (1994) affirmed that such individual difference variables are important to a wider understanding of career behavior of all individuals. Thus, for example, the study of the career issues of women has identified a large number of variables relevant to the career behavior of men as well as women (Fitzgerald et al., 1995). This chapter will present a review of recent developments in the career theory of women, racial and ethnic groups, and lesbians and gay men, as well as theories exploring socioeconomic issues.

WOMEN'S CAREER DEVELOPMENT

The previous two decades have seen a significant increase in theoretical and empirical work focusing on women's career behavior. Limitations in early explanatory work, including its almost exclusive basis on studies of men, were acknowledged by Holland (1966), who advocated a "special but closely related theory for women" (p. 13). While Super (1957), the first major theorist who identified women's separate vocational issues, attempted to classify women's career patterns, his work was predominantly descriptive. Osipow (1975) commented on the lack of usefulness of traditional theories of career behavior for special groups (including women) in that several basic assumptions on which they were founded were not relevant. For example, traditional career theory is based on the assumption that an array of career choices is available to all individuals, who are in turn motivated to pursue their personal interests in making certain choices. A comment on the state of vocational psychology in relation to class made by Tyler (1967) highlights the inadequacy of application to women: "Much of what we know about the stages through which an individual passes as *he* prepares to find *his* place in the world of work might appropriately be labelled the vocational development of white middle class males" (p. 62). Gilligan's (1979) classic article entitled "Woman's Place in Man's Life Cycle" emphasized the inadequacy of many theories of psychology for understanding women's lives in that they implicitly adopt maleness as the norm and fail to account for the unique social and family situation of women and the related demands on them.

Fitzgerald and Crites' agenda-boosting 1980 article on the career psychology of women was pivotal in outlining key issues for research and theory building. While many theorists (Holland, 1985a; Super, 1990) subsequently attempted to include applications to women within their theory with modifications over time, criticisms remain about the failure of much career development theory to account for the lives of women adequately. Further, in much of the recent literature, women are still referred to as a "specific group" (Isaacson & Brown, 1993) or a "special subgroup" (D. Brown, 1990), and theories are discussed as they apply to "women and people of colour" (Sharf, 1992, 1997), indicating that women's career development remains a consideration separate from mainstream career theory. In their major review of the career psychology of women, Betz and Fitzgerald (1987) concurred with many other authors (Gallos, 1989; Gutek & Larwood, 1987; Marshall, 1989) in noting that although the field has burgeoned in the past 20 years, much more work needs to be done to develop theoretical understandings that highlight the unique experience of women's career development. More recently, Osipow and Fitzgerald (1996) have continued to advocate the examination of variables not relevant to men as a "viable theoretical stance" for the future (p. 261).

However, the literature generally remains in conflict on what constitutes "career" for women, or whether indeed we need separate career theories (D. Brown, 1990; Gallos, 1989). Larwood and Gutek (1987) cautioned that advocating a separate career theory for women should not imply that women's career issues are any less important than those for men or those who do not fit the male model. Indeed, these authors maintained that existing theories also do not account for the career experiences of many males and suggested that a broad model of women's career development may also improve our knowledge of the career development of a larger group of males: "In effect, a good model of career development for women may be the more general model for both sexes"

(p. 174). Gallos (1989) maintained that developmental concerns are missing from many proposed models of women's career and suggested that theorists and researchers need to observe and study women's distinctive developmental needs and voices in defining how women see their world, their choices, and their opportunities.

Thus, there remains considerable theoretical uncertainty about the nature and development of women's careers. The discussion here is based on three key assumptions. First, while there is considerable support for the premise that our understanding of the career behavior of women has changed, much more needs to be done. Second, there is consistent support in the literature for the assumption that meaningful work is central to women's lives (Betz, 1994a; Cook, 1993). Third, many variables, both internal and external, operate to inhibit or facilitate women's career behavior. Thus, this section of the chapter will explore definitions of women's careers and present a brief background on issues relevant to understanding women's career behavior. Finally, it will explore five main theoretical approaches that have offered explanations and predictions of women's career behavior: development of specific theories for women, adaptation of traditional theories, attempts to develop comprehensive theories for women and men, development of models that focus on specific individual difference variables important to the career choices of women, and development of sociocognitive models that have application to women.

DEFINITIONS OF CAREER FOR WOMEN

Definitions of career until recently were separate for females and males. It was assumed that males' careers were chosen shortly after adolescence and remained quite static throughout life, whereas females' careers were chosen as a temporary measure until the full-time "career" of motherhood and homemaking. Poole and Langan-Fox (1997) asserted that the traditional interpretations and definitions of career have prevented the formulation of a theory explaining women's career development. Although these notions have largely changed, what constitutes career for women remains in conflict.

Fitzgerald and Crites (1980) and Betz and Fitzgerald (1987) maintained that defining homemaking as a career choice—that is, "equating of a nonstructured noncompensated set of activities (i.e., housekeeping, which has no requirements for entry, no structured standards for performance, nor even necessarily any broad agreement on the nature and extent of the tasks involved) with the standard notion of occupation[—]appears to render the terminology scientifically useless" (Betz & Fitzgerald, 1987, p. 89). While one of the arguments proffered for not accepting this definition is that women will continue to be undervalued in the paid workforce, other writers have suggested that valuing traditional women's work only by the rituals of traditional notions of male employment is also a gross underestimation (Gallos, 1989; Marshall, 1989). Gallos (1989) insisted that women's notions of career are a rejection of male notions, that a career is not a "lock-step linear progression of attainments directed by a focus on 'the top'; not a job sequence aimed at upward mobility and success at all costs; not job complacency, fear of professional success or low needs of achievement; not simply a mechanical issue of learning how to juggle marriage, children and women" (p. 125).

An alternative approach to defining career for women is to focus on a definition that is broad enough to cover the life span and that includes women and men. Raynor (1982) broadly defined career in phenomenological psychological terms: "What we do defines who we are, and who we are is determined by what we do" (pp. 208–209).

Feminist analyses (e.g., Rose, 1986) suggest that what has been traditionally identified as "men's" work is largely contrived and artificial, whereas "women's" work is necessary to the survival of the human race. Indeed, Marshall (1989) suggested that a new phase of feminism is "looking again at roles into which [women] have been socialized, particularly those to do with relationships and the family. Instead of seeing these roles as of low social worth because that is how a patriarchal society defines them, women are reclaiming their positive aspects" (p. 277). Similarly, by focusing on competencies that are required by or developed by different work, including domestic work, the external measures of occupational title or level of remuneration can be transcended. Within this scenario, women's competencies developed from domestic work are transferable and can be acknowledged as such.

We agree with Fitzgerald and Weitzman (1992) that "the career development of women, although not fundamentally different from that of men, is demonstrably more complex due to a socialisation process that has emphasized the dichotomy of work and family since at least the Industrial Revolution of the 19th century" (p. 125). Another important issue is the heterogeneity of women; their differences from each other. Fitzgerald et al. (1995) raised questions about the dearth of information we have about women of color, lesbians, and poor women and again emphasized that in learning more about the career psychology of individual differences, we will also learn more about commonalities. We believe that the breadth and complexity of the definition of career for women needs to be emphasized within the framework of the competency and contribution of all women's work as acknowledged and undertaken by each individual woman. An approach that allows an exploration of the complexity of interrelationships that influence career development, such as that offered by the systems theory framework, is an important addition to our understanding and our practice in relation to this acknowledgment.

ISSUES IN WOMEN'S CAREERS

Traditionally, career preparation activities focused on males, on the assumption that women's foray into the world of work would be a brief gap filler between school and marriage and full-time homemaking. Opportunities in the workforce were also structured around this assumption. Indeed, women in certain organizations were obliged to resign upon marriage until as recently as the early 1970s (Limerick, 1991). Nevertheless, the period following World War II has seen what has been referred to as "a quiet revolution in women's participation in the paid workplace" (B. White, Cox, & Cooper, 1992, p. 1). This increased workforce participation has emphasized the importance of career for women.

However, while the number of women in the workforce has increased, the nature of their participation continues to differ greatly from that of men. Women's employment is more likely to be part time than men's and to be concentrated in a small number of occupational categories. In addition, women tend to enter and remain in low-paying, low-status positions. These differences are suggestive of structural opportunity differences operating in relation with gender differences.

In 1974, L. S. Hansen detailed what she perceived as theoretical limitations in relation to women's career development. These included societal trends and changing life patterns, as well as obstacles to the career development of women, such as sex-role socialization, role conflicts about marriage and work, focus on marriage, lack of work orientation, and sexism and sex discrimination. In a positive prophecy, she suggested that a focus on women "perhaps . . . will not be necessary in another 12 or 15 years" (p. 1). However, 20 years later, Eccles (1994) commented on the ongoing differentiation between women and men in occupations and the continued underrepresentation of women in high-status occupational fields. She commented that "many factors, ranging from outright discrimination to the processes associated with gender role socialization, contribute to these gendered patterns of educational and occupational choices" (p. 585). Despite the growth in the field of career development theory during the past 20 to 25 years, there is only minimal change in the career experiences of most women.

In their 1995 review, Fitzgerald et al. identified concepts that had been labeled as unique to women's career development as "pretheoretical developments" (p. 68). These concepts that prompted the interest of theorists and researchers included career versus homemaking orientation, career salience, traditionality of career choice, and career patterns based on the relationship between work and family in women's lives. While more recent conceptualizations have moved on from the either/or classification of home or career, women's traditional roles continue to be important in career choice and adjustment issues. This movement away from a dichotomous classification has prompted voluminous work on multiple roles and an attendant discussion on role conflict. Despite changes in women's roles, research cited by Fitzgerald et al. continues to show an inverse relationship between being married and number of children with every known criterion of career involvement and achievement and illustrates that "this continues to be the main difference between women's career development and that of men" (p. 73).

Betz (1994a) also outlined a summary of key issues, which she categorized as barriers and facilitators, relevant to women's career development. For each of these, she distinguished between individual or internal (often the result of gender-role socialization) barriers and facilitators and environmental barriers and facilitators. Examples of internal barriers may include role conflict and mathematics anxiety, and examples of external barriers may include occupational stereotypes, gender-biased counseling, and restrictive career assessment tools and practices. A given factor can be either a barrier or a facilitator, depending on whether it is present or absent. The concept of barriers and facilitators is useful in that suggestions for interventions and changes arise from ongoing discussion about their absence or presence in the contexts of women's career development.

THEORETICAL APPROACHES

DEVELOPMENT OF SPECIFIC THEORIES FOR WOMEN.   While the necessity of a separate theory is not agreed to by all writers in the area (Astin, 1984; Brooks, 1990; Fitzgerald & Crites, 1980), Osipow (1983) concluded in his major review that "substantial differences exist to warrant attempts to develop distinctive theories for each gender" (p. 263). In supporting her argument for a separate career theory for women, Gallos (1989) emphasized that women's distinctively different voice and needs lead to a different perspective on career and different choices, priorities, and patterns, all of which need to be recognized and understood.

Early acknowledgment of the need to explain career development differentially for men and women and of the limitations in existing theories resulted in two attempts to propose issues relevant to specific theories for women (Psathas, 1968; Zytowski, 1969). Psathas (1968) emphasized that his work "does not attempt to develop a theory of occupational choice for women but rather describes a number of factors which appear to operate in special ways for women" (p. 257). These factors included marriage, intention and fulfilment; family finances; social class; education and occupation of parents; values; and social mobility and mate selection. Importantly, Psathas, a sociologist, noted that the theoretical frameworks in existence are limited by their failure to focus attention on the social and economic factors that influence the psychological act of choosing. In commenting on the importance of the setting in which choices are made and the salience of sex-role and stereotyped expectations within this setting, he was one of the first writers to call attention to the importance of context in career decision making. A unique, albeit controversial aspect of Psathas's work was his proposition that the presence of large numbers of women in jobs such as teaching, nursing, and secretarial work was related to women's desire to marry upward and thereby secure status.

Like Psathas (1968), Zytowski (1969) focused on the link between sex role and occupational role and emphasized the role of marriage, motherhood, and homemaking. He offered nine postulates in an attempt to characterize the vocational development of women. Because of postulates that "the modal life role for women is described as that of homemaker," "the nature of the woman's role is not static; It will ultimately bear no distinction from that of men," and "vocational and homemaker participation are largely mutually exclusive," his work has been criticized for the limited roles afforded to women, for the suggestion that work role and home role are mutually exclusive, and for the suggestion that career roles for women are less important than home roles (Perun & Bielby, 1981; Vetter, 1973). The postulates proffered by Zytowski also ignore the subtle and powerful nature of gender-based socialization in limiting choices for women, both in the choice between career and homemaker and in choices within the range of available occupations.

Other characteristics of Zytowski's model emphasized the perceived central role of homemaking and illustrated the limited vision of women's workforce capacity. In formulating patterns of women's participation in the workforce, he identified three variables by which patterns could be characterized: age of entry into the workforce, span of participation, and degree of participation, which was related to the traditionality of the occupation that the woman entered. Therefore, a "mild" career pattern reflected early or late entry for a short time span and in a traditional occupation, a "moderate" pattern reflected early entry for a long time in a traditional occupation, and an "unusual" pattern reflected early entry for a long time span in a nontraditional occupation. Interestingly, a nontraditional occupation was characterized as representative of a high degree of participation in the workforce.

ADAPTATION OF TRADITIONAL THEORIES.   While Fitzgerald and Crites (1980) acknowledged that women's career development needs require special consideration and are more complex, they maintained that the career development of women is not fundamentally different from that of men. However, in critiquing traditional career theories for their focus on white, middle-class men (Gallos, 1989; Larwood & Gutek, 1987), others maintained that minor changes to existing theories were not sufficient. Several theorists previously discussed have attempted to incorporate women's issues into their theoretical formulations. We will focus on the major contributions of Super and Holland.

Super's (1957) original theory formulation (see Chapter 3 of this book) was the first theory to address women's career issues. In acknowledging the central role of homemaking in women's lives and the related increase in numbers of women entering the workforce, he identified seven categories of women's career patterns: the stable homemaking pattern (women who married early into full-time homemaking); the conventional career pattern (work until marriage and then homemaking); the stable working pattern (work in the paid workforce for life); the double-track career pattern (ongoing combination of career and homemaking roles); the interrupted career pattern (a return to work, usually following children leaving home); the unstable career pattern (irregular movement in and out of the workforce); and the multiple-trial career pattern, indicating a multiple-change work life. While these patterns have changed since their first formulation, they were an important attempt to illustrate the relationship between work and family throughout women's lives.

Super also proposed specific developmental stages (see Chapter 3) through which an individual passed in formulating career decisions. Each of these stages required the completion of developmental tasks. Later statements (e.g., Super, 1980) acknowledged that these stages may be encountered at more than one time in life. The stage approach was less than satisfactory in understanding women's work behavior because it was based on a male pattern of career planning uninterrupted by marriage and childrearing. Osipow (1983) noted that the exploration stage, for example, was often not truly engaged in by most women, since career plans were made pending marriage plans; rather, women often engaged in exploration and career planning following childrearing if they were entering or reentering the paid workforce.

Super's modified theoretical formulation (1980) also suggested the notion of a "lifespace," in which the many varied roles that contribute to a broad notion of career (child, student, leisurite, worker, citizen, homemaker) could be acknowledged. These additional classifications offered a useful way of understanding the complex patterns of behavior that are women's career patterns. However, a shortcoming remained in terms of explaining the motivation of women to engage in the various life roles. Super's empirical work suggested the importance of self-concept and work importance. However, while Super maintained that career choice was essentially a decision based on self-concept, no account was taken of differences between the sexes in the relationship between self-concept and work. Yet as Perun and Bielby (1981) argued, "We cannot assume that the process of self-concept development . . . is identical for both sexes" (p. 248). Women's self-concept may be affected by the work-family decision and subsequent role conflict. In supporting the notion of work importance, Super presented data (Super & Nevill, 1984) indicating that the importance of work as a major life role is more significant in relation to career maturity than either gender or social class. Irrespective of the broad available roles for women that Super has suggested, Fitzgerald and Weitzman (1992) emphasized that "traditional socialization processes do not prepare women for the complex nature of the choices they will make or the life roles they will face" (p. 135).

Holland's theory of vocational choice (1985a, 1992; see Chapter 2 of this book) posited that an individual's knowledge of self and the world of work interact to facilitate career choice. The individual engages in a complex process during which elements of personality are related to specific occupational frameworks. The theory proposed a hexagonal model of individual and workplace personalities (RIASEC; Realistic, Individual, Artistic, Social, Enterprising, and Conventional). Holland (1996) described his theory as a "one-size-fits-all-groups approach" (p. 9). While he suggested that research supported this proposition, he was provocative in adding that "some people, including some well-educated middle-class White women, disagree" (p. 9). However, it is indisputable that the pervasiveness of gender-role socialization continues to concentrate women in low-level jobs and out of jobs that require, in particular, thorough grounding in mathematics and science. Further, as Fitzgerald and Weitzman (1992) have pointed out, it is clear that certain occupational environments remain essentially closed to women, particularly the Realistic and Investigative environments, while women are found in large numbers in clerical and service occupations. These authors also raised questions about the notion of congruence between personality and occupational characteristics for many women. For example, personal preference may be compromised because of family or financial security demands. They referred to the concepts of "satisficing" and "optimization" to explain the compromise involved in choosing a job that is not wholly congruent with career interests on the basis of congruence with other role (e.g., family) demands.

The major theoretical basis of stereotypes in formulating decisions about occupational interests remains a major limitation in applying Holland's theory to women. While his 1985 work attempted to illustrate the application of the typology to distinguish between women who became homemakers and those who became career women, it remains limited in failing to acknowledge the powerful restrictive impact of gender socialization. Research cited by Betz (1994a) emphasized the impact of early socialization of girls into certain occupational fields and the impact of encouraging girls to undertake particular directions in education and training that effectively close entry to a wider range of occupational fields.

ATTEMPTS TO DEVELOP COMPREHENSIVE THEORIES APPLICABLE TO WOMEN AND MEN.   In varying ways, commencing with Super (1957) and Psathas (1968), much work has acknowledged the importance of a broad array of environmental influences in women's career choice and development. Nieva and Gutek (1981) distinguished between women's career preferences and their ultimate jobs, stressing that while personality accounts for preferences, many demographic and economic variables account for the latter. This integration of individual and environmental influences in explaining career behavior was further developed in two theoretical models of the 1980s, Astin (1984) and L. S. Gottfredson (1981). Astin's (1984) model was one of the major attempts to propose a comprehensive theory to explain the career development of women and men. She was invited to prepare "a comprehensive yet parsimonious theoretical statement" (p. 117) on women's career development. She aimed to present "a beginning formulation of a theoretical model that can enhance our understanding of women's career behavior" (p. 117). She believed that her subsequent sociopsychological model could be used to explain the occupational behavior of women and men, maintaining that "work motivation is the same for men and women, but they make different choices because their early socialization experiences and structural opportunities are different" (p. 118).

Astin's model incorporates four major constructs: motivation, work expectations, sex-role socialization, and the structure of opportunity. She proposed that an individual's motivation for work behavior is related to the need for survival, pleasure, and the making of a societal contribution. Career choices are therefore related to accessibility of various occupations and the individual's expectation that these three needs will be met. She acknowledgeed that these expectations are related to early gendered socialization and the structure of opportunity which interact with each other. Factors incorporated within the structure of opportunity include distribution of jobs, sex-typing of jobs, discrimination, job requirements, the economy, family structure, and reproductive technology. Astin emphasized that changes in the structure of opportunity (e.g., in reproductive technology) can lead to considerable change in women's career expectations.

Astin's theory has drawn mixed responses. Favorable comment has been chiefly directed toward the concept of structure of opportunity and the attempt at theoretical integration (Gilbert, 1984; Harmon, 1984). However, cited limitations include the failure to take into sufficient account the differences in workforce realities for women and men and the institutional and structural barriers to women's careers (Gilbert, 1984). Gilbert (1984) also noted that assuming the male model of work as a person's central role contributes to considerable conflict between work and family, since there is a considerable disjunction between our present institutional structures and family roles. While referring to Astin's model as "a shiny fresh minted penny" (p. 141), Farmer (1984) nevertheless called for the need for "caring values" to be incorporated into the career domain "rather than at odds with it" (p. 142). Further, Kahn (1984) lamented the reduction in importance of the family role at the expense of the work role. Astin's model can also be criticized for its deterministic nature, such that external forces are perceived as shapers of individuals' career futures.

Despite its being an invited contribution, very little empirical work has attempted to test Astin's model, with a number of reviews citing no studies (D. Brown & Brooks, 1990b; Hackett & Lent, 1992). A recent study by Poole, Langan-Fox, Ciavarella, and Omodei (1991) found support for Astin's model in confirming the importance of socialization, structure of opportunity, and expectations and in supporting the need to consider gender differences in socialization and structure of opportunity. These authors recommended refinement of Astin's model and suggested a contextualist framework that would link individual development to location in historical time. It is interesting that Fitzgerald et al. (1995) were critical of Astin's study, chiefly because of the limited nature of the variables used to test Astin's constructs. They noted, however, that this was also a reflection of the general difficulty in operationalizing the theory's constructs, particularly structure of opportunity, and suggested that it might be more useful to view it as a general conceptual framework than as a theory that was subject to more formal scrutiny.

The developmental model proposed by L. S. Gottfredson (1981, 1996) was discussed in detail in Chapter 3. It is included in this discussion because Gottfredson's work focused on processes of circumscription and compromise relevant to women and men. She developed self-concept theory further by proposing that self-concept is a combination of psychological variables and environmental variables involved in career choice. She proposed that self-concept (being composed of gender, social class, intelligence, interests, and values) interacts with occupational images (sex type, prestige, and field of work) to determine an individual's occupational preferences. Together with perceptions of job accessibility that incorporate perceptions of opportunities and barriers, a range of acceptable alternatives is formulated. Thus, her model highlights the relevance of sex-role socialization of women and men, whereby individuals make decisions based on sex type of occupations and perceptions of opportunities and barriers. Gender type, for example, influences career choice because individuals narrow their perceived appropriate occupational alternatives on the basis of societal notions of gender-appropriate careers. In addition, Gottfredson asserted that the age at which individuals will narrow their occupational alternatives is between 6 and 8 and that once these limits are set, individuals will rarely consider outside them. In addition, Gottfredson asserted that individuals make compromises between preferences and employment realities and that when these compromises are made, individuals sacrifice first their interests (field of work), then their desired prestige levels, and last their preferred sex type. This proposition reinforces the perceived importance of gender-role stereotypes in career choice.

It is interesting that in 1986, Gottfredson widened her discussion on the issue of gender in career development. She suggested a broadening of the problem to an analysis of factors that identify individuals who are "at risk" in relation to career choice. These factors included cultural or geographic isolation and poor education and may be relevant to women and men and individuals from racial and ethnic groups. Her rationale was that specific group issues may also be relevant to specific individuals. However, Hackett and Lent (1992) cautioned that different "risk" factors may operate differently for women and men and that such a framework may be restrictive.

DEVELOPMENT OF MODELS FOCUSING ON INDIVIDUAL DIFFERENCES.

A number of other theoretical models have proffered explanations about women's career behavior that focus on individual differences between women and men on specific variables. These include the work of Farmer (1985), Betz and Fitzgerald (1987), and Fassinger (1985, 1990). Farmer's work focuses on applications to men as well as to women, but it has been included in this category because the initial focus was on issues and concerns relevant to women.

Farmer (1985) proposed that background characteristics and personal variables interact to foster achievement and career motivation. Background variables (gender, race, social class, school location, age) interact with personal psychological variables (self-esteem, values, homemaking attitude and commitment, success attributions) and environmental variables (societal attitude to women working, support from teachers and parents). These variables in turn were hypothesized to influence three motivational factors: level of aspirations, mastery strivings, and career commitment. Research testing this model has generally supported the salience of background factors such as gender-based attitudes, support, and commitment to career and family in career aspirations and choices. For example, Farmer (1985) noted that gender differences were greater for career centrality than for aspirations and mastery. This finding is indicative of the greater role conflict evident in career commitment than in aspirations and mastery. While career commitment increased from 1980 to 1990 because of the supportiveness of the environment, Farmer, Wardrop, Anderson, and Risinger (1993) noted that women may reject more demanding careers because of the perceived role conflict. This adjustment of aspirations is similar to the notion of "satisficing" discussed earlier (Fitzgerald & Weitzman, 1992).

In their major review of the career psychology of women, Betz and Fitzgerald (1987) summarized the literature and identified four sets of factors that influence women's career choices. Contrary to Astin and Farmer, these authors believed that theoretical models needed to be specifically focused on women's issues so as not to neglect any important variables. The factors deemed to be particularly crucial in promoting realism of career choice included individual variables (self-concept, ability, liberated sex-role values), background variables (parental support, parents' education level and occupational status, work experience), educational variables (women's schools, higher education, continuation in mathematics), and adult lifestyle variables (timing of marriage, number of children). These variables were hypothesized to be causally ordered. A limitation of this work is its focus on higher ability women, particularly the university educated.

Fassinger (1985, 1990) tested the Betz and Fitzgerald model and proposed several refinements. Her 1985 study found ability, achievement orientation, and feminist orientation to be independent variables influencing family and career orientation and career choice, leading to a revision of the original model. In her 1990 study, higher ability levels interacting with aspects of personal agency (e.g., instrumentality and self-efficacy) and sex-role attitudes, specifically a feminist orientation, influenced career orientation and career choice. Fassinger attempted to include a more heterogeneous sample, thereby widening the generalizability of the model. She also incorporated broader methodological approaches in her study in a bid to overcome psychometric problems in measuring the variables.

DEVELOPMENT OF SOCIOCOGNITIVE MODELS.   Hackett and Betz (1981) were the first to apply Bandura's 1977 theory to career development. A more recent theoretical formulation, social cognitive theory of careers (Lent et al., 1994; discussed in more detail in Chapter 4) has drawn on the revised work of Bandura (1986). Each one has direct application to the career behavior of women.

Self-efficacy refers to the belief or expectation that one can successfully perform a certain task or behavior. Hackett and Betz (1981) recognized that women's socialization mediates the cognitive processes that are crucial in career decision making:"[Women] lack strong expectations of personal efficacy in relationship to many career related behaviors and thus fail to fully realize their capabilities and talents in career pursuits" (p. 326). Betz (1994b) continued in this vein in describing the importance of self-efficacy in career behavior: "Because many behaviors or behavior domains are important in educational and career development, efficacy expectations are postulated to influence choice, performance, and persistence in career related domains" (p. 35).

Hackett and Betz (1981) attempted to explain the influence of socialization on career behavior by using the four sources of experiential information about personal self-efficacy developed by Bandura (1977): performance accomplishments, vicarious experiences (e.g., through role models), verbal persuasion (i.e., the support and encouragement of others), and emotional arousal with reference to a behavior or domain of behavior (the higher the arousal or anxiety, the lower the self-efficacy). As an example specifically related to women's educational and career behavior, if a woman had a level of success in mathematics, was aware of other women successful in mathematics-related fields, received support and encouragement from others, and had a low level of mathematics anxiety, she would be expected to develop high self-efficacy expectations in relation to mathematics.

In formulating their theory, Hackett and Betz (1981) reviewed evidence that showed the differences in relation to the efficacy information received by women and men. This information difference resulted in a broader variety of career options exposed to men than to women. Research by Betz and Hackett

(1981) assessing occupational self-efficacy found significant gender differences in occupational self-efficacy expectations when traditionality of occupation was taken into account. Men's occupational self-efficacy was equivalent for both traditionally male- and female-dominated occupations, whereas women's occupational self-efficacy was lower than men's for traditional men's occupations and higher than men's for traditional female occupations. In addition, these gender differences were predictive of the range of occupations considered. A considerable number of studies have supported these findings, emphasizing the theoretical and empirical support for the role of perceived self-efficacy as a mediator of gender differences in career and educational behaviors. In addition, the theory has practical utility in that the sources of self-efficacy are amenable to group and individual intervention.

More recently, Lent and colleagues (Lent & Hackett, 1994; Lent et al., 1994, 1996) have formulated a social cognitive theory of career to explain how academic and career interests develop, how individuals make and enact career-related choices, and how the construct of personal agency operates in terms of career outcomes. Built on the work of Bandura (1986), this theory focuses on self-efficacy, expected outcome, and goal mechanisms and how these reciprocally interact in an ongoing manner with individual factors (such as cognition), environment factors (such as support structures), and behavioral and learning factors. Fitzgerald et al. (1995) have outlined the ways in which this theoretical model can contribute to the career psychology of women. These include the importance of deliberately including a focus on contextual factors that have been emphasized as important for understanding the career development of women, people of color, working-class people, and others for whom existing frameworks offer less than satisfactory explanation.

WOMEN'S CAREER DEVELOPMENT—OTHER VIEWS.   Finally, other authors have identified shortcomings in existing theoretical models, or "missing theoretical construct(s)" (Forrest & Mikolaitis, 1986, p. 79), and have proposed areas that require further theoretical and empirical work. Gallos (1989) echoed the comment of Farmer in the previous section and called for career theory to consider women's distinctive developmental needs and voices. Among many questions she posed for researchers to consider was, "What does a long-term career underpinned by an ethic of caring look like?" (p. 128).

Forrest and Mikolaitis (1986) proposed the integration of a "relational component of identity" into existing career theories, defining this concept as "a guiding principle, although not necessarily a consciously organized one, that influences heavily one's perceptions and actions toward self and others" (p. 79). They derived the notion of relational identity from the work of Chodorow (1978), Gilligan (1977, 1982), and Lyons (1983), noting that "women reflect their sense of identity primarily in terms of their connection to others" (p. 80), whereas men describe their sense of self by "differentiating themselves from others in terms of abilities and attributes" (p. 80). Gilligan (1982) asserted that a convergence between the connected self and the separate self was illustrative of development toward maturity. Because this construct is central to the self for both women and men, Forrest and Mikolaitis emphasized the importance of its incorporation into existing theories of career development. They offered an example by studying the theory of Holland, noting that women and men whose self-descriptions were connected or separate would be likely to choose related occupational fields. For example, women and men who would describe themselves as "connected" or who viewed relating to people as important would be likely to choose occupations within the service area, such as teaching or nursing. However, the imbalance of women and men within these occupations may be explained by the greater support for women to be "connected" in their self-descriptions and for men to be separate. Such differences may go some way toward explaining some of the differences in the numbers of women and men in various occupations. In a similar vein, a mismatch between self-identity and work environment may explain job dissatisfaction for females and for males.

While Forrest and Mikolaitis (1986) called for the inclusion of this construct into theory development, there has been little further work. It may be a narrow construct that has been more broadly illustrated by discussion of the interaction between internal psychological constructions and social and environmental constraints. Recent discussions about social construction of individual variables suggest that relational identity is socially constructed.

More recently, Poole and Langan-Fox (1997) focused on women's careers and identified several concepts that were not present in existing theories—namely, disconnection, transitions, constraint, conflict, and compromise. They also noted the importance of building the notion of context into the career theory literature at the micro and macro levels. Thus, they proposed two frameworks to explain career development: a contextualist framework and the notion of "lifecareer," "in which both men and women have multiple options, various pathways, career networks, even career disconnections (e.g., unemployment, retrenchment) which are seen as legitimate journeys over the life course, and not perceived as deviant patterns" (p. 39).

SUMMARY

While there has been considerable development in theoretical work on the career behavior of women, the construction of a unified picture remains difficult, as in career theory generally. The above discussion presents a field that remains complex, disparate, and developmental, with existing theorists continuing to incorporate women's issues into their frameworks or rejecting the value of doing so and with individual differences models addressing different dimensions. For example, Farmer (1985) focused on three dimensions of achievement motivation, Astin (1984) elaborated a more broad sociopsychological model, and Betz and Fitzgerald's (1987) factors relevant to the realism of women's career choices continue to be refined (Fassinger, 1990). Despite these problems, the frameworks discussed in this section have highlighted the importance of relevant background factors such as gender, ethnicity, educational and occupational level of parents, and socioeconomic status to women's career behavior. Similarly, they have addressed in different ways the importance of socialization processes. While internal traits and attitudes have also been shown to be important in women's career-related behavior, the interaction of these with processes of socialization has not been adequately addressed. For example, if relational identity is socially constructed, can it be incorporated within a male identity? How do women learn gender-role attitudes that are career positive, family positive, or amenable to a balance of both with minimal conflict?

These questions have begun to be answered by the sociocognitive approaches of Hackett and Betz (1981) and Lent and Hackett (1994). These approaches can address the intricacy of internal socialization processes through the inclusion of cognition in their models. In addition, they incorporate contextual issues into their explanations. Finally, they address another problem with existing work—that is, the static nature of current descriptions and explanations. Hackett and Lent (1992) discussed this succinctly when they reminded us that "social changes impact social roles generally, and women's roles in particular. These shifts may shorten the shelf life of past research findings; they also highlight the need for researchers to attend to current social realities and their interaction with career development processes" (p. 439). The introduction of the importance of a triadic reciprocity that is ongoing in the social cognitive approach (see Chapter 4) identified the repeated and ongoing change that the individual and society are undergoing and the importance of its inclusion in theorizing about career development.

Despite these issues, theoretical work in the career psychology of women has drawn attention to variables that were previously unspecified. As discussed previously, an important contribution of this work has been the increased understanding of issues relevant to the career development of men. In focusing on gender as a group variable, theorists have also identified the importance of the heterogeneity of each gender group and indeed of individuals generally. Fitzgerald et al. (1995) presented this important development as follows: "Thus from a focus on the ways in which women are different from and similar to men, the question arises, How are we different from—and similar to—one another? And what implications does this have for our relationship to work and family?" (p. 102). As such, career theory has also focused on individuals of varying class, color, intellectual and physical ability, and sexual orientation. The fields of racial and ethnic background and sexual orientation have seen particular growth in recent years and will be included in the following sections.

THE CAREER DEVELOPMENT
OF RACIAL AND ETHNIC GROUPS

As discussed above, career theory has given little attention to racial and ethnic groups. In each of these fields, traditional career theory is based on erroneous assumptions, several concepts are irrelevant, and important contextual career determinants have been excluded. In particular, as with other groups in this chapter, the assumption that options and choices are available to individuals without some form of social discrimination operating to distort individual characteristics is violated with respect to racial and ethnic group members.

While research in the area is hampered by problems such as definitional concerns with respect to the terms *race*, *ethnicity*, and *minority group*, the confounding of race and ethnic group with socioeconomic level, and the conceptualizing and measuring of variables from a white middle-class perspective, several clear patterns have been emerging. These include the differential representation of racial and ethnic groups in certain occupational areas and higher unemployment rates for certain groups (Smith, 1983). For example, as with women, the assumption that the sociopolitical environment enables all individuals equal access to choose according to their interests and abilities is fallacious and misleading. Smith (1983) reported that racial and ethnic minority youth in America have less occupational information than other groups. An Australian study by Poole and Cooney (1985) reported that there was no difference in the awareness of occupational possibilities in a group of adolescents, regardless of gender, socioeconomic background, or ethnic background. However, gender and socioeconomic background restricted the consideration of the occupational possibilities perceived as relevant to and achievable by each individual. Further, a report on the review of Aboriginal employment and training programs in Australia (Miller, 1985) showed that Aborigines have more restricted employment opportunities and higher unemployment than white Australians. In addition, the retention rate in secondary schooling is considerably lower for Aborigines than the national rate. Similar data on racial and ethnic groups in America are reported by Fitzgerald and Betz (1994) and Arbona (1990).

A number of reviews (Brooks, 1990; Fitzgerald & Betz, 1994; Hackett & Lent, 1992; Leong, 1995) have concluded that there is no model specifically developed to explain the career development of ethnic and racial groups. While several theorists have acknowledged effects of race and ethnicity in their models (L. S. Gottfredson, 1981; Holland, 1985a; Super, 1990), these have not been fully integrated into theoretical propositions. Leong and D. Brown (1995) and Leong (1996b) have been critical of existing theories in relation to their reliance on attempting to confirm internal validity at the expense of external or ecological validity.

Like the theories of women's career development discussed earlier in this chapter, career theories can be grouped into three categories in terms of their relevance to racial and ethnic groups: traditional theories that have tried to incorporate minority issues into their conceptualizations, broader theoretical models that may be applicable across cultures, and recent conceptual proposals that are attempting to incorporate cultural validity through culture specificity. In the first category, we will discuss the work of Holland (1985a) and Super (1990). In the second category, we will explore self-efficacy theory (Hackett & Betz, 1981) and the sociocognitive model of Lent and Hackett (1994), social learning theory (L. K. Mitchell & Krumboltz, 1996), and the broad sociopsychological model of L. S. Gottfredson (1981). In the third category, we will include Osipow and Littlejohn (1995), who aimed to focus on subtle differences in "minor" variables relevant to career theory and this group rather than on the larger variable of race. Finally, we will discuss the recent culture-specific conceptual proposals regarding American Hispanics (Arbona, 1990) and African Americans (Cheatham, 1990).

In their major review of theoretical issues in cross-cultural career development, Leong and Brown (1995) emphasized the narrow population for which most career theory has been developed, the limited nature of the theoretical assumptions, the failure to recognize broader "sociopolitical, socioeconomic, social-psychological, and sociocultural realities of cross-cultural individuals" (p. 146), and the inappropriateness of much use of the terms *race*, *ethnicity*, and *minority*. Leong and Brown (1995) recommended the use of the terms *ethnic group* and *cultural group*. In relation to the failure to acknowledge the broader context, these authors emphasized that the factors that influence the career choice process of these groups may not yet be addressed by current theories.

EXISTING THEORIES WITH CROSS-CULTURAL PERSPECTIVES

As in the previous section, we will focus on the major theories of Holland and Super. Holland (1985a, 1992; see Chapter 2 for an overview of the theory) acknowledged that factors such as age, race, class, and gender may restrict career options and that in these cases, individuals will choose the next most dominant feature of their personality in implementing their career choice. A number of studies have shown that poor African Americans are found in low-level realistic jobs when Holland's typology is applied (Arbona, 1989; Miller, Springer, & Wells, 1988), but work with other ethnic groups has not been conducted. It is interesting that the effect of this compromise process over time on job satisfaction or personality was not pursued in Holland's formulation. Some evidence that African Americans and other ethnic groups may experience lower congruence than other Americans has been reported by M. Brown (1995).

Although Holland (1985a) asserted that the structure of interests conforms to the hexagon "even when the data, sexes and cultures vary" (p. 119), research has reported conflicting findings. A review of research by J. C. Hansen (1987) concluded that "the structure of interests of international and cross-ethnic populations seems to correspond to Holland's model almost as well as does the structure of interests of Whites" (p. 173). More recently, however, two studies with Mexican engineers (Fouad & Dancer, 1992) and African American college students (Swanson, 1992) have shown only mixed support for the hexagonal structure. A revised position has subsequently been posited by J. C. Hansen (1992), who commented that while there is a "broad pattern of structural similarity across cultures," there are "specific sample differences [that] reflect the individual differences of cultures" (p. 188). This conclusion was strengthened following a structural meta-analysis of 20 American ethnic matrices and 76 international matrices from 18 countries by Rounds and Tracey (1996). These authors found that Holland's model did not fit well for the ethnic groups in America or for international samples. Recent work with disadvantaged black South African students has also supported this view (M. B. Watson, Stead, & Schonegevel, 1997).

Like Holland, Super (1990) attempted to acknowledge issues of ethnicity in his formulation, although he did not expand on the process of their influence. Although there have been many questions about the cultural validity of some of his key constructs, there is a need for much more research into the usefulness of Super's theory for ethnic groups (Fouad & Arbona, 1994; Leong & Brown, 1995). While self-concept as a determinant of career choice is a key component of Super's theory, a number of writers have suggested that poverty and discrimination are more valid determinants for ethnic groups (Osipow, 1975; Smith, 1983). In addition, in many cultural groups, self-concept is inextricably entwined with cultural attitudes, beliefs, and values. In particular, Leong and Serafica (1995) commented that the degree of an individual's acculturation may affect the role of the self-concept in career development differentially. For example, in some ethnic groups, occupations are chosen on the basis of family and culture-of-origin goals rather than implementation of an individual's self-concept. Similarly, ethnic discrimination may not only restrict the availability of occupations but also affect occupational self-concept and more general self-concept. The way in which these processes may work is also in need of more research.

Two other constructs that are key elements of Super's (1990) theory are developmental stages and career maturity. Leong and Brown (1995) commented on the lack of research on developmental stages of ethnic groups. In addition, the concept of mastering tasks within developmental stages is likely to be unrelated to many cultures. Leong (1993) concluded that the concept of stages would apply more to members of racial and ethnic groups who had acculturated more into the dominant white culture.

Smith (1983) first emphasized the inherent cultural bias of the concept of career maturity. He argued that the tasks measured by career maturity inventories may not be common to all ethnic groups. More recently, Fouad (1994) commented that Super's career maturity construct may be more relevant for individuals in ethnic groups who have developed an ethnic identity. It is important to acknowledge that ethnic groups are often also found in lower socioeconomic groups. As such, this concept also may need revision with respect to different ethnic and cultural groups and with the confound of socioeconomic status partialed out of the data.

BROADER THEORETICAL MODELS

As discussed earlier in this chapter, L. S. Gottfredson (1986) proposed a framework offering categories for conceptualizing risk factors that create career choice problems. While not intended as a theoretical model, it defined risk factors as "attributes of the person or of the person's relation to the environment that are associated with a higher than average probability of experiencing the types of problems under consideration" (p. 143). These categories of risk are influences that cause people to be different from the general population (e.g., low IQ, low self-esteem, cultural segregation, poverty), factors involving differences from one's own social group (e.g., socioeconomic disadvantage, racial or ethnic group, physical impairment), and factors involving family responsibilities (e.g., primary provider). Such a framework is broad enough to offer factors that may inhibit career development for a variety of groups of people and individuals.

This 1986 discussion on risk factors was an extension of L. S. Gottfredson's major (1981) theoretical model (see Chapter 3). Gottfredson's circumscription and compromise theory was one of the few that explicitly acknowledged the effect of social factors on career choice. She asserted that careers are circumscribed in terms of sex type at a young age, prestige in later childhood, and interests and values during the teen years. Thus, the acknowledgment of gender and prestige as important variables in career choice has relevance to a discussion of cross-cultural career development.

Gottfredson's other important process, compromise, is also relevant to cross-cultural career development. She asserted that compromise occurs as a function of perceived compatibility between one's occupational self-concept and both jobs and the perceived accessibility of jobs. In the case of ethnic groups, jobs compatible with the occupational self-concept may be seen as unavailable because of discrimination. As discussed earlier, this process may be even more complex in that discrimination awareness may also affect the development of occupational self-concept.

The learning principles inherent within social learning theory (Krumboltz, 1979; L. K. Mitchell & Krumboltz, 1990, 1996), such as associative and instrumental learning, are essentially fundamental behavioral principles and therefore are likely to be universal. In the most recent major presentation of the theory (L. K. Mitchell & Krumboltz, 1996), an African American case example is used to illustrate the universality of learning principles. As such, the process element of this theory has the potential to be applicable to racial and ethnic groups. However, the content elements of the theory, such as self-observation generalizations, need to be further related to particular racial and ethnic groups.

The self-efficacy theory of Hackett and Betz (1981) also has potential to be applicable to ethnic groups (Lent & Hackett, 1987). In brief, the theory asserts that career self-efficacy expectations are beliefs about one's ability to perform certain occupational behaviors and that these expectations determine one's actions and efforts in relation to those occupational behaviors. While more research is needed, studies have shown the relevance of self-efficacy in academic and career behavior of different cultural groups (Arbona, 1995; Hackett, Betz, Casas, & Rocha-Singh, 1992). However, M. Brown (1995) has commented that discrimination and social bias can influence one's expectations of outcomes quite independently of the effectiveness of one's behavior.

Rather than focusing on the effects of the major variable of race per se, Osipow and Littlejohn (1995) examined some of the other variables that permeate career theory and identified their effects with respect to race. The authors included self-concept (discussed previously) and its close relationship with identity stage development, commenting on the fluctuating phases of acceptance of mainstream society and minority culture. Osipow and Littlejohn (1995) emphasized the lack of attention paid to these issues in the career theory literature. Several questions thus remain unanswered, such as "What is the relationship between minority identity development and career choice? Are there correlations between worldview or ethnic identity and career achievement? And how does level of acculturation influence career development?" (p. 259). The work environment and the variable nature of opportunities available to many racial and ethnic groups were also explored by these authors. Closely linked with the work environment is the lack of opportunity of individuals from these groups to develop self-efficacy in relation to many occupational areas. In conclusion, these authors emphasized the inadequacy of attention of many current theories in relation to the application of these variables to this group.

CULTURE-SPECIFIC CONCEPTUAL MODELS

Finally, in an attempt to clarify the career behavior of particular ethnic and cultural groups, theorists have developed culture-specific models to highlight relevant career development issues. In commenting on this focus with particular minority groups, Arbona (1996) emphasized that

> we need to identify the specific elements of each minority group's experience that contribute to the proposed relationship among race, ethnicity, culture, and career development variables. . . . Only then will we be able to determine if there is sufficient overlap across groups to warrant talking about the career development of ethnic minorities as a group. (p. 47)

In the same vein, Hesketh and Rounds (1995) also commented on the value of specific theories that are capable of generalization: "There may be value in our developing theories through the ongoing process of comparing and contrasting different cultures. In this way, the universal aspects of the theory will be apparent, as will the need for specific components to deal with particular cultural contexts" (p. 385). While Leong and Brown (1995) discussed culture-specific models extensively, the discussion here will be restricted to two models (Arbona, 1990; Cheatham, 1990).

In reviewing the relationship between career theory and educational development and academic achievement as they interact with ethnicity and social class, Arbona (1990) concluded that career theories may have some use for Hispanics of average academic achievement for whom the worker role is salient, regardless of socioeconomic level, but that they are not relevant to clients who have limited access to education and for whom concepts of career choice are limited. She proposed a model suggesting that the salience of structural barriers and problems of access is more relevant than interests and aspirations to occupational mobility in diverse Hispanic groups. That is, she suggested that contextual factors may be more relevant than individual factors for members of this group. A focus on the heterogeneity of Hispanic Americans also led her to call for research examining subcultural factors influencing career behavior.

Cheatham (1990) proposed a model based on the concept of Afrocentrism. He stressed the interplay between African American culture and European American culture and identified several cultural dualisms that he suggested needed to be measured so that their relationship with career behavior could be documented. One of these dualisms concerned the cultural construction of values. For example, he stated that Afrocentric cultural values of affiliation, collectivity, interdependence, and work were in stark contrast to dominant European American or Western values of individualism, competition, and mastery over nature as opposed to harmony with nature. Another cultural difference was the

Western adherence to measured time (indicated by the often-repeated saying "a race against the clock") as opposed to experiential lived time.

THE CAREER DEVELOPMENT
OF LESBIANS AND GAY MEN

There has been a dearth of attention directed toward the unique career development issues relevant to lesbians and gay men, a minority group that receives more negative bias than any other (Herr & Cramer, 1992). However since a 1989 article on career counseling with lesbians (Hetherington & Orzek), texts such as that of Herr and Cramer (1992) and several research and review articles (Morgan & Brown, 1991) have appeared. In 1991, the *Counseling Psychologist* (Fassinger, 1991) devoted a special issue to counseling lesbian women and gay men, and a special section of the *Career Development Quarterly* (Pope, 1995) was recently devoted to the issue. Specific texts (e.g., Diamant, 1993) have also appeared. Internal and environmental issues relevant to the career development of these individuals and separate from those relevant to heterosexuals have been suggested (Fassinger, 1995; Hetherington, 1991). Before our exploration of these issues, we will briefly discuss broad contextual issues relevant to lesbians and gay men.

It is clear that many issues for lesbians and gay men are similar to those identified for women and racial and ethnic minority groups. Chung (1995) supported the suggestion by Morgan and Brown (1991) that minority career development theories (e.g., those related to women and racial and ethnic groups) may be appropriately used to explain the vocational issues of lesbians and gay men. However, lesbians in particular live in a patriarchal and heterosexist world; several authors (Hetherington & Orzek, 1989; Morgan & Brown, 1991) have commented on the combined minority status of lesbians in dealing with gender and sexual orientation issues, in what Betz (1994a) has referred to as "double jeopardy" (p. 19). Fassinger (1995) also referred to the triple minority status experienced by colored lesbians.

It is also important, as in the discussion with women and racial and ethnic groups, not to assume heterogeneity of gay people generally or each gender-based group. For example, Etringer, Hillerbrand, and Hetherington (1990) found that gay men have the greatest uncertainty about vocational choices and are more dissatisfied with their choices than nongay men or lesbian women. Further, lesbians are more likely to be in lower paying jobs than gay men and to be employed below their skill and educational level (Elliott, 1993a, 1993b; Morgan & Brown, 1991).

Given the importance of self-concept and identity formation in all major theories of career development, several issues relevant to identity development for lesbians and gay men add an extra level of complexity. First, Fassinger (1995) commented that in relation to lesbians, the demands of identity issues may result in the neglect of career development issues. Since lesbian identity is not usually clarified until late adolescence or adulthood, the inclusion of an individual identity into career planning may not occur until after important early periods of career development (Morgan & Brown, 1991).

Second, the identification of oneself as gay may eliminate a number of potential career options, particularly those in which being gay has marked negative consequences (e.g., teaching and the military). Third, many lesbians may experience estrangement from families, a major influence on women's career development. Finally, the coming-out process often results in "a temporary (but dramatic) decrease in self-esteem and new complexities in self-concept" (Fassinger, 1995, p. 155). These effects have complex implications for career development for lesbians and gay men (Hetherington, 1991; Hetherington, Hillerbrand, & Etringer, 1989).

In addition to these individual issues, Hetherington (1991), Fassinger (1995), and Elliott (1993b) have identified environmental issues relevant to the career development of lesbians and gay men. These include occupational stereotyping (assumptions that certain occupations are lesbian and gay specific) and occupational discrimination (rejecting or discouraging lesbians and gays in particular fields). Morgan and Brown (1991) discussed Astin's (1984) concept of opportunity structure (discussed earlier in this chapter) in relation to lesbians' occupational stereotyping. They also noted its usefulness in acknowledging how changing societal and political views relevant to gay people and occupations may affect the opportunity structure. The possible late development of a gay identity may also affect an individual's perception of opportunity structure.

Additional issues raised by Fassinger (1995) include the difficulty of having one's occupational identity strengthened by role models, since so many lesbians and gay men remain closeted; the negative bias in testing and counseling; and the null environment (Betz, 1989) in education and the wider social environment. The null environment is described by Betz as "an environment that neither encourages or discourages individuals—it simply ignores them" (p. 17).

However, in her discussion of vocational issues for lesbians, Fassinger (1995) also identified some positive aspects of identity that lesbians bring to the process of career choice. In particular, she noted that lesbians exhibit more liberal gender roles than heterosexual women (Hetherington & Orzek, 1989; Morgan & Brown, 1991). As a result, they may illustrate greater flexibility in choosing a broader array of occupations. Research with women discussed previously has shown that traditional gender roles can limit women's career choices (Betz & Fitzgerald, 1987; Fitzgerald et al., 1995). These propositions have not been tested. However Morgan and Brown (1991) discussed L. S. Gottfredson's (1981) circumscription and compromise theory and its applicability to lesbians. In particular, Gottfredson explored the premise that in limiting career options, individuals will give up interests first, status second, and sex type of the career last; that is, they will hold to sex type the most. Given the more liberal gender roles of lesbians, Morgan and Brown (1991) contended that they may be less influenced by sex type of an occupation and may focus more on interests and status. This may result in more realistic choices that exhibit congruence with interests. Economic necessity, with lesbians aware of the necessity of being self-supporting, may also explain career choices in male-dominated fields.

Morgan and Brown (1991) also explored the theories of Farmer (1985) and Astin (1984) and commented on their applicability to lesbians. They noted that

Farmer's three factors influencing career development (background variables, person psychological variables, environmental variables) are applicable to lesbians. In particular, they added sexual orientation to Farmer's background variables, androgyny and valuing independence to her personality variables, and support for a lesbian per se and for lesbians in particular occupations to her environmental variables.

In relation to Astin's theory, Morgan and Brown (1991) focused on the differential timing of the coming-out process for lesbians (and gay men) and how this would affect the perception of the opportunity structure. In addition, the work motivation and work expectations of lesbians may be different than those of heterosexual women, who may have an expectation of getting married and working in the home.

In relation to gay men, Chung and Harmon (1994) found that gay men's career interests and aspirations were less traditional than those of heterosexual men. Their sample of educated men scored higher on the Artistic and Social scales of the Self-Directed Search (Holland, 1985b) and lower on the Realistic and Investigative scales than a heterosexual sample matched for age, socioeconomic status, education level, student status, and ethnic background.

Attempts to apply existing theories to the career experience of lesbians and gays has to date been conducted only in relation to lesbians (Morgan & Brown, 1991). Chung (1995) emphasized the need for a guiding theory for the vocational experience of lesbians and gay men. Fassinger (1995) echoed previous work (Fitzgerald et al., 1995) illustrating that research on women has expanded our knowledge of the career development of men as well. She suggested that research on the career choice process of lesbians may assist in untangling the effects of gender roles relative to other variables that influence women's career planning generally. Morgan and Brown (1991) reiterated this assertion and also suggested that "the development of a theory of lesbian career development, based on the experiences of the diverse population of lesbians, might shed new and different light on our paradigms for all women's career development" (p. 289).

SOCIOLOGICAL VARIABLES

In addition to women, racial and ethnic groups, and lesbians and gay men, little theoretical attention has been given to the complexity of socioeconomic status in relation to career development. One of the often-repeated criticisms of psychological theories of career development is their failure to focus in a detailed way on sociological variables. D. Brown (1996b) commented that of the psychological theories presented in their career theory text, only the work of L. S. Gottfredson (1996, discussed in this book in Chapter 3) incorporated sociological variables in a detailed way in her theory. Other theorists (e.g., Lent et al., 1996; Super et al., 1996) mentioned the relevance of sociological variables such as social class and educational options but only in a nonspecific way.

Sociologists have made significant contributions to our understanding of factors relevant to career development. In this approach, career development is viewed in relation to its contextual or situational determinants, such as social class membership, economic opportunities, and the organization of the world of work.

In direct contrast to the traditional assumption that the individual has unfettered capacity and means to make career decisions, Roberts (1968, 1977) and others have challenged the notion of career decision making and have questioned whether all people do have the capacity to choose a career. In advocating a situational approach based on an explanation of the role of broad macrovariables such as social class and labor market accessibility, Roberts (1977) claimed that "it is not choice but opportunity that governs the manner in which young people make their entry into employment" (p. 145), thus being one of the first to discuss the notion of opportunity structure (see also Astin, 1984; Lent et al., 1996). Roberts believed that socioeconomic factors act as filters of relevant information in several areas, including type of education received and information obtained, values held, observable role models, possible courses of action, and level of encouragement. Such a view challenges career theorists to explore ways of ensuring equality of opportunity for all people so that they have the opportunity to make decisions, in addition to hypothesizing about how career decisions are made.

In addition to specific sociological variables, theorists within this category have focused on status attainment, whereby the father's occupation and education are seen as a measure of status and are related to occupational level of offspring (Blau & Duncan, 1967). Considerable research has supported this model, with Hotchkiss and Borow (1996) concluding that "few models in social research have held up so well under such extensive scrutiny" (p. 288). However, recent work has challenged the comprehensiveness of the model, in particular in relation to women and racial and ethnic groups. Structural theorists, consisting of sociologists and economists, have attempted to broaden our understanding of the influence of social systems and have advocated focusing on a variety of features of the social structure that are related to individual career functioning. These structural features include discrimination, occupational and job segregation, the supply and demand of labor, the size and location of employing organizations, and a range of other work and labor market factors.

In sum, "The sociological framework for analyzing career paths of individuals considers the interplay between individual choices and constraints on those choices imposed by the operation of the labor market" (Hotchkiss & Borow, 1996, p. 325). The new structural emphasis reflects a broader consideration of social structural factors and complements the relevance of these factors to the individual choice processes emphasized by psychological theories. These structural theories have exposed reasons for the differential access to and outcomes from the labor market in a number of gender, racial and ethnic, and socioeconomic groups in society. The relevance of these structural issues has been incorporated to varying degrees into psychological theoretical models.

Another area within sociological theory is the issue of chance, described by some as "accident theory" (Minor, 1992). Chance is defined as "an unplanned event that measurably alters one's behavior" (Miller, 1983, p. 17). Bandura (1982) explored in detail the potential influence of chance encounters with individuals and the effects that unforeseeable events can have on individuals. Other factors that can be related to chance include being born with certain genetic endowments, being born into a family with particular socioeconomic status and perhaps in a particular geographic location, and even being born in a particular era, such as that of a depression or a war. Psychological theorists have paid little attention to a discussion of chance, despite the relative frequency of its occurrence in individuals' lives (Bandura, 1982). This may be because it is somewhat at odds with the focus of psychological theories on individual planning and control over the future. Chapter 5 showed that Krumboltz, Lent et al., and Roe and Lunneborg are the only theorists that have attempted to include a discussion of chance factors, such as genetic endowment, in their theories.

CONCLUSION

The work in this chapter on women, racial and ethnic groups, lesbians and gay men, and socioeconomic groups raises some important concerns for theory development generally. First, there is much heterogeneity within these groups, based on gender, socioeconomic status, and other variables. For example, our discussion of ethnic groups did not include women. Theoretical and empirical work is only beginning to explore the interaction between ethnicity and gender. For example, Bingham and Ward (1994) outlined five areas that they believed may affect the career development of women of color. These include relevant information about the workplace, factors related to family commitment, community factors such as language and role models, influence of socialization, and impact of sexism and racism. These authors highlighted the relevance of these factors to the career counseling process with women from ethnic groups (Bingham & Ward, 1996).

Second, future theory development needs to expand on the specifics of individual differences and the structural and cultural factors that influence the theoretical and applied usefulness of career theories. Betz and Fitzgerald (1994) identified the following important individual difference categories—gender, race, ethnicity, social class, and sexual/affectional orientation—and suggested three approaches by which these can be addressed. They emphasized the need to explore the applicability of a given theory to a particular group, rather like the work that has been done in this chapter. This notion also echoes the "specific to universal" path of theory development (Arbona, 1996; Hesketh & Rounds, 1995) discussed in the ethnic group section of this chapter. It is also reflected in our discussion of women's career theory, where we noted that theoretical and empirical work on the career behavior of women has enhanced our knowledge of aspects of men's career development.

Betz and Fitzgerald (1994) suggested that research should explore the relevance of individual difference and structural and cultural variables that affect the predictive value of a theory. They advocated the careful examination of each theory to analyze the roles that these structural and cultural factors play in the conceptualization and measurement of the important constructs of the theories.

As with career theory generally, the theoretical picture with respect to career development of women, racial and ethnic groups, lesbians and gay men, and individuals from different socioeconomic backgrounds is one in which no one theory presents a comprehensive theoretical rationale for and explanation of career behavior. However, each theory has addressed important individual variables and important social and environmental variables and has started to address key aspects of cognitive process and issues related to the interaction of these variables and processes over time. Such a picture stresses the valuable nature of the theoretical contributions that have been made, and any further work within individual theoretical frameworks can only enhance their theoretical and practical worth.

However, there is a need for an overarching framework in which the contribution of each of these theories can be noted by theorists, researchers, and practitioners. Betz and Fitzgerald (1994) advocated that "structural and cultural factors [serve] as a focal point for both theoretical development and integration" (p. 114). The framework suggested by Betz and Fitzgerald (1994), emphasizing individual difference and structural and cultural factors, is a useful overarching framework for theory questioning and for guiding research, although it does not explicate the processes by which these factors interact.

This part of the book has presented a detailed and comprehensive review of career theories, noting the lack of coherence and integration among the major theories and emphasizing issues that existing theories have failed to address adequately. It has highlighted the value of exploring career theory with a focus on particular groups and of developing an overarching framework. In Part 2, we will present an overarching framework for career theory based on systems theory. Before that (Chapter 9), we will detail previous attempts at integration of career theory issues and the recent moves toward convergence (Chapter 7) and will explain key elements of systems theory (Chapter 8).

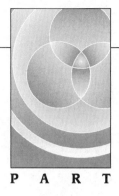

II

THE MOVE TOWARD INTEGRATION AND CONVERGENCE

7

TOWARD INTEGRATION
IN CAREER THEORY

As previously indicated, reading in the field of career development can quickly become overwhelming for the uninitiated as they are confronted with an array of theories addressing many issues and espousing a range of perspectives on career development. This array of theories may engender comments such as: "But which one is right?" "Who do I believe?" "How can I know what to think?" and "They all sound good to me." Alternatively, the careers professional may become an adherent of one theory at the expense of the others. Thus, the practitioner's response to the existing body of literature may range on a continuum from confusion to narrow-mindedness, since the links between theories traditionally have not been made clear.

Discussion in Chapter 1 emphasized the segmented and disparate nature of much of career development theory and the conceptual overlap between existing theories. Theorists have responded to this issue in a number of ways over many years. Their responses have included proposals for integrative frameworks and adoption of elements of other theories into their own in an attempt to forge links between theories. In particular, the two major theoretical perspectives of Holland and Super have shown ongoing adjustments in this direction. For example, Holland (1985a) commented that his model works best when considered in context and also acknowledged the impact of chance factors. In describing the development of his Archway model, Super (1990, 1994) acknowledged the contributions of many writers, including Roberts (1977) and Vondracek et al. (1986). In addition, both Holland and Super commented on the importance of Krumboltz's learning theory in contributing to refinements in their work. Osipow (1983, p. 313) observed that "most writers have chosen to emphasize the roles of one or two variables over those of others, but nearly all have acknowledged that many factors operate to influence career development"—a comment that he reiterated in 1990. As a whole, the existing literature reflects the multifaceted base and complexity of the concept of career development. But until recently, there has been only minimal effort to synthesize the theories.

In this chapter, we will review the underlying epistemological base of vocational psychology and discuss how changes in worldviews are contributing to the development of linking of theoretical concepts. We will also look at the historical trend toward convergence of career theory, beginning with early approaches to further the integration of concepts in career development. A number of proposed bridging frameworks that have been proffered will be explored. Finally, we will trace the more recent moves toward theory convergence (since 1990) that have contributed to renewed activity and vitality in the careers field.

Underlying Worldviews

The move toward convergence in career theory reflects disenchantment with its disunity. It also reflects a change in an underlying worldview, or root metaphor. This underlying philosophy is a guide to all our theories of human behavior. A worldview has been described by Lyddon (1989) as serving the role of organizing day-to-day experiential data. Pepper (1942) identified what he viewed as four competing root metaphors: mechanism, organicism, formism, and contextualism. *Mechanism* refers to the perspective that attempts to explain phenomena in mechanical terms. For example, such explanations suggest that we reason in direct linear routes from the general to the particular and vice versa and that we focus on cause and effect. In this view, the world operates in much the same way as a machine. Problems arise when some part of the machine is malfunctioning. *Formism* is related to the process of forming phenomena into explainable structures. *Organicism* sees human development as an orderly maturational unfolding process. It is the basis of prominent stage-based models in developmental psychology, and particularly of the work of Super and Gottfredson in vocational psychology. Any problems in the unfolding are thought to be related to the individual. For example, within the stage-based models of career, the individual is seen as responsible for movement toward the next stage, however the characteristics of that stage have been predetermined by a theorist. Collin and Young (1986) pointed out that "career theories have so far been largely informed by the root metaphor of either organicism and/or mechanism" (p. 843).

However, *contextualism* is increasingly being suggested in a number of fields in the social sciences—for example, by Collin and Young (1986) and Vondracek et al. (1986) in career psychology and by Steenbarger (1991) in counseling psychology. A contextual worldview focuses on the world simply as "events" in a unique historical context. These events occur "out there," but how they are viewed is linked to the perspective of each individual. Furthermore, the contextualist worldview does not conceive development as maturational and as unfolding in stages but rather as an ongoing process of interaction be-tween the person and the environment. Within this process, random or chance events contribute to an open-ended, unpredictable state of being. An outcome of these elements of the contextualist worldview is the view of the individual as an active, self-building and self-renewing "self-organizing system" (D. Ford, 1987), as opposed to a passive organism subjected to maturational and devel-opmental stages and/or environmental forces. Career work within the contextualist worldview focuses on individuals interacting with their social and environmental contexts. Career development is not viewed as an intraindividual developmental process.

The contextualist worldview is reflected in the constructivist epistemol-ogy as opposed to the traditional objectivist or positivist epistemology. To ex-plain these two positions, positivists emphasize rationality based on an objec-tive, value-free knowledge: objectivity over subjectivity, facts over feelings. Constructivists argue against the possibility of absolute truth. However, to say that the constructivist approach is the opposite would be to oversimplify. Constructivism is directly derived from the contextualist worldview in that the "reality" of world events is seen as constructed from the inside out by the indi-vidual (i.e., through the individual's own thinking and processing). These con-structions are based on individual cognitions in relation with perspectives formed from person-environment interactions. "They are both individual and interactional, creating order for the person and guiding interactions with the environment" (Steenbarger, 1991, p. 291). Constructivism therefore views the person as an open system, constantly interacting with the environment, seek-ing stability through ongoing change. The emphasis is on the process, not on an outcome; there is no completion of a stage and arrival at the next stage, as in stage-based views of human development. Mahoney and Lyddon (1988) em-phasized the change and stability notion as follows: "Embedded with self-change is self-stability—we are all changing all the time and simultaneously remaining the same" (p. 209).

While there is ongoing discussion in different disciplines about the "cor-rectness" of each of these ways of viewing the world, it is clear that there is no "right" way. Savickas (1995) emphasized the disagreements over which is the "right" epistemology and presented an illustrative outline of the historical pre-cursors to the philosophies of science that have informed the development of career theory. He reasserted the view that "vocational psychologists are being challenged to revise their core philosophy of science and to reform their field into an interpretive discipline" (p. 18). As in other disciplines (e.g., social work; see Franklin & Nurius, 1996), a number of authors have developed theoretical and research approaches that can be grouped under the postmodern or constructivist perspective. These approaches may all focus on different aspects and often have different names (e.g., *perspectivism, interpretivism, constructivism*), but they are all derived from similar perspectives. They include the work on hermeneutical perspectives in career theory (Collin & Young, 1988; Young & Collin, 1988) and in research (Young & Collin, 1992). Hermeneutical approaches focus on bringing together the meaning or underlying coherence of, in this case, an individual's career or the career experiences of a group of individuals. The career story is the text to be interpreted for what meaning we can glean from it. Other approaches include Peavy's (1992) work on constructivism in career counseling and Young and Borgen's (1990) work on subjective methods in the study of careers. In particular, the social cognitive career theory (SCCT; Lent et al., 1994) has been derived directly from assumptions of constructivism.

Following the emphasis on psychoanalytic and behavioral theories, constructivism has been acknowledged as the third major theoretical development in cognitive science (Mahoney & Patterson, 1992), a development that emphasizes human agency in individuals' construal and shaping of their experiences. It is this feature that distinguishes constructivism from the earlier movements and is now a major influence on human development theory and practice. Its specific influence in the development of career theory is evident in our earlier discussion of career theories. Lent and Hackett (1994) asserted that cognition can be used as a "fulcrum for theoretical convergence" (p. 83). However, before further developing the influence of the root metaphor of contextualism and the specific influence of cognitive constructivist approaches, we will explore earlier attempts at integration. In doing this, we will attempt to chart the historical process of integration in career psychology.

STAGES IN INTEGRATION AND CONVERGENCE

Savickas (1995) discussed three stages that a science follows in its transition from "early to late science" (p. 6). Early beginnings tend to encourage the development of diverse theories and approaches, with each scientist emphasizing the uniqueness of his or her own contribution. This can be seen in the early development of career theories, in which each theory focused on a different aspect of career behavior or a different part of the "map" (Krumboltz, 1994). During the second stage, relationships between theories and approaches are acknowledged, and scientists attempt to integrate diversity and eliminate the inevitable conceptual overlap. Three substages of this stage may be recognized: rapprochement, convergence, and bridging.

Rapprochement involves a cessation of competition and an introduction of a process of collaboration, in which researchers work together for commonalities across theories. "As rapprochement strengthens, the goal for knowledge production broadens to include not just the discovery of the novel but the interrelation, organization, and simplification of existing knowledge" (Savickas, 1995, p. 5). This rapprochement is evident in the increasing acknowledgment of the influence of context in refinements of Super (1980, 1990) and in Holland's (1985a) acknowledgment of the developmental nature of career.

Following rapprochement, *convergence*, which involves development of a common language for describing theoretical constructs, can begin. After completing Chapters 2 through 4, the reader will be aware that often theorists describe similar constructs using different language. For example, we noted the similarity between Krumboltz's (1994) self-observation generalization and Super's (1990) discussion of self-concept. However, it is also clear that theorists have chosen to share language rather than to confuse their work with additional terms. For example, Astin (1984) referred to *opportunity structure*, a construct also referred to by Roberts (1977), and both Lent et al. (1994) and Vondracek et al. (1986) have adopted the term *contextual affordance*.

The third substage within the second stage involves *bridging*. This phase requires work across theories, whereby key aspects of the existing theoretical base are organized. Savickas (1995) emphasized the importance of maintaining the integrity of existing theories as well as the growth toward unification. Examples of bridging frameworks will be discussed later in this chapter.

A final stage of unification involves a synthesis that uses a new "superordinate umbrella, coherent theoretical gestalt, metatheoretical framework or conceptually superior theory" (Beitman, Goldfried, & Norcross, 1989, p. 139). The systems theory framework that we propose in Chapter 9 is an example of such a framework.

Attempts at integration of career theory constructs have been located from as early as the 1950s. These have included attempts at interdisciplinary integrative frameworks, theorists' integration of elements of others' theories into their own, and development of new theories that attempt to build on previous theories. Examples of each of these will be presented, with an indication of whether they are representative of rapprochement, convergence, or bridging. A number of theoretical frameworks that have been suggested as suitable bridging frameworks in career theory will then be outlined.

INTEGRATIVE FRAMEWORKS

The interdisciplinary nature of contributions to career development theory has meant that writers have been attempting to construct integrative conceptual frameworks for some time. In this instance, a conceptual framework is seen as an umbrella concept for an overall theoretical field that is explained by a number of specific limited theories. "Conceptual frameworks do not usually have determinable empirical consequences, although their component models (limited to theories) typically contain statements about reality which may be open to empirical test" (Warr, 1980, p. 161). In this section, we will review five theoretical integrative frameworks: (1) Blau, Gustad, Jessor, Parnes, and Wilcock (1956); (2) Campbell (1969); (3) Hesketh (1985); (4) Pryor (1985a, 1985b); and (5) Sonnenfeld and Kotter (1982).

The first framework that we identified was that proposed by Blau et al. in 1956. These authors recognized the importance of contributions from psychology, economics, and sociology in understanding career choice and developed an inclusive conceptual framework. They provided a comprehensive outline of factors, drawn from the three disciplines, that had been advanced as relevant to the process of career choice. These were comprehensive and included genetic endowments, physical conditions, sociopsychological attributes, social structure, personality development, historical change, and socioeconomic organization. While acknowledging the importance of these factors, the authors noted that little is known about the relationships between them.

This article by Blau et al. (1956) was important for its inclusion of psychological and contextual antecedents in career choice. Although it stopped short of identifying the nature of the relationships between the variables, it highlighted the importance of understanding these relationships: "The identification of isolated determinants, however, cannot explain occupational choice . . . . [T]he exact relationships between [causal factors] have to be determined by empirical research before a systematic theory can be developed" (p. 532). Blau et al. did not claim to be advancing a theory but rather a conceptual framework. While it was not proposed to integrate existing theories, it did attempt to integrate crucial antecedent factors in occupational choice. Also, even at this early stage in the development of career development models, the importance of repeated decision making and the relevance of earlier choices to future choices were acknowledged: "A series of successive choice periods must be successively analyzed to show how earlier decisions limit or extend the range of future choices. This requires the repeated application of the schema at crucial stages in the individual's development" (p. 541).

Campbell (1969) also dealt with the problem of identifying a comprehensive framework for career behavior. He noted that the parameters identified in the literature crossed discipline boundaries and that the resultant contributions from different disciplines created a segmental picture. In searching for a "broad umbrella to cover the dimensions of vocational behavior" (p. 22), he proposed the adaptation of the conceptual framework of human ecology, which he termed "vocational ecology . . . the study of *man* as *he* adjusts to *his* vocational environment which includes the interrelated influences of sociological, psychological and economic forces" (p. 22). Campbell's identification of contextual factors as relevant to career choice, like Blau et al.'s (1956), was an important addition to writings in the field. However, the suggestion that individuals adjust to these contextual factors allows little room for individual self-determination.

These first two frameworks seem to reflect a merging of the substages discussed earlier in this chapter. They are representative of bridging frameworks, although aspects of their construction are external to the theoretical field. Each of these frameworks was attempting to link relevant constructs in career development, as opposed to relevant theories.

The merging of theoretical constructs can be seen as an example of bridging. The first of the following two frameworks is an example of exploring one theory as a base for a broader theoretical framework. The second framework is an example of the merging of two theories.

In searching for a framework for vocational psychology, Hesketh (1985) emphasized the complexity of career behavior and the improbability that any one theory could adequately explain it. She advocated the generation of empirically testable specific theories, or microtheories, and the development of a conceptual framework that provided a structure to integrate findings from research. She identified the following three themes that underlie existing theory in vocational psychology: intervening factors, the role of the individual (how active the individual is), and the degree of emphasis on content or process. She then examined the theory of work adjustment in relation to these themes as a possible starting point for an integrative framework. Her review of work adjustment theory led her to call for a greater integration of the content and process of career development in theoretical work. She also highlighted the "dynamic active and reactive modes on the part of individuals and organisations" (p. 28), but she acknowledged the need for more research into the nature of these interactions. While applauding the work adjustment model for its parsimony in providing a framework for important issues in individual's career behavior, she also identified some shortcomings. Despite the simplicity achieved by this attempt to begin an integrative framework, it is clear that the need for such a framework remains. More recently, the work adjustment theory has also been suggested as a possible base for a bridging framework, as will be discussed later in this chapter.

Also in 1985, Pryor (1985a) proposed what he termed a "composite" theory of career development and choice. He commented on the separateness of theorizing in vocational psychology from other fields in psychology, emphasizing that "dividing the person up into bits and theorising separately about each piece is a fundamental denial of the totality of the human being" (p. 226). He saw Krumboltz's (1979) early attempts to apply social learning theory to career decision making as a useful addition to career theory, although he criticized its early articulation on two points: an inadequate conceptualization of self and a neglect of developmental factors. He therefore attempted to integrate this theory with L. S. Gottfredson's (1981) circumscription-and-compromise theory to formulate a "composite theory." While also acknowledging limitations in Gottfredson's theory (Pryor, 1985b), Pryor (1985a) proposed that an integration of the two theoretical formulations would give a more complete account of career development and choice.

Rather than focusing on individual theories, or combinations of two theories, Sonnenfeld and Kotter (1982) attempted a far more expansive attempt at integration. They identified four waves in the evolution of career theory:

1. the social structure approach, in which career outcomes were set from birth as a result of parent's social class
2. a focus on the relationship of individual traits to career choice
3. a focus on the stages of individuals' careers and
4. the life cycle approach, in which the focus was on the interrelationships between career and other areas of an individual's life across the life span

The increasingly dynamic nature of career theory and the increasing number and array of variables relevant to career choice were inevitably contributing to a picture of considerable complexity. Sonnenfeld and Kotter (1982) therefore advocated a fifth approach, an attempt to integrate all factors and show how they contributed to a bigger picture. They developed a two-dimensional model, with life space on one axis and time on another, to illustrate the interaction between occupational, personal, and family factors in career development. Nine major sets of variables operating within the two axes included educational environment, the individual's personality, childhood family environment, adult family/nonwork history, adult development history, work history, current work situation, the individual's current perspective, and current family/nonwork situation. While the model serves an illustrative purpose, it offers little in the way of theoretical underpinnings. Further, its assumption of a linear maturation of career theory based on an organicist worldview (Lyddon, 1989; Pepper, 1942) has also been criticized (Collin & Young, 1986).

THEORISTS' MODIFICATION OF THEORIES AND NEW THEORIES

The narrowness of the traditional base for individual career development theories and those theories' failure to take into account broader contextual influences were discussed in Chapter 1. As early as 1965, Lyon warned that "current theories of career development will soon be obsolete if they fail to take the social context into their formulations" (quoted in Osipow & Fitzgerald, 1996, p. 328). More recently, this issue of including context has been addressed by career development theorists and is another one of the early indications of a move toward theory integration.

While many have suggested the need to focus on contextual factors (Bailyn, 1989; Collin & Young, 1986; Poole, 1992; Poole et al., 1991) and have proffered contextual models (Vondracek et al., 1986), there has been no ongoing development of a specific theoretical framework. Several writers have proposed a rationale for a contextual model, with various suggestions, inclusions, and foci. For example, Bailyn (1989) proposed that the immediate context of work and the context of time need to be included in studying careers, and Schein (1984) suggested that cultural influences on the concept and importance of career are also an important type of contextual influence that affects our understanding of career development.

In acknowledging changing labor markets, government policies, and ongoing unemployment, Poole (1992) reinforced the importance of recognizing the context of change as "embedded in an inextricably linked, interdependent field of internal and external influences" (p. 234). She then supported the development of a contextualist framework that would link individual development to opportunities and constraints in different time periods, "in which individual career planning and career attainment is conceived as a dynamic and interactive process between developing individuals and the changing contexts in which their lives are lived, negotiated, and constructed" (Poole et al., 1991, p. 623).

Existing theories do take account of the social, economic, and environmental context, with Super's (1990) reality testing, Holland's (1985a) focus on personality and work environments, and social learning theorists' attention to individual and environment (Krumboltz, 1979; L. K. Mitchell & Krumboltz, 1990). But none of these theories develops and conceptualizes the nature of these influences that act as a contextual medium for individual decision making.

Moves toward convergence in theories of career development can also be seen in the attempts to integrate these perspectives of context, as well as life span and social systems, into career development theory. As Jepsen (1992, p. 101) commented, "greater attention is being given to people of all ages, stages and cultures," thus addressing some of the criticisms of early theory. This convergence indicates that "there can be little doubt about career being embedded in, and influenced by, historical, cultural and social contexts" (Jepsen, 1992, p.

115). The most significant of these attempts include Super's (1990, 1992) life span, life space approach, L. S. Gottfredson's (1981, 1996) theory of occupational aspirations, and Vondracek et al.'s (1986) developmental-contextual approach. Each of these will be discussed in turn as an illustrative attempt at theory integration.

It is interesting that one of the pioneers of career development theory made a significant attempt at theory integration or, as Savickas (1995) suggested, rapprochement. Super had often referred to his theory as segmental in that he focused on specific constructs such as self-concept, career maturity, and work values. In a 1992 article entitled "Toward a Comprehensive Theory of Career Development," he acknowledged the need for "not two, but three" (p. 59) models to explain career development. These included the life-span, life-space model depicted in Super's Rainbow and the determinant/choice model depicted in his Archway (see Chapter 3). Super indicated that these two models also needed a decision-making model to form an integrated theoretical approach. Finally, he noted that three elements of career development needed integration for a unified theory to develop, thereby naming those theories whose components were crucial to any integrated career theory. These were trait-and-factor theories (Dawis & Lofquist, 1984; Holland, 1985a), his own developmental theory (Super, 1990), and the social learning theory of career decision making (L. K. Mitchell & Krumboltz, 1990). More recently, Savickas (1997) suggested that Super's construct of adaptability could be a useful bridge between the individual differences, developmental, self, and contextual segments in life-span, life-space theory.

Another example of rapprochement is in the work of L. S. Gottfredson (1981), who "integrates a social systems perspective with the more psychological approaches" (p. 546). In doing so, Gottfredson's theory "accepts the fundamental importance of self-concept in vocational development, that people seek jobs compatible with their images of themselves. Social class, intelligence and sex are seen as important determinants of both self-concepts and the types of compromises people must make" (p. 546). As well as acknowledging many influences on career development, Gottfredson (1981) identified four stages through which young people pass, thus focusing on time. These stages—orientation to size and power, orientation to sex roles, orientation to social valuation, and orientation to internal, unique self—also illustrate an emphasis on the individual in context. As indicated earlier, Gottfredson (1986) also proposed an "at-risk" framework in which she identified a wide range of possible influences on career development. Thus, in her work, she acknowledged the importance of the concepts of time and context to career development and illustrated the integration of concepts from different disciplines, such as sociology and psychology.

The concepts of time and context are also recognized in the developmental-contextual approach of Vondracek et al. (1986). These authors stressed that their approach to career development was not a theory but a general conceptual model. First, they emphasized that career development lies within the field of human development and therefore that the focus of life span development is key. Second, they contended that to understand career behavior, it is essential to view the contextual (socioeconomic and cultural) influences on career and their ever-changing nature. Finally, an important concept within the model is the embeddedness of human life within multiple levels of analysis, such as biological, individual-psychological, organizational, social, cultural, and historical levels, and the ongoing dynamic interactions between the individual and these areas of context. According to this approach, career development is facilitated by the interplay between an active organism and an ever-changing environment. This approach is an example of rapprochement and perhaps convergence in that similarities with existing theoretical offerings are recognized and links between disciplines and theories are developed.

BRIDGING FRAMEWORKS

Most writers acknowledge that a conceptual tool for bridging theories, or an overarching framework, needs to be identified and developed. Savickas (1995) identified six frameworks that have been proposed as having the potential to be developed as bridging frameworks for career theories: (1) developmental contextualism, (2) learning theory, (3) person-environment transaction, (4) work adjustment theory, (5) developmental systems theory, and (6) systems theory. We would add to this list social cognitive career theory and action theory. We will review each of these frameworks briefly.

DEVELOPMENTAL CONTEXTUALISM.   The theoretical model of Vondracek et al. (1986) was presented in detail in Chapter 4. It was also discussed earlier in this chapter as an example of a model developed on the basis of merging new ideas. In the context of the present section, it is important to focus on the developmental-contextual perspective as derived from both the developmental organic perspective and the contextualist perspective. Vondracek et al. (1986) acknowledged two limitations of pure contextualism in their theoretical formulation. First, this worldview sees the components of life as totally dispersive. Vondracek et al. believed that development must be more than mere change and that "a worldview that stresses only the dispersive, chaotic, and disorganized character of life would not readily lend itself to a theory of development" (p. 24). Hence, these authors combined two perspectives in their formulation of developmental contextualism. Second, contextualism emphasizes the current event and the importance of the relation between the elements. A developmental analysis offered by these authors emphasizes the changes that exist in the relations between elements over time.

Developmental contextualism therefore emphasizes ongoing change both within the organism and within the environment and the interaction between the two. Thus, the perspective emphasizes change and dynamic interaction. Further, it acknowledges the internal stability of the organism and the reciprocal influence of the organism and the context.

Also, in discussing the interaction between the individual and the environment, Vondracek et al. (1986) emphasized the self-determinism and agency of the individual. The developmental-contextual approach holds that the environment engenders chaotic and reflexive changes in an individual's behavior, but it also emphasizes that the environment is facilitated or constrained by the unique characteristics of the individual. Within the model, the individual is an active organism operating in a constantly changing environment—hence the concept of dynamic interaction. An individual's career development is a reflection of the continuous interplay of person and context at all possible levels. Thus, this approach can include elements of content and process.

LEARNING THEORY.   Most theorists have championed learning theory as crucial to any integrated theory, since it is such an important underpinning of individual behavior. For example, Holland (1994) suggested that "the most promising integration would be to insert the Krumboltz learning theory into every other vocational theory" (p. 45). Earlier frameworks (e.g., Pryor, 1985a) also highlighted the value of merging learning theory with other theories. Super (1990) referred to learning theory as the cement that bonded the segments of his Archway, and Subich and Taylor (1994) referred to it as "a central glue in explaining the learning processes underlying other career theories' core constructs" (p. 171). However, Savickas (1995) asserted that its value lies more in providing a more fine-grained analysis of existing constructs than in providing a framework for an overarching intertheory analysis.

PERSON-ENVIRONMENT TRANSACTION.   A number of authors have identified person-environment (P-E) transaction as a central unifying principle for converging theories (Rounds & Hesketh, 1994; Spokane, 1994; Walsh & Chartrand, 1994). However, these authors have also acknowledged that P-E is defined differently across related theories and that this definition needs to be sharpened before any convergence work is undertaken.

THEORY OF WORK ADJUSTMENT.   The theory of work adjustment (TWA) was conceived as useful in integration of career theory as early as 1985 (Hesketh, 1985). As Dawis (1994) has stated, TWA was initially constructed to integrate several related concepts from different areas in psychology: ability, reinforcement, satisfaction, and person-environment correspondence. As such, it was initially constructed as an early example of convergence. Dawis (1994) illustrated the already strong correspondence between TWA and Holland's (1985a) theory. The only major difference is the focus of Holland's work on career choice and of TWA on work adjustment. In that both TWA and Krumboltz's (1994) theory are based on learning theory, there are already points of convergence.

DEVELOPMENTAL SYSTEMS THEORY.   Vondracek and Kawasaki (1995) further developed the developmental-contextual model using the living systems framework (LSF; D. Ford, 1987). This framework furthers our understanding from the description of human behavior to an understanding of the underlying processes—the "how and why of the behaviors that determine the work lives of individuals" (Vondracek & Kawasaki, 1995, p. 118). Vondracek and Kawasaki (1995) illustrated the value of both developmental systems theory (DST; D. Ford & Lerner, 1992) and motivational systems theory (MST; M. Ford, 1992) for furthering our understanding of adult career development in particular. At this stage, however, the authors have not incorporated the principles of these theoretical frameworks into a comprehensive overarching theoretical framework for career theories. Rather, they have shown how DST and MST can be used to understand the vocational behaviors of adults.

SYSTEMS THEORY.   The potential of the LSF of D. Ford (1987) as an overall theoretical framework has been illustrated by Krumboltz and Nichols (1990). These authors applied the LSF to provide an inclusive "map" for specific career decision-making frameworks. The value of the framework as identified by these authors is its ability to integrate all of the determinants of human development and specifically of career choice and career development. Its contribution to date has been to examine the four governing functions in decision making—information-processing, storage, directive, and regulatory/control processes—in the specific realm of career decision making. In addition, the LSF emphasizes the relationship among these functions in decision making and other relevant individual subsystems. For example, an individual from a rural area may have less access to career information so their information processing may be limited. Krumboltz and Nichols (1990) commented that "although the LSF does not specify the full complexity of human decision making, it provides us with a map of a larger area than we generally consider in current theories of career behavior" (p. 189). Its explication to date, however, introduces this larger area into career behavior without a clear explanation of its links. These authors believe that existing career theories could be embedded within the overall LSF, but this suggestion has not been developed further.

Both Blustein (1994) and Bordin (1994) have acknowledged the value of systems theory as a basis for a convergence framework. In particular, these authors drew from the work of the family systems movement (Bowen, 1978). Bordin (1994) suggested that to effect synthesis of career theories, a broader perspective, such as the family system, "can encompass all theories" (p. 61). Again, this application has not been further developed.

SOCIAL COGNITIVE CAREER THEORY.   As discussed previously in this chapter, Lent and Hackett (1994) viewed their emerging social cognitive career theory (discussed in detail in Chapter 4) as a model that could integrate existing theoretical constructs. Their model focuses on a number of constructs that exist in other theories and brings them together within the framework of Bandura's (1986) theory. In particular, the authors asserted that their theory converges with existing theories in relation to a focus on personal influences in career development and on the importance of learning experiences and self-efficacy in the career development process.

CONTEXTUAL EXPLANATION OF CAREER.   In describing their contextual explanation of career (see Chapter 4), Young et al. (1996) acknowledged that the concept of context is understood in various ways. These authors proposed a framework informed by Pepper (1942) for understanding key aspects of many contextual approaches to career. Further, they proposed action theory as a means of integrating aspects of contextualism. These authors defined the basis of contextualism as "the recognition of a complex whole constituted of many interrelated and interwoven parts, which may be largely submerged in the everyday understanding of events and phenomena" (p. 479). Context consists of multiple complex connections and interrelationships, the significance of which is interpreted according to an individual's perspective. Young et al. identified several aspects of the contextualist metaphor crucial to their contextual explanation of career. These include an emphasis on the goal and content of acts, acts that are embedded in their context. Change is integral within this perspective, and "because events take shape as people engage in practical action with a particular purpose, analysis and interpretation are always practical" (p. 480). Finally, these authors maintained that reality is constructed from the present event outwards, thereby rejecting the systems theory notion that reality is constructed only in relationship with an individual's own internal representation and that only a contextual truth is possible. Thus, these authors drew on some key concepts of systems theory and rejected others.

A significant feature of the work of Young et al. (1996) was the attempt to classify the various career and counseling theories that have adopted parts of the contextualist approach. In doing so, they classified the model of Vondracek et al. (1986) as representative of a systems approach in that it addressed the concept of dynamic interaction between the person and the context, although they acknowledged that it was not strictly a systems approach.

It is clear that the developing worldview of contextualism and the development of constructivism in cognitive psychology have been important influences in the move toward integration and convergence of career theories. The 1990s have seen a focus of energy in this direction, and it is to the efforts in this area that we will now turn.

THE 1990S FOCUS ON CONVERGENCE

The beginning of the 1990s saw a number of review articles, originating in the 20-year anniversary of the *Journal of Vocational Behavior*, which seem to have accelerated moves toward convergence. Osipow (1990) identified the similarities and differences between theories in an article entitled "Convergence in Theories of Career Choice and Development: Review and Prospect. " Osipow identified four theories that he asserted remained the most influential—namely, the work of Holland (1985a), Dawis and Lofquist (1984), Super (1980), and A. M. Mitchell, Jones, and Krumboltz (1979). He named common themes in these theories in the areas of biological factors, parental influences, outcomes, personality, methods, and life stage influences but noted that the emphases and importance of each of these themes varied in different theories. Osipow concluded that the theories are evolving to resemble each other in several ways but that differences remain and each offers practical utility for different populations. These key theories identified by Osipow are similar to those identified by Super (1992).

The notion of integration of theory was also raised in a later retrospective article in the same journal by Borgen (1991). Borgen identified what he referred to as "converging trends toward an integrative career psychology" (p. 279). These included a greater focus on the personal agency of individuals, the developing potential of cognitive psychology to contribute to integration, and the increasing similarity being observed between theoretical constructs and explanations.

Another 1991 review article for the same journal by Hackett et al. raised the need to identify common constructs and outcomes and to assess commonalities and relationships in existing theories. These authors emphasized that it was time to investigate proposals for integration of career theory and particularly to identify the variables important to an overarching theory of career development (p. 28).

Super (1990) commented on the understandable segmental nature of much theory development in the area of career psychology "in view of the size of the problem" (p. 221). He acknowledged that theories that attempt to encompass too much may suffer from superficiality and that future theories of career development "will be made up of refined, validated and well-assembled segments, cemented together by some synthesizing theory to constitute a whole which will be more powerful than the sum of its parts" (p. 221). Super (1992) added to this discussion, commenting that no theory is in itself sufficient and that to adequately address the complexity of career development, contributions from each of the major theories are necessary (see earlier in this chapter).

This development in discussion about integration and convergence led to the publication of other articles advocating ways to integrate theory. In emphasizing the need to create integrative and comprehensive theoretical syntheses of career theory, Gelso and Fassinger (1992) also acknowledged the potential of the contextual perspectives of personality and developmental psychology. In particular, they discussed the research and theoretical potential of the process-person-context framework of human development (Bronfenbrenner, 1988).

A major development in the move toward convergence was the convening of a conference specifically on the issue, an indication of its significance to career development theorists. In particular, attention focused on convergence between career development theories, empirical research, and career development theory and practice. Papers from this meeting of invited scholars in the field were published in Savickas and Lent (1994), who noted that the project sought "to facilitate theory convergence, stimulate theory unification research, and prompt more explicit use of theory in guiding vocational research" (p. 3). The editors also noted that the book was the first attempt to facilitate "rapprochement among career theories" (p. 5).

A review of the papers by the prominent theorists in the Savickas & Lent (1994) volume shows that there is no agreement in the field about the value of convergence. While Super (1994) reiterated the existing diversity in conceptualization of his theory, Holland (1994) was emphatic in rejecting the concept of convergence and recommending the reformulation of existing theory. Krumboltz (1994) also expressed concern about the need for convergence, providing a map analogy of the state of career theory whereby each theory includes parts of the terrain (career development) and leaves out others. This analogy formed the basis for his conclusion that theories are chosen for different purposes. Dawis (1994) distinguished between theory unification and theory convergence, calling the former a "will-o'-the-wisp" (p. 42). He suggested that there are two approaches to demonstrating convergence: "first, showing equivalence or similarity or overlap, and second, showing linkage, which could include superimposing a larger framework on the linkages" (p. 33). Spokane (1994) emphasized that while convergence on terminology may be achieved, it is much more difficult to achieve convergence in underlying philosophy. Finally, Bordin (1994) highlighted an area of consensus in career development, the importance of the individual. As previously discussed, he also suggested the potential of the family system to serve as a platform for theory convergence.

In reviewing the success of the convergence conference, Lent and Savickas (1994) noted that there was some variation in understanding of the meaning of convergence and that this diversity might have contributed to the differing views. They commented that understanding of the term ranged from construction of one grand theory to "an effort to explore points of commonality, to account for the relationships among seemingly diverse constructs, to promote more comprehensive theories, and, where possible, to reduce redundancy and promote parsimony" (p. 266). Vondracek and Fouad's (1994) conclusion to their group discussion at the convergence conference echoed that of Lent and Savickas. While commenting that not enough is known to converge theories and that convergence may inhibit a counselor from constructing his or her own theory of vocational behavior, these authors noted that "there was agreement that it was most important to acknowledge the contributions of various theories and to recognize areas in which they were complementary, while still recognizing that much work remained to be done to better explain vocational behavior and more effectively help clients" (p. 208). In advocating an overarching framework of career theory, we support this conclusion. Such a framework can highlight commonality and diversity in existing theories, while encouraging further work on the areas that require it.

Other participants at the convergence conference identified areas not adequately accounted for in existing theoretical formulations (reviewed in more detail in Chapters 2–6) that need to be accounted for within a framework of convergence of theory. For example, Fitzgerald and Betz (1994) identified inadequacies within current theory, such as the irrelevance of current concepts of career development to large groups of people (e.g., women and people of other races) and theoretical constructs that ignore structural and cultural factors. These sentiments were echoed by Vondracek and Fouad (1994). They proposed that the concept of cultural and structural factors be used to "provide an overlay to, or new perspective for, the consideration of career theories" (p. 113). Other concepts raised as important inclusions in a comprehensive theory included the family system (Bordin, 1994; S. D. Brown & Watkins, 1994), contextual affordance (Lent & Hackett, 1994; Spokane, 1994; Walsh & Chartrand, 1994), and the person-environment interface (Blustein, 1994; Rounds & Hesketh, 1994; Spokane, 1994).

ADVANTAGES AND DISADVANTAGES OF CONVERGENCE

As discussed, not all theorists are in agreement about the need for convergence, its definition, and the form it should take. Others may be supportive of the project as worthwhile for the career field but maintain that it is premature because of the limited existing empirical base. Several advantages and disadvantages can be identified.

Convergence might be advantageous, first, because no single theory can fully explain the complexity of career behavior (Hesketh, 1985; Osipow, 1983; Super, 1992) and because a comprehensive framework might assist career counselors in practice. Second, without a comprehensive theory, research resources and endeavors tend to be divided among efforts to gauge outcomes from individual interventions derived from different theories. Third, the credibility of an overall field is not enhanced by the lack of a comprehensive and unified picture and the presence of several theories vying for the position of *the* theory of career development. Although, as Osipow (1990) emphasized, existing theories all have an important contribution to make, appropriately address different issues, and are appropriate for different problems, a unifying framework can enhance the potential for seeing a "big picture."

Disadvantages of a convergence project have been raised by a number of authors (D. Brown & Brooks, 1996b; Holland, 1994; Savickas, 1995). They include suggestions that unification may discourage the creation of new theories and that constructive theory building a step at a time is better. Integration without careful thought may result in unrelated constructs being drawn from different theories and contributing to further ambiguity. Related to this concern is that convergence may lead to the ignoring of interesting elements of existing theories. Other comments include that convergence needs to be an empirical exercise rather than a literary one and that a political agenda may be forced through a unification project. In addition, comments have been raised about the limitations of a convergence project—that it can only result in a "convergence in terminology, not in philosophy or theory" (Savickas, 1995, p. 10). A final disadvantage is that as science moves toward postmodern approaches and related pluralism, unifying or single approaches are out of tune.

THE PRESENT POSITION OF CAREER THEORY

It is clear that the field of career development theory is dynamic and undergoing change. While theoretical integration and convergence is the major issue, a number of related concerns need to be addressed. Sonnenfeld and Kotter (1982) noted that all of the major career theories are predominantly psychological, with some also drawing from sociological disciplines. Thus, little attention has been paid to relevant input from other disciplines. A number of authors (Collin & Young, 1986; Sonnenfeld & Kotter, 1982; Van Maanen, 1977) have maintained that working within discipline boundaries restricts the maturation of career theory. Arthur et al. (1989) emphasized the extent of the impact that other disciplines (e.g., economics and political science) could have on our understanding of careers, and they call for a greater attempt to identify organizing principles of career theory. The greater input from disciplines other than psychology in career theory is also necessary because career practitioners increasingly need to be aware of economic, sociological, and political issues that affect clients' career decision making.

Despite a significant history in the development of theory to account for career development, the theory remains disparate and segmented. While the move toward incorporating constructs and processes derived from the root metaphor of contextualism has resulted in a greater convergence in the sharing and modifying of theoretical concepts in traditional and newly emerging theories, separate models are still being proposed (e.g., Peterson et al., 1991). The only major exception is that of Lent and Hackett (1994). There is still no coherence in the career theory literature, which can still be viewed as competing theories searching for the truth in career development or, more generously, as a number of theories continuing to focus on specific aspects of career development within a whole that is not yet clearly specified.

Several common themes emerge from the discussion on integration and convergence of career theory to date. Some of these are the need for theory to include many concepts and issues that have not yet been adequately accounted for (e.g., developmental phases of career, different groups, cultural and structural factors). In addition, just what form such integration and convergence will take remains unclear, whether one grand theory; several segmented theoretical contributions under one umbrella, such as developmental theories; frameworks or models identifying theoretical commonalities; or a more loose identification of complementary contributions and conceptual relationships. In addition, there is little agreement in the field about the value of, or future of, convergence. Borgen (1991) asserted that "vocational psychology has unprecedented prospects for integration" (p. 280), whereas Holland (1994) viewed the activity as futile. According to D. Brown and Brooks (1996b), the divide between constructivism and positivism meant that "convergence among theories and the development of an integrated theory seems less likely today than ever" (p. 11). However, Borgen (1995) believed that "a field can thrive with apparently opposed paradigms and epistemologies" (p. 430), arguing that "we can have both—expanding our insights through perspectivism but also building on the empirical strengths of traditional research" (p. 429).

We acknowledge each of these themes and believe that systems theory, also related to the root metaphor of contextualism, can provide the basis of an overarching framework within which commonalities and relationships can be identified. Thus, against this background, we propose that systems theory provides the key to a unifying metatheoretical framework within which to locate and use the extant theoretical insights on career development.

A systems theory framework diminishes some of the earlier cited disadvantages of convergence. Because it is an overarching framework focusing on all the parts as well as the whole, new or revised theoretical developments need not be discouraged. With the individual as the central focus, constructing his or her own meaning of career, constructs of existing theories are relevant as they apply to each individual. The systems theory framework encourages pluralism in that each individual's career is the prime concern. Finally, the framework also allows for relevant constructs and meanings from other disciplines.

CONCLUSION

This chapter has discussed the philosophical underpinnings of existing career theory and recent changes to this philosophy. Related changes to thinking about individual career theories and the overall picture of career theory have been presented. Attempts to integrate the disparate field have been identified, and the more recent activities that focus on convergence in the field have been detailed. There is little dispute that some combination of constructs and theories is necessary to provide a coherent and practical overarching picture. Systems theory has been suggested as an overarching framework to unify existing theories. The next chapter discusses systems theory. In Chapter 9, we present the framework that we have developed to provide a metatheoretical synthesis of the existing career theory literature.

CHAPTER

8

SYSTEMS THEORY

As discussed in Chapter 7, systems theory has been proposed as a potential overarching framework for career theories. This chapter will briefly describe the history and development of systems theory and its emergence from, and contrast with, the traditional worldview. While systems theory is perceived as the basis for the construction of a new worldview, its development from different sources and in different disciplines has led to varying assumptions about systems themselves, how they are organized, and their essential properties. Thus, this chapter will outline key elements of systems theory and will briefly illustrate each one in terms of career theory. Finally, existing attempts to relate systems theory to career behavior will be presented. This chapter sets the base for our macro-level analysis of systems theory as an overarching framework for career development theory. Chapter 9 extends this analysis, presents the framework, and illustrates its application at the micro level of individual career development.

THE DEVELOPMENT OF SYSTEMS THEORY

The emergence of systems theory has essentially been a reaction to the traditional classical, analytic, or positivist worldview on which much of our thinking has been based. This traditional view assumes that the world operates in much the same way as a machine and that within that structure, each part operates in a particular way to accomplish an outcome. All action is related to a carefully balanced interdependent model of linear cause and effect. The classical worldview concentrates exclusively on that which is observable, insisting that the only valid knowledge is that gained through sense perceptions. Principles of this worldview include the focus on objects as separate and observable, the belief that natural unhindered development will always yield progress, and the belief that such progress is incremental and linear.

Criticisms of this worldview have included the failure of linear stage-based models to adequately account for the complexity of human development. In addition, development based on invariant sequences of maturational unfolding cannot account for situational and contextual influences on a person's development, such as environmental changes, or for the rich diversity of individual differences based on factors such as gender and culture. Further, much change is random and unpredictable.

In contrast, the systems worldview values the whole, a system that is more than the sum of individual parts. Rather than focusing on cause and effect between parts, it views a pattern of interrelationship as more important. Progression within this pattern is not always linear; the complexity of a system is far too great. The application of systems theory to learning changes our traditional view. The concept of knowledge acquisition—that is, of adding to our existing body of knowledge—becomes dated. Rather than assuming a quantitative view of knowledge—that is, of knowing "more"—it views knowledge in a qualitative way. Within this perspective, new knowledge is incorporated into existing frameworks in a relational and associative way.

Further, not all change is incremental: enduring change may also be sudden. For example, brief therapy has been modeled on this principle. Interventions within this mode of operating are designed to heighten the existing situation through actively confronting it, with a view to bringing about enduring change.

The complexity of systems theory reflects the complexity of science. Thus, simple definitions are difficult to construct (Plas, 1992). However, by way of definition, the following statement is reflective of the interconnecting concepts that underpin systems theory:

> This newer thinking is much more concerned with patterns of functioning. Searching for the causes of human activity ceases to be important. Inductive and deductive logic make room for other types of rationality, such as reasoning by analogy. Understanding human language patterns is critical. Everything is viewed as dynamic rather than static. Spontaneous change can be expected under certain circumstances. Working with wholes instead of pieces of the whole is fundamental. (Plas, 1986, p. 3)

From this theoretical viewpoint, the human system is viewed as purposive, ever-changing, and evolving toward equilibrium. The human system, itself a complexity of interrelated subsystems, interacts with other systems and subsystems, living and nonliving. Human life consists of ongoing recursive processes involving disorganization, adaptation, and reorganization. Knowledge about self and the environment is an emergent process as the individual interacts with the world (Mahoney & Lyddon, 1988).

GENERAL SYSTEMS THEORY

Attempts to view life as composed of systems appeared as early as 1925 (Whitehead, 1925) and in the early work of von Bertalanffy (1940). However, von Bertalanffy, acknowledged as the founder of the systems movement, published his first statement of general systems theory (GST) in 1968. The aim of the GST movement was to encourage the development of theoretical systems that would be applicable to more than one of the traditional parts of knowledge. Von Bertalanffy posited that certain principles are valid for systems in general, irrespective of their inherent content and energy. He also was critical of traditional deductive and inductive reasoning processes that led to identification of parts rather than wholes and to a focus on linear causal explanations. Rather, he encouraged a reasoning process based on analogy, with a focus on a search for patterns.

While GST has essentially not emerged and has been consistently criticized, the prevalence of systems thinking across a large number of disciplines "establishes 'systems' as a meta-discipline" (Checkland, 1979, p. 129). Indeed, Checkland maintained that the major contribution of the systems movement has been, not the development of an overarching theory, but applications to problem areas in specific disciplines. A negative corollary, however, has been the variation in its development across disciplines, so much so that Checkland (1981) also commented on the difficulty of establishing a coherent view of the systems movement as a whole.

Contributors to systems theory have come from the fields of physics (Capra), biology and anthropology (Bateson), and psychology (Bateson; Berger & Luckmann; and Ames, Cantril, Hastorf, & Ittelson, known as the "transactional functionalists"). The development of field theory by K. Lewin has also had an important influence on the development of systems theory in psychology. More recently, the work on living systems by D. Ford (1987) and M. Ford and D. Ford (1987) has furthered the construction of an integrated framework of human development and the evolution and understanding of systems theory. Developmental systems theory (DST) and motivational systems theory (MST) have illustrated the applicability of systems theory principles to human behavior. The complexity paradigm, or the science of complexity, has also been influential in applying the principles of systems theory to an understanding of world change. The major contributions of each of these researchers, thinkers, and movements will be discussed, since their work has formed the basis of, and has contributed to a greater understanding of, many of the key concepts of systems theory.

FRITJOF CAPRA

Two important contributions to systems theory were made in the work in quantum physics of Fritjof Capra (1975, 1982): the notion that all things are interconnected and the notion that no object can be studied in isolation, since all phenomena exist only in relation to each other. Focusing on one aspect only, therefore, is likely to cause other aspects to be missed or undervalued, and uncertainty is an inevitable outcome. In studying subatomic phenomena—that which cannot be seen—Capra discovered that the building-block approach to classical physics was no longer applicable. He emphasized the importance of the relationship between the observer and the observed; for example, an electron can be identified only with complex laboratory equipment. As a result, he maintained that the phenomena being studied can be represented only by that relationship. Therefore, the reality we come to know is inseparable from the relationship between the observer and the observed.

In describing this, Capra also became aware of how our language is limited in being developed for and available to describe only experiences based on our senses: we have no language to describe experiences independent of our physical senses. In reflecting on the consequences of studying objects that could not be seen, touched, or heard, Capra (1982) stated that

> the worldview emerging from modern physics can be characterized by words like organic, holistic and ecological. It might also be called a systems view, in the sense of general systems theory. The universe is no longer as a machine, made up of a multitude of objects, but has to be pictured as one indivisible, dynamic whole whose parts are essentially interrelated and can be understood only as patterns of a cosmic process. (pp. 77–78)

GREGORY BATESON

Bateson, a biologist, anthropologist, psychologist, and theoretician, contributed considerably to our understanding of systems. During the 1950s, Bateson and his colleagues pioneered an approach to treating schizophrenia that focused on the system (the family) rather than the patient (the individual) (Bateson, Jackson, Haley, & Weakland, 1956). Bateson believed that schizophrenia was a problem related to communication within the family rather than an individual disease—a notion that was the forerunner of family therapy. As a result, one of his key contributions to systems theory was the suggestion that communication patterns are functionally representative of the system. This communication is not necessarily linear; there are feedback loops in messages between system members (Bateson, 1972).

Bateson's study in biology led him to expand his notions about communication patterns to broad "connecting patterns." He believed that biological patterns and communication patterns all served to connect (Bateson, 1979). Within the focus of communication, Bateson also drew attention to the limitations of our language and emphasized the need for people operating from a systems perspective to focus on the primacy of language and its meaning.

Bateson's work also led him to conclude that there is no such thing as objective knowing—a notion shared by many systems theorists. Since we cannot know objective reality, all knowing requires interpretation. Bateson concluded that the understanding we have of any event is determined and often therefore restrained by the individual's interpretive framework—that is, preexisting experiences and suppositions. He maintained that our interpretation of events is determined by its fit with patterns that are already known to us. Further, he maintained that events that cannot be patterned are not selected for incorporation into our reality; they will simply not exist as facts.

Related to these concepts of interpretive frameworks, connecting patterns, and the role of language is another important contribution from Bateson to systems theory, that of the need to develop processes of reasoning by relationship, or by analogy. Bateson called this process *abductive reasoning*, in contrast to the processes of inductive reasoning (from the part to the whole) and deductive reasoning (from the whole to the part). Abductive reasoning emphasizes relationships and similarities of patterns. For example, we are used to the sentence stems "that reminds me of" and "that is just like." In describing someone as "just like" our brother or sister, we are using abductive reasoning—that is, commenting on similarities in patterns of behavior or patterns of appearance.

BERGER AND LUCKMANN

The relationship between the knower and the known that has emerged from early systems theory was further explicated by Berger and Luckmann (1967) in their classic book *The Social Construction of Reality*. These authors argued that reality is a function both of what is actually there and of the relationship between the individual who is perceiving and what he or she is perceiving. Since the individual is operating within a physical and social system, as is the reality he or she is perceiving, these two systems merge as the observer becomes part of the reality that he or she is observing.

TRANSACTIONAL FUNCTIONALISTS

Ames and his colleagues conducted experiments in visual perception (Cantril, Ames, Hastorf, & Ittelson, 1949) and, later, social perception (Hastorf & Cantril, 1954). In his trapezoidal rooms, objects closer to the observer (at the front of the room) appeared smaller, rather than larger, than objects farther away (at the rear of the room). These experiments again illustrated that perception of reality occurs as a result of the relationship between the observer and the observed. Ames and his colleagues concluded that knowing a reality without observer "contamination" is theoretically impossible: "We have believed that our knowledge discloses the innate constitution of things apart from their relationship to us. We fail to realise that we can know nothing about things beyond their significance to us" (Ames, 1960, p. 4). Reality, then, is a result of the transaction between the observer and the observed.

KURT LEWIN

Proponents of field theory aimed to draw analogies between the physical sciences and the social sciences. K. Lewin (1951) developed the notion of the "life space," a notion designed to represent all the psychological factors operational at any given time for each individual. Lewin drew life spaces and plotted psychological movements toward goals and actions. Field theory's contribution to systems theory is in its focus on the total system in understanding individual behavior: an individual's behavior is a combination of intrapersonal variables influenced by variables located outside the individual and operating within his or her life space.

FORD'S LIVING SYSTEMS FRAMEWORK

As discussed in Chapter 7, the work of D. Ford (1987) is becoming increasingly used as a model for theory integration. Writers agree that the Living Systems Framework (LSF) proposed by Ford is too complex to be summarized adequately (Vondracek & Kawasaki, 1995). We agree wholeheartedly and strongly recommend that interested readers refer to Ford's own works. D. Ford (1987) began his framework development by comparing mechanical control systems to human systems. He attributed human qualities to these control systems, hence the notion of living systems. These human qualities included human capability for biological self-construction (e.g., development of physical and mental capacities), behavioral self-construction (e.g., directing one's behavior toward a specific goal), and self-renewal. The framework includes the many structures, processes, and functions that interweave to become what we know as human behavior. In constructing it, Ford has drawn on decades of work in developmental psychology and related fields. As such, Ford's framework is an example of abduction, an exploration of patterns and relationships in various disciplines and subdisciplines to develop a framework based on similarities and differences.

The LSF aims to represent all aspects of humanness operating on all levels in all contexts. It has been constructed by drawing on normative and nomothetic knowledge about human behavior as well as idiographic knowledge. It is therefore "a comprehensive theory of human functioning and development that integrates scientific and professional knowledge about the characteristics of people in general (nomothetic knowledge) and the organization and operation of these characteristics in individual persons (idiographic knowledge)" (M. Ford, 1992, p. 19). The individual is conceived both as a whole and as a sum of component parts; change in the individual occurs to maintain stability. The LSF also emphasizes that human behavior is a function of the interaction of the person and context. Change in the organism is conceived as both developmental and transformational, thereby incorporating the key elements of developmental psychology and systems theory.

Because of the complexity and comprehensiveness of the framework, it is most instructive to use the words of M. Ford and D. Ford (1987) to summarize:

> The Living Systems Framework (LSF) is designed to represent all aspects of being human, not merely a particular facet of behavior or personality. . . . It describes how the various "pieces" of the person—goals, emotions, thoughts, actions, and biological processes—function both semi-autonomously as a part of a larger unit (the person) in coherent "chunks" of context-specific, goal directed activity (behavior episodes). It also describes how these specific experiences "add up" to produce a unique, self-constructed history and personality (i.e., through the construction, differentiation, and elaboration of behavior episode schemata), and how various processes of change (self-organization, self-construction, and disorgani-

zation-reorganization) help maintain both stability and developmental flexibility in the organized patterns that result (steady states). Thus the LSF cannot be easily characterized in terms of traditional theoretical categories. Rather, it is a way of trying to understand persons in all their complexly organized humanness. (pp. 1–2)

This definition reflects the holism of systems theory, in that all aspects of the person are seen as integrated into a whole. It also is suggestive of the fluidity of the individual system and the notion that both flexibility and stability are incorporated within change.

DEVELOPMENTAL SYSTEMS THEORY

DST (D. Ford & Lerner, 1992) was formulated to extend developmental contextualism (the basis of the theoretical model of Vondracek et al., 1986, discussed in Chapter 4). In particular, it aims to extend the focus of the individual to all relevant aspects and to the processes by which individuals function. It represents a synthesis between developmental contextualism and the LSF of Ford and has been discussed further in Chapters 4 and 7.

MOTIVATIONAL SYSTEMS THEORY

MST (M. Ford, 1992) was developed to provide a theoretical integration of the many motivation and behavior theories in existence (e.g., actualization theory, social learning theory, social cognitive theory, attribution theory, self-efficacy theory, optimal theory, and expectancy valence theory). As such, its aim is very similar to that of the systems theory framework described in the next chapter. In recognition of the plethora of closely related theories and concepts,

> the primary theoretical rationale for Motivational Systems Theory (MST) is the urgent need for a conceptual framework that addresses the consensus, cohesion, and integration in the field of motivation. MST attempts to bring coherence to the field by providing a clear, concise and comprehensive conceptualization of the basic substance and organization of motivational patterns and by showing how other theories can be understood within this integrative framework. (M. Ford, 1992, p. 244)

As discussed in Chapter 7, MST has been used specifically within the career theory literature by Vondracek and Kawasaki (1995) and Krumboltz and Nichols (1990) to integrate aspects of career development. MST acknowledges the interplay between the individual and the environment in any progression toward career-related goals and the centrality of motivational factors to an individual's functioning.

COMPLEXITY THEORY

More recently, a number of writers representing what has been termed the emerging science of complexity have further developed criticisms of the dominant paradigms' static and reductionistic representations of human behavior. Contributors to this complexity paradigm state that human beings are complex adaptive systems and that traditional explanations limit our potential to understand human behavior. Their ideas are published in works such as *Complexity: The Emerging Science at the Edge of Order and Chaos* (Waldrop, 1992), *Complexity: Life at the Edge of Chaos* (R. Lewin, 1994), *Chaos: Making a New Science* (Gleick, 1987), and *The Quantum Self* (Zohar, 1991). Although no one theory represents this worldview, Leong (1996b) outlined the characterizing features of complex adaptive systems as a way of illustrating elements of complexity theory. Such systems are nonlinear, multivariate, nonequilibrium, open, pattern forming, adapting, evolving and coevolving, and self-organizing. Each of these features can be seen to be an extension of the worldviews that underlie systems theory and are forming the basis of new understandings of career development.

Senge (1990) asserted that systems theory thinking was needed more than ever because of the overwhelming complexity of our times. He viewed systems theory as "a discipline for seeing wholes, . . . a framework for seeing relationships rather than things, for seeing patterns of change rather than static 'snapshots'" (p. 68). Senge identified two forms of complexity: detailed complexity and dynamic complexity. *Detailed complexity* relates to the number of variables considered in a situation; *dynamic complexity* reflects the complexity of the interrelationships and feedback patterns between the variables. All human behavior involves both detailed complexity and dynamic complexity. Traditional theories of career development focused on the detailed complexity, whereas theories influenced by constructivist and systems theory perspectives are increasingly focusing on both detailed and dynamic complexity. Senge has also applied principles of systems theory and techniques derived from these principles to the development of personal mastery (the development of inner leadership and personal empowerment) through the creation of more effective mental models and an understanding of the detailed and dynamic complexities of one's role in systems.

ISSUES IN SYSTEMS THEORY

The introductory section of this chapter has described the development of concepts and principles inherent in systems theory. It clearly illustrates the complexity of this perspective. However, Senge (1990) believes that systems thinking offers a language that can restructure how we think and can therefore be useful in providing a "discipline for seeing the 'structures' that underlie complex situations" (p. 69), the wholes and relationships that can more readily foster an understanding of complexity. Since systems theory is only a relatively recent phenomenon, the identification of a coherent set of principles is still emerging. Constructing a definitive list of the elements of systems theory is therefore an almost impossible task.

However, before discussing some of the key elements of systems theory, it is instructive to consider two important underlying themes in systems theory that have been mentioned in the preceding section: the limitations of our knowledge and of our assumptions about how we know, and the limitations of our language in describing our knowledge and understandings. Language and epistemology are at the core of understanding the elements of systems theory, so it is important that we address these themes.

ASSUMPTIONS ABOUT KNOWING

Common to many of the contributors to systems theory presented in the first section of this chapter has been the questioning of assumptions about how knowing occurs. These theorists, philosophers, and researchers have forced us to reconsider whether it is possible to know an unencumbered essence of any reality. The limitations of our sensory functions and our contextual environment have been highlighted by many.

For any observation, there must be an observer, who is operating from a particular frame of reference and within a particular time, place, and cultural framework and who is using a particular language to describe the observation. Each of these factors influences the nature of the reality that is observed and how it is described. Objectivity and pure knowing is impossible; all knowing requires a process of interpretation. The underlying epistemology of systems theory holds that the only reality is the reality construed by the observer in interaction with the observed. This perspective is related to that of postmodern constructivism, which seeks to gather multiperspectival data in an attempt to glean richer knowledge from many perspectives. It is the acceptance of this limitation to knowing that has prompted discussions on the validity of external, "available-to-all" observations. Within systems theory, validity is attained through interobserver reliability. Therefore, if a number of observers reach an acceptable level of agreement about the occurrence of a phenomenon, one can be more sure about the conclusions drawn (Lincoln & Guba, 1985).

LIMITATIONS OF LANGUAGE

As we have discussed, reality is a function of the observed and the observer. The validity of an observation, according to a systemic perspective, is based on observer agreement; this agreement cannot be maximized unless the language of the observers has some similarity and equivalence of expression. Thus, language is a vital influence on the perception and description of reality (Berger & Luckmann, 1967). For example, these authors argued that we construct reality through our use of shared and agreed meanings communicated via a common language; therefore, our ideas and beliefs are socially constructed. In a similar vein, Savickas (1995) emphasized that "linguistic concepts and their definitions do not mirror reality; they inscribe meaning" (p. 22). Thus, he preferred the term *construct* over the term *concept*, in that *construct* incorporates the personal and cultural component of meaning making, whereas *concept* suggests that something was discovered and named and is now objective knowledge. A clear example of the role of language in inscribing meaning can be found in the discussion of definitions of *career* in Chapter 1.

Language, then, is an important intermediary in our perception of reality—so much so that Dewey and Bentley (1949) believed that to name is to know. These authors stated that language and our knowledge and understanding are inextricably intertwined—key factors in knowing include that there is a relationship between the observer and the observed and that language represents the transaction between the two. For most people, there are many instances in life when naming an observation, whether it is an emotion within the self, a sensory experience, or some other occurrence, is hampered by being "at a loss for words." In other cases, words of other cultures are said to be more adequate descriptors of phenomena than words of Western English; idioms are often unique to cultural and temporal experiences. These are examples of the relationship between language and understanding described by Dewey and Bentley and of the limitations of language. In systems theory thinking, then, it is important to be aware of this relationship between language and our knowing and of the limitations of each.

SYSTEMS THEORY ELEMENTS

The following constructs will be discussed as key elements of systems theory: wholes and parts, patterns and rules, acausality, dynamic reciprocity, discontinuous change, open and closed systems, abduction, and stories. Each will be briefly discussed as it applies to understanding career theory and career behavior. In addition, each will be specifically explained in relation to a practical example in Chapter 9.

WHOLES AND PARTS

A fundamental element is a focus on the unity of the system, on a whole that is greater than the sum of its parts. Each component or subsystem of a whole is partially dependent on and partially independent of the whole of which it is a part. It is important not to break a system into parts, since the coherence of the systemic operation will be changed. Further, although reductionist strategies of breaking a system into parts to understand it are intuitively sensible, key parts and key processes of systemic operation and patterns of relationship may be lost, and individual subsystems inevitably will seem different when isolated from the whole.

Kraus (1989) has defined a system as "a whole which functions as a whole by virtue of the interdependence of its parts" (p. 6). Thus, in terms of career development, individuals and their contexts would be regarded as a whole, and the interactive process between individuals and their contexts would be regarded as the interdependence of parts. Using a systems approach, "We are much more likely to view individuals as parts of ongoing interpersonal contexts than as discrete organisms seeking need fulfilment from the environment" (Kraus, 1989, p. 6).

Traditional career theory has tended to focus on specific discrete concepts relevant to individual career behavior. If we focus on only one aspect relevant to career decision making—for example, intrapersonal aspects such as self-concept—others will inevitably be undervalued or ignored, and the nature of their interaction almost certainly will be. The proponents of the recent movement toward convergence (see Chapter 7) have emphasized the importance of viewing the whole of career behavior and the relationship between all relevant parts to each other and to the whole. This approach requires considering contributions from all theories when exploring an individual's career decision making processes.

PATTERNS AND RULES

Related to a focus on the whole system is a focus on patterns, or what Miller-Tiedeman (1989) referred to as a web of interrelationships. Plas (1986) defined a pattern as "an identifiable arrangement of relationships . . . that have recognizable gestalts; that is, the arrangement of relationships within a pattern produces an organization that is experienced as a whole" (p. 73). Relationships occur both within the components of a subsystem and among the components of a system. D. Ford (1987) maintained that relationships within system components are more complex than those between system components; that is, intrapersonal processes are more complex than interpersonal processes.

While patterns are not unique to human systems, rules are a special form of a pattern that has been constructed by human systems—for example, codes of conduct and communication. Rules vary according to different systems; for example, different families have different rules, and societal and cultural norms also vary. In relation to career behavior, it is important to recognize both individual patterns (e.g., resistance to change) and contextual patterns (e.g., ongoing change). Likewise, it is important that career theories be flexible enough to account for individual and contextual patterns and changes within these patterns. On a broader level, the review of frameworks in Chapter 7 illustrated the existence of identifiable patterns between theories within the whole of the career theory literature.

ACAUSALITY

A corollary of the systems theory focus on patterns and relationships occurring within wholes is the reduction in attention given to causality. In describing the organization and functioning of mechanical structures, it is instructive to focus on their causal interdependence. For example, pulling the cord of a lawn mower causes the ignition to activate, the fuel to begin its path through the engine, and the other functions, such as gears and cutting tools, to mobilize. There is a direct line of cause and effect, and a breakdown at one point can be traced back to its cause. However, humans are living systems and function in processual rather than structured ways. Capra (1982) illustrated the complexity of human systems in commenting on medical science:

> This nonlinear connectedness of living organisms indicates that the conventional attempts of biomedical science to associate diseases with single causes are highly problematic. . . . The systems view makes it clear that genes do not uniquely de-

termine the functioning of an organism as cogs and wheels determine the working of a clock. Rather, genes are integral parts of an ordered whole and thus conform to its systematic organization. (p. 269)

In relation to career theory, there is considerable restriction in existing theories that have focused on causal explanations of career behavior, such as "This is because of that" or "As a result of this, that is likely to occur." While causality provides a useful way of making sense of much behavior, understanding living systems as organic wholes requires less of a reliance on this concept. In addition, a recognition of the many interrelated influences relevant to career development highlights the limited and reductionistic nature of causal explanations.

RECURSIVENESS

Following from the limitations identified in relation to causality is the rejection by systems theorists of linearity. This postulate is as difficult to come to terms with as many of the others we have discussed, since much of our conceptualization about time, space, and development is expressed in linear terms. For example, we go from here to there, and we develop along linear dimensions of height, weight, and growth. Developmental psychology and stage theories of career are reliant on the linear construct to describe their behavioral understandings, and the field of psychopathology has traditionally focused on causal linear explanations for mental problems. Attempts by systems theorists to convey the meaning of nonlinearity have again been illustrative of limitations within our language. Senge (1990) emphasized the limitations of our language and at the same time its importance in shaping our perceptions: "What we see depends on what we are prepared to see. Western languages, with their subject-verb-object structure, are biased toward a linear view. If we want to see systemwide interrelationships, we need a language of interrelationships, a language made up of circles" (p.74). Dewey and Bentley (1949) used the term *circularity*, described as "not merely round the circle in one direction; the course is both ways round at once in full mutual function" (p. 109). Circularity, however, is problematic in that it is suggestive of an irreversible and therefore deterministic relationship between a present relationship between variables and a future relationship. Others have described functions involving feedback and feedforward (D. Ford, 1987; Senge, 1990), and the family therapy literature refers to "mutuality" (Goldenberg & Goldenberg, 1991).

Plas (1986) drew on the term *recursive*, which Bateson had used extensively, as an appropriate starting point to describe nonlinearity:

> A recursive phenomenon is the product of multidirectional feedback, which occurs as functional and arbitrarily identifiable parts of a system emerge in transaction across time and space. A recursion is nonlinear; there is mutuality of influence. Any event that can be identified within a recursive human network can be viewed as the product of experience and anticipation. That is, any isolated movement or moment can be seen to be influenced by events in the past, present, and future. (p. 62)

Although past, present, and future are linear constructions, they are influential in our present thinking and behavior in a recursive manner.

Recursiveness advances the concept of dynamic interaction further in that it does not presume reciprocal interactions, although it does stress mutuality. Thus, feedback and feedforward mechanisms may not occur in a reciprocal manner in all interactions.

In relation to career theory, it is clear that the historical development of theories is related to the ongoing mutuality of influence between theorists and between theorists and researchers. In the same way, the various constructs and processes identified by career theorists as relevant to career development are mutually and recursively influential in an individual's career behavior. Recent formulations of career theory based on contextualism focus on related processes, such as dynamic interaction (Vondracek et al., 1986) and triadic reciprocity (Lent et al., 1996), but each of these remains linked to notions of linear direction and causality.

DISCONTINUOUS CHANGE

Yet another feature of systems theory is its emphasis on ongoing change—that is, a dynamic rather than static perspective. A system is always in a state of flux through continuous informational transaction with the environment that has the ability to affect it. Prigogine (1980), a chemist, referred to the process of maintaining and changing that occurs in open self-organizing systems through ongoing interaction with the environment as *negative feedback loops* in which regulatory processes maintain stability and balance of the system. When the energy flow becomes too complex through either volume or speed, a positive feedback loop emerges toward reorganization or growth and development of the system.

This process is a key element in understanding systems theory. Systems theory makes the assumption that, in a context of ongoing change, systems regulate themselves to maintain stability. Thus, the self-organizing and self-constructing nature of the living system makes possible the maintenance of stability through appropriate transformation of environmental information, or self-renewal (Capra, 1982).

Within systems theory, change is not necessarily construed as progress. The term *progress* contains assumptions about linearity, and much change occurs without entailing progress. Change is often construed as slow and long term: growing, developing, evolving. However, systems theory also accounts for the occurrence of sudden or spontaneous change that occurs after a breakdown of the processes of accommodation in transactions with the environment. When this occurs, the system develops a new set of patterns to accommodate change, breaks down, or develops a completely new form of system organization and functioning.

This change to a new form of system functioning is termed *discontinuous change* and has been identified as occurring during major life crises. Systemic family therapists have developed strategies to attempt to introduce such change into systems where tried ways of functioning are no longer working. Within this framework of thinking, career theorists also need to acknowledge the contribution of futurists. Individual behavior must change along with the rapid changes occurring within the workplace environment, and career planning must become increasingly flexible and adaptable. As Super (1992) commented, "We are evidently entering an age of emerging rather than preset goals" (p. 61). Such frequent change, as well as the occurrence of chance happenings, or happenstance, may produce discontinuous change within an individual system.

Open and Closed Systems

It is the relevance of the environment that makes human systems open rather than closed systems. A closed system is impenetrable and therefore impermeable to information introduced from outside, whereas an open system is permeable. "An open system can be understood only in relation to its necessary and actual environments. Trying to understand people's functioning separate from their contexts would be the same as treating them as closed systems" (D. Ford, 1987, p. 50). Since an open system depends on the existence of an environment, transactions with aspects of the environment relevant to the system are always involved in its functioning (see also the previous discussion on Prigogine).

The environment has been described and organized in a number of ways. The following three conceptualizations have been influential in the development of the framework described later in this book. Each of the following conceptualizations can be seen to be influenced by systems theorists and by field theory (K. Lewin, 1951). D. Ford (1987) spoke of the hierarchical organization of environmental components and organized them as family, communities and institutions, and society and culture. Blustein (1994) referred to two levels of context: the immediate familial and interpersonal context and the broader societal context represented by such factors as culture, socioeconomic background, and other environmental influences.

Another way of categorizing environments relevant to the present discussion is that proffered by Bronfenbrenner (1977). He conceived the ecological environment "as a nested arrangement of structures, each contained within the next" (p. 514). These structures were microsystems, mesosystems, exosystems, and macrosystems. The *microsystem* is described as "the complex of relations between the developing person and environment containing that person (e.g., home, school, workplace, etc.)" (p. 514). A *mesosystem* is a system of microsystems and includes the various settings in which an individual participates. The *exosystem* includes nonspecific formal and informal structures "which do not themselves contain the developing person but impinge upon or encompass the immediate settings in which that person is found, and thereby influence, delimit, or even determine what goes on there" (p. 515). Examples given by Bronfenbrenner include the neighborhood, the mass media, government agencies, and the world of work. Finally, the *macrosystem* "refers to the overarching institutional patterns of the culture or subculture, such as the economic, social, educational, legal, and political systems, of which micro-, meso-, and exosystems are concrete manifestations" (p. 515). Vondracek et al. (1986) emphasized the complexity of the environmental influences of human development and suggested that the Bronfenbrenner model "can lead to a more orderly, systematic, and comprehensive understanding of the context as it impacts career development" (p. 65). We have also drawn from the work of Bronfenbrenner in the development of the systems theory framework to be described in the next chapter.

ABDUCTION

As discussed earlier, another element in systems theory is an emphasis on forms of reasoning by analogy. Both inductive reasoning, or reasoning based on deriving a general principle from a specific case, and deductive reasoning, which applies a general principle to a particular case, are linear in their application. In contrast, according to Bateson (1979), abductive reasoning involves processes of lateral thinking and is concerned with patterns and relationships. Patterns are explored for their relationship within each other and for their relationship to other similar patterns. For example, the process that has created the systems theory approach to career development is an example of abductive reasoning. Systems theory has been explored in detail, and principles that may assist in providing an overarching theoretical framework for existing career theories have been studied and applied. Similarly, theories of career development have been studied in detail for their patterns and relationships.

STORY

The concept of "story" in systems theory was originally derived from Bateson (1979), who defined it as an individual's explanation of the relevance of a particular sequence of connectedness in his or her life. Bateson went further and acknowledged that stories represent communications about patterns that connect all living things. Through stories, individuals make meaning of their lives and actively construct their lives. Systems therapists focus on individual and group (e.g., family) constructions of their reality; through these constructions, attempts are made to understand patterns and relationships. Recent therapeutic approaches that have focused on stories and narrative (e.g., White & Epston, 1989, 1990) can be seen to be derived from this notion. Thus, White and Epston (1989) suggested that "rather than propose that some underlying structure or dysfunction in the family determines the behavior and interactions of family members, the interpretive method would propose that it is the meaning that members attribute to events that is determining of their behavior" (p. 13). Therefore, helping clients story, or restory, experiences to give them different meanings will assist them in understanding the experiences.

Further researchers informed by social constructionist principles have used narrative as a research tool to capture the context richness and subjectivity of individuals' career lives (Young & Collin, 1992). These narrative approaches can also be used in career counseling, although they have not been applied extensively to date. In career theory, each theoretical formulation can be seen as

derived from and representative of individual and group stories, or constructions of meaning (see Vondracek, 1990).

SYSTEMS THEORY PERSPECTIVES IN CAREER THEORY

Although career theorists and researchers have not used systems theory to provide an overarching theoretical framework for the field of career development
before this book, systems theory has influenced their thinking for over a decade. These applications have been at three levels. First, several authors have
acknowledged the potential of systems theory for furthering the integration of
career theory and practice. Second, other writers have incorporated specific
aspects of systems theory into their theoretical formulations. Finally, theoretical frameworks of human development derived from general systems theory
have been adopted as frameworks within which to further understand specific
aspects of human career behavior. Each of these will be discussed in turn.

ACKNOWLEDGMENT OF POTENTIAL OF SYSTEMS THEORY

In acknowledging the increasing integration of various disciplines in career
psychology, Osipow commented, as early as 1983, on an emerging "systems
view of career behavior" and pointed out that "with a highly sophisticated systems approach to career development, questions about the role of the biological, social, and situational factors in occupational behavior would become more
explicit and . . . understandings of the interactions between these views would
be more likely to emerge" (p. 314). A similar perspective is offered in the most
recent version of the Osipow theory overview (Osipow & Fitzgerald, 1996).

Osipow (1983) stated that "the systems approach is in a position to take
the most useful concepts of each theory of career development and apply them
to the understanding of individual behavior" (p. 320). The emphasis in systems
theory is on the importance of a whole that is greater than the sum of its parts,
the interrelationships between elements or subsystems of the system, and the
changes that occur over time as a result of these interactions. The application of
systems theory to career development would allow linking and coherent inclusion of existing concepts, thereby not devaluing existing theoretical contributions. A distinct advantage of systems theory is that it can be applied to all
people. This addresses a major criticism leveled at much of the career development theory, which does not adequately, if at all, apply to women, minority
groups, and groups from non-middle-class backgrounds.

Collin and Young (1986) reviewed a number of approaches informed by
what they termed a contextualist worldview (as identified by Pepper, 1942): the
ecological/systems, the biographical, and the hermeneutical. "Each approach
has its own identity, literature, and methods, and none is without hurdles to
overcome" (p. 843). However, all three share a similar epistemology and are
perceived by these authors as "three faces of a coherent whole" (p. 843). The
ecological systems framework identified by these authors emphasizes a mu-

tual and reciprocal interaction between the individual and the environment and the role of the individual as an active agent. While traditional notions of development remained linked to concepts of linear stages and causality, an ecological systems framework accounts for discontinuity. For example, in times of change, individuals change their actions, and as these responses are reinforced and fed back to the system, renewed equilibrium and self-renewal of the individual system occur. Collin and Young (1986) emphasized the twofold value of an ecological/systems perspective: it presents an epistemological shift that focuses on how parts fit together and interact rather than how they are causally connected, and it is useful for integration. The authors highlighted one of the issues related to systems theory as it is currently conceptualized—namely, that it is particularly abstract. They argued that for this reason the ecological perspective, a special instance of systems theory, is more useful in representing human phenomena. Of the many useful contributions of this article, the complexity of terminology used to explain approaches that are derived from similar perspectives is clearly illustrated.

Each of the authors (Collin, 1985, 1990; Young, 1983) has adopted the nested-systems description of the environment discussed earlier in this chapter (Bronfenbrenner, 1977) as an appropriate metaphor for an individual's career. These authors (Collin, 1985; Collin & Young, 1986) acknowledged the usefulness of systems theory as a framework for career, particularly in its capacity to explain complex, interrelated events. Collin (1985) identified the need for an overarching theory to join disparate and incomplete theoretical constructs and suggested that "an open system model of 'career' could generate a comprehensive, appropriate and grounded theory" (p. 48).

More recently, Bordin (1994) and Blustein (1994) both have acknowledged the value of systems theory in contributing to a greater convergence of the existing theories of career development, particularly within the frameworks of the family systems movement (Bowen, 1978). These authors have been discussed in more detail in Chapter 7. In developing a domain-sensitive approach to counseling and career counseling, Blustein and Spengler (1995) also drew on what they referred to as "systems theories" and their ability to "provide an epistemological lens with which to view a given phenomenon" (p. 313). In relation to career intervention, these authors emphasized the interplay and interdependence of systems relevant to human behavior and the resultant change in parts of the system following an intervention and change in other system parts. In a discussion of the future of career theory and practice and convergence, Herr (1996b) commented that this "may also depend on greater attention to the importance of the explanatory power of general systems theory as the various parts of the individual's environments are understood in their interactive effects on behavior" (p. 16).

SPECIFIC INCORPORATION OF SYSTEMS THEORY PRINCIPLES

A number of theoretical formulations have specifically incorporated elements of systems theory. We will discuss the work of Miller-Tiedeman (1988, 1989) and Hershenson (1996). Miller-Tiedeman's (1988, 1989) work has been reviewed in detail in Chapter 3. The theory is raised here as an illustration of the influence of systems theory on a specific career theory. Miller-Tiedeman (1988) described her "lifecareer" theory as "the general personal process that can accommodate both conventional career theory and the more comprehensive organizing themes of the new science" (pp. 33–34). Being critical of the narrow, other-determined state of existing career theories, she developed her theoretical formulations on the basis of the scientific shift to quantum theory, systems theory based on the work of Prigogine (1980) and Capra (1982), and universe process theory, which emphasizes self-determination. Many of the principles described earlier in this chapter are embodied in her theoretical propositions.

Hershenson (1996) refined his work adjustment model, which he had developed primarily as an example of theory-practice integration, to include a greater acknowledgment of contextual and environmental variables and developed what he referred to as "an adaptation . . . to a systems format" (p. 443). In particular, he incorporated the principles of the framework of Bronfenbrenner (1977) to illustrate the relevance of a number of nested systems in understanding work adjustment. Thus, he referred to subsystems of the person (work personality, work competencies, work goals), elements of the work setting (behavioral expectations, skill requirements, rewards and opportunities), and components of work adjustment (work role behavior, task performance, worker satisfaction) as all operating within and across the systems of family/living, reference group/socialization, school/learning, and cultural and economic context to facilitate work adjustment. He also applied elements of systems theory in his discussion on counseling for work adjustment, noting the interwoven nature of an individual's systems and the effects of interventions on related systems in an individual's behavior. Therefore, once an individual's career problem is determined, a related change in the relevant system will facilitate a change in another part of the individual's system.

FRAMEWORKS SPECIFICALLY DERIVED FROM SYSTEMS THEORY

Finally, a number of theoretical conceptualizations designed to further explain human vocational behavior have drawn specifically on frameworks derived from systems theory. In particular, we will focus on the work of Vondracek and his colleagues (Vondracek & Fouad, 1994; Vondracek & Kawasaki, 1995; Vondracek et al., 1986), and Krumboltz and Nichols (1990).

The developmental-contextual approach to career development proffered by Vondracek et al. (1986) has been influenced by systems theory philosophy. These authors emphasized the importance of the context in human development, and their life span orientation allowed for change over time. Further, the concepts of embeddedness of relevant systems in each other and interaction of these systems with each other (dynamic interaction) are clearly derived from the worldview that informs systems theory. Vondracek and Fouad (1994) illustrated the influence of systems theory in discussing interventions within the developmental-contextual framework, suggesting that intervening at different levels of context can change the relevance of a particular variable. This principle of intervening within one system to bring about change in a related system has been clearly illustrated in family therapy practice (Bowen, 1978).

More recently, the work of Vondracek and Kawasaki (1995) in furthering the developmental-contextual model using the LSF (D. Ford, 1987) is an example of work directly derived from systems theory. The LSF of D. Ford (1987) has also been applied by Krumboltz and Nichols (1990) as an overall theoretical framework, or inclusive "map," for specific career decision making frameworks. Both of these formulations have been discussed in more detail in Chapter 7.

SYSTEMS THEORY AND RELATED CONCEPTUALIZATIONS

Clearly, systems theory is becoming increasingly influential in career development theory. This influence varies in degree. It has the potential to contribute to our understanding of the detail and dynamic complexity of career development. Specific theoretical models have been modified to incorporate some aspects of systems theory, although complete development of systems elements has not occurred. Further, frameworks that have been developed using principles of general systems theory (e.g., D. Ford, 1987) have been used as conceptual frameworks for understanding the "what" and "how" of human behavior in relation to careers (Krumboltz & Nichols, 1990; Vondracek & Kawasaki, 1995).

There are many conceptual similarities between systems theory and the contextual approach of Young et al. (1996), the developmental-contextual approach (Vondracek et al., 1986), and the recent DST (Vondracek & Kawasaki, 1995). For example, while contextual approaches emphasize the need to acknowledge the influence of the multiple embedded levels of the environment in human behavior, systems theory places more focus on the nature and process of this influence, "seeing interrelationships rather than linear cause-effect chains, and seeing processes of change rather than snapshots" (Senge, 1990, p. 73). Vondracek et al. (1986) emphasized that development theory must be at the heart of career theory; systems theory emphasizes that meaningful change is not always ordered or developmental. In addition, systems theory suggests that linear and causal relationships are restricted in their explanatory power of much human behavior.

While Vondracek et al. (1986) developed the notion of dynamic interaction to depict the mutuality of the influence of variables relevant to career development, the concept remains limited. Influence between variables may not always be reciprocal, and the bidirectional model of causality embedded in Bandura's (1986) triadic reciprocity is also bound by linear and causal principles. It is here that the systems theory element of recursiveness, or multidirectional nonlinear feedback, is particularly relevant. Senge (1990) also spoke of two types of feedback relevant to the mutual flow of influence: *reinforcing feedback*, which propels an organism forward in a direction, and *balancing feedback*, which focuses actions toward the desired goal. Both types of feedback show

how actions can reinforce or counteract (balance) each other. Central to this feedback loop process is the notion that delays can interrupt the flow of influence. Furthermore, systems theory allows for nondevelopmental or nonlinear change processes and thus for circumstances of chance.

The contextualist worldview also stresses the "now" of an event, and in doing so fails to attribute sufficient importance to the effect of both the past and future as influences on the individual, the context, and their interrelationship. Systems theory focuses on learning to recognize types of structures that recur, being influenced by past, present, and future factors.

CONCLUSION

The field of career development, like many other fields of psychology, has a variable and complex theoretical base. The need for an integrating strategy has been emphasized by many writers in the area, culminating in the conference on convergence in career development theories (Savickas & Lent, 1994). While the complexity in the status of theory reflects the complexity of career behavior, the need for a corresponding complex grand theory, or group of theories, is not supported by all writers. Vondracek et al. (1986) commented that "the ultimate result of embracing an interdisciplinary, systems theory type view of career development will be a shift from simplicity to complexity" (p. 6), with related research and measurement concerns. However, we believe that the adoption of an integrative framework based on systems theory (described in the next chapter) can provide coherence to the field by providing a comprehensive conceptualization of the many existing theories and concepts relevant to understanding career development. The systems theory framework is not designed to be a theory of career development; rather, systems theory is being introduced as the basis for an overarching framework within which all concepts of career development described in the plethora of career theories can be usefully positioned and used in theory and practice.

9

A SYSTEMS THEORY FRAMEWORK OF CAREER DEVELOPMENT

The purpose of this chapter is to outline our systems theory framework (STF) of career development—a specific attempt to provide a synthesis of the existing theoretical literature using a metatheoretical structure. As discussed, systems theory offers the potential to focus on different theories as being parts of a whole and to search for relationships and patterns between variables as they are relevant to the individual. The framework will be presented in stages, each highlighting significant influences on career development and relationships with existing theoretical literature. Seven advantages of the framework will be discussed, and the application of the framework to practice in the case of one individual will be presented.

It is important to acknowledge at the outset the twofold purpose of our STF. First, it can reflect a macropicture of career theories, illustrating the contribution of each one of the theories and its interrelationship with others. Second, it presents a framework of the influences relevant to an individual's career development, showing the many complex and interrelated systems within which such development occurs.

DEVELOPMENT OF THE FRAMEWORK

In 1992, we (McMahon, 1992) first presented the concept of a STF as a contextual model for understanding adolescent career decision making. Since then, we have further argued that context is an integral part of systems theory and that decision making is an integral part of career development. We published the initial STF in 1995 (McMahon & Patton, 1995) and modified it in 1997 (Patton

& McMahon, 1997). The framework presented here has again undergone substantial revision.

The STF was developed to be a useful overview of important influences on career development as identified by the many theorists, researchers, and practitioners who have contributed to our understanding in this field. It aims to identify two broad components of career theory, content and process. Under *content*, the framework identifies variables applicable to the individual and to the context, thereby outlining key influences on career development. We deliberately chose the word *influence* to describe intrapersonal and contextual factors relevant to the career development process, since we believe it is less static than *factors* and is a dynamic term capable of reflecting both content and process. An influence acts as input into an individual's system and can relate with the system in a number of ways. Within a systems theory perspective, an individual could perceive an influence as a barrier or as a facilitator in relation to career development.

Under *process*, the framework identifies the existence of recursive interaction processes within the individual and within the context, as well as between the individual and the context. This recursive interaction contributes to the microprocess of decision making and the macroprocess of change over time. Finally, the process component of the framework identifies the relevance and importance of chance.

In our STF for career development, the common elements reflected in the convergence of the literature are also shared by a systems theory perspective. The content influences in the framework are (1) the individual system and (2) the contextual system; the processes influences are (1) the recursive nature of the interaction between the individual and the contextual system, (2) change over time, and (3) chance. The framework is presented according to these elements to demonstrate the components of a systems theory perspective on career development, their interrelationship, and their contribution to wholeness.

THE INDIVIDUAL

The review in Part One of this book highlighted the increasing emphasis in the literature of the importance of the individual as the center of the career choice and development process. Thus, the individual is the center of the STF. The importance of the individual as the focus of career development is reflected in a number of perspectives. Traditionally, the role of the individual in career decision making has been central (Ginzberg, 1972), but this role has typically been passive, with the individual being shaped by his or her ability, gender, socioeconomic status, and other related influences (e.g., L. S. Gottfredson, 1981; Roberts, 1977). However, several developments encouraged the active involvement of the individual. These included the practical work of Holland (1973) in developing the "self-directed search," which encourages individual involvement in the career decision-making process. The theoretical work of Bandura (1977, 1986) in developing the concept of self-efficacy emphasized an individual's ability to act on his or her environment rather than merely responding to environmental experiences: "Reinterpretation of antecedent determinants as predictive cues rather than as controlling stimuli has shifted the locus of regulation of behavior from the stimulus to the individual" (Bandura, 1977, p. 192).

This perspective has been mirrored in the work of Vondracek et al. (1986), who emphasized the uniqueness of the individual and his or her context and the resultant uniqueness of the interaction between each individual and that context. They concluded that, "as a consequence, we may only speak probablistically of the effects a given person may have on his or her context, and of the nature of the person's development that will therefore ensue" (p. 78).

The worldview presented in Chapters 7 and 8 also stresses that there is "no objective, ordered social reality outside the individual's construction of it through subjective and intersubjective meanings" (Collin & Young, 1986, p. 842). As discussed in Chapter 8, such a view of the world presents the individual as defining and determining his or her own reality and negates the traditional view of causality in relation to effects of the environment. Miller-Tiedeman and Tiedeman (1990) extended the view of individuals as constructors of their own lives in asserting that "lifecareer" needs only to make sense to the individual.

More recently, organizational psychologists have suggested that the role of individuals in their own career development is becoming more important due to changes in the workplace. Hall (1996) describes his "protean career" as that which is "driven more by the individual than the organization. This would call for frequent change and self-invention and would be propelled by the desire for psychological success rather than by externally determined measures of success" (p. xvi).

In his Archway model, Super (1990) identified the person as the central component, or "keystone." Similarly, in the STF presented in this chapter, the person is the most central feature. Super (1990) used the term *self* in his model, but we prefer to use the term *individual* in our framework to suggest the uniqueness of a person and his or her situation and to reflect the conception of personal agency that is embedded in current theoretical perspectives. In addition, following the work of D. Ford (1987), Leong (1996b) asserted that "each individual is in and of him or herself a complex adaptive system" (p. 341). It is in this context that we view the individual in the STF.

Thus, the center of the STF is a circle representing the individual. The circle contains a range of intrapersonal features influencing career development that are possessed by all individuals but are different for each individual. Influences shown in Figure 9.1 include both some of those more frequently featured in the descriptions of a number of writers and some that have traditionally been neglected.

THE INDIVIDUAL SYSTEM

Many of the influences represented in Figure 9.1 are represented in existing career theories and have been discussed in relation to those theories in Chapters 2 through 6. Personality is central to the work of Holland (1985a) and the five-factor theory (McCrae & John, 1992). Interests and beliefs are also central

F I G U R E 9.1 The individual system

to Holland and to both social learning theory (L. K. Mitchell & Krumboltz, 1990) and social cognitive theory (Lent et al., 1994). Values have recently received renewed emphasis (D. Brown, 1996a). In his life-span, life-space approach and his Archway model (described in Chapter 3), Super (1990) included many of these influences, including specifically role self-concept. The development of stage theories by Super (1953, 1957, 1990) and L. S. Gottfredson (1981, 1996) illustrates the importance of age. While age is seen as a limiting variable within systems theory, we include it because of its relationship to existing constructs. From the standpoint of systems theory, we need to move beyond the view of age in terms of a linear and chronological sequence of stages to a perspective in which the implications of age vary with other influences, such as social influences, and may change over time. For example, a certain age does not always reflect a particular stage in development. Finally, knowledge of the world of work has been inherent in career theory since the work of Parsons (1909) and remains a key factor in recent theories, such as the cognitive information-processing theory (Peterson et al., 1991, 1996).

The insufficient attention to gender, ethnicity, and sexual orientation in career theorizing has been highlighted in Chapter 6. Recently, however, the issue of the importance of gender has been raised in the work of a number of authors (e.g., Astin, 1984; Betz & Fitzgerald, 1987; Fassinger, 1985, 1990; L. S. Gottfredson, 1981, 1996; Hackett & Betz, 1981). The career development needs of ethnic groups (Arbona, 1990; Cheatham, 1990; L. S. Gottfredson, 1986; Hackett & Lent, 1992; Osipow & Littlejohn, 1995; Smith, 1983) have also been emphasized. Following the recent attention in career counseling research directed toward the particular career development issues of lesbians and gay men (Croteau & Hedstrom, 1993a; Elliott, 1993a, 1993b; Hetherington & Orzek, 1989) and the identified inapplicability of theories of women's career development to lesbians (Morgan & Brown, 1991), sexual orientation has also been included as an important individual influence.

Disability has also been given scant attention in the theoretical literature to date, with some mention in the work of L. K. Mitchell and Krumboltz (1990) and Lent et al. (1994). We believe it is timely to include disability in the framework as an influence in its own right rather than as an adjunct to ability. In addition, these authors commented on physical attributes and talent in relation to career choice. Finally, health has been seen as important indirectly through Krumboltz's attention to genetic endowments. A holistic view of the individual needs to emphasize physical and mental health in relation to career choice and development. Work adjustment theory (Dawis & Lofquist, 1984) in particular drew attention to the potential relationship between job satisfaction and physical and mental health. In addition, there is a voluminous literature on the physical and psychological health effects of unemployment (e.g., Feather, 1990; Fryer & Ullah, 1987; Herr, 1992; Osipow & Fitzgerald, 1993).

The relationship of health to employment and unemployment is one example of the interaction between many of the intrapersonal influences in this circle and sociocultural influences. For example, being born as female or male is a chance occurrence, but gender is a socially constructed variable. The cultural construction of values also emphasizes the relationship between intrapersonal and sociocultural influences. World-of work-knowledge is related to access to resources and can be seen to be related to gender, socioeconomic status, geographic location, and other influences. Such knowledge is particularly crucial in our globalized environment. With unemployment particularly affecting certain age groups more than others, age and environmental-societal influences are related. Finally, in many ethnic groups, we acknowledge that the family is a major focal group in development, not the individual.

THE CONTEXTUAL SYSTEM

In terms of systems theory, an individual is a system in its own right, with the influences in Figure 9.1 representing its subsystems. However, an individual as a system lives, not in isolation, but rather as part of a much larger system. In fact, life roles exist only in relation to this larger system. Thus, the individual as part of a larger system coexists with a broad contextual system that is itself composed of smaller subsystems. We have broken this broader system into two subsystems, the *social contextual system* (the other people systems with which the individual interacts) and the *environmental/societal contextual system* (the environment and society). In presenting a STF, it is useful to represent these separately. They are represented in Figures 9.2 and 9.3 respectively.

We acknowledge the influence of the systems of Bronfenbrenner (1977) discussed in the previous chapter in the construction of the parts of our system. Thus, the social system is representative of Bronfenbrenner's "microsystem," and the environmental/societal system is representative of his "exosystem" and "mesosystem." While we acknowledge the pervading influence of a macrosystem of broader attitudes, values, cultural influences, and major societal systems as identified by Bronfenbrenner, within the present framework, we see these as pervading each of the other systems rather than as a system that can be identified separately. Such an approach is more in keeping with the recognition of recursiveness, or recurring interaction between systems.

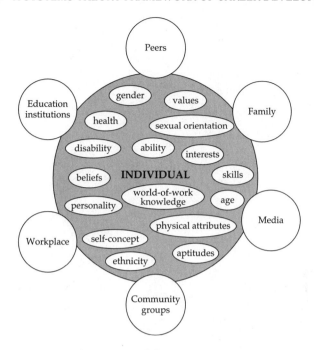

F I G U R E 9.2 THE SOCIAL SYSTEM

THE SOCIAL SYSTEM

Figure 9.2 represents the principal social influences with which individuals interact or from which they receive input. Jepsen (1989) commented that "an adolescent's social environment is comprised of several primary social groups to which most adolescents belong, especially the family of origin, the several subgroups in schools such as classes and activity groups, and the peer friend group" (p. 73). These groups have been described as the principal agents of socialization by Borow (1984). Although this comment refers to adolescents, the influence of these groups is pervasive throughout life, as acknowledged in Super's (1990) Archway model.

Vondracek et al. (1983) identified the important contextual variables that we have categorized within the social system as community structure and size, school climate, and family context variables, such as birth order and family size, maternal and paternal employment status, and paternal encouragement. These authors also highlighted the interaction between systems by emphasizing that socioeconomic status and ethnicity of family are relevant influences.

The media have received scant attention in the career theory literature, with Jepsen (1989) being one of the few writers to identify the media as a socializing influence. In fact, much information from the environmental/societal system is transmitted to individuals through the media. The media are also significant as a filter of information in terms of what they report and how they report. In terms of career development, the workplace and education institutions may influence individuals directly or indirectly. The role of employing organizations in individual career development is also important and needs to be acknowledged (Hall, 1996; Herriott, 1992).

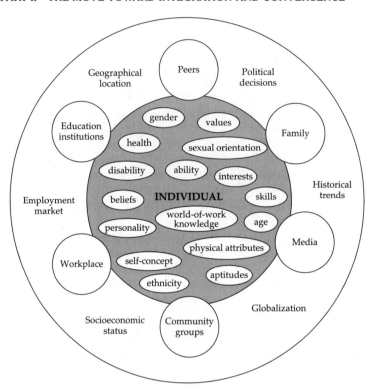

F I G U R E 9.3   THE ENVIRONMENTAL-SOCIETAL SYSTEM

Each of these social structures is also the source of values, beliefs, and attitudes that may be conveyed to the individual in a variety of ways. The influence of these groups can be long lasting and can vary over time. For example, changes within curriculum, such as the recent inclusion of vocationally oriented programs in educational institutions, can alter perceptions and opportunities of individuals. In addition, students who engage in vocational programs that take them into education and workplace environments outside the school may be less influenced by the school as a result. Similarly, career development programs instituted at an organizational level can have an impact on individual career development. Within each of these systems, formal and informal structures that incorporate mentoring arrangements may also be relevant.

The composition of the social system will change throughout life as the individual moves into and out of groups—for example, changing schools or jobs or moving to a new town. In the present framework, the social systems that are common to most individuals have been represented. However, most individuals will belong to significantly more groups, such as interest groups, service clubs, and self-help groups, and this will inevitably lead to membership in different peer groups.

Thus, it is essential in considering the social system of an individual to explore the exact nature of the systems within which he or she exists. The systems theory framework can serve as a starting point for this process.

THE ENVIRONMENTAL-SOCIETAL SYSTEM

The individual also lives within a broader system, that of the society or the environment. The influences represented in Figure 9.3 may seem less directly related to the individual, yet their influences can be profound. Many of these influences have been highlighted in the work of a number of career theorists (e.g., Lent et al., 1994, 1996; L. K. Mitchell & Krumboltz, 1990; Roe & Lunneborg, 1990; Vondracek et al., 1986).

As suggested in the reviews in Chapters 2 through 4, geographic isolation has been underrated as an influence in career development. Rural isolation may influence the nature of schooling received, employment opportunities, the availability of role models, and access to information (Collett, 1997). The influence of geographic location can also be experienced within cities, where the better "name" of some suburbs than others affects the employment opportunities of residents. Some suburbs are also better serviced than others. For example, residents' opportunities may be restricted by limited transport to and from work and study. There is often a close link between political, socioeconomic, historical, and geographic influences in cities and in rural locations.

Decisions of governments on issues such as social security benefits, funding for schools and universities, industrial agreements, and workplace restructuring may have profound effects on individuals or the members of their immediate social system. Political and historical influences may also account for the beliefs, values, and attitudes held by age cohorts, such as the values held by school leavers at times of high employment compared with those at times of high unemployment.

Inclusion of employment markets in the framework provides an opportunity for employment to be seen as part of the broader life context. Although closely related to political, socioeconomic, historical, and geographic influences, employment market trends can be a significant influence on the demand for tertiary courses and can influence the curriculum of schools, colleges, and universities.

Opportunities in the employment market have also been significantly affected by rapid advances in technology. Thus, technological change forges a link between employment market and historical influences. In a similar way, environmental awareness has influenced the employment market, the school curriculum, and tertiary courses. Changes to the employment market, such as award restructuring, enterprise agreements, the increasing proportion of contract positions versus tenured positions, and workplace-based education and training, brought about largely by political influences, should also be noted as significant influences on career development. Increasing unemployment, especially for specific groups, such as young people and the middle aged, is also an important influence in the environmental-societal system. These employment market influences increase the need for ongoing career planning and lifelong learning.

The importance of acknowledging the restrictions imposed by the sociopolitical environment has been emphasized by a number of authors (Osipow, 1975; Smith, 1983; Vondracek & Fouad, 1994). The effect of these influences on people is profound and they have been included in this framework to highlight their significance. Roberts (1977) emphasized that socioeconomic influences affect values held, education received, information obtained, and observable role models.

Globalization has only recently been given attention in the career development literature (Hall, 1996; Hansen, 1996, 1997; Herr, 1996a). It is relevant in relation to changing organizations and changing workplaces and in the broader context in which we all live. Hansen (1996) nominated ten global issues that she considered most relevant in the career counseling context: "Technological Change, Environmental Degradation, Human Rights, Multiculturalism, Migration, Changing Gender Roles, Violence, World Population, Issues, Spirit and Meaning, and New Ways of Knowing" (p. 25). The effects of globalization are far reaching—for example, in the areas of information about the world of work, provision of jobs in particular areas, and the importance of transferability of skills. Further, globalization and technology are continuing to have unimagined and far-reaching effects on our lives in relation to access to information, communication, and the process of applying for jobs and engaging in career counseling through the facilities of the Internet. Such developments propose ongoing challenges for career counselors.

RECURSIVENESS

The influences contained in the STF are representative of the multitude of influences on career development. A STF would not be complete without acknowledgment of the process of influence both within and between these systems. We have chosen the systems theory term *recursiveness* (described in the previous chapter) over others used throughout the literature. We have rejected the notion of reciprocal interaction, which we referred to in earlier versions of our work (McMahon & Patton, 1995; Patton & McMahon, 1997), since it is clear that many of the influences are not reciprocal in size or direction. The concept of "triadic reciprocity," defined in the work of Bandura (1986) and the social cognitive theory (Lent et al., 1994), remains linked to notions of causality, and we believe that this concept limits our thinking about the movement of the influences between and within the systems in our framework. Vondracek et al. (1986) referred to the concept of dynamic interactions in describing "the fact that complex, multidirectional relations exist between an individual and his/her context, and that changes in one of the multiple sources of development . . . will influence changes in all others" (p. 187). We believe that this concept comes closest to describing the process of interaction, focusing on the multidirectionality of influence and the relationships between all systems. However, a limitation of the concept of dynamic interaction is that it is closely linked to contextualism, which is based on the present moment. The person-context relation described is therefore only that occurring at one point in time. In addition, the relation at this point in time may influence future relations in a deterministic manner. Thus, interaction between person and context is viewed as a snapshot, and development is seen as "a longitudinal series of snapshots" (Vondracek et al., 1986, p. 82) rather than an ongoing, ever-changing process.

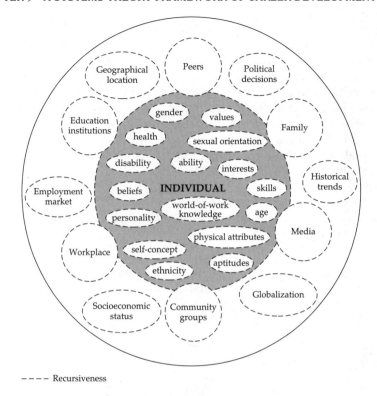

– – – – Recursiveness

F I G U R E   9.4   RECURSIVENESS

However, we believe that recursiveness incorporates many key aspects of influences, such as their being nonlinear, acausal, mutual, and multidirectional, as well as including the ongoing relevance of the past, present, and future. Each of the systems and subsystems is an open system and is therefore permeable to influence. Thus, the broken lines in Figure 9.4, indicating permeability, represent this recursive phenomenon occurring between the influences. Significantly, as the nature of the influences changes, so too does the degree of influence. The influences of the intrapersonal system are also not static, and a recursive interaction takes place between these influences as well as between them and the influences of the social and environmental/societal context. Thus, in terms of practice, career development facilitators become part of the interconnected system of influences affecting the career development of individuals (described further in Part Three). In addition, a change in one part of the system or in one system produces a change in another part of the system, and individuals and their systems will experience their own recursiveness.

CHANGE OVER TIME

It is well accepted in the literature that career development is a life span phenomenon (Super, 1990; Vondracek et al., 1986). In addition, career development involves ongoing decision making. Thus, change over time refers to decision-making processes and accounts of change over time. This is shown on the systems theory framework in Figure 9.5 as a broader system of time within which the individual and his or her particular systems move. This circular depiction emphasizes the nonlinear nature of an individual's career development process and the integral role of past, present, and future influences in the decision-making and broader change process. In fact, the path of career development is one of constant evolution and may incorporate forward and backward movements. This evolution is referred to in the extant theory as "emergent career decision making" by Super (Freeman, 1993), "successive approximations" by Holland (Freeman, 1993), and "mini-decisions" (Herr & Cramer, 1992) and is indicated by shading in Figure 9.5 as change over time in the system influences.

The recursive interaction between individual and the social and environmental-societal systems reflects the reformulation of career theory away from a basic linear model to incorporate aspects of the life cycle and changing demands

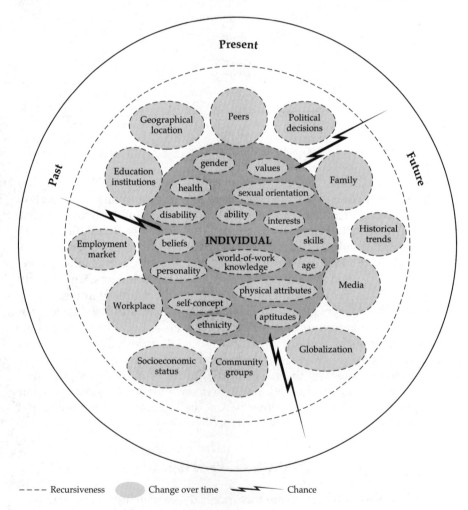

F I G U R E 9.5 CHANGE OVER TIME

of life roles (Levinson, 1978; Sonnenfeld & Kotter, 1982; Super, 1990). Nicholson and West (1989) maintained that traditional theories have focused too much on exploration and career entry decisions at the expense of change and transitions. While linear development may have given way to a notion of sequential recurring stages, definitions of career continue to emphasize the cumulative nature of the process. The "successful" career is still viewed as one that has advanced vertically as opposed to having moved horizontally, and the concept of a "backward" career move remains in the literature. While job or career change no longer is seen to reflect career uncertainty or immaturity (e.g., Super & Knasel, 1981, rejected the concept of maturity in favor of the concept of career adaptability), the restrictive expectation persists that career development can be measured against a time scale.

In formulating a suggestion to address this problem, Marshall (1989) advocated the inclusion of elements of "female" values in career theory: "a more cyclical interpretation of phases, based in notions of ebb and flow, of shedding and renewal" (p. 285). Marshall discussed the cyclical view of personal development, in which going back to retrace steps and relearn material offers new learnings because of the different place in the life pattern. She presents as a model of this pattern of career development the diversity of women's life patterns, which reflect a "wide variety of combinations and sequences, often appearing to start afresh as they give up status in one arena to take on a novice role in another. From this perspective, the connecting thread is the individual's life, not a building image of increasing social status" (p. 287). This perspective is reflective of important principles and processes embedded in systems theory.

The process of career development needs to be considered in relation to the influences of stage of life and family life cycle, concepts taken from developmental psychology and family therapy respectively. Future considerations, such as anticipated lifestyle and employment market trends, may also influence the career development of an individual. Ellyard (1993) commented that

> rapid technological and social change means that work skills are made redundant at increasingly fast rates. Up to 50 per cent of the skill required in the newer knowledge based industries in particular, become redundant every 3 to 5 years. In the next 20 year period 50 per cent of all job categories are likely to change. Half of these will involve job categories now existing which will disappear. The other half will involve new job categories, not yet existing which will be created. (p. 3)

Thus, to consider career development without looking forward to the emerging future is indeed short-sighted.

Implications of the broad process of change over time, change that reflects the coexistence and recursive action between the individual and the broader systems, are far reaching. An individual's "lifecareer" (Miller-Tiedeman & Tiedeman, 1990) will be less predictable and will demand greater adaptability, flexibility, and mobility of the individual. In addition, the importance of individual acceptance of lifelong learning is crucial. The role of career development facilitators in this process is also crucial. Both of these issues will be explored in detail in Part Three.

CHANCE

Chance needs to be considered in a STF and is represented in Figure 9.5 by random flashes. Although unpredictable, the influence of chance can be profound, and its importance as a possible influence on career development needs to be acknowledged and included in the framework (L. K. Mitchell & Krumboltz, 1990; Roberts, 1977; Roe & Lunneborg, 1990). Chance is defined as "an unplanned event that measurably alters one's behavior" (Miller, 1983, p. 17) and can be referred to as luck, fortune, accident, or happenstance. As discussed in Chapter 4, L. K. Mitchell and Krumboltz (1990) included genetic endowments as an occurrence of chance. In addition, Vondracek et al. (1986) introduced the notion of chance in referring to the probabilistic nature of development and hence career development.

Given the complexity of influences in relation to career development, it is unreasonable to assume that the individual's career development will always be planned, predictable, or logical. Chance can affect any part or combination of parts of the system. For example, an accident or illness may produce a disability, a chance meeting may open up new employment prospects, and a "manmade" or natural disaster may reduce or increase job opportunities.

The broader perspective of systems theory allows for the inclusion of chance as yet another influence to be dealt with as it arises and is acknowledged. Within the systems theory perspective, however, the emphasis on chance is that it occurs only as it is perceived by the individual observer. It is constructed through the interconnectedness of the system; this implies that change in one part of the system brings about change in another part of the system. However, from the perspective of an individual, the interconnectedness may not be obvious or visible; thus, an event may be unexpected and explained as a chance occurrence.

ADVANTAGES OF A SYSTEMS THEORY FRAMEWORK

There are several advantages in a STF approach to integrating career theories and integrating theory and practice.

1. *The important contribution of all career theories can be recognized.* It has been acknowledged that theorists have developed theories emphasizing aspects of career development over others and that often these aspects of career behavior have been approached from different standpoints (Savickas, 1996a). Many of the extant theories focus on components of career development, thus providing depth to what is a broad and multifaceted field. The breadth of the field of career development may preclude there ever being one overarching theory (Hesketh, 1985; Super, 1990). Regardless of whether this occurs, there will still be a need to recognize the input of the components.

2. *A STF can place extant theories in the context of other theories, and their interconnections can be demonstrated.* While this advantage is related to the first one, it extends it in a subtle way. By viewing the whole picture of interconnecting influences on career development, a systems theory perspective can also

recognize the interconnections between theories and view them in the context of other theory. Thus, the place of all extant career development theory can be recognized, since systems theory has the capacity to provide a metatheoretical bridging framework (Savickas, 1995) for presenting a theoretical overview while acknowledging the worth of individual theories. For example, Holland (1985a) described the categories of interests and their relationship with work environments; L. K. Mitchell and Krumboltz (1990) contributed to our understanding of how these interests are formed. Social cognitive career theory (Lent et al., 1994) describes detailed cognitive processes relevant to career decision making; the cognitive processing model (Peterson et al., 1996) describes additional metacognitive processes.

3. *A systems theory perspective recognizes the contribution to career development theory and practice of other disciplines.* As discussed, career development theory has been criticized for not crossing boundaries into other disciplines (Arthur et al., 1989; Collin & Young, 1986; Sonnenfeld & Kotter, 1982; Van Maanen, 1977) and therefore not capitalizing on the benefits that this could bring to the advancement of the field. The STF has applications both between and within disciplines and brings with it a richness that is not available through more narrow, single-focus theories. For example, in discussing the influence of family on an individual's career development, reference can be made to family therapy principles. Similarly, principles from fields such as economics and political science can be incorporated in exploring the environmental-societal system. Thus, the STF offers the potential for integrating psychological and sociological theories of career.

4. *Systems theory brings to career development a congruence between theory and practice and new approaches for use in career practice.* The theory-practice rift was emphasized by Lent and Savickas (1994), who concluded that change theories from counseling may usefully be integrated into career interventions. Systems theory is already a well-established concept in other counseling fields, such as family therapy. As a result, its application to career development brings with it well-established techniques that can be used by practitioners. For example, the systems theory principle of intervening in one part of a system to bring about change in another part of a system is practiced in family therapy. The process of intervening in an organizational system to repattern relevant influences is reflected in R. Taylor's (1997) description of a university program that was designed to change career pathways of socioeconomically disadvantaged adolescents.

5. *The emphasis in career development is placed on the individual and not on theory. Therefore, systems theory can be applicable at a macro level of theory analysis, as well as at a micro level of individual analysis.* The importance of theoretical perspectives of the individual within the STF was discussed at the beginning of this chapter. With a systems theory perspective, the role of the practitioner is not to be the expert and to predict or foresee but rather to assist individuals through dialogue to understand themselves and their own intrapersonal and systems-based influences and to construct the story of their own lives. As individuals make sense of these influences, they are assisted to construct their own career development processes and engage in action accordingly.

The STF is also an important framework for the micro purpose of individual theory applicability. It therefore also addresses the concern raised by Richardson (1993) about the potential need for separate theories for individuals according to the diversity of their locations. Richardson lamented the "overwhelming plurality of specific locations . . . [and] the anxiety engendered by what seems to be a collapse of comforting, if limited, bodies of generalized knowledge into a confusing relativism and multiplicity of parts about which little is known or can be known" (p. 429). However, a separate theory is not necessary for each individual. As individuals are placed at the center of their own process, they can work to identify their own meaning from the theories. Thus, the complexity of the field and of the process can be reduced for both the individual and the career counselor, and career counseling and career education interventions can become system input for the individual to act on and process. This perspective is not too different from that advocated by Vondracek and Fouad (1994).

6. *A systems theory perspective enables practitioners to choose from the theory that is most relevant to the needs and situation of the individual.* A systems theory perspective encourages practitioners to focus on the individual and his or her relevant systems and processes. Thus, their approach cannot be predetermined by adherence to a single-focus theory, and their reliance on a single assessment instrument or technique is likely to be reduced. Therefore, interventions are more likely to be tailored to the needs of the individual rather than to the theoretical or methodological preferences of the practitioner. While the current state of theory suggests that certain theories are useful for different purposes (Krumboltz, 1994; Osipow, 1994), the integration of theory within an overarching framework can facilitate this process.

7. *Systems theory offers a perspective that underlies the philosophy reflected in the move from positivist approaches to constructivist approaches.* The philosophy underlying systems theory is related to the contextualist worldview discussed in Chapter 7. A significant difference between logical positivism and constructivism is that "there are no absolutes; thus, human functioning cannot be reduced to laws or principles, and cause and effect cannot be inferred" (D. Brown & Brooks, 1990b, p. 11). Thus, the objectivity of a logical positivist approach that can often be supported by test results is replaced by subjectivity. Individuals are encouraged to define themselves and their environment and to refer to the subjective sources of their knowledge. This philosophy has great implications for the development of career theory and for the conduct of career counseling and career guidance, and will be further discussed in Part Three.

IMPLICATIONS OF A SYSTEMS THEORY PERSPECTIVE

The proposal of a systems theory perspective and a STF is not designed to compete with or devalue existing career theories. Rather, its significance lies in its capacity to place the emphasis back on the individual and to unite the various theories under one framework. Systems theory provides the breadth necessary to unite the theories, while the individual theories provide the depth needed to account for specific concepts. Thus, systems theory and the existing theories are complementary and can coexist compatibly. Despite the multitude of influences, it is the individual that is most important. Super (1990) confirmed this importance in commenting that it is the individual "in whom all the personal and social forces are brought together" (p. 203).

However, a systems theory perspective has several implications for career theory, for our understanding of career, for career decision making, and for the relationship between theory and practice.

IMPLICATIONS FOR EXTANT THEORY

A STF gives coherence to the myriad influences on career development and the many theories on career development. The framework enables their place in the system to be illustrated in relation to other theories. The framework demonstrates the recursive interaction between the theories that need no longer be viewed as discrete, disparate, or segmental.

In addition, we have been emphasizing the value of the STF in providing a framework for integrating theory and practice by giving the individual and not the theory the central role in the career development process. This approach has been advocated by a number of authors (e.g., Leong, 1996b). Due to the uniqueness of individuals and their systems, "Theories cannot be right or wrong, but only more or less useful" (Stoltenberg & Delworth, 1987, p. 3).

In relation to the issues of gender, racial and ethnic groups, sexual orientation, and socioeconomically disadvantaged groups, a STF provides adequate attention to the recursive nature of the interaction among the variables that influence differential opportunity structure, including psychological variables and economic and sociopolitical variables. In addition, a systems theory perspective focuses on the dynamic interactions between the individual and historical, social, political, economic, cultural, technological, and organizational influences in understanding career decision making and planning.

IMPLICATIONS FOR OUR UNDERSTANDING OF CAREER

With its interactive and nonreductionist approach to careers, the STF can broaden the narrowness of existing career definitions. A practical example of this is changing from the existing "nontraditional careers for girls" emphasis to an emphasis on reclaiming the diversity of women's lives and fostering the development of broad choices, including, if chosen, the homemaker role. The broader context in career theory can support a focus on contextual breadth as opposed to linear depth in discussing careers. Further, a systems theory perspective of career development acknowledges the importance of knowledges and methodologies from other disciplines in furthering our understanding of career.

With the emphasis on the individual, a systems theory perspective allows for multiple meanings and explanations of the purpose of work and its significance to people. From a systems theory perspective, it is less relevant to make value judgments about part-time work, job sharing, homemaking, casual work, and unemployment because a STF graphically illustrates the current constellation of influences that account for the present status of an individual's career development. Thus, all career options can be validated and explained in terms of system influences. Career can therefore be defined broadly as a life pattern determined by recursiveness of life influences. Put simply, career could be viewed as the pattern of influences that coexist in an individual's life over time.

As discussed in Chapter 1, a number of authors (Collin & Watts, 1996; Herr, 1992; Miller-Tiedeman & Tiedeman, 1990; Richardson, 1993, 1996) have proposed a more flexible approach to defining career. The STF enables such flexible definitions. In addition, the nature of our times requires them, for individuals need to be more flexible in their own career constructions, given the many changes occurring in the systems with which they relate. Embedded in this need for flexibility is the concept of lifelong learning, illustrated by Collin and Watts (1996), who asserted that "the concept of career needs to be reconstrued as the individual's development in learning and work throughout life" (p. 393). Thus, within the worldview that underlies systems theory and related constructivist approaches, career can be defined as a lifelong process in which patterns and relationships between work and other areas of life are constructed within the learner in an ongoing way.

IMPLICATIONS FOR THE PROCESS OF CAREER DECISION MAKING

The process of change over time is facilitated through the evolving processes of career decision making, which cannot be explained in terms of models that apply to all people. Rather, career decision making is unique to each individual. It represents the processing of information constantly being received throughout the system through a combination of conscious and unconscious processes. The components and requisite cognitive functions in career decision making have been identified in a number of theories (Lent et al., 1994, 1996; L. K. Mitchell & Krumboltz, 1990; Peterson et al., 1996; Young et al., 1996). These processes produce subjective and objective evaluations by the individual that may or may not be able to be articulated. Practitioners may assist this process by encouraging the individual to make links between the many systemic influences and between the past, present, and future. Incorporating systems theory-based assumptions into theorizing and researching about careers will assist in identifying how individuals learn about and make decisions within a context—that is, how the interconnections between the individual's subjective experience and their systems operate.

IMPLICATIONS FOR PRACTICE

For practitioners using a STF, the purpose of theory changes as it becomes a source of multifaceted constructs and possible related influences. The meaning of these constructs and relationships is constructed by the individual within a process facilitated by the career practitioner. Theories and assessment measures can no longer be used as predictors of development or direction; rather, they are used to feed information into the system for processing by the individual.

Individuals determine prominent themes and dominant stories relevant to their career development, and they process and make sense of these with the counselor acting as facilitator. Thus, "Knowledge or reality is constructed by the individual. Importance is not placed on events or combinations of events as much as the transformation of these events into meaningful information which is then incorporated into prior knowledge" (Stoltenberg & Delworth, 1987, p. 5).

APPLICATION OF THE SYSTEMS THEORY FRAMEWORK

While the STF has already been depicted in this chapter, its adaptability and elasticity are more apparent when it is applied to the career development of a particular individual at various points in his or her life. The STF can be used to map an individual's career story throughout his or her career development. Individuals can be encouraged to draw the framework as they narrate the story of their career development. To illustrate the adaptability and usefulness of the framework as a tool for career development facilitators, we offer an example of its application to one person's life.

The example chosen is that of a typical young man growing up in a rural area during the 1970s. This individual is from a low-income family in which neither parent completed secondary schooling and both parents have struggled to provide for their family. The individual, the eldest child of the family, has reached the end of compulsory schooling. Postcompulsory schooling is not available locally because the government education department closed the senior secondary school due to low student numbers. Postcompulsory secondary education would necessitate either a two-hour bus trip morning and night to a neighboring town or boarding in that town, an option that is not viable for the family because of the young person's age and their financial situation. Another alternative is to complete postcompulsory schooling through distance education via correspondence. While the young person has done well at school and is motivated to continue at school, the family decide for financial reasons that the offer of a secure job with a company in the town is the best option. It is the parents' hope that this good job will mean that life will not be such a struggle for the young person as it has been for them. The company recognizes the ability and potential of their new employee and is supportive of his completing secondary schooling by correspondence. They allow some time for exams and study. Figure 9.6 depicts the dominant influences on the career development at school-leaving age. For this young person, the transition from secondary school to beyond was influenced by age, gender, ability, socioeconomic status, family, geographical location, the employment market, and political decisions.

Once the young person completes secondary education, promotional opportunities become available in the company. The young man's family now consider him old enough to leave home and are encouraged by the future promised by the company. Mobility is not a problem for the individual, who has no ties and is able to take advantage of opportunities in a number of other locations. While the individual is not participating in formal education, he regularly participates in in-service training provided by the company. In addition, a

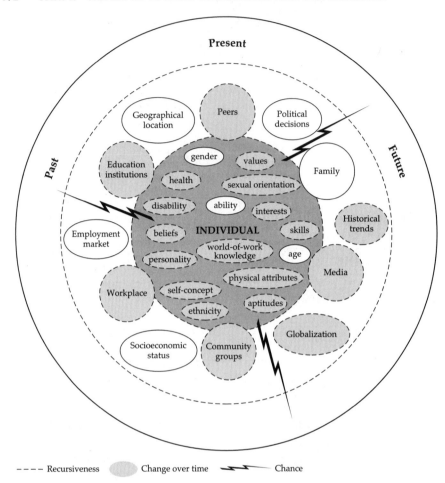

F I G U R E   9.6   DOMINANT INFLUENCES AT SCHOOL-LEAVING AGE

senior executive of the company has recognized his potential and taken him "under his wing." Thus, ten years after leaving school, the individual is on a promotional track. This is illustrated in Figure 9.7. While some of the same influences remain dominant, they have changed over time. For example, geographic influences are still significant but are now related to the individual's mobility and the opportunities associated with that, whereas previously geographic location restricted opportunities. New influences have emerged, such as the employer who is acting as a mentor. The individual continues to learn. However, this occurs less formally through experience in the company and company in-service training. Thus, knowledge of the world of work has increased and has resulted in several promotional opportunities. Up to this point, the individual has followed a traditional vertical path of career development.

During the next ten years, the individual continues working for the company, which has now established branches in several overseas countries. As a result, the individual has been able to spend extended periods of time overseas with responsibility for establishing new branches and making connections with

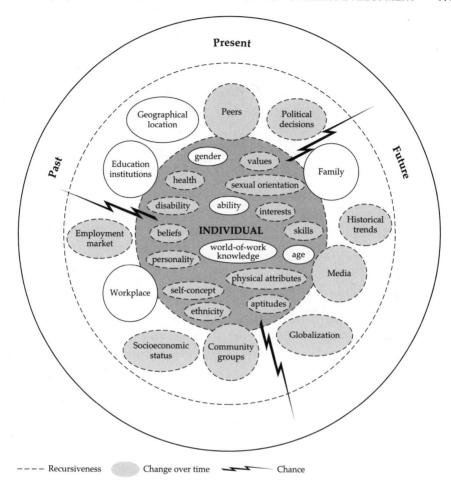

F I G U R E   9.7   DOMINANT INFLUENCES 10 YEARS AFTER LEAVING SCHOOL

other companies. However, during this time, the individual has also married, and he is now in the position of having a young family and not wanting to travel as much. The decision to spend more time with the family has led to reduced promotional opportunities. Working for the company is now less satisfying, since others, less senior, are in the decision-making positions. In addition, the individual has identified several satisfying and challenging aspects of his work in which he would like to specialize. Since he is now based in a large city and is traveling less, he enrolls in part-time study. He is beginning to feel less secure in the company, since it is restructuring its operations. In addition, he is feeling less satisfied with work and is beginning to think about opportunities outside the company. However, he feels limited by the financial constraints of a mortgage and raising a family. Figure 9.8 illustrates the constellation of influences 20 years after leaving school. Learning has continued both formally and informally, although the individual feels that his career has plateaued. Globalization has emerged as an influence. Family has reemerged as a dominant influence, although its nature is different. The individual has defined his inter-

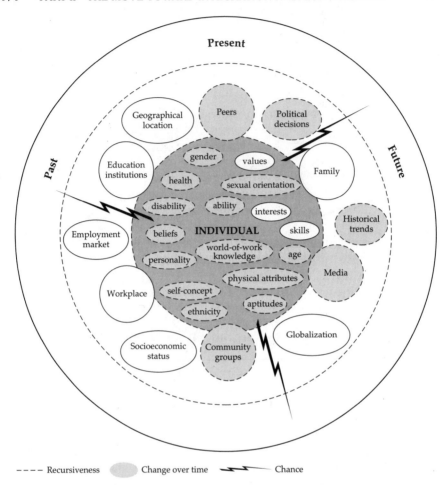

- - - - Recursiveness   Change over time   ⚡⚡   Chance

F I G U R E   9.8   Dominant Influences 20 Years After Leaving School

est area more clearly and realizes how much he values having some control over his work.

As restructuring in the company continues, the opportunity arose for the individual to work on a permanent part-time basis. This has provided a sense of security as well as the opportunity to explore other work options, such as contract work. Peer networks and professional contacts developed during his work life have enabled the individual to secure several contracts, and he is now committed to building his own business. He enjoys the challenge and decision making associated with this. The specialized nature of the contract work is providing a sense of satisfaction because it is of great interest to him. Also, he is now feeling secure in the knowledge that if he is laid off or offered a voluntary early retirement package, he has other options. Figure 9.9 represents the constellation of influences 30 years after leaving school. The influence of family remains constant. While security has always been an important value for the individual, the importance of other values such as challenge and responsibility

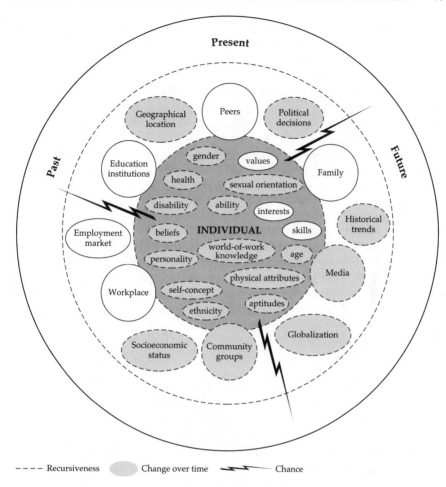

F I G U R E 9.9 DOMINANT INFLUENCES 30 YEARS AFTER LEAVING SCHOOL

are now highlighted. The pattern of career development has changed and is no longer that of ascent through an organization.

Thus, throughout the individual's life, the STF has been able to account for his career development. The constellation of dominant influences has varied, and the degree to which the influences have affected his life has changed. In addition, the nature of the influences has changed over time. It can be clearly seen that the influences cannot be construed as negative or positive, but rather as "push" or "pull" factors in relation to certain decisions and the individual's career path.

SYSTEMS THEORY CONSTRUCTS APPLIED

The previous example illustrates how a STF can be a useful tool for understanding the complexity of influences operating in the career development of an individual. It is also useful in illustrating the constructs of systems theory previously discussed in Chapter 8. Each of the constructs will be presented here.

WHOLES AND PARTS.   The frameworks depicted in Figures 9.6 through 9.9 present a picture of the whole system of which the individual system is a part. To separate the part from the whole leads to a misleading picture of the individual's options. For example, at school-leaving age, consideration of the individual system only and the interests and abilities of the individual would suggest that he continue at school. Combining the evidence from this part of the system with evidence from another part—that is, his future ambitions— would make continuation at school seem even more logical. However, when the information from these parts (subsystems) is considered in conjunction with information from the whole system, particularly the social system and the environmental / societal system, the individual's continuation at school seems less logical, although still an option. Thus, it can be seen that to operate on information from less than the whole system can be potentially misleading.

PATTERNS AND RULES.   In the family depicted in Figure 9.6, there is no pattern of continuing to postcompulsory education, even though there are no family rules precluding it. However, there is an established pattern of a solid work ethic that is closely related to the family role and a related emphasis on family values and security. Although the individual depicted in the example followed a significantly different career path from that of either parent, he maintained the established pattern of hard work and the importance of his family role. In addition, security remained as an important value throughout his career.

ACAUSALITY.   While it is easy to identify significant points in the career development of the individual depicted in the example, it is not easy to identify the exact reason for the outcome. For example, not continuing at school cannot be attributed solely to the family's socioeconomic circumstances. Geographic location, political decisions, age, employment market, the individual's motivation and ability, and family influences all played a part. Thus, the decision to take up an offer of a job cannot be accounted for by a causal or linear explanation such as "He did not continue because the family could not afford it." Understanding the outcome requires acknowledgment of many interrelated influences operating at the time of the decision in the system of the individual.

RECURSIVENESS.   The previous explanation also illustrates the recursiveness that occurs within and between the elements of a system. The ever-present influences of the framework are interrelated and therefore act on each other. Thus, there is a mutuality of influence. However, as an influence changes, its degree of influence on other elements of the system also changes. For example, the degree of influence of globalization on the individual during his early life was not marked. However, as globalization grew, new opportunities opened up for the company and in turn for the individual. Thus, the company and in turn the individual, participated in globalization through expansion in other countries. While there is a mutuality of influence, the degree of influence is not reciprocal. Rather, a recursive pattern of interaction occurs.

DISCONTINUOUS CHANGE.   Globalization is an example of discontinuous change. Another is the change in the family system of the individual. For example, discontinuous change occurred when the individual left home, again when he married, and again when he had children. In each case, the system, while still a system, would not be the same again.

OPEN AND CLOSED SYSTEMS.   The previous discussion of the application of the STF illustrates the permeability of the boundaries of the subsystems, which are open to influence from other subsystems. For example, the individual system was influenced by the social system and the employment market. This illustrates the operation of an open system—that is, a system that is open to input from the surrounding systems. Closed systems are not open to such input and have impermeable boundaries.

ABDUCTION.   Previously, the family values of hard work, security, and the importance of family were discussed as a pattern of living shared by the individual and his parents. Abduction is a process of reasoning by examining patterns and relationships. Thus, the individual's values did not just occur. They can be related to patterns within his family of origin. Similarly, the career pattern of the individual 30 years after leaving school did not just occur. Rather, it reflects changing patterns in the nature of work, the organization of business and industry, and fulfillment of the individual's own needs. Abductive reasoning looks for patterns and relationships between the individual's system of operating and interrelated systems—for example, the family or the employment market.

STORY.   To understand these patterns and relationships, counselors encourage individuals to tell their story—for example, to talk about what life was like growing up, family attitudes to work, work history, and how they have coped with change in their lives. Through story, patterns and relationships can be derived and interconnection forged between previously unconnected events in an individual's life. Story also enables patterns and relationships to be forged between the rich system of influences on the individual. Through story, individuals construct their own meaning about experiences and their own reality. The STF depicted in this chapter can be useful in assisting the individual to tell his or her story.

THE INDIVIDUAL AS A LEARNING SYSTEM

As evidenced in Figures 9.6 through 9.9, all of these influences are brought together in the individual. Individuals are both participants in their systems and receivers of information from their systems. As the individual interacts with the other elements of the system, he or she collects new information. This is combined with previous information to form new knowledge. Thus, the individual can be viewed as a learning system. The creation of knowledge is a process that resides within the individual and is an emergent process influenced by language, time, place, and culture. For example, throughout this individual's career development, learning and the creation of knowledge were ongoing. Sometimes the influences on learning were overt, as in participating in a course of study, and sometimes they were covert, as in development of family values, although these may never have been discussed or taught. At times, the input was formal education, such as school or university study, and at times it was informal, such as observations about work, life experience, recognition of personal preferences, and input from the media or mentors. As a result, the individual learned about himself as well as the world of work at a general level and specifically in terms of interest areas. Any individual's learning creates a unique perspective or worldview that is reality for him or her and may differ from the reality of other individuals.

Thus, the use of systems theory thinking challenges traditional ways of knowing and opens up the possibility of multiple perspectives. This is reflected in the many perspectives on career development presented in the career theories. Many theorists have constructed individual worldviews on career development. Individually, they represent parts of a complex system. However, as evidenced by the example of the application of the STF to the career development of an individual, the parts need to be viewed in relation to the whole. Thus, systems theory thinking, with its focus on the whole, has much to offer our understanding of career development at both practical and theoretical levels.

CONCLUSION

Using systems theory, "elements of the social, personal, and economic situation within which individuals operate may be more explicitly analyzed, and the relationships of the larger systems to one another may be more clearly understood than in the traditional approaches to behavior, which tend to emphasize only one major segment of the individual or the environment" (Osipow, 1983, p. 320). Thus, systems theory provides an opportunity to develop a framework to represent the complex interrelationships of the many influences on career development.

A systems theory perspective also addresses many of the criticisms of the career theory literature. It represents a conceptual move to provide a metatheoretical framework for integrating existing theories and integrating theory and practice. Significantly, systems theory offers a framework for the blending of what different disciplines can bring to career theory and a congruence between theory and practice, applicable to all individuals, that did not previously exist. The application of the STF in integrating theory and practice within the crucible of the individual will be developed further in Part Three.

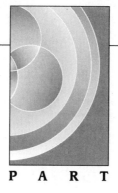

III

SYSTEMS THEORY AND CAREER PRACTICE

10

LIFELONG CAREER DEVELOPMENT LEARNING

As discussed in Parts One and Two of this book, debate about the integration or convergence of career theories continues (Savickas & Lent, 1994). Similarly, debate has ensued about the integration of career theory and career practice (Savickas & Walsh, 1996). Through the application of a systems theory perspective, Part Two of this book established that theory integration can be forged within the individual. It is the individual in and by whom application of career theory is made and integration occurs. The individual provides the unifying theme in practice and can be seen as the crucible for the integration of theory and practice. With a systems theory perspective, the individual is placed at the center of career development practice, since he or she is the constructor of his or her own career.

This theme is reflected in the work of Knowdell (1996), who drew on the metaphor of different types of transportation to illustrate the changes confronting career decision makers since the 1950s. According to Knowdell, the 1950s career was a ride on a train along steady and stable tracks to a particular destination. But during the 1970s, as the world of work began to change, career became more like a journey on a bus in that buses respond to changing traffic conditions and may change routes along the way or even destinations, though still operating on a schedule determined largely by the bus company. In the next century, the appropriate vehicle for the journey will be the "all terrain vehicle" (p. 184), as the individual will be in the driving seat and will need to "take the controls and 'drive' his/her own unique career toward success" (p. 184). Knowdell claimed that "those who learn to 'drive' their own careers will get there" (p. 191), and he expressed concern for those who do not.

In a similar vein, Herr (1992) reminded us that careers do not exist in the same way as jobs and occupations but rather are the creations of individuals. Thus, it is reasonable to propose that "individuals should regard themselves as being self-employed" (Collin & Watts, 1996, p. 391), since they are expected to "manage their own career" (Savickas, 1997, p. 256) and in doing so to take responsibility for their own learning and "career-long self-development" (Collin & Watts, 1996, p. 391). The new meaning of career as a "process, not a structure" (Watts, 1996c, p. 44) can apply to all individuals, not just those in hierarchical organizational structures, and can occur laterally, vertically, and inside and outside of organizations. As explained in Chapter 9, the individual makes career decisions and choices over time in relation to the interaction in his or her life of a complex network of influences, as illustrated by the systems theory framework. Career in itself could be regarded as a system that is constantly molded by the interaction of influences.

The comments of Collin and Watts (1996) draw attention to three key issues: the new understanding of career and the changing context of career development, the responsibility of individuals to chart their own path of career development in a time of change, and the relationship between career development and learning. This view of career development and the centrality of the individual in the process brings with it significant challenges to the way in which career development practices need to be conceptualized and conducted.

This chapter sets the scene for Part Three of this book. In particular, it examines the changing context in which career development and career development practice occur. It argues that if individuals are to chart satisfying career development courses for themselves, they will need to engage in lifelong learning. Using lifelong learning as a central theme, this chapter draws attention to the need to rethink career practices and the traditional role of career practitioners. All chapters in Part Three will be presented through the filter of systems theory thinking. Where relevant, practical examples of the application of systems theory will be provided.

Chapters 11, 12, 13, and 14 will focus on specific aspects of lifelong learning. Chapter 11 will discuss the establishment of learning systems, using the example of training of career counselors. In Chapter 12, the focus will be on career development learning in school systems. Chapter 13 will discuss the facilitation of lifelong learning in a changing context through career counseling, and Chapter 14 will focus on the lifelong learning of career counselors through supervision. Although it is recognized that career development learning is also facilitated in organizations, and although the themes presented are relevant in any career development learning setting, the inclusion of organizational career development is beyond the scope of this book. This area is addressed in other work, such as that of Kidd (1996), Law (1996b), and Senge (1990).

THE CHANGING CONTEXT

There would be little debate about descriptions of today's work environment as "turbulent" (Lester, 1996, p. 193; Mirvis & Hall, 1996, p. 72). The world of work in the latter part of the 20th century is a dynamic place, described by Jones (1996) as "harsh and challenging" (p. 453). Gone is the security many workers have experienced and relied on, since "the traditional concept of a 'job for life' is dying" (Watts, 1996a, p. 231). In its place is an environment of uncertainty and constant change, reflected in Borow's (1996) description of "current widespread trends toward corporate downsizing, wholesale layoffs, and drastic reductions in long-term career-ladder positions, and toward part-time jobs carrying no benefit and no future" (p. 8). Thus, the employment market is increasingly characterized by a growth in the number of self-employed, part-time, and contingent (short-term contract or casual) workers and teleworkers and the numbers of people who are becoming unemployed or underemployed.

In addition, "the nature of work has changed; it has become more automated, profit oriented, competitive, and dynamic. Job security, to the extent that it exists, rests primarily on marketable skills, not on job seniority or on the paternalism of a company" (Jones, 1996, p. 455). In this regard, Knowdell (1996) commented that "gone are the days when the young entry level worker, with little education, went to work for a company, learned and mastered their product and lived 'happily after'" (p. 187). By comparison, workers of today, and indeed the future, can expect to change jobs several times, work for a number of organizations, and experience times of underemployment and unemployment. Some of this will occur as a result of the individual worker's choice, but some will be forced on him or her and brought about by company policies of downsizing, restructuring, and outsourcing. Thus, workers find themselves in a "foreign" world of work, facing a complex array of issues for which many are ill prepared. To some extent, this stems from the changing nature of the relationship between organizations and workers from one based on tenure and mutual loyalty to one based on economically driven short-term contracts. Most individuals will have to find and hold a job not only once but repeatedly during their lifetime. As a result, workers can no longer rely on the same beliefs, skills, and values to be successful and satisfied in their careers.

Most writers commenting on the changing world of work draw attention to issues such as globalization of the workforce, a growing global labor surplus, organizational transformations in the workforce, the rise of a contingent workforce, the rising importance of the knowledge worker, growing awareness of linkages between career experiences and mental and physical health, family responsibilities and life options, the appearance of government policy and legislation, and demographic trends related to new entrants to the workforce. The challenges posed by such trends include job insecurity, unemployment and underemployment, and the related issue of economic security. Some challenges, such as balancing work and family roles and issues of discrimination and harassment, reflect recursiveness between individuals and their social system. Others, such as "fighting for a job or career advancement in a highly competitive environment; and adjusting to boring, low-paying, dead-end jobs that offer little hope for the future" (Jones, 1996, p. 453), reflect recursiveness between the individual and environmental/societal system. Related to these, and also illustrating recursiveness, are issues of mental health related to increasing workplace stress.

This recursiveness of interaction between elements in the system is creating issues that previously received little consideration from career development practitioners. Traditionally, the clients most commonly seen by career counselors were those experiencing difficulty choosing an occupation (Wijers & Meijers, 1996). However, the issues previously discussed clearly point to a broadening of the role of career development practitioners, away from the traditional role of counseling for workforce entry in a "job-for-life" world and toward the provision of a range of career-related interventions for diverse individuals throughout the life span. Against this background, Watts (1996a) commented that "the profession of career counseling, and the concept of career to which it relates, are creatures of the industrial age" (p. 230). It is therefore essential that this constantly unfolding world be understood as the backdrop to career guidance and counseling activities and that counselors not only understand it but guide their clients according to the new reality.

Within this changing world, Watts (1996a, 1996c) claimed that career counseling has a much more significant social role to play in modern-day society than ever before. This has coincided with its forging of close links with personal counseling and its potential not only to provide vocational advice but to deal with such broader career-related issues as workplace stress and conflicting life roles. Thus, the potential client market of career counselors has broadened at a time when the complexity of issues with which they are dealing has also broadened. In addition, the world of work is more complex and less secure, and individuals are turning to career counselors in greater numbers. At the same time, business organizations and governments have also realized the potential role for career counselors in this changing world.

So important is this issue that a special section of the *Career Development Quarterly* was devoted to a discussion on "public policy and career counseling for the twenty-first century" (Savickas, 1996b, p. 3). Such thinking prompted M. Taylor (1994) to comment that "counseling is not a luxury but a basic need for a healthy population" (p. 307). Bimrose and Wilden (1994) suggested that "careers guidance has been identified as centrally important to the economic recovery of the nation [England]" (p. 373), a sentiment that has also been expressed by others (Hansen, 1996; Herr, 1992; Krumboltz, 1996). In the American context, Krumboltz (1996) claimed that "the economic welfare of the nation depends on its citizens learning career-relevant skills and characteristics and learning to adapt to a constantly changing work environment" (p. 75). In some countries, such as Canada, evidence of this thinking is already being manifested in the form of a national career development strategy (Bezanson & Heibert, 1996).

Thus, the work of career development practitioners is increasingly being seen as influenced by national and even global perspectives. For example, Herr (1992) claimed that

> as individual nations become increasingly interdependent players in what is clearly becoming a global economy, they share concerns about strategies to develop functionally literate and productive work forces; mechanisms to help youth make the transition from school to work and to distribute persons among available occupations; procedures to help persons make the adjustment to work effectively and

obtain job satisfaction; plans to deal with high rates of youth unemployment and / or rapidly aging work forces; and methods by which employers and work settings can be increasingly attentive to the needs of employees, seeing them in holistic rather than fragmented ways. (p. 255)

Herr's statement effectively illustrates the recursiveness between influences of the environmental / societal system, the individual, and the role of career development practitioners as they attempt to confront the issues of the future. Indeed, if practitioners are not responsive to these changes and the demands of future trends, they will become increasingly redundant.

CONSUMERS OF CAREER DEVELOPMENT SERVICES

Herr's (1992) statement also alludes to the changing nature of the client group with whom career development practitioners interact. In this changing society, it is essential that career guidance and counseling be available to all individuals throughout their life span (Collin & Watts, 1996; Herr, 1992) and at a reasonable cost. Much of the available career guidance and counseling traditionally has been provided to young people in secondary schools; such restricted service provision is no longer adequate.

Chapter 6 has previously drawn attention to the career development needs of women, racial and ethnic groups, and gay men and lesbians. The systems theory framework also depicted other groups whose career development needs are determined by an interaction of individual and contextual needs but whose issues have not yet been sufficiently theorized—for example, people with disabilities. Increasingly, the needs of the unemployed and underemployed also need to be taken into account in career development practice (Patton, 1996). The emergence of a society in which approximately one-third of people are privileged and in a reasonably secure form of employment, one-third are unemployed, and one-third are marginalized and insecure is often discussed. It is this diverse group that will be presenting as consumers of career guidance and counseling services.

The services required by individuals at different points during their career development will vary depending on their responses to the stresses and strains of the work environment and the circumstances of their career development at that point—for example, emotional problems, being laid off, or parenting. The changing nature of the client population also means that career development services will need to be provided in a variety of settings, such as workplaces, community agencies, and universities, as well as the traditional location of schools. In this regard, Herr (1992) noted that career counseling or career guidance is becoming increasingly more comprehensive in terms of its content and processes and the characteristics and settings that it serves. The growth of outplacement services is an example of how the career guidance and counseling industry can be responsive to changing market needs.

Service provision to a range of individuals with unique needs in diverse settings poses challenges to career development practice if it is to meet effectively the needs of a client group for whom the concept of career development no longer means a preset vertical path within an organization. However, the changed and changing environment and the rapidity with which change is occurring raise questions about the ability of traditional approaches to career practice to respond. In relation to career counseling, Borow (1996) commented that "these grim developments call into question the idealized picture of career counseling and planning process that our textbooks and journals often present" (p. 8). A basic premise of career theories that was criticized in Part One of this book is that career options exist for all and that certain career patterns are attractive to everybody. When these views are also part of practice, it is clear that our theory and practice assumptions are not in step with the current situation, let alone future trends.

THE CASE FOR LIFELONG LEARNING

As evidenced in the discussion throughout this chapter and in Chapter 9, consumers of career development services will increasingly be viewed as lifelong learners. The links between the concept of lifelong learning and career development have strengthened in recent years, since learning is the only way for individuals to keep pace with the rapidly changing society in which we live. It is imperative that individuals be encouraged and know how to learn and that they take responsibility for learning throughout their life span (Collin & Watts, 1996; Cornford, Athanasou, & Pithers, 1996). Indeed, Mirvis and Hall (1996) claimed that the new career will require "learning a living" (p. 80) rather than simply earning a living. Echoing sentiments expressed earlier in this chapter, Cornford et al. (1996) claimed that engagement in lifelong learning "appears to offer benefits in terms of economic productivity" as well as "longer-term benefits for the individual" (p. 43).

From a systems theory perspective, investment in and gains from the learning of individuals have benefits at a broader societal level. Cornford et al. (1996) claimed that lifelong learning "has been advocated by progressive educators and UNESCO since the early 1970s, but only recently have governments seriously started to consider its implementation" (p. 43). Their interest in promoting lifelong learning has to some extent been prompted by increasing globalization and competition from international competitors. Thus, career development practice is increasingly being seen as part of the broad environmental/societal system and as a mechanism for facilitating lifelong learning, and career development practitioners as operating at the interface of the individual and his or her environment.

It is not an overstatement to claim that lifelong learning is a necessity. Krumboltz and Ranieri (1996) claimed that lifelong learning "is needed in the present age for workers to develop their capabilities and to adapt to a changing workplace" (p. 37). Thus, the concept of lifelong learning is increasingly being seen as an intrinsic part of the career development process—a notion reflected in Charland's (1996) comment that "lifelong learning is a way of living fully in our time, and that is the gift of changing economy" (p. 132). Charland reminded us that learning is "a need that doesn't diminish with age" (p. 129). It could be argued that this need has been brought into sharp focus by the rapidly changing world in which we live. Lifelong learning is essential because the constantly changing conditions of the modern world have made necessary the continuing acquisition, renewal, and upgrading of knowledge, skills, and attitudes (Candy, Crebert, & O'Leary, 1991).

Ellyard (1993) reminded us that traditionally, the life of an individual has been seen as having three stages—schooling and formal education, the working life, and retirement—and that learning in the second and third stages has been viewed as "not nearly as significant or as important as the learning one obtains in the first age" (p. 2). However, with the changing emphasis to lifelong learning, it becomes increasingly important that individuals leave school "with a desire to be a lifelong learner, a love of learning, and be capable of learning because they have the skills to access knowledge, such as literacy and numeracy" (p. 5). In addition, the processes of formal education should also develop in individuals the confidence to be a lifelong learner. Thus, it is imperative that our young people be adequately prepared for this context in which they will be living and working.

At the same time, the potential of career counseling and career guidance to be an educative process is being realized—an important shift in emphasis. This trend is clearly reflected by Krumboltz (1996), who claimed that the goal of career counseling is to "facilitate the learning of skills, interests, beliefs, values, work habits, and personal qualities that enable each client to create a satisfying life within a constantly changing work environment" (p. 61). Thus, the challenge for career development practitioners will be to foster client learning and to "generate learning experiences for their clients that involve a wide array of personal as well as career issues" (p. 75). Career counselors need to rethink their role and view their clients as lifelong learners, themselves as facilitators of learning, and their interaction as a learning system. In addition, it must be remembered that traditional learning experiences have not adequately catered to all learning styles, and that individuals whose learning styles have not been accommodated are at risk of not becoming lifelong learners. Therefore, it is essential that learning experiences support the learning processes of all individuals.

Many career guidance practitioners and some career counselors may draw on psychoeducational models in their work. Opportunities abound for creativity in the design of learning experiences that meet the needs of the individual learner. These may include formal courses and training or informal learning both in the workplace and through everyday activities. As Feller (1996) reminded us, "Opportunities to learn are everywhere" (p. 150)—a notion in keeping with a systems theory perspective and a reflection of the closer links that are being forged between education and industry and the promotion of organizations as sites of learning (Senge, 1990). The practicalities of rethinking our roles will be discussed in more detail in the following chapters.

PREVIOUS ACKNOWLEDGMENT OF LIFELONG LEARNING IN THE CAREER LITERATURE

It would now seem that the concepts of career development and lifelong learning are inseparable, as reflected in Collin and Watts's (1996) description of a career as the process of an "individual's development in learning and work throughout life" (p. 393). But although lifelong learning is presented as a relatively new concept, it could be argued that learning has always been a theme of career development theory.

Since the days of Parsons (1909), learning has been an implicit part of career decision making. In his approach, learning encompassed learning about the self and the world of work. It centered on a point in time rather than being presented as a lifelong process. But in the person-environment fit approaches, the concept of learning was extended through the notion of adjustment. Adjustment to attain a closer fit was performed on the basis of decisions made about personal needs and work environment needs. Needs emerged as a result of personal learning. For example, Holland (1992) proposed the term *successive approximations* to account for the changes that individuals make during their career development to enable them to be more satisfied in their work. These approximations result from greater self-awareness in terms of needs. Self-awareness can be construed as part of a personal learning process, and it is reasonable to propose that self-learning underpins the person-environment fit approach.

The developmental theories proposed stages during which tasks were completed, generally on the basis of learning about the self or the environment. For example, Super (1990, 1992) proposed that learning theory is the unifying feature of his segmental framework that applies to people of all ages. With relation to the contextual theories, individuals learn from their environment either directly or indirectly. These processes of learning are illustrated by the social learning theory of career decision making (discussed in Chapter 4).

WHAT IS LEARNED

Career development theory draws attention to the possibilities of the content of lifelong learning—for example, learning about interests, values, or family-of-origin influences; learning about the world of work; and learning about processes, including decision making, communication, and teamwork. Walz and Feller (1996) suggested that every worker needs a "core set of survival skills," including "resilience, the capacity for continuous learning and improvement, the ability to network and team, skill in using technology effectively, willingness to take calculated risks and learn from setbacks" (p. 431). Pena (1997) concurred and added to this set of skills the need for individuals to have the skills of managing the processes of change. Given the potential for individuals to work in a number of organizations, Pena also advocated that individuals learn about transitions and understanding "business dynamics" (p. 35) so that they can "fit in." Collin and Watts (1996) described the processes such as those listed previously as the skills of career self-management. Learning about processes related to career self-management is of particular importance in an era in which career is conceptualized as a process and knowledge dates rapidly. In addition, many theories draw attention to the sources of learning, such as family, school, the workplace, and peers. Processes and a variety of learning sources are reflective of the dynamic and interactive nature of career development. Thus, learning can be seen as a bridge between career theory and practice that is created by

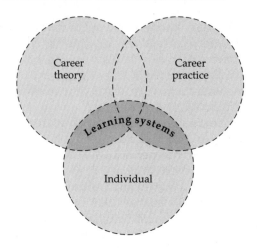

F I G U R E   10.1   INDIVIDUAL CAREER DEVELOPMENT AND LEARNING

the individual, who is central to the learning process. It is the individual who is the central learning system. This is illustrated in Figure 10.1.

The individual is viewed as an open system who receives input from interrelated systems for processing. As self-organizing systems, individuals incorporate the new input into existing life narratives and organize or reorganize their viewpoint. Knowledge acquisition or learning is not cumulative; rather, it builds on and is filtered by that which we already know. Thus, knowledge acquisition is qualitative, and individuals define their own reality (Chapter 8 draws attention to the changing worldviews and the place of knowledge in these). Learning is a highly individualized process, the individuality of which needs to be respected. This opens the way for constructivist approaches to be used in career development practices. For example, learning is filtered through the narratives or stories of the individual's life (these are addressed in more detail in Chapters 11 and 13).

THE LANGUAGE OF LEARNING

It can be seen from the discussion so far that lifelong learning is central to the career development of the individual and that the individual is central to the learning process. However, the traditional terms of *counseling, education, training,* and *supervision* have connotations of "doing to others" who have little responsibility in the process. These language connotations support a process whereby "language helps define cognition, experience, emotions, and relationships by connecting an individual to another in predetermined ways" (Owen, 1991, p. 309). Thus, for example, terms such as *teacher* and *student* or *client* and *counselor* predetermine the relationship between those individuals as a hierarchical one, with the teacher or counselor in the dominant position in the learning process. However, if the individual is viewed as a lifelong learner in charge of his or her own learning and career development, such traditional terms must be replaced by terms that place the emphasis on the learner. In the context of therapy, Owen (1991) explained that "as the use of language conjures up experience (and vice-versa), the use of healing language in therapy frees clients to experience new parts of themselves and act differently with the people around them" (p. 314). Thus, what is needed in career practice is a language that frees individuals to construe themselves as self-directed and responsible for their own learning and a language that frees professionals to act differently than they have acted in the traditional roles of teacher and counselor. This then raises the question of the role of traditional "doers" in relation to the learner. For the purposes of this book, the term *career development facilitator* has been selected and will be used where appropriate. We believe that the term provides a sense of thematic unity between career practices, even though they may be conducted in different ways. The term *facilitator* also relates to a process rather than directly to the learner and therefore does not define their relationship in the same way as *teacher* and *counselor* do. Thus, the learner can be placed at the center of the learning process to take from it what is appropriate to his or her needs. Language issues are an important part of systems theory and will be further referred to elsewhere in Part Three.

IMPLICATIONS FOR CAREER DEVELOPMENT FACILITATORS

As reflected in this chapter, the changing nature of the context of work, the nature and needs of the client population, and the settings for career guidance and counseling have implications for the work of career development facilitators. On a broad level, career guidance and counseling practices are "shaped by the economic conditions and political belief systems that prevail in any nation" (Herr, 1992, p. 256). However, career development practices are dominated by what has worked and been done in the past, and their adequacy to "address the career development and workforce preparation needs of tomorrow's citizens" has been questioned (Savickas, 1996b, p. 3). Harris-Bowlsbey (1996a) not only questioned our practices but claimed that they fail to help "people of all ages, colors, and characteristics to not only make satisfying, well-informed choices but, even more importantly, learn and internalize a process for doing that again and again across the life span" (p. 363). Clearly, this is a situation that needs to be addressed if career guidance and counseling practice are to find a place in the 21st century.

Present career development services can no longer rely solely on the practices of the past but must be guided by the needs of the future. It is not adequate for career development facilitators to respond only to the changing economic circumstances of the individual nation and increased globalization. They must also proactively initiate forward-thinking career development services that are in keeping with the trends and policy issues of the environmental/societal system if they are to prepare their clients for the emerging future. Pryor (1991) warned of the need for career counselors to confront these policy challenges so that decisions are not made by organizations on the basis of economic and administrative exigencies rather than client needs.

Thus, the emerging direction and shape of career services reflect the recursive nature of systems theory thinking. Not only is there an interplay between past, present, and future influences, but there is also a constant interplay between economic, social, and workplace changes at global, national, state, and local levels, the career development needs of individuals, and the responses of career development facilitators.

The role of the career development facilitator is undergoing massive change in a context that is also experiencing complex and rapid change. Collin and Watts (1996) suggested five implications of these immense societal changes for career guidance and counseling practices:

1. Career guidance must be accessible to individuals throughout their working lives.
2. The role of career education in initial education must be strengthened and recast as the foundation for lifelong career development.
3. In career guidance methodology, more attention must be paid to the constructivist approaches, helping individuals to develop their subjective career narratives.
4. To provide a formal frame for career narratives but also to maintain the dialectic between subjective and objective careers, career guidance services must support individuals in regular recording of achievement and action planning.
5. Closer links must be forged between career guidance and at least three other areas: financial guidance, relationship counseling, and stress counseling. (pp. 394–395)

Viewed systemically, some of these implications may be addressed by individual career counselors, some by the career counseling profession itself, and some by government and education institutions. Thus, better career development learning outcomes for individuals can be achieved by actions brought about at any level of the systems that are relevant to their career development.

Career guidance and counseling practices are increasingly being viewed as services that must be accountable. Corresponding with this are moves toward public agency fee charging and privatization of services, both of which contradict the long-held social equity tradition of career guidance practices (Pryor, 1991) and raise questions about how the marginalized and unemployed will pay. Steenbarger and Smith (1996) suggested that career services must collect data on service quality in terms of client satisfaction, outcomes, and counselor performance to justify their requests for financial support. Such data gathering is likely to become increasingly important for survival in future service-based environments.

These trends demonstrate that the workplaces of career development facilitators are not exempt from the changes and challenges of the postindustrial society. As a result, individuals in this profession find themselves managing their own workplace changes as well as providing support for others. Thus, like other individuals in the community, career development facilitators must become lifelong learners. This issue will be discussed in Chapters 11 and 14.

LEARNING SYSTEMS

Systems theory and the concept of lifelong learning propose a change in the way we think about traditional career development practices, each of which may be viewed as an open system. Each of the activities of counseling, education, training, and supervision constitutes a learning process, and each occurs as a result of the interaction of at least two individuals. This interaction takes place within a number of interrelated relevant systems. Therefore, all of these processes will be discussed as learning systems in the following chapters. For example, the counseling relationship is a recursive system of interaction operating within the broader system of the lives of the counselor and client, the organization, and society.

CONCLUSION

From a systems theory perspective, the emphasis on the individual as a lifelong learner necessitates a change in thinking about career education, training, counseling, and career counselor supervision practices. As discussed earlier, these processes need to adopt language changes that will reflect the individual's place at the center of the process. Thus, the titles of the following chapters have been carefully selected to reflect language relevant to the changing context discussed in this chapter. Training will be viewed as a learning system in which theory and practice can be integrated. Career education will be discussed as a career development learning process existing within the broader school system. Career counseling will be conceptualized as a therapeutic system. Supervision will be discussed as a means of facilitating the lifelong learning of the career counselor.

11

CAREER DEVELOPMENT LEARNING SYSTEMS

The previous chapter detailed the complex and rapid changes occurring through-out our society as we move into the postindustrial era and the resultant impact of these changes on the career development of all individuals. It is also clear from the discussion in Chapter 10 that lifelong learning is not an option but a necessity, the importance of which cannot be overstated. Learning occurs through all life stages and in all human settings and is the key process by which development occurs. Thus, learning is central to both training and counseling. However, as discussed in Chapter 10, terms such as *student* and *trainee* connote certain modes of interaction between individuals, and as we move toward an era of self-directed learners, these terms are no longer appropriate, given the type of interaction they connote. Therefore, in this chapter, the terms *learner* and *career development facilitator* will again be used. *Learner* also connotes a con-tinuity throughout life, whereas terms such as *trainee* disempower individuals during certain periods of their lives.

This chapter will discuss the nature of knowledge and learning and the use of experiential learning as a means of facilitating learning and establishing learning systems. In addition, it will discuss current perceptions of the training of career counselors. It will also demonstrate that learning processes are means of forging links between theory and practice and between learning and facili-tating. Examples of learning processes will be provided. In particular, a section of the chapter will describe the establishment of a learning system appropriate for facilitating the preparation of career counselors, including an example of a learning process and discussion of the content and assessment of learning.

THE NATURE OF KNOWLEDGE AND LEARNING

"Learning is the process whereby knowledge is created through the transformation of experience" (Kolb, 1984, p. 38) rather than a process of taking in and storing. Knowledge is constructed in relation to past experience, previous learning, and ongoing interaction in the world. This view of knowledge draws on Capra's notion of interconnectedness (discussed in Chapter 8), highlights weaknesses in content-based didactic teaching, and emphasizes the need for learning processes that can facilitate interconnectedness. The recall of previous experiences can facilitate learning by providing an interpretive framework such that new information is fitted into the patterns of the past, a view explored by Bateson (see Chapter 8). Learning occurs through the "active extension and grounding of ideas and experiences in the external world and through internal reflection about the attributes of these ideas and experiences" (Kolb, 1984, p. 52). Individuals actively participate in the creation of their own reality through their relationship with their environment and thus are proactive in their own construction of their knowledge. Learning is a holistic event involving thinking, feeling, perceiving, and behaving, and results in the creation of knowledge and meaning through the medium of language. Thus, knowledge is both an evolutionary result and an interactive process.

Kolb (1984) outlined four critical aspects of the learning process from the experiential perspective, all of which are closely related to the discussion on systems theory in Chapter 8. Specifically, they are

1. the emphasis on the process of adaptation and learning as opposed to content and outcomes
2. the view of knowledge as a transformation process, being continuously created and recreated, not an independent entity to be acquired or transmitted
3. the idea that learning transforms experience in both its objective and subjective forms
4. the idea that to understand learning, we must understand the nature of knowledge, and vice versa (p. 38).

This understanding of learning and knowledge poses a challenge to traditional methods of teaching in which the underlying assumption has been that "learning is brought about by instruction." However, "Instruction does not cause learning. At best it can support and nurture it" (Cunningham, 1992, p. 42). Thus, it is the construction process that must be nurtured, not the acquisition and processing of knowledge.

THE TRAINING DILEMMA

Current concerns about career counseling and training must be viewed against this understanding of knowledge and learning. At a time when the services of career development facilitators are perhaps more in demand than ever before and the profession of career counseling has the potential to establish a firm foothold in the environmental-societal system, it is troubling that serious concerns have been expressed about the training of career counselors and the lack of interest among new counselors in the field of career counseling specifically (Heppner, O'Brien, Hinkelman, & Flores, 1996).

PERCEPTIONS OF CAREER COUNSELING

Krumboltz (1996) posited that

> career counseling is the most complex type of counseling because the counselor must possess all the skills of other counselors and, in addition, know employment trends, methods of preparing for work roles, career assessment techniques, and methods for changing work-related behavior, emotions, and cognitions. (p. 59)

Other writers describe career counseling as a process that assembles personal identity and meaning, which are fundamental to an individual's survival, family lifestyle, and well-being.

These more holistic views of career counseling are in stark contrast with the traditional approach to career counseling, which is founded on the Parsonian tradition (see Chapter 13), where the focus is on values, interests, activities, and information-gathering skills rather than the intertwining of "occupational and family systems" (Davidson & Gilbert, 1993, p. 153). Sadly, however, the positivist Parsonian tradition of matching methods dominates practice and has influenced those entering our profession. For example, Krumboltz (1996) claimed that career counseling is of "diminishing concern" to "neophyte counselors" and that they perceive it as "boring and uninteresting" (p. 59)—observations also made by Betz and Corning (1993) of their graduate students.

In addition, the perceived contrast between personal and career counseling (see Chapter 13) that has recently been discussed in the literature (Subich, 1993), such that career issues are seen as "rational," whereas personal issues are seen as "emotional," and such that the two domains are perceived as separate (Betz & Corning, 1993), has also provoked concern. A disturbing outcome of these perceptions is that "younger professionals continue to move away from the career-related domain" of counseling psychology (Blustein, 1992, p. 714) and that newly qualified counselors not only express a lack of interest in career counseling but report less ability in the requisite skills (Heppner et al., 1996). However, findings such as these are not new; Pinkney and Jacobs found in 1985 that counseling psychologists and graduate student counselors were more interested in personal counseling than in career counseling.

PERCEPTIONS OF CAREER COUNSELOR TRAINING

These findings, particularly those related to new graduates, raise questions about the nature of the training they have received and about whether anything has changed in career counselor training settings over the last ten years. Heppner et al. (1996) found that while trainees' experiences of career counseling were positive, their "most negative experiences were disparaging remarks about career counseling from faculty and supervisors and their formal course work in career development" (p. 105)—a poor reflection on those who should be advocates for the profession. The study also found that the quality of training was low. We concur with these authors in advocating that training processes be considerably improved.

A LEARNING PERSPECTIVE ON THE DILEMMA

Many of the concerns previously expressed have to do with the approach to learning that training in career counseling has traditionally reflected. The Parsonian tradition emphasizes content and the objective acquisition of knowledge, a perspective grounded in the traditional or positivist worldview. There is no room in this tradition for meaning making within individuals as they process their new input. In addition, this tradition emphasizes the transmission of knowledge rather than the transformation and creation of knowledge within the individual. Increasingly, the adequacy of the traditional matching approaches in dealing with the complex issues of career development and workforce issues is being questioned (Savickas, 1996b). Indeed, we could also question whether this approach is meeting the needs of learners, the consumers of career counselor training, who are indicating disenchantment with the profession and their training.

Criticisms of the positivist Parsonian tradition and the separation of personal and career counseling reflect an awareness of the need to ground learning in the broad range of past and present experiences of the individual. They also reflect concerns about insufficient emphasis on subjective processes—an area in which career counseling training has been out of step with a systems theory view of learning and knowledge. In addition, it is clear that the traditional approaches are based on additive perceptions of learning rather than on the integrative view of learning that underpins systems theory. Failure to take a holistic view of learning in both training and career counseling has resulted in lack of interest on the part of the learners, for whom the oversimplification of process does not fit.

Harris-Bowlsbey (1996b) claimed that the profession of career counseling is "at a crossroads at a time when its services are more desperately needed than at any other time in history" (p. 57). This situation raises questions about the direction that training must take if it is to assume its predicted role in the 21st century. As Heppner et al. (1996) reminded us, those providing training "will continue to be powerful influences on the development of interest and proficiency in career counseling among counseling psychology trainees" (p. 123). However, training that continues in the positivist traditions of the past will seriously jeopardize the future of the profession. It is time to review the profession's attitude to learning.

EMERGING SOLUTIONS

Solutions to this dilemma are already emerging. In career counseling, there have been calls for a move toward holistic approaches (Betz & Corning, 1993; Krumboltz, 1993; Richardson, 1993), which in turn necessitates a move toward holistic approaches in training. Heppner et al. (1996) provided insight into how training can become a quality experience and a positive influence on those participating in it. Their suggestions, which reflect the contemporary interest in holistic approaches, include

- broadening trainees' understanding of career counseling away from its equation with "placement activities alone" (p. 119).
- using creative, holistic, and developmental approaches to teaching.
- employing teaching staff with demonstrated interest, innovation, and creativity.
- designing different teaching strategies.
- integrating career and personal counseling by "making career counseling more personal and more integrated with the person's non-vocational life" (p. 121).
- viewing the career counseling process more holistically.
- raising the importance of developing a working alliance with career clients.

Blustein (1992) supported these sentiments by concluding that

- Vocational behaviors must not be seen as a discrete phenomenon.
- Vocational functioning needs to be placed in a broader contextual framework.
- "The centrality of vocational issues in human behavior across the life span" (p. 721) needs to be communicated to students in an "exciting and compelling" manner.
- "Supervisors of counseling practica need to help students learn how to integrate a more complete view of clients, encompassing all of the major domains of their lives (e.g., current relationships, family-of-origin, educational and vocational functioning)" (p. 721).

It is clear from all these suggestions that there is a need to move away from a dependence on didactic teaching toward small group processes based on creative holistic approaches.

TRAINING—A PREFERRED VIEW

Heppner, O'Brien, Hinkelman, and Humphrey (1994) suggested that creativity is a possible key to "ensure that students develop an interest in vocational counseling and clients receive excellent service" (p. 85). Their suggested approaches include guided imagery, metaphor, career genograms, time line analysis, and collage and other art mediums. It is their hope that "these tools may encourage vocational educators and counselors to shift the career counseling paradigm from assessment, match and terminate sessions to dynamic creative and challenging interchanges" (p. 79). While these approaches are appropriate for individual interventions, they lend themselves just as well to training large numbers through the use of structured small group work.

These approaches are consistent with Peavy's (1992) proposal of a "caring curriculum for educating career counselors" (p. 225) that is based on critical self-reflection. He suggested that a curriculum for educating counselors should embody the same goals as career counseling (discussed in Chapter 13). Just as clients are encouraged to reflect on their career story and construct knowledge that leads to a greater range of possibilities, those training to be career counselors should be encouraged to do the same. Peavy suggested that constructed knowledge is "contextual, emotional, intersubjective, passionate, rational, evolving, relational, ethical, and values-based" (p. 225). Learning experiences that enable the creation of knowledge in this way build a greater understanding of the career counseling process and increase the experience of clients.

Career counseling training programs that have adopted these approaches have reported positive outcomes. For example, Warnke et al. (1993) reported that they created a classroom environment that maximized learners' development and enhanced their relationship with clients. In addition, they reported that "each class member had an opportunity to self-disclose, to offer and receive feedback and support, to process emerging views about career counseling, and to become both a teacher and a learner" (p. 185). McMahon (1997a) has reported similar positive outcomes.

Such approaches address concerns previously expressed in this chapter about career counseling practice. The holistic approach is reflective of systems theory thinking, and the creative activities suggested are examples of constructivist approaches that have been advocated by several writers (Collin & Watts, 1996; Young & Valach, 1996).

EXPERIENTIAL LEARNING— A PREFERRED APPROACH TO TRAINING

A problem with constructivist approaches is that they are based on a worldview that is more developed philosophically than methodologically (Granvold, 1996). As a result, they have yet to offer much in the way of specific techniques. However, this is not inconsistent with their belief that the relationship between client and counselor is of prime importance, a relationship that can be deemphasized when the therapist places emphasis on technique at the expense of the client. This is a significant point in that one of the criticisms of career counseling has been its lack of emphasis on the therapeutic relationship (see Chapter 13).

Constructivists use a range of experiential exercises to invite learners to "explore, examine, appraise, experience, define, and redefine themselves, their life experiences, and their directions in life both inside and outside" the learning session (Granvold, 1996, p. 351). Thus, experiential learning has much to offer as an approach to training that is in line with calls to move toward constructivist approaches in career counseling.

The emphasis in experiential learning is on development toward a life-long goal and related self-direction as the organizing principle for education. This is consistent with Peavy's (1992) discussion of agency and fruitfulness and the belief in "persons as self-organizing authors of their own lives" (p. 220). It is clearly the emphasis needed if our education and training are to develop life-long learners who can drive their own careers. "Lifelong learning and career-development programs can find in experiential learning theory a conceptual rationale and guiding philosophy as well as practical educational tools" (Kolb, 1984, p. 18).

Kolb (1984) posited six propositions that characterize experiential learn-ing, each of which is closely related to the worldview that underpins systems theory. Each will be briefly explained.

1. *Learning is best conceived in terms of process, not outcomes* (Kolb, 1984, p. 26). In this approach, learning is not the memorizing and storing of facts. Rather it is the forming and reforming of ideas through experience. Thus, knowledge is constructed by the individual, and outcomes cannot be predicted.

2. *Learning is a continuous process grounded in experience* (Kolb, 1984, p. 27). This is possibly one of the most significant concepts about experiential learn-ing. In essence, it acknowledges that learners come into a situation with prior experience and that new learning is grounded on this prior experience. Thus, the learning process needs to facilitate processes of tapping into the experi-ences on which learners' beliefs and personal theories are founded, examine and test them, and then integrate new ideas into their belief system. "Ideas that evolve through integration tend to become highly stable parts of the person's conception of the world" (Kolb, 1984, p. 28).

3. *The process of learning requires the resolution of conflicts between dialecti-cally opposed modes of adaptation to the world* (Kolb, 1984, p. 29). This proposition recognizes four modes of experiential learning: concrete experience, reflective observation, abstract conceptualization, and active experimentation. These four modes form the basis of the four-stage experiential learning cycle through which new knowledge, skills, or attitudes are achieved. Effective learners need all four modes. In essence, learners must be able to "involve themselves fully, openly and without bias in new experiences, . . . reflect on and observe their experi-ences from many perspectives, . . . create concepts that integrate their observa-tions into logically sound theories, . . . [and] use these theories to make deci-sions and solve problems" (Kolb, 1984, p. 30). Any one or all of these processes may govern the learning process at a given time. This cycle opens the way for a richness of learning processes that accords with the creativity in career counse-lor training that commentators have advocated (Heppner et al., 1994). In addi-tion, learning processes that draw on these four modes of learning cater to the learning styles of all individuals in the learning system.

4. *Learning is a holistic process of adaptation to the world* (Kolb, 1984, p. 31). Kolb (1984) described learning as "the major process of human adaptation" (p. 32) and as involving the integrated functioning of the human system, in-cluding thinking, feeling, perceiving, and behaving. Basically, as an open sys-tem, an individual continually receives input that interacts with his or her in-

terpretive framework, with the outcome of learning and knowledge. This reflects Granvold's (1996) claim that learning is brought about by "perturbations produced by the interactions with the world" (p. 347). Thus, as the individual system receives input, it begins a process of "evolutionary self-organization—a dynamic organization-reorganization activity" (Granvold, 1996, p. 347). Knowledge development, specifically self-knowledge, is assumed to follow this pattern.

5. *Learning involves transactions between the person and the environment* (Kolb, 1984, p. 34). As evidenced in the discussion of proposition 4, learning involves a "transactional relationship" between the individual and his or her environment that has dual meaning. First, it has subjective and personal meaning for the individual, as in the case of an experience of joy. Second, it has objective and environmental meaning. These two meanings transact in an active self-directed process.

6. *Learning is the process of creating knowledge* (Kolb, 1984, p. 36). Knowledge is created through the interaction of subjective and objective experiences in the process called learning. Thus, knowledge is a continuous process of creation and re-creation.

PREPARING CAREER COUNSELORS

CREATING A LEARNING SYSTEM

From a systems theory perspective, any situation in which learning takes place may be construed as a learning system. Learning systems may occur incidentally, as in the case of an individual interacting with another person or another influence from his or her system, or they may be intentionally constructed. Examples of intentionally created learning systems include those found in workplaces, classrooms, and other learning sites, such as counseling clinics.

A system designed to facilitate career development learning contains a career development facilitator and a learner or learners, all of whom have prior personal experience of career development and some of whom may have experience in career development theory and career counseling. It is recognized that each learner brings a unique perspective to the learning process and indeed will leave with a unique perspective (Bednar, Cunningham, Duffy, & Perry, 1992). Thus, while the formation of the learning system and the provision of learning experiences may be intentional, the nature of the learning constructed by the unique perspective of the individual learner cannot be intentionally planned.

DEVELOPING A LEARNING ALLIANCE.   Learning is best facilitated by a constructivist learning environment. Fundamental to developing a learning system is the development of a relationship—a learning alliance. Just as the quality of the relationship is critical to a constructivist approach to counseling (discussed in Chapter 13), so it is important in a constructivist approach to training. Thus, as with any relationship, care must be taken, while establishing a learning system, to build a sense of trust in the training group so that important sharing and learning can take place. The use of group processes and experiential learning techniques enables learners to become both participants in and contributors to their own and each other's learning. This is an essential component of creating a constructivist learning environment because it enables a multiplicity of perspectives to be shared, and these contribute to the construction of understanding (Bednar et al., 1992). Without a trusting, safe, and caring environment, this sharing may not occur.

CLARIFYING THE PROCESS AND LEARNING OBJECTIVES.   Given that this type of learning environment may be new to some people, it is important that the nature of the learning process be clarified when the learning system is first formed so that the members of the system understand how learning will be facilitated, what their role is, and what the role of the facilitator is. It also must be recognized that each learner in the group will have his or her own needs. The learning process is guided not by preset content-related learning and performance objectives but rather by the needs of the learners in relation to their experiences with the world. Therefore, it is important that learners be given an opportunity to articulate their needs. Thus, facilitation becomes a process of balancing group and individual needs while facilitating a learning process. However, it is also useful to provide opportunities for groups to discuss and review their experiences of learning in the group so that adjustments to the learning process can be made.

THE LIFE OF THE LEARNING SYSTEM.   In traditional group learning situations, group process has been described as progressing through stages, such as the much-cited stages of forming, norming, storming, and performing (Watson, Vallee, & Mulford, 1980). While such linearity is not in keeping with a systems theory perspective, these stages draw attention to the fact that at different times groups will have different needs that should be taken into account by the facilitator.

THE LEARNING APPROACH.   Creative approaches using the structure of experiential learning can cater to the learning styles of all individuals. They can also provide opportunities for personal reflection, sharing, and self-learning. However, students are always advised to share only that personal information that they feel comfortable sharing. The issue of confidentiality needs to be discussed.

AN EXAMPLE OF AN EXPERIENTIAL LEARNING PROCESS

The following example describes an experiential learning process that we have used to teach career counseling. It illustrates the relationship that can exist between the individual learner, the facilitator, theory, and practice. It is important to remember that learners are told in advance that the activities will require them to participate in personal reflection and sharing with others. They are advised to share only what they feel comfortable sharing.

This example demonstrates the incorporation of Kolb's (1984) four modes of learning into the experiential learning activity. The learning activity is con-

L E A R N I N G   A C T I V I T Y

USING THE SYSTEMS THEORY FRAMEWORK TO EXPLORE CAREER DEVELOPMENT

This process enables learners to reflect on the influences on their career development and to note the changes and consistencies over time.

PART 1—GROUNDING IN EXPERIENCE.   Learners are asked to reflect on their life at school-leaving age. The facilitator guides a reflection process using a series of questions to encourage learners to reflect on themselves at that time, the subjects they studied, extracurricular activities, interests, abilities, the type of person they were, and any cultural considerations. They are then asked to think about the significant people in their lives at that time, including friends, family, teachers, acquaintances, and TV and movie role models. Following this, they are asked to think about their socioeconomic circumstances, where they lived, and what work or further education opportunities were available. The guided reflection is completed in stages, and after each stage, the learners write relevant information on a blank copy of the systems theory framework. The facilitator uses a set of overhead transparency overlays of the systems theory framework as presented in Chapter 9 to guide the activity. Learners then complete another framework for their current stage of career development and take time to compare the two and look for patterns, similarities, and differences.

PART 2—MULTIPLE PERSPECTIVES OR REFLECTIVE OBSERVATION.   With a partner, learners examine their diagrams and compare and contrast them. Each learner uses his or her counseling microskills to help the other explain his or her diagrams and extract meaning from them. Thus, in trying to be helpful to their partners, learners keep in mind the four dimensions of career counseling suggested by Peavy (1992): relationship, agency, meaning making, and negotiation.

PART 3—CREATING CONCEPTS; INTEGRATING OBSERVATIONS INTO LOGICALLY SOUND THEORIES.   Each pair joins with another pair, and the two pairs share their observations. On the basis of their comparisons, learners develop a list of observations or generalizations about career development. In the whole group, learners present and discuss their generalizations about career development.

PART 4—MULTIPLE PERSPECTIVES.   The facilitator provides input on definitions of career development and the systems theory framework.

PART 5—REFLECTIVE OBSERVATION.   Learners resume work in their small groups and discuss the application of the input in their own lives.

PART 6—MAKING DECISIONS AND SOLVING PROBLEMS.   In small groups, learners discuss the question: "How could you apply this exercise to your practice as career counselors?"

PART 7—MULTIPLE PERSPECTIVES.   In the whole group, learners present the applications to the rest of the group.

ducted in several parts and illustrates how the elements of experiential learning can be interwoven through the learning activity.

The example also illustrates the recursiveness of the learning system between theory, practice, individual learners, and the facilitator. Learning is centered on the learners and their experiences. The learning process elicits the experiences and interpretive framework of the individual learner, through which new information is received. Learning and knowledge unique to each individual result. In addition, the example illustrates the role of the facilitator as being less directive, in keeping with constructivist thinking.

Parts 6 and 7 of the learning process are critical in that they facilitate the link between learning in the classroom and later work as a counselor. For example, participants may suggest that clients could participate in the same reflective process with a counselor. Thus, learning in the classroom can be seen to have direct application to work as a career counselor, participation in the process enables participants to see the relevance of the process to their clients, and participants' role in facilitating the reflection of another in the classroom empowers them to use the process with clients in their later work.

THE CONTENT OF LEARNING

The complexity of the society in which we live and the complexity of career counseling, described by Krumboltz (1996) and others, necessitates that those learning to become career counselors be provided with a broad range of learning experiences that reflect the breadth of content applicable in this field. For example, the National Career Development Association (1992) list ten areas related to career counseling in which learners should demonstrate their competency: career development theory, individual and group counseling skills, individual/group assessment, information/resources, program management and implementation, consultation, special populations, supervision, ethical/legal issues, and research/evaluation. It is not the intention of this chapter to list all of the content areas. This is done elsewhere (see, e.g., Hutton & Splete, 1995). However, this chapter will briefly address several key learning areas.

SELF-LEARNING.   Throughout life, learning experiences are integrated by individuals so that they "shape" to some extent their philosophy of life or the meaning they attribute to experience. It is through this interpretive framework that new input is received and output is channeled. Thus, a counselor's interaction with a client—for example, how he or she responds to input from the client and reacts toward the client—is determined by the counselor's interpretive framework. Therefore, counselors' hopes for their clients can be reflections of their own values or, in Corey's (1991) words, "The goals and therapeutic methods of the counselor are expressions of his or her philosophy of life" (p. 20). An essential part of career counselors' training, therefore, is to investigate their own individual experience and learning and uncover beliefs, values, and attitudes that could affect the counseling process. The learning activity discussed previously is an example of a mechanism for this process.

MULTICULTURAL LEARNING.   Learners live in a diverse multicultural society, and it is critical that they be taught "to incorporate a multicultural perspective into the practice of career counseling" (Swanson, 1993, p. 48). Multicultural diversity, as described by Swanson, is interpreted more broadly than in the traditional focus on racial and ethnic minorities. In her view, multiculturalism includes issues related to "gender, life-style, sexual orientation, age, socioeconomic status, religion, and physical disability, as well as race and ethnicity" (p. 42). This definition draws attention to the diversity of clients, particularly the groups who have been traditionally neglected in the career field (discussed in Chapter 6). In addition, it has been recognized that individuals may belong to several groups. Such diversity necessitates that the emphasis in counseling be on individuals and the meaning they ascribe to their lives. Thus, learning programs need to reflect commitment to preparing learners to work in culturally sensitive ways with a multiculturally diverse client group by integrating appropriate multicultural learning experiences.

CAREER DEVELOPMENT THEORY.   A sound base in career development theory is essential for those preparing to become career counselors. As illustrated in Figure 10.1, the individual learner is the site in which theory integration and integration between theory and practice are forged.

COUNSELING THEORY AND PRACTICE.   One of the criticisms of career counseling discussed previously is that it may neglect the relationship with the client and oversimplify the career counseling process. Those preparing to be career counselors need to be skilled counseling practitioners as well as having a knowledge and understanding of career theory and practice. Greater links need to be developed between these two disciplines.

USE OF TECHNOLOGY.   While the use of technology in career counseling will be discussed more in Chapter 13, it is important that learners be aware of its potential as a learning tool and be skilled in its use. In fact, technology is now an integral part of progressive learning environments. From a constructivist point of view, information-processing technologies facilitate learning that enables the learner to actively use knowledge and skills (Perkins, 1992) and decreases the emphasis on didactic patterns of interaction between learners and facilitators.

CAREER ASSESSMENT.   Career assessment still holds a significant place in career counseling. Therefore, learners still need to be trained in test administration and related ethical considerations. However, a systems theory approach to learning necessitates a different approach to assessment, and narrative forms of assessment have emerged as useful tools. For example, the learning activity presented earlier in this chapter could be used as a form of narrative assessment. This will be discussed further in Chapter 13.

EMPLOYMENT MARKET, SOCIAL AND ECONOMIC TRENDS.   As evidenced in Chapter 10, career counselors are working in a rapidly changing world, where consumers of their services are demanding information on labor market trends that will help them chart their course. While consumers need to be encouraged to seek such information for themselves, career counselors also need to be familiar with this information and its sources. In addition, they have an ethical responsibility for the storage and continued updating of such materials.

ASSESSMENT OF LEARNING OF COUNSELORS IN TRAINING

Assessment using experiential or creative approaches clearly calls for rethinking traditional ways of assessing and grading learners' work. From a constructivist perspective, learning and knowledge are created in the individual and cannot be predetermined or predicted. Therefore, as mentioned previously, learning objectives are not used. Rather, they emerge in each individual learner in relation to his or her experience of the world (Bednar et al., 1992). "Assessment is not a separate activity carried out after instruction, using some pseudo-scientific instrument purported to reveal the truth of a student's accomplishment" (Cunningham, 1992, p. 39).

Thus, it is not adequate to set papers or essays on the basis of content. These assess accumulated fact, not knowledge or learning. Assessment must be grounded in realistic settings or tasks and must evaluate how knowledge has been integrated into an individual's perspective and practice. Two elements guide the evaluation of learning and are illustrated in the following questions: (1) "To what degree does the learner's constructed knowledge of the field permit him/her to function effectively in the discipline?" and (2) To what extent can the learner "defend his/her own judgements?" (Bednar et al., 1992, p. 29). Techniques such as keeping a journal and practically applying learning to one's work or life situations are more appropriate assessment tools. In addition, they forge links between theory and practice. Learners can also be involved in establishing assessment criteria or developing their own ways of demonstrating their learning. For example, they can critique videotapes of themselves engaged in counseling. It should also be remembered that the "one size fits all" approach discussed in Chapter 12 will not be appropriate to the assessment of learning. Different forms of assessment may be needed to cater to the needs of individual learners.

If we are using experiential or constructivist conceptualizations of learning, objectification of learning through scaled grading is also not appropriate. Learning is mapped onto prior experience, and learning and knowledge are evidenced by the learner's being at a different point from the one at which he or she began. However, given the elements of evaluation mentioned previously and the ethical responsibilities we have for preparing professional counselors, competency-based assessment may be appropriate—that is, the assessment that a learner is either competent or not yet competent. Students can be involved in establishing the criteria and methods under which they will be assessed, either individually or en masse. Involvement in the assessment process requires learners to be reflective practitioners who are able to gauge their own progress and learning needs and as a result be more adequately prepared as lifelong learners.

To extend the example from earlier in this chapter, the learner may video-tape how he or she used the systems theory framework as a means of qualita-tively assessing the career development of a client. Thus, assessment of learn-ing illustrates a recursiveness between the individual system, the classroom learning system, and the therapeutic system. For example, the content of an-other learning experience could be related to forming a therapeutic alliance. The learner may then choose to make a video demonstrating how he or she has applied his or her learning. In conjunction with peers or the facilitator, the learner may review the video and thus extend his or her learning even further by iden-tifying in which areas he or she is competent and how he or she would develop competency in other areas. In both cases, the assessment is applied learning rather than the testing of accumulated fact. While these ideas are not new, a constructivist approach to learning would place a higher priority on these meth-ods of assessment than on other forms.

EXPERIENTIAL LEARNING VIEWED FROM A SYSTEMS THEORY PERSPECTIVE

Only a systems theory perspective, using the tool of experiential learning, pro-vides a bridge between theory and practice, teaching and learning, teaching methods and counseling practices, personal and career counseling, and indi-vidual and group counseling. Importantly, unlike the approaches discussed in previous research (Heppner et al., 1996; Pinkney & Jacobs, 1985), this approach is empowering for learners. Their understanding of career development is en-hanced through detailed personal and professional development based on their own experiences. They can see the relevance and place of their prior knowl-edge and skills as links are made between theory, practice, and experience. Throughout the training process, learners act as both facilitators and learner, thus having an opportunity to apply their previously learned skills and con-stantly build on them. The following seven points emphasize the value of this approach in the preparation of career development facilitators.

1. The learning processes forge links between theory and practice. Learn-ers are engaged in activities, including self-reflection, that provide an experi-ence onto which theory can be mapped. Thus, learners are able to construct meaning and knowledge by connecting career theory with their own experi-ences. In addition, their learning is facilitated through a multiplicity of per-spectives. Learners therefore are also more able to understand the process of counseling from the client's perspective.

2. The learning processes provide learners with a range of techniques that can be used with individual clients or groups. The learning activities used in the learning system, such as the systems theory framework activity described earlier, can be used by the learners in their own work with clients. In addition, the ability to facilitate group processes addresses the concerns expressed in Chapter 10 about the provision of career services to an increasing number of

people at a reasonable cost. Conducting career services using group processes provides a possible solution.

3. The skills of counseling are an integral part of the learning processes that are undertaken, and this in turn provides modeling of their importance in the career counseling process. Krumboltz (1993) commented that "career and personal counseling are inextricably entwined—let's act as if we believe it" (p. 148). Training using a systems theory perspective and specific creative approaches is a clear demonstration in the belief that career and personal counseling are inseparable.

4. Learners build working alliances with each other as they process the learning activities and in so doing draw heavily on the counseling skills they have previously learned, thus forging links between personal and career counseling. For example, developing a learning alliance, as discussed previously, is modeled in the classroom and sets a standard for the learner's work with clients. Importantly, this addresses a criticism that in career counseling, "often there is not enough focus on the counselor's deliberate building of the working alliance" (Meara & Patton, 1994, p. 165).

5. The breadth of issues addressed in the group processes and the multiplicity of perspectives to which learners are exposed reflect the complexity and advances in career development theory, specifically the place of work in people's lives (Richardson, 1993, 1996). In addition, the complexity of influences that affect an individual's career development and the concepts of lifelong career development and career in the broad context of a person's life can be illustrated.

6. The emphasis in learning is clearly placed on the individual, thereby illustrating the inseparability of the "career" and the "personal" in our systems theory framework. As Richardson (1993) stated, it is not tenable to "separate the study of career from the multiple and interacting strands and trajectories of development that make up the texture of lives over the life span" (p. 431).

7. Importantly, these learning processes encourage a collaborative relationship rather than one in which the client is "subordinate," a situation that Healy (1990) described as an obstacle in career appraisal. Quality relationships such as that illustrated in the example of the learning activity discussed earlier are conducive to the use of narrative approaches in career counseling (a topic that will be discussed more in Chapter 13).

CONCLUSION

Career counselor educators can be "part of both the problem and the solution" (Heppner et al., 1996, p. 121) of the training of career counselors. In this regard, O'Brien and Heppner (1996) suggested that training programs are vital to increasing the interest and performance of graduates in career counseling. Systems theory thinking and the use of creative approaches and experiential learning will ensure that career development facilitators will be a part of the solution.

12

CAREER DEVELOPMENT LEARNING IN SCHOOL SYSTEMS

The systems theory framework presented in Chapter 9 emphasized the importance of school to the career development system of individuals. McMahon and Patton (1997b) noted that this influence can be intentional or unintentional and that it is generally random, "as students are left to make their own links between school and career development" (p. 26). One important way in which the career development of all young people can be intentionally influenced by schools is through the provision of opportunities for career development learning.

As discussed in Chapters 10 and 11, the language used to describe career development practices needs to place the individual learner at the center of the process. The terms used to describe those responsible for career guidance in schools vary and include *career teacher, career coordinator, career counselor,* and *career adviser.* However, the change of focus from teaching to learning necessitates the use of more appropriate terms to describe the role. Gysbers (1990) suggested that teachers be regarded as "advisors, learner managers, or development specialists" (p. 6). However, from the perspective of lifelong learning, in which the focus is on the learner, we believe that the most appropriate term to be used is *career development facilitator.*

Since learning may occur through formal or informal processes, the term *program* has been intentionally omitted. It is the purpose of this chapter to discuss career development learning in schools from a systems theory perspective and in the context of lifelong learning. The chapter will begin with an application of the systems theory framework to schools.

APPLYING THE SYSTEMS THEORY FRAMEWORK TO SCHOOLS

As discussed earlier, schools are an influence on the career development of individuals who, in our view, are learners and direct consumers of the learning experiences provided. As such, schools are a subsystem of the system of interconnected influences on each individual student (as depicted in Figure 9.2).

However, the systems theory framework can be applied to schools as it can to individuals. Figure 12.1 illustrates that schools are systems in their own right, each containing a multitude of subsystems, including administration, teachers, learners, year-level cohorts, curriculum documents, and school policies. If they exist at all, career development learning and career development facilitators are a small subsystem of a school system.

During the industrial era of the 19th century and the early part of this century, school was viewed as a part of a linear progression through certain life stages. For example, young people were expected to start school by a certain age, and a minimum school-leaving age for compulsory schooling was set. Terms such as *school-to work-transition* reflect this view. Such language assumes the separateness of the two systems. In fact, the transition from one system to the other was traditionally the focus point for vocational guidance activities. The notion of a linear progression is also reflected in the curriculum, which traditionally has been developed by education authorities remote from individual schools. This has been a developmental curriculum through which all students pass, spending a year at each level with no opportunity to move through at their own pace, in what Charland (1996) described as "a one-size-fits-all exercise" (p. 133). However, there is ample evidence, discussed later in this chapter, that this approach is not meeting the needs of many young people and is not adequately preparing them for the future.

Consequently, the traditional linear progression is being challenged, and schools are being encouraged to forge close links with employer groups and their local communities. In addition, parents are being encouraged to participate more in education. Recursive interaction between the school system and its social and environmental-societal systems is being fostered. Examples include work experience programs, links to apprenticeships, school/industry partnerships with flexible, individually determined pathways, and community-based learning activities. Thus, the school must also be viewed as a subsystem of a much larger system. This is depicted in Figure 12.1, which also illustrates change over time and the recursiveness between the influences of past, present, and future time, the environmental-societal system, and the school system. The following discussion will first examine career development learning from a time perspective. Second, the school will be presented as a subsystem and also as a system in its own right. Third, elements of the system, including the learners and the career development facilitators, will be discussed. Throughout the discussion, recursiveness and change over time will be illustrated. In addition, a practical exercise based on the systems theory framework will be provided for practitioners who wish to review career development learning in their school.

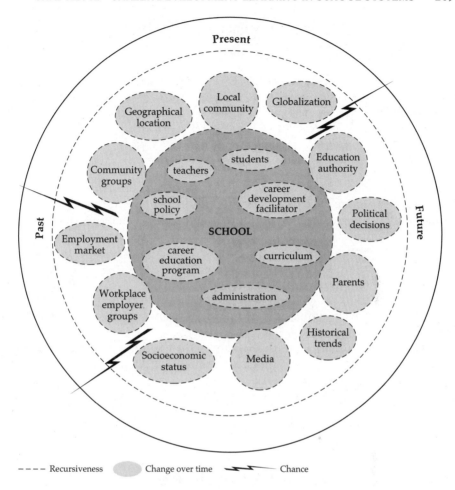

--- - Recursiveness   ⬤ Change over time   ⚡⚡⚡ Chance

F I G U R E   12.1 THE SCHOOL SYSTEM

THE TIME PERSPECTIVE

Time spent in school is but one phase of a lifelong process of career development. However, the importance of that phase cannot be overstated. As discussed in Chapter 10, there is a pressing need for individuals who want to be satisfied in their careers to become lifelong learners and to drive their own careers. If this is the foundation of a satisfying future for our young people, then schools have a major part to play in laying the foundation. Therefore, the needs of the future must drive our practice in schools, and not the tried-and-true content and methods of the past.

It is disturbing that "as we move into a post-industrial, global economy, much of what America's young people learn and experience as students is almost totally disconnected from what they will be expected to know and do as adults" (Crow, 1996, p. 136). If, despite all of the information available on the needs of the future world of work, this is the best our school system can do, then we are badly letting down our young people, and many will move into the future disenfranchised.

THE INFLUENCES OF THE PAST

Clearly, education needs to be framed in the context of future needs. However, our education system was shaped in the industrial era. As such, it has been a lockstep system organized around content and time, in which students have been regarded as the products of their schooling (Crow, 1996). Links between courses and levels in schools and between school programs and the knowledge and skill base required by students when they leave school are seldom shown. The vertical structure of schools, such that students move through one level at a time and are either college or workforce bound, is also an industrial-age concept and not an accurate reflection of the society that young people are entering, in which vertical career paths are now almost nonexistent. In addition, those who do not fit into this system are viewed more or less as "faulty products" (e.g., as unmotivated or incapable). The school system itself is seldom questioned. Thus, these young people are at risk of dropping out and being disenfranchised even more as they enter into a knowledge world centered on lifelong learning.

Within this industrial worldview, career education and guidance programs are merely extracurricular activities taking time away from the curriculum that really matters and that is assessable. Collin and Watts (1996) described career guidance in the industrial era as a "marginal social institution, largely concentrated around the transition from education to employment" (p. 394). This concentration was appropriate only for a bygone era, that of high employment in a "job-for-life" world.

THE SITUATION OF THE PRESENT

Despite the limitations of operating in an industrial-age school system, much effort has been devoted to developing guidance programs that facilitate career development learning in schools. Gysbers (1990), tracing the trend of guidance in America through the 20th century, claimed that it was not until 1972 that the "lack of an appropriate organizational structure for guidance in America's public schools was finally being addressed" (p. 1) through the development of guidance programs.

Guidance had its genesis in schools in the 1920s. At that time, the emphasis was on vocational guidance, particularly occupational selection and placement. Described by Gysbers as the "services model" (p. 3), the approach emphasized six major services: orientation, assessment, information, counseling, placement, and follow-up. Such an approach was founded in the traditions of the positivist matching approaches to counseling (discussed in more detail in Chapter 13). But by the late 1920s, a need for guidance for personal adjustment had been realized, and the "process model" (p. 3), with its emphasis on counseling and the counselor, emerged.

As this trend continued, vocational guidance gradually became subsumed under a broader concept of guidance that also incorporated educational and personal-social guidance. During this period of development, guidance was increasingly seen as an ancillary service in schools, and the emphasis was on the position rather than the program of guidance offered. During the 1960s and 1970s, the concept of developmental guidance programs began to emerge, stimulated partly by concerns about the efficacy of existing guidance services, accountability, and evaluation, and partly by renewed interest in "vocational-career" guidance and developmental guidance. The first manual for a comprehensive guidance program model was completed in 1974 (Gysbers & Moore, 1974).

The work of Gysbers and Moore (1974) is significant in several respects. First, these authors adopted the term *career* in its broadest sense to incorporate all the roles that an individual may assume in various settings throughout the life span and challenged the tendency to use the terms *career* and *occupation* synonymously. Second, they used the term *development* "to indicate that individuals are always becoming" (Gysbers, 1990, p. 9). Third, their emphasis on life career focused on the individual in relation to his or her life context. Fourth, in their emphasis on development, in conjunction with life career, they took a holistic view of the individual (e.g., including emotional and physical needs) and his or her uniqueness in that respect. They defined life career development as "self-development over a person's life span through the integration of the roles, settings and events in a person's life" (Gysbers, 1990, p. 8). In addition, Gysbers and Moore's (1974) comprehensive guidance program model recognized the need for guidance for all students and not just secondary school students at transition points, as had been the case under the service model. Implementation of comprehensive guidance programs has continued through the 1980s and into the 1990s (Gysbers & Henderson, 1997). The work of Gysbers and Moore (1974) typifies what Herr (1992) described as a "major shift from career counseling and career guidance as a random one-on-one support process to career counseling or guidance as a program that is accountable for specific educational or career-related outcomes" (p. 270). In this context, Herr mentioned the recent development of national guidelines and competency statements that outline the content of career guidance programs. He also acknowledged advances in the identification of career guidance goals and resources and the evaluation of career guidance outcomes. However, the implementation of such programs seems to be in the early stages, and although programs of materials and national guidelines are available, comprehensive guidance programs vary widely, "from minimal at the one end to exemplary at the other" (Shears, 1996, p. 10).

The peripheral position of career development learning in schools shows the difficulties under which career guidance and counseling practitioners have worked in trying to implement such programs. McMahon (1997b) described this situation in Australia, claiming that the rhetoric surrounding career education had not been matched by either funding or implementation policies. Thus, career guidance and counseling have generally not received appropriate enabling support. Watkins (1994b) suggested that coordinators of such programs have been rendered impotent by the following unstated directives:

1. Give them no structure to work in.
2. Give them no budget.
3. Give them no symbolic support from senior managers.
4. Subject them to wholesale "role-sending": "You're the expert: your job is to do it," "You're stealing time from me," "You're just a co-ordinator: I'm the real thing," "We need someone to do this—you'll do."
5. Make sure you never make a clear statement about their role and what it is meant to achieve. (p. 146)

While this situation is far from desirable, it is one that many career development facilitators would recognize.

   In the past, career guidance and counseling practitioners have been the only voices extolling the virtues of career development learning as preparation for young people's futures, and they have been peripheral to mainstream education, the dominant focus of the industrial era. However, the inadequacies of our education system in preparing young people for the world of work have been brought into sharp focus by problems of high youth unemployment and school-to-work transition problems. As the social and economic significance of this situation has been realized, so too has it been realized that "the social significance of career guidance could potentially be much greater in the post-industrial era" (Collin & Watts, 1996, p. 394). Thus, the place of career guidance and counseling for students in our schools is being strengthened as a result of increasing awareness of its integral part in individuals' environmental-societal system and its potential advantages to individuals and to society generally.

   Charland (1996) described a career as "basically continuing education." If this is the case, and if individuals are expected to become lifelong learners, then they must become active in their learning process at school, and they must be enthusiastic about continuing learning throughout life beyond their school years (Ellyard, 1993). However, their learning is still predominantly teacher directed according to a preset curriculum with a focus on additive knowledge. Thus, while the implementation of comprehensive guidance programs in schools is commendable, such programs, to be successful, must use processes that develop lifelong learning strategies and must emphasize learning based on the incorporation of knowledge into an individual's frame of reference.

MOVING TOWARD THE FUTURE

Significant advances have been made, but they have been constrained by the context of the industrial system described earlier, and there is still a long way to go. Crow (1996), envisioning a restructured school system, described a learning environment with a customized curriculum organized into "multilevel, interdisciplinary learning communities where the operant word is learning and everyone learns from everyone else" (p. 138). Learning systems such as these were discussed in more detail in Chapter 11. Connections are made between learning in school and learning in the broader community. Career development learning is an integral part of the curriculum. In a reversal of industrial-era notions, learners are viewed as consumers of a product, education. Built into this system are regular meetings between students and staff about improving learning for everyone and ensuring that the product is meeting the needs of the consumers. Within this system, young people begin a career portfolio at a young age and can relate their learning experiences to their career path. Learners exit this system with what Crow (1996) termed a "certificate of mastery" (p. 139), indicating both their competencies and a career plan that takes them at least a year beyond school. However, they will also need to be empowered to continue this recording and planning process throughout their lives. The importance of recording achievement and action planning throughout life cannot be overstated, for such documents become a source of continuity for individuals through a life of many changes and a mechanism by which learners can become managers of their own careers. As Law (1996c) explained,

> Recording and planning can provide a means for reinstating the concept of "career" in contemporary society. Recording and planning may help people to become learners who can represent themselves and their experience, develop plans on the basis of what they learn, and negotiate with others concerning the new opportunities which implement these plans. Such people are forging for themselves a genuinely developing career—whether conducted in employment or the wider work scenario. It may be one of the most valuable means we have for enabling people to make continuing sense of increasingly discontinuous experience. (p. 267)

While this description of learning in the future may be viewed as idealistic or impractical, its contrast with the present system provides a reminder of how far the present education system has to progress if it is to prepare its consumers adequately for a changing world.

In addition to significant changes in the nature of learning and schooling, changes in the emphasis of learning are required. Whereas learning in the industrial system focused on content, learning in a postindustrial system needs to focus on processes. For example, learning increasingly must focus on the processes of learning, thinking, planning, problem solving, working in teams, negotiating, communicating, monitoring, evaluating, and using technology (Ellyard, 1993; Staley & Carey, 1997; Walz & Feller, 1996). In addition, Ellyard (1993) was adamant that "failure to become literate or numerate ensures failure in a modern technological world" (p. 5) because it denies one access to rapidly changing information bases. Thus, the present industrial-age school system is no longer adequate to prepare our young people for the present, let alone the future. It may be time for yet another restructuring of the school system, this time guided by the career development needs of the lifelong learners of the 21st century.

THE SCHOOL AS A SUBSYSTEM

Schools do not exist in isolation, and increasingly closer links are being forged between schools and the social and environmental-societal systems. Plas (1986) drew attention to the connection between the school and the larger system and the exchanges that occur between them. However, it is of concern that at a time when more emphasis is being placed on the need for career development learning, "legislators, principals, parents, and even some counselors are still confused, if not woefully uninformed, about the contributions of school counseling programs and the role of school counselors" (Borders & Drury, 1992, p. 487). These authors also noted that informative resources, though available, are scattered and that it is difficult for school counselors to advocate, plan, or evaluate their comprehensive guidance programs.

McCowan and McKenzie (1994) noted that "school programs should be in synchronisation with the communities they serve. That is, they should take account of local situations, conditions and initiatives" (p. 32). Such comments are particularly pertinent to career development facilitators in relation to both the changing social system and the changing environmental-societal system. In addition, Pryor (1991) drew attention to the need for career guidance professionals to become involved in policy issues, since it is through policy that funding provisions are determined. He maintained that as massive social changes have occurred, guidance has become politicized, and the challenge now is for career guidance providers to balance their responsibilities to their clients with their responsibilities to their employers.

While the school should be responsive to the community that it serves, the community can also respond in some ways to the needs of the school. There is a resource role for parents, employers, and other members of the broad school community to play in the career development of young people. For example, members of the social system may act as role models or interpreters for learners or parents. A strong recursive link between the school and the community that it serves will help to strengthen the career development learning of its young people. The role of the career development facilitator is pivotal if profitable exchanges are to occur.

ACCOUNTABILITY

The closer links between career development learning, schools, and the wider system have drawn attention to the need for accountable practice and demonstrated outcomes. In this regard, Beavers (1995) stated that guidance professionals "can no longer avoid the demand that we be accountable by pretending that guidance and counselling goals and methods are of such an esoteric nature that they are not amenable to evaluation" (p. 8). In addition, he claimed that career facilitators must be able to demonstrate the positive student outcomes of their programs in order to receive ongoing funding.

The move toward comprehensive guidance programs is significant in that it has provided a mechanism for addressing these concerns. This is reflected in the elements of Gysbers' (1990) program model, which include definition and philosophy, rationale, and assumptions. Integral to his assumptions is the reminder that "planning, designing, implementing, and evaluation must continue even long after the program is put in place" (p. 13).

McCowan and McKenzie (1994, 1997) advanced the concept of evaluation even further by suggesting that outcomes be demonstrated in terms of knowledge, skills, and attitudes that learners acquire. In addition, they suggested that these outcomes "address the four social contexts of school, family, labour market, and society/economy" (p. 42). This is a timely development, given that government policy and funding for schools and career development learning are increasingly being linked to outcomes. In terms of the outcome/funding link, it is essential that modern guidance programs be developmental programs of activities, with an emphasis on an individual's competencies, and resulting in learner outcomes that can be assessed.

Accountability necessitates responsiveness to the needs of the changing social and environmental system. Herr (1992) reminded us that the changing social and environmental system determines the responses needed from career guidance services and that these responses will differ at different points of an individual's life career. In this regard, Borders and Drury (1992) discussed program renewal, which relates to the systems theory concept of change over time. Specifically, the needs of learners and those who have sociopolitical influence over curriculum offerings change in response to trends in the social, economic, and political systems. Therefore, it would be unwise for career development facilitators not to respond. It is essential that they maintain programs that are seen as responsive, effective, and relevant.

Career development learning, then, must be subject to ongoing evaluation, monitoring, and review (Borders & Drury, 1992; Gysbers, 1990; Gysbers & Henderson, 1997; McCowan & McKenzie, 1994, 1997). The provision of this information to others in the social and environmental-societal system will ensure that career development learning is better understood and that its outcomes meet the needs of the individual, school, social, and environmental-societal systems. As a result, career development learning is more likely to maintain a place in the school curriculum. It is therefore imperative that career development facilitators advocate for career development learning and can articulate its purposes, content, and outcomes to all members of the school system.

THE SCHOOL AS A SYSTEM

The previous discussion examined the recursive links between the school system and the social and environmental-societal systems. However, the elements of the school system also need consideration. This section will focus on the role of the career development facilitator, the learners, and career development learning.

THE CAREER DEVELOPMENT FACILITATOR

Given that career development learning is often considered as peripheral to rather than an integral part of the school curriculum (as mentioned previously), the career development facilitator is faced with many challenges. It seems that despite political documents to the contrary, career guidance, more than any other area, must continually justify its place in the curriculum. Thus, the role of the career development facilitator in schools is multifaceted and involves tasks such as public relations, teaching, curriculum development, acquisition and maintenance of career resources, staff development, and professional development (National Board of Employment, Education and Training, 1991), all of which demonstrate recursive links with other elements of the social and environmental-societal system.

In this regard Cornford et al. (1996) described career development facilitators as "intermediaries" (p. 43) between members of the system, including clients, employers, educational bodies, and government agencies, and claimed that they have a role to play in promoting current thinking about work and learning. Thus, career development facilitators have a resource role in providing current information to parent and employer bodies as well as to teachers and others in the school system. This illustrates the need for career development facilitators to extend their responsibilities beyond the school.

However, career development facilitators frequently are the only people on a school staff with a background and interest in career development. Therefore, the onus is on them not to have a narrow view of career development or of guidance programs but to view such programs in the context of the broader system. This means that career development facilitators must have a sound background in teaching and learning, career development theory, career education, curriculum development, and international, national, and state trends in education policy and the employment market. In other words, they need to comprehend their role from the perspective of systems theory and be able to convey this message to other members of the system.

However, comprehending their role from a systems theory perspective necessitates understanding the emerging worldview and new ways of construing teaching and learning. These new requirements have implications for the training of those new to the profession, as well as for practicing professionals (see Chapter 11). While ongoing training and upgrading of knowledge and skills is intrinsic to their role as lifelong learners, it is essential that their new learning challenge the thinking of the past. Chapter 14 discusses supervision as a means of addressing the ongoing personal and professional development needs of career development facilitators.

The career development facilitator has an important role to play in attending to the career development needs of particular groups within the school community, such as the groups discussed in Chapter 6. The career development facilitator may need not only to be culturally aware but also to raise the awareness of other members of the staff. Awareness of the social context of the school community, and hence the composition of the student body, may necessitate the use of varied approaches.

THE STUDENTS—LEARNERS AND CONSUMERS

A systems theory view of education draws attention to the need to recognize individuals as having unique learning needs. The "one-size-fits-all" approach fails to address the needs of many young people in our school system. In particular, the career development learning needs of women, racial and ethnic groups, gay men and lesbians, and people with disabilities have not been adequately addressed by our school system. Young women, for example, have not been well prepared for vertical career paths, which traditionally have not suited their patterns of career development. However, awareness of special needs and sensitivity to those needs may result in the development of appropriate career development learning programs (Ettinger, 1996). Leong (1996a,1996b), in discussing the needs of culturally different clients, claimed that there was a need to "integrate both the universal approach exemplified by traditional mainstream psychology and the cross-cultural approach" (Leong, 1996a, p. 278).

Additional issues are raised by socioeconomic status and rural location. The review in Part One of this book highlighted the lack of attention to these issues. For example, "The school experiences of poor children are likely to be qualitatively different from those children of high income homes" (Brantlinger, 1992, p. 281), and "Fewer students from rural locations enter and complete tertiary study compared with their urban peers" (Collett, 1997, p. 77). Borders and Drury (1992) discussed research findings indicating that the students who are most likely to need guidance are the least likely to receive it. For example, students from lower socioeconomic backgrounds, from rural areas, or from minority groups have less access to career development facilitators. However, the authors also concluded that in the future these groups would make up a large proportion of the population. This issue must be addressed by career development professionals, particularly if they are to meet the American School Counselors Association guidelines for equity in school counseling programs, which require that all students have equal access to the full range of services provided by the profession, including counseling, resource access, and educational and occupational information.

It is frequently commented that the curriculum is generally directed toward the preparation of young people going on to higher education (Pautler, 1996). Especially given equity concerns, this is an issue that needs to be addressed. Pautler suggested that all students, including work-bound youth, have transition plans as described earlier in this chapter. With the focus in the systems theory framework on the central role of the individual in his or her own learning, it is important that learning systems be developed for all individuals. In addition, an intervention aimed at certain individuals in the school system, such as disabled learners, will have an effect on other elements of the system through a recursive process and may produce new outcomes.

One frequent outcome for those whom the school system has traditionally not served is that they drop out of education. While young people drop out for many reasons, risk factors such as poverty or learning disabilities seem to have a detrimental effect on children's experience of schooling, and higher dropout rates are experienced by students of African American, Hispanic, and low socioeconomic backgrounds (Wirth-Bond, Coyne, & Adams, 1991). Similar findings have been reported in Australia (Miller, 1985). These risk factors indicate the recursiveness that can occur between the intrapersonal and the social systems of the individual and the school system. In a knowledge world where lifelong learning is fast becoming a reality, these young people are at considerable risk. In particular, "Dropouts are 7½ times as likely as graduates to be dependent on welfare, and twice as likely to be unemployed and to live in poverty" (Wirth-Bond et al., 1991, p. 131). While schools may not be able to address the issues presented by the broader system, they are able to address the learning needs of these students within the school system. Thus, schools must be able to identify these students and intervene in appropriate ways to provide them with a chance of a more satisfying career path.

Gysbers (1996) suggested that school counselors should strive to seek greater understanding of various population groups with special needs. First, they should identify special-needs individuals and groups within the school and clarify the nature of their needs. Second, they should attempt to understand these individuals' needs and the life outcomes of not meeting these needs. Knowledge at both of these levels will inform the school counselor about practical ways in which to address the special needs identified, bearing in mind the cautions about the "one-size-fits-all" approach discussed earlier. In addition, Gysbers urged that school counselors advocate for those in special population groups and suggested that "career mentors" (p. 19) might be helpful to students. He claimed that school counselors who advocate for these groups are likely to produce the best results. Patton (1997) concurred and claimed that it is important for career development facilitators to "develop systematic programs for students, teachers, parents, community leaders and others, and to act as advocates in the arena of public policy" (p. 91). Her comment illustrates the recursiveness of the system and the potential of the career development facilitator to act on the social or environmental-societal system to effect change for the individual system. For example, working with parents can empower them to advocate with school or government authorities, which in turn may result in better learning outcomes for individuals with special needs.

The shift toward beginning comprehensive guidance programs in elementary school is important, given that many stereotypes develop at a young age (L. S. Gottfredson, 1981; McMahon & Patton, 1997a). However, from a systems theory perspective, for change to occur in a lasting way, it may be necessary to involve not only the young people but also influential members of their communities, including parents. Sensitivity to the needs of these individuals may require that the career development facilitator take on roles other than counselor or teacher, as suggested previously.

LEARNING CONTENT AND PROCESSES

Career programs in schools often do much to help students explore their interests and abilities. However, it seems that despite broadening of the definitions of career and career development, and despite a recognition of these concepts' complexity, the prevailing influence in career education in schools is still the matching approach of trait-and-factor theory. While the matching approach has merit, it alone cannot account for the career choices that students make. It is a product of the industrial era and the prevailing views and influences of those times, such as differential psychology. Now, however, as evidenced by the development of comprehensive guidance programs, the need to take a more holistic view of career development has been recognized. This is consistent with a systems theory view of career development programs.

Holland (1985a) agreed that in relation to his theory, vocational predictions work better when variables such as age, socioeconomic status, and chance are taken into account. Super (1990), in his life-span, life-space approach, and Vondracek et al. (1986), in their developmental-contextual approach, acknowledged not only a broad range of influences but also the lifelong process of career development. Isaacson and Brown (1993) commented that "the school and its guidance program" have a role to play "in assisting the individual to maximize development as a person" (p. 38). This can only occur if career education moves away from its origins in the matching approaches and information provision and toward programs that are developmental and that attend to the processes and tasks of career development. In addition, career education must be provided for all students.

There is no debate in the literature that career development is a lifelong process. McMahon and Patton (1994) found that career development was a concept understood by children and adolescents from preschool to year 12. However, career development programs, as they are currently taught, are much more likely to be found in secondary schools than in elementary schools. Given that young people understand the concept of career development (McMahon & Patton, 1994), that children as young as five years can express occupational dreams (Phipps, 1995), and that career preferences are formed early (Poole & Low, 1985), it seems that valuable opportunities to influence the socialization and career development learning of many young people are being missed. Therefore, appropriate career development learning must be provided for young people of all ages.

IMPLEMENTING CAREER DEVELOPMENT LEARNING SYSTEMS

As discussed in Chapter 11, the systems theory perspective challenges traditional positivist views on knowledge and learning, teaching and learning, the content learning, the outcomes of learning, and the approaches used to facilitate learning. It requires a shift in worldview. For example, the place of didactic teaching is reduced, necessitating a change in role from that of teacher to that of career development facilitator. Correspondingly, there is a change from an emphasis on information provision to an emphasis on construction of knowledge using learning processes. The role of learner changes from one of passive recipient to one of active participant and constructor of one's own learning. This is reflected in a shift from preset learning objectives to learning objectives generated by each individual in relation to his or her environment. Learning from this perspective is centered on the needs of the individual learner, a feature that has implications for individualization of learning. Thus, Crow's (1996) vision of a restructured school system discussed earlier in this chapter is very much in keeping with systems theory thinking.

Experiential learning has much to offer in facilitating career development and opens the way for activities including group processes, tracking of career development using time lines, role plays, and genograms. In addition, it opens up possibilities for grounding career development learning in the real-life contexts of the family, social, and environmental-societal systems. All of these strategies provide opportunities for learners to explore their career narratives. This is in keeping with Collin and Watts's (1996) proposal that "more attention needs to be paid to constructivist approaches" (p. 394) that help individuals to develop their subjective narratives. Through this approach, learners are able to make links between past and present and to make plans for the future. In particular, Collin and Watts suggested that this approach focus on three tasks: "helping them to 'authorise' their careers by narrating a coherent, continuous and credible story; helping them to invest their career narrative with meaning by identifying themes and tensions in the story line; and learning the skills needed to perform the next episode of the story" (p. 394). Through this approach, individuals can uncover differences between their subjective and objective careers. This is an important concept because, as Savickas (1991) observed, some individuals are not aware that they have a career. In addition, it has been strongly suggested that learners be encouraged to keep records of their achievements and of their action plans (Collin & Watts, 1996; Law, 1996c).

The holistic perspective of systems theory challenges the practice of dividing the curriculum into discrete areas and in particular challenges the traditional separation of career and other learning. A systems theory perspective lends itself to integration of career development learning into the curriculum. Thus, a systems theory approach is in keeping with the long-held view that career development learning works best when integrated into the curriculum rather than as a marginalized extra (Gysbers, 1990; McCowan & McKenzie, 1994, 1997). McCowan and McKenzie (1994) commented that career development facilitators should be able to link career education "to curriculum and classroom practices and these in turn to student development and the world of work" (p. 33). Such interconnectedness reflects a systems theory perspective.

Career development learning from a systems theory perspective provides a means of integrating school and postschool options, since the emphasis is on the skills of career self-management, a lifelong task. This is reflected in suggestions that career development learning contain both content learning and process learning. Content learning includes self-awareness, self-confidence, and political awareness. Process learning includes skills that are transferable throughout the social and environmental-societal systems, such as self-promotion, exploring and creating opportunities, action planning, networking, decision making, negotiation, coping with uncertainty, and transfer skills (Collin & Watt, 1996). In addition, learning needs to be viewed from a developmental perspective. An emphasis on process and on the learner being at the center of the process is in accordance with constructivist approaches. In addition, career self-management skills enable young people to move into the future as lifelong learners prepared to manage their own careers. In fact, this is the ultimate evaluation of learning from a systems theory perspective—that is, how well learners can apply their constructed knowledge in the real-life situations that they encounter.

Under the present school system, it would seem that the needs of learners are not adequately being met. While there is evidence of a new emphasis on career guidance at sociopolitical levels, the response of schools is still guided by the traditional worldview, which may not effectively meet the needs of the future. Thus, schools must review their traditional approach if they are to cater to their diverse consumer group effectively.

REVIEWING CAREER DEVELOPMENT LEARNING IN SCHOOLS FROM A SYSTEMS THEORY PERSPECTIVE

It is timely to review our practice in schools from a systems theory perspective. A significant feature of a systems theory approach is understanding the interconnectedness of the systems discussed in this chapter, in particular the school, individual, social, and environmental-societal systems. In addition, these systems need to be set in a time perspective. Systems theory thinking may be used to review career development learning and the role of career development facilitators. The following provides an example of a process for such a review in the form of questions designed to encourage career development facilitators to reflect on their practice. The reflection will be presented in sections according to the elements of our systems theory framework.

THE TIME PERSPECTIVE

As discussed previously, there is an increased need for our school system, and in particular career development learning, to be shaped by the needs of the future.

- What time perspective is currently guiding learning in my school?
- In what ways am I informing others in the system about the employment market and the society of the future?
- What time perspective is guiding the career development learning that I facilitate?

THE ENVIRONMENTAL-SOCIETAL SYSTEM

The recursiveness between the role of the career development facilitator and the environmental-societal system has been demonstrated throughout this chapter. Career development facilitators need to understand this recursiveness and the nature of the influences to facilitate career development learning proactively.

- What are the major influences affecting career education at national, state, and local levels?
- What are the policies affecting youth, training, and higher education that will affect the career development of the young people with whom I work? How do these affect the role that I need to play in my school?
- What resources may be accessed from national, state, and local bodies?
- What programs or funding are available that may benefit specific groups of learners with whom I work?

THE SOCIAL SYSTEM

Recursiveness between the career development facilitator and the social system of the school has the potential to enhance the career development learning outcomes for young people.

- In what ways can I encourage parents and members of the wider school community (e.g., employers) to be involved in the career development learning of the young people in my school system?
- In what ways can I facilitate understanding of lifelong learning and career development with parents and members of the wider school community?
- What links have been forged between the school system and the local community system?
- In what ways is the school system responsive to the needs of the local community system?
- What roles do school personnel play or need to play in relation to the broader school community?

THE SCHOOL SYSTEM

Career development learning occurs within the context of a school and needs to be reflected in the school goals (McCowan & McKenzie, 1994). It also needs to meet the needs of its particular group of learners. The following questions may guide a review of the learners in a particular school system.

Increasingly, students are being seen as consumers of a product, education. How well the school system meets their needs has important implications at sociopolitical levels. Therefore, it is important to pay attention to the needs of the consumer population.

- Who are the learners who attend your school, and what are the specific needs within your learner population?
- Which learners are encouraged and which are discouraged from attendance?
- How is the uniqueness of individual learning styles recognized and catered to?
- What happens to those learners whose needs are not catered to?
- Are the learners prepared to be and capable of being lifelong learners?
- How is career development learning viewed by the learners?
- What input do the learners have into career development learning?
- Is the concept of lifelong career development understood by learners?
- Is the career decision making in which learners participate set within the perspective of lifelong career development?
- What provision is made for follow-up with individual learners?
- Are the learners empowered with the processes of career self-management?
- Are the learners equipped with an understanding of the future world of work as well as the present world of work?
- Is lifelong career development learning available to all learners in your school?

CAREER DEVELOPMENT LEARNING

On the basis of the systems theory framework, career development learning should provide an awareness of the following: the lifelong nature of career development, the range and nature of the influences on career development, processes for coping with the ongoing changes experienced throughout career development, and an awareness of the future world of work. In addition, programs need to be developmental and to attend to the needs of particular individuals or groups of individuals. Career development facilitators reflecting on career development learning in their school could be guided by the following questions:

- What is the place of career development learning in your school?
- Who in the school supports career development learning?
- What is the role of the career development facilitator in the school?
- How is the position of career development facilitator viewed by the school administration?
- How is the position of career development facilitator viewed by the other staff?
- How are time, resource, and staff allocations determined by the school administration?
- Is the focus of career development learning on career decision making or career development?
- In career development learning, what emphasis is placed on influences other than interests and abilities?
- Is the concept of lifelong career development understood by the school staff?

CAREER DEVELOPMENT FACILITATORS

Career development facilitators are also lifelong learners involved in a process of lifelong career development, a process shaped by a range of past, present, and future influences. It is important for career development facilitators to have an understanding of the influences on their own career development, the values and attitudes they hold, and their current stage of career development. Personal reflection would include examination of the following questions.

- Am I a lifelong learner who is continually updating my own learning, including personal learning, trends in career development theory, world-of-work knowledge and trends, and teaching and learning practices?
- What values and attitudes do I hold in relation to career development and the world of work?
- What is the pattern of my own career development?
- Do I understand the relationship between career education and career development?
- Do I oversimplify career development learning?

- Do I facilitate learning about the processes involved in career development as well as providing information?
- Do I understand the use of experiential learning techniques?
- Do I understand the systems worldview that is challenging the traditional positivist worldview?
- Do I understand the implications of the systems worldview in terms of my own personal views of learning and career development practice?

CONCLUSION

Career development learning in schools establishes a pattern of lifelong learning in the context of lifelong career development. The content and process of career development learning are recursively linked to the needs and circumstances of the social and environmental-societal systems in which school systems exist. An examination of the systems theory framework demonstrates its applicability in the school setting. Specifically, it can be used to inform the input and processes of career education programs, review the roles of career development facilitators, and examine the relationships between students, career development facilitators, the school, and the broader school system. Awareness and understanding of the systems theory framework can only enhance the work already being done by career development facilitators.

Application of the systems theory framework will serve to move career development learning away from reliance on the matching approaches of the traditional worldview and the industrial era and toward an approach that is in keeping with the emerging worldview and the future. In particular, it will place the emphasis on individual learners and empower them to be lifelong learners and constructors of their own careers.

13

THERAPEUTIC SYSTEMS

Career counseling "operates at the interface between personal and societal needs, between individual and opportunity structures, between private and public identities" (Watts, 1996a, p. 229). Increasingly, it is being seen not only in terms of its individual worth but in terms of its economic worth to nations, as a sociopolitical activity. Such thinking challenges career counselors to think about their profession in a way not previously imagined. In addition, it provides evidence that the radical economic and societal changes experienced in the postindustrial era are not just the topic of "abstract musings" (Peavy, 1996, p. 142) but will have a lasting impact on our profession.

As demonstrated in Chapter 10, the stage is set for the profession of career counseling to take a pivotal role in the lives of individuals and society. However, its readiness for this role is in question (Savickas, 1996b). Peavy (1996) claimed that counseling was "badly in need of revisions in order to attain synchronicity" (p. 142) with the changes in society and with the complex issues confronting individuals. It seems that career counseling is in a similar, if not worse, position.

Much attention has been paid in Part Three of this book to what Lent (1996) described as a "collective wake-up call" (p. 59). Challenges such as the redefinition of career, the rapidly changing society and its increasingly complex needs, demands being made on career counseling at sociopolitical levels, and the need to examine service delivery require a response. Complacency would be to the detriment of not only the profession but also those who need its services (Harris-Bowlsbey, 1996b). However, taking up the challenge will ensure that the profession of career counseling has a stimulating future and a vital role to play in the lives of the individuals and nations it serves.

It seems that as the environmental-societal system is looking for answers to the challenges it has set, our profession is grappling with issues of its own. Debates such as those about the links between personal and career counseling and between career development theory and practice have been featured in recent publications (e.g., Collin & Watts, 1996; Feller & Walz, 1996; Savickas, 1995, 1996b; Savickas & Lent, 1994; Savickas & Walsh, 1996; Subich, 1993). Savickas (1995) described these debates as schisms and focused particularly on those between career theory and practice, career theory and research from other psychological sciences, and career counseling and psychotherapy.

This chapter will not discuss these debates at length, since that has been done in the aforementioned publications. Rather, it will focus on the practice of career counseling, the service it can provide to the consumers of the future, and its readiness to take a leading role in the future. However, such a discussion needs to be set in the context of the history and debates of the career field. These will be examined briefly, and trends emerging out of the debates will be discussed as possible paths to the future. In addition, the systems theory framework will be used as a means of conceptualizing these trends.

BEHIND THE SCENES

At its genesis in the early 1900s, vocational guidance, as it was then known, was unified theoretically and practically in the work of Frank Parsons (1909). As shown in Part One of this book, his work has been followed by a proliferation of theories that have added great depth to the career field. For much of that time (as discussed in Part Two), theory and practice were based on the logical positivist worldview of the trait-and-factor or matching approaches. Since that time, theories of increasing complexity, such as the segmental model of Super (1990, 1992), the developmental-contextual approach of Vondracek et al. (1986), and the social cognitive career theory of Lent et al. (1994), have been proposed to accommodate expanded definitions of career and career development and to locate career in the context of people's lives.

Despite this, the relevance of career theory to the lives of many individuals has been questioned (see Chapter 6), not only at a theoretical level but also at a practical level (Harmon, 1996; Herr, 1996a; Holland, 1996; Richardson, 1993, 1996; Savickas & Walsh, 1996). It has been suggested that the gulf between theory and practice is so great that they may be regarded as different sciences. Yet in the move toward a postindustrial society, with changes in the social and environmental-societal systems posing considerable challenges to career development facilitators, it is crucial that guiding principles be appropriate and relevant.

According to Osipow (1996), connecting theory and practice is difficult because career theory is abstract while career practice is concrete, and career development theorists "have sought to apply theory to counseling only as an afterthought" (p. 404). It could be argued that the gap between theory and practice has widened because practice, having direct contact with changes in the economy and society, must respond in concrete ways. For example, D. Brown and Brooks (1991) have suggested that "practitioners have been far ahead of scholars" (p. v) in locating the career role in the context of other life roles. Thus, it seems that both the ability of career theory to respond to and address the issues of a rapidly changing world of work and its utility for practitioners is being questioned.

CENTER STAGE: THE TRAIT-AND-FACTOR APPROACH

Despite advances in theory and practice, the dominant paradigm of career development facilitators is still that of the original trait-and-factor approach, evidence that they have been slow to move from the familiar and comfortable positivist process of giving information and matching the person to the job (D. Brown & Brooks, 1996b). In an Australian study that analyzed what counselors actually do in career counseling interviews, N. B. Taylor (1985) concluded that the approach being used was still predominantly the trait-and-factor approach. In an overview of career counseling, Peterson et al. (1991) stated that career counseling appears to have changed little since the days of Parsons. They stated that counselors typically listen to concerns about making career decisions, seek to understand these concerns, assist in making connections to opportunities, formulate alternatives, and help clients evaluate occupational alternatives to arrive at tentative choices.

Rounds and Tracey (1990) contended that while the trait-and-factor approach today has been modified by person-environment fit theory, it is still predominantly a problem-solving approach with emphasis on diagnosis and assessment. This is evidenced in Williamson's (1939, 1965) six-step process of career counseling, which includes analysis, synthesis, diagnosis, prognosis, counseling, and follow-up. *Analysis* is the process whereby the counselor collects data about the client, which is then summarized (*synthesis*) to identify "career problems" (*diagnosis*) that are categorized as "no choice; uncertain choice; unwise choice; discrepancy between interests and aptitudes" (Isaacson & Brown, 1993, p. 372). *Prognosis* involves predictions about the possible success of the individual with regard to his or her goals. *Counseling* occurs if the individual has career problems or has made an inappropriate choice. *Follow-up* examines the viability of the individual's course of action. This approach reflects career counseling's beginnings as a process that was counselor directed, in which the counselor was the "expert" and counseling was centered on career choice only. Decision making was thought to be a rational process, and there was a narrow focus on matching interests, abilities, and world-of-work knowledge. In addition, counselors using this approach paid little attention to the broad system in which the individual operated.

A desirable outcome of this rational approach is that clients learn a basis for present and future problem solving and decision making. However the trait-and-factor approach is guided substantially by the process and the professional rather than by the individual client. In fact, Rounds and Tracey (1990) commented that "the first four steps were the province of the professional" (p. 4). However, this approach is one of the few that is linked to studies of vocational behavior and also to a counseling theory, that of problem solving.

More recently, trait-and-factor counseling has been informed by person-environment fit theory. This has brought about a shift from the descriptive matching models, with their emphasis on congruence, to a more dynamic, process-oriented model emphasizing person-environment fit. However, while the dynamic person-environment fit models have made a conceptual contribution to career theory, they have not yet contributed in a significant way to career counseling practice.

The trait-and-factor approach has been the subject of much criticism (Krumboltz, 1994). Researchers (e.g., Healy, 1990; Krumboltz, 1993) argue that an overemphasis on this model has led to the popular perception that career counseling consists of nothing more than a quick and simple matching process—what Crites (1981) described as "three interviews and a cloud of dust" (p. 49). As Krumboltz (1994) commented "Trait-and-factor theory . . . paints a picture, creates an image, and draws a map that oversimplifies the complexities of helping people with a wide range of career problems" (p. 15). "Oversimplification" is one of the most common criticisms and centers on the elements of diagnosis, psychometric information, and occupational classification and information.

This criticism overlooks the fact that the trait-and-factor approach is informed by the recognized counseling problem-solving approach and is conducted by trained counselors (Rounds & Tracey, 1990). But despite its grounding in a problem-solving framework, trait-and-factor theory does not help us to understand the increasingly complex issues brought about by today's world of work, such as job-related phobias, sexual harassment, job burnout, dual-career families, unemployment, and job seeking. It also does not address the emotional aspects of these issues.

Thus, the trait-and-factor approach to career counseling finds itself in the curious position of being both much maligned and at the same time commonly used. This unusual position is possibly best understood from the systems theory perspective in terms of time. Trait-and-factor approaches evolved at a time when occupational choice was the predominant issue and was brought to career counselors by clients once in a lifetime (this is reflected in the term *vocational guidance*, which was prevalent at that time). In today's world, however, people change jobs several times in a lifetime, and occupational choice is only one of a myriad of concerns that individuals bring to career counselors. Thus, the map (to use Krumboltz's metaphor) of career counseling has broadened since the time of Parsons and Williamson. Rather than covering the whole map, the trait-and-factor approach now only occupies a small section. Therefore, as evidenced by current practice, there is still a definite place on the map for trait-and-factor counseling.

However, the complexity of the new map, as evidenced by the broadening of career development theory to include approaches encompassing the social and environmental-societal systems and lifelong career development, is not reflected in traditional approaches of career counseling. Savickas (1996a) asked, "How do counselors apply theories that are partial and simple to clients who are whole and complex?" (p. 193). Their sentiments have been supported by others (e.g., Osipow, 1983; Vondracek et al., 1986) who have raised similar concerns. Savickas (1996b) argued that the trait-and-factor approach is unlikely to meet the needs of clients living in the complex world of the future; D. Brown and Brooks (1991) questioned the emphasis that it places on the career to the exclusion of other life roles; and Vondracek et al. (1986) claimed that it is incompatible with their developmental-contextual model, which is more illustrative of the complexity of career development, and that more sophisticated approaches to career counseling are required.

A SCENE CHANGE

As previously indicated, the practice of career counseling has lagged behind that advocated by more recent approaches to both career development theory and counseling practice. This is evidenced by the dominant approach used in career counseling, the trait-and-factor approach, which is based on problem solving. Savickas (1993) urged that career counseling "keep pace with our society's movement to a postmodern era" (p. 205). While counseling practice is moving toward what has been described as the "fourth wave" (O'Hanlon, 1993, p. 3)—that is, the constructivist approaches, including narrative therapy—career counseling is still very much based in the problem-solving mode, which O'Hanlon connected with the "second wave."

Recent discussion on career counseling reflects a move toward constructivist approaches (Collin, 1996; Richardson, 1996; Young & Valach, 1996), which according to Collin (1996) will present a new challenge to career counselors. This challenge is twofold. First, traditional views of career and career development have been questioned, and new definitions have emerged (see Chapter 1). Second, these changes necessitate new ways of thinking about the practice of career counseling that are in keeping with the new worldview. Savickas (1993) suggested that these trends reflect a move away from "seeking truth to participation in conversations; from objectivity to perspectivity" and that career counseling is "reforming into an interpretive discipline" (p. 205).

Thus, career counseling can be seen as an evolving profession. In reality, it has emerged as a profession in its own right only comparatively recently. Herr (1997) explained that for much of its history, career counseling was rarely differentiated from vocational or career guidance and that it was not until the 1960s and 1970s that the term *career guidance and counseling* gave counseling and guidance equal attention. Further, he claimed that only in the last 20 years have calls been made for an expanded role of career counseling in response to changes in society and for changes in definitions of career counseling. Herr stated that the principal content of the new career counseling is the "perceptions, anxieties, information deficits, work personalities, competencies, and motives that persons experience in their interactions with their external environment." He claimed that career counseling is not a singular process but comprises a range of interventions and that it "is no longer conceived as a process principally focused on ensuring that adolescents make a wise choice of an initial job." It can, for instance, be "one of a program of interventions . . . to deal with emotional or behavioral disorders that accompany or confound a person's career problem" (pp. 85–86).

Herr (1997) noted that these changes in the content and processes of career counseling have not occurred in a vacuum but rather are responses to the prevailing conditions in society. This awareness is reflected in Watts's (1996a) suggestion that closer links be forged between career counseling and other forms of counseling that have emerged in response to society's changing needs, such as financial counseling, stress counseling, and relationship counseling. Watts's reasoning illustrates the recursiveness of systems theory. For example, he suggested that "social change is generating considerable uncertainty and ambiguity for individuals" (p. 234) and that these promote anxiety and stress with which career counselors can assist. In addition, he claimed that individuals will increasingly have more responsibility for financial management in relation to "pensions and other forms of social insurance" (p. 234). He also explained that negotiating work roles and family and relationship roles is becoming more complex because they are so entwined. This recursiveness is illustrated in Figure 13.1, discussed later in this chapter. Thus, Herr (1997) described the emergence and development of career counseling as "a process in process" (p. 92).

The changing nature of career counseling is also exemplified in the recent debate about the fusion of career and personal counseling (Hackett, 1993; Krumboltz, 1993; Manuele-Adkins, 1992; Subich, 1993). This debate represented the first serious challenge to the problem-solving traditions of career counseling and drew attention to the need for career counseling to change its practices to be more relevant. It is too simplistic to adopt the approach that individuals can separate career issues from personal issues; as Savickas (1993) stated, "Career is personal" (p. 212).

From a systems theory perspective, there is no debate because the uniqueness and wholeness of the individual is of paramount importance in counseling, and the elements of the individual's subsystems cannot be separated from each other. Burlew (1996) explained that "there is no way to separate issues with which clients come into counseling because they're housed in one body, one mind, and one soul" and that "you can't pull a person apart and dissect mind and spirit issues as clearly as you can separate, for example, the heart from the rest of the body" (p. 375). Imbimbo (1994) suggested that the distinction between career counseling and personal counseling may actually be more in the counselor's perception of the role than in the client. For example, in the six-step process described by Williamson (1939, 1965) the counselor could follow a standard process with each client regardless of his or her needs. Thus the process could become rote and repetitive. Alternatively, a counselor guided by a constructivist view could enter each encounter with a client as a unique experience directed by the client rather than by a formula.

WAITING IN THE WINGS: CONSTRUCTIVISM

As previously mentioned, there is an emerging trend toward the use of constructivist approaches in career counseling, a trend that may make career counseling more relevant and responsive to the times and to the individuals who are its consumers. Such a move can counter the popular perception of career counseling as a simplistic process. The move toward constructivism has to some extent been heralded and influenced by discussion about the fusion of career counseling and personal counseling.

D. Brown and Brooks (1996b) identified four assumptions underlying the emerging constructivist position in career development:

1. All aspects of the universe are interconnected; it is impossible to separate figure from ground, subject from object, people from their environments.
2. There are no absolutes; thus, human functioning cannot be reduced to laws or principles, and cause and effect cannot be inferred.
3. Human behavior can only be understood in the context in which it occurs.
4. The subjective frame of reference of human beings is the only legitimate source of knowledge. Events occur outside human beings. As individuals understand their environments and participate in these events, they define themselves and their environments. (p. 10)

These assumptions are clearly in keeping with the elements of systems theory discussed in Chapter 8. In particular, systems theory emphasizes interconnectedness and the importance of wholes rather than parts. Thus, individuals cannot be separated from their context, and behavior cannot be accounted for in a linear way. Knowledge is constructed within individuals in relation to their experience and cannot be taught. Therefore, theory cannot be applied to individuals; they construct their own personal theory.

Approaching career counseling from a constructivist perspective possibly represents one of the biggest challenges yet experienced by career counselors—"a formidable challenge to the assumptions about reality, knowledge, and causality" (Granvold, 1996, p. 345) held by adherents of traditional positivist approaches to career counseling. Fundamental to the constructivist approach is that human knowing is proactive and that individuals actively participate in the creation of their own reality. In career counseling, this occurs through the use of language and dialogue with the counselor. Language is fundamental to the creation of meaning and knowledge. Knowledge is shaped through dialogue between the career counselor and the client. It is through language that individuals construct their own reality. The process of dialogue between counselor and client and the construction of a new reality is termed *coconstruction*. Thus, through language, individuals construct the story of their careers. Several aspects of the constructivist approach will be discussed in relation to career counseling. They are the nature of the counseling relationship, the nature of the counseling process, the use of language, and the use of narrative approaches. The nature of career assessment within this approach will be also be discussed.

THE NATURE OF THE COUNSELING RELATIONSHIP

Traditional career counseling approaches have seen the counselor take on what may be described as an expert role of solving the client's problems, explaining through assessment, or providing advice. The emphasis in career counseling has been on the "communication dimension" at the expense of the "relationship dimension" (Savickas, 1993, p. 210). Career counselors therefore have been criticized for not paying enough attention to the working alliance or relationship with the client (Meara & Patton, 1994). However, with a constructivist approach, the quality of the relationship is essential, and characteristics such as acceptance, understanding, trust, and caring are critical (Granvold, 1996). In addition, counselors make little attempt to be seen as an authority or to draw conclusions from information (Gergen, 1993). This approach poses a significant challenge to counselors operating from the matching tradition. For example, while assessment data may be gathered, they can no longer be objectively presented as a statement of fact to clients. Rather, their meaning has to be interpreted through language by the individual in dialogue with the counselor. In addition, what can be viewed as assessment is more varied. For example, an individual's own career story could be included as assessment data.

THE NATURE OF THE COUNSELING PROCESS

Traditional positivist approaches to counseling have placed the counselor in a central position, often as a provider of information or in a directive role. However, constructivists are less directive, provide less information, and facilitate a process of exploration and restructuring. This is a process in which the counselor and client join to construct and reconstruct meanings considered important in the client's life through processes such as information sharing, interpretation, supportiveness, encouragement, structuring, and challenge (Granvold, 1996).

Using this approach, there is a shift away from "fixing" the presenting problem. Rather, the approach has a "structural/process orientation" (Granvold, 1996, p. 348), whereby the personal meaning ascribed by the client to the problem is explored and possible new meanings are constructed, from which goals are developed and outcomes achieved. Peavy (1992) advocated replacing the term *outcomes* with the term *fruitfulness* and suggested that the career counseling process should be fruitful—that "it should provide a re-construing or changed outlook on some aspect of life" (p. 221). Savickas (1993) described a move away from trying to "fit" individuals into a mainstream culture and toward affirming diversity and enabling individuals to plan their own lives. In addition, he suggested that increasingly career counseling will be about "life design and the place of the work-role within a constellation of life roles" (p. 212).

From a constructivist perspective, Peavy (1992) suggested four dimensions for career counselors to keep in mind if they are to be helpful to clients: relationship, agency, meaning making, and negotiation. All of these, according to Peavy, can be framed as questions by the career counselor. When working with clients, career counselors can ask themselves:

1. How can I form a *cooperative alliance* with this client? (Relationship factor)
2. How can I encourage the *self-helpfulness* of this client? (Agency factor)
3. How can I help this client to *elaborate and evaluate his or her constructions and meanings* germane to [his or her] decisions? (Meaning-making factor)

4. How can I help this client to *reconstruct and negotiate* personally meaningful and socially supportable realities? (Negotiation factor) (Peavy, 1992, p. 221)

Thus, constructivists place emphasis on the life span developmental history of the client as told by the life story that the client brings to counseling. In the example presented in Chapter 9, the individual's present can be understood only by understanding his past and anticipated future. His dilemma of the present is influenced (among other things) by his values, which can be traced back to his family of origin, and by his desire for more autonomy in his work in the future.

Emotion is also important, and its inclusion in the process responds to criticism that emotion and social meaning have been missing from career counseling (Young & Valach, 1996). Clients are encouraged to explore and express their emotions through a range of interventions, including experiential interventions. In particular, approaches from gestalt therapy and psychodrama such as empty-chair technique, behavior rehearsal, guided imagery, and role plays may be used. In addition, techniques that center on the use of language may also be used.

Peavy (1992) suggested that the term *experiment* be used instead of *intervention* and that career counseling be viewed as a "fruitful experiment," since the "helping alliance itself is an experimental structure" (p. 222). "Experiments" are any planned interventions that the counselor may use in cooperation with the client "in order that the client may come to think, act, and feel more productively in relation to some dilemma or trouble in life" (p. 222). Peavy suggested that there are four levels of experiments: imaginal or embodied, thinking, simulated, and real-world experiments. Guided fantasy or focusing activities are examples of imaginal experiments, whereas repertory grids, critical self-reflection, genograms, and the systems theory framework can be used to facilitate thinking experiments. Simulated experiments can be facilitated by processes from gestalt therapy and psychodrama such as role play and two-chair technique. Real-world experiments are generally done outside the therapy setting and involve interactions with individuals other than the therapist, as in the case of work experience, work shadowing, or applying for a job.

LANGUAGE

Recognition of the precision of language and its power in constructing meaning is an important contribution of the constructivist movement (as has previously been discussed in Chapter 11). In essence, language constructs our reality and the meaning we make of the world (Berg & De Shazer, 1993). According to Herr (1997), language is important because it forms the basis of our professional interactions with clients and because it helps to define our profession. The second claim warrants further comment.

Herr listed a number of terms that relate to our profession, including *employment counseling* and *appraisal*, and explained how their meaning has varied across time and across cultures. Similarly, the language used to describe our profession has been variously described. In its early days, *vocational guidance* was the term used, since counseling had not yet emerged as a profession, and the terms *career* and *vocation* were used synonymously. Over time, and in response to advances in our field, the terms *vocational psychologist, vocational counselor,* and *career counselor* emerged. In addition, the terms *school counselor* and *guidance counselor* began to be used. Thus, as professionals for whom the basis of our interactions with our consumers is language and the unifying theme is career development, we find ourselves in a position of having many occupational titles, none of which denote exactly what we do. This is an issue that needs clarification. How can our consumers know what to expect from our services or which professional group provides a better service? How do consumers make sense of the competition? What do all these professionals do that is so different, and what can consumers expect from one that they cannot expect from another? Do we, the professionals, know who we are and what we have to offer?

Maybe having many occupational titles is appropriate given our complex times. Throughout Part Three of this book, it has been suggested that an appropriate term for the profession would be that of *career development facilitator*. This term provides a conceptual link between theory and practice and draws attention to the theme underlying our profession. In addition, it provides a developmental perspective at a time when increasing numbers of customers will be returning to us at different times of their lives. It also reflects current thinking on career as process, for facilitation relates to process and not the nature of the relationship. While we accept that ours is but one suggestion of an occupational title, the issue warrants further thought.

Because of our unique experiences, we can never know with any certainty that we understand what another person means. "Meaning is arrived at through negotiation within a specific context, for example the therapeutic context" (Berg & De Shazer, 1993, p. 7). Throughout a therapeutic encounter, language and discourse are used to arrive at new meanings, which in turn lead to change. For example, individuals may ascribe a certain meaning to their behavior, but then, through the counseling discourse, construct a new meaning or multiple meanings that enable them to view themselves differently and in turn act differently. New meanings bring about change, and thus it is through language that change occurs (Berg & De Shazer, 1993).

As evidenced in the previous discussion, our knowledge about ourselves is socially constructed, not only through language but also by culture (Lynch, 1997). In the traditional worldview, there was a place for objective universal truths—for example, about the role of women. However, the emerging worldview, with its emphasis on the individual as part of an interconnected whole, has brought about challenges to objective universal truths and "grand narratives" and has increased the importance of "local narratives," or meaning from a particular context (Lynch, 1997). It is no longer possible, if it ever was, to "apply one grand narrative to everyone" (Savickas, 1993, p. 211). Thus, the life narratives of individuals represent their own reality. Counseling is based on these life narratives. Typically, a counseling relationship becomes a therapeutic conversation, in which the counselor and the client join as coconstructors of a new reality.

THE NARRATIVE APPROACH

This use of language in counseling is often referred to as the narrative approach. Stories or narratives are a unique derivative of systems theory thinking and are key to constructivist approaches. They represent a mechanism for human knowing in that individuals "construct their identities from the symbols or meanings on offer within their culture" (McLeod, 1996, p. 178). Richardson's (1993, 1996) call for explorations of the place and meaning of work in different people's lives suggests one type of story that may be uncovered in career counseling. In addition, through story, the patterns and themes of an individual's life can be uncovered, and connections can be forged between previously unconnected events. Gysbers, Heppner, and Johnston (1998) described career development as "the drama of the ordinary because it is unfolding and evolving every day" (p. 12). They suggested that because of its "ordinariness," individuals may lose sight of its dynamic nature and impact on their lives. The use of story is a way of "identifying and analyzing life career themes" (Gysbers et al., 1998, p. 236), uncovering the meaning that individuals ascribe to interwoven parts of their lives, and focusing on individuals' subjective careers. "The power of stories to capture attention and convey meaning is reemerging as an important component in career counseling" (Krumboltz, Blando, Kim, & Reikowski, 1994, p. 60).

It is assumed that an individual's need to seek counseling is brought about by life stories or self-stories that are "incomplete, confused, or have negative or tragic outcomes" (McLeod, 1996). In addition, a narrative approach may enable individuals to tell stories that have been silenced. For example, some individuals may not have told their stories of incidents of workplace harassment or work-related stress because they had no one to tell or were prevented from telling by someone, possibly someone in authority. Counselors may look at the characteristics of the story being told—for example, if a story is meaningless, repetitive, life-denying, or subservient (McLeod, 1996). The type of story provides clues to the themes and patterns of an individual's larger life story and the meaning he or she makes of his or her life. Thus, counseling becomes a dialogue of coconstructing new meaning and/or writing new chapters. In using this approach, as in most other forms of counseling, counselors use counseling microskills, such as empathic reflection; interventions, such as psychodramatic enactments; and metaphor. But above all, a quality relationship is essential.

NARRATIVE ASSESSMENT

The use of narrative approaches challenges career counselors to examine the type and place of career assessment in their counseling. The use of assessment remains one of the biggest differences between personal and career counseling. However, the use of narrative approaches and potentially narrative forms of assessment breaks down what has traditionally been a barrier to the merging of the two forms of counseling.

The use of assessment in career counseling grew out of the psychology of individual differences previously discussed in Chapter 2. Thus, to a large extent, assessments in counseling "reflect old science" (R.W. Bradley, 1994, p. 224) and the traditional worldview underlying the trait-and-factor approaches. In fact, the use of assessment has traditionally been a major factor in defining the career counseling relationship. For example, the career counselor, with answers based on the objective data provided through quantitative assessment instruments, can be seen as an expert to whom the client deferred. Thus, as career counselors make increasing use of narrative assessment with the postmodern shift from objectivity to subjectivity or from scores to stories (Savickas, 1993), the counseling relationship will be defined differently. Goldman (1994) suggested that most career counselors could make better use of narrative assessment, since many are not well qualified in quantitative assessment.

In essence, narrative assessment is intended to encourage individuals to tell their own career stories (Borgen, 1995) and to uncover their subjective careers. The subjective component has traditionally been overlooked in career counseling, and Savickas (1992) suggested that we can lessen the separation between personal and career counseling by adding the subjective component through the use of qualitative assessment. In addition, he claimed that qualitative assessment "emphasizes the counseling relationship rather than the delivery of the service" (p. 337). Goldman (1990, 1992) listed the characteristics of qualitative assessment as follows:

1. Clients play an active role rather than that of "passive responder" (Goldman, 1990, p. 205).
2. Qualitative assessment is more integrative and holistic.
3. Qualitative methods emphasize learning about oneself within a developmental framework.
4. Qualitative assessment methods work well in groups.
5. Qualitative assessment reduces the distinction between counseling and assessment.
6. Qualitative assessment is valuable for relating to individuals of "different cultural and ethnic groups, socioeconomic levels, sexual identities, and to people with disabilities"(Goldman, 1990, p. 206).

The four most popular methods of qualitative assessment are autobiographies, early recollections, structured interviews, and card sorts. While these methods are not new to counselors, many of them are new to career counselors. In addition, the method of constructing life lines is useful in assisting clients to review their life histories. Goldman (1992) suggested that counselors can develop their own qualitative assessment instruments. The systems theory framework presented in Chapter 9 is an example of a tool that can be used in qualitative assessment. Clients can be encouraged to draw the constellation of influences in their system at various points in their life, such as school-leaving age. By then drawing their current constellation of influences and comparing them, they can explore their narratives or stories of their life career. Gysbers et al. (1998) comprehensively described the use of genograms and occupational card sorts as qualitative assessment tools. While it is not suggested here that one form of assessment is better than another, qualitative assessment has been discussed as a form of narrative approach to career counseling and as an important part of career counseling. It could be argued that narrative assessment should form a part of every career counseling encounter.

THE SET DESIGN: A SYSTEMS THEORY PERSPECTIVE

The systems theory framework can provide a map for career counseling in that it accommodates not only the perspectives of the traditional predictive theories but also those of the more recent constructivist approaches. A further strength of the systems theory perspective is the link it forges between theory and practice. The use of a systems theory framework for understanding career development has implications for the practice of career counseling. As evidenced by the discussion in this chapter, the use of a systems theory perspective requires career counselors to make the difficult move from the comfortable traditional worldview to the emerging worldview with its different account of causality (Bratcher, 1982). Bratcher commented that career counselors will be expected to combine some of the directive approaches of the past with the ability to think in circular rather than linear terms (as discussed in Chapter 8). The notion of subtle circular feedback processes shaping and reshaping systems is common in some fields of counseling but comparatively new in the field of career development.

It is evident from the discussion in this chapter and the nature of the interaction between the client and the counselor that the counseling relationship can be conceptualized as a system in its own right. In fact, counselors become an element of the system of influences on the career development of the individual, and the individual becomes an element of the system of influences on the counselor. In this system of interaction, the counselor and the individual use language to coconstruct the meaning of career for the individual. Language has a central role to play in the career counseling profession, described by Herr (1997) as a verbal profession. In counseling, the term *therapy* is often used to refer to the constructivist approaches. In fact, the term *family therapy* was coined to describe the discipline that first recognized the use of systems theory in counseling. Peavy (1996) suggested that the terms *counseling* and *therapy* refer to the "same process of personal reality construction and reconstruction" (p. 142) and that both center on meaning, with language as the medium. This conceptualization has informed the selection of the title for this chapter, "Therapeutic Systems." The therapeutic system that we have conceptualized is illustrated in Figure 13.1.

The figure portrays the potential complexity of career counseling and its place in the social and environmental-societal systems. Just as the career counselor exists within his or her own ever-changing system of influences, so too does the client. Career counseling constitutes the meeting of two separate systems and the formation of a new system, the therapeutic system. The boundaries of each system must be permeable enough so that a relationship can develop and dialogue and resulting meaning can occur, yet impermeable enough for both parties to maintain their individuality. Thus, the boundary between the counselor system and the client system needs to be maintained. However, as the relationship between members of the therapeutic system develops, the boundary between the client system and the counselor system may become less clear. Counselors who lose sight of this are in danger of imposing their own values on clients or manipulating them or, alternatively, being manipulated by the client. Thus, career counselors need a clear understanding of their own narratives formed through interaction with their own system of influences, past,

F I G U R E 13.1 THE THERAPEUTIC SYSTEM

present, and future. They also need to facilitate exploration of the client's life narratives, including the meaning of career and work in the client's life. Thus, the creation of meaning through dialogue is illustrative of the therapeutic system as a learning system.

Narratives are shaped through interaction with language and culture. Client populations in career counseling are increasingly diverse in terms of both their ethnic and cultural backgrounds and the nature of their concerns (Borders, 1996). Counselors also have diverse backgrounds. A systems theory perspective and associated narrative approaches enable the diversity to be addressed by engaging in a dialogue centered on the client's own narrative. Narrative approaches and their emphasis on the quality of the relationship are in keeping with recent thinking on multicultural counseling (discussed in Chapter 11). For example, Patterson (1996) described a change in the multicultural literature that reflects a return to recognizing counseling as an interpersonal relationship based on awareness of the uniqueness of the individual. It is now recognized that all individuals belong to and interrelate with multiple groups, and the counselor must be aware of the unique pattern of these influences in each client if counseling is to be successful.

Increasing globalization is "leading to increased homogeneity and a world view representing the common humanity that binds all human beings together as one species" (Patterson, 1996, p. 230). But career counselors still need to develop multicultural sensitivity and competence (Betz, 1993; Swanson, 1993) to avoid what Leong (1993) described as "culturally inappropriate" goals and process. For example, some cultures may be more oriented toward family or community than the individual, and in some cultures, such as the Chinese culture, the role and place of the counselor may not be easy to define (Back, 1997). Leong (1993) suggested approaching cross-cultural encounters without preconceived ideas about the individual or his or her culture, an approach that accords with the systems theory framework and the narrative approach of exploring meaning through language.

Career counseling takes place within a therapeutic setting, such as a school, a business, or a private counseling office. This setting may influence the type of clients counseled (e.g., rehabilitation clients), the cost of the service, record keeping, and the nature of the service provided. In fact, it may define the therapeutic relationship. For example, all clients may be "processed" in a similar way. In addition, the setting may affect the level of professional support available to counselors—for example, supervision, a subject that will be discussed more in Chapter 14.

At a broader level, career counseling takes place within the environmental-societal system. As previously discussed, career counseling is increasingly being seen by governments as essential to the future well-being of individuals and nations in the rapidly changing world. While this emphasis will raise the profile and expectations of career counselors, it will also place demands on them to provide accountable practices with outcomes that reflect responsiveness to the needs of society. Influences at this level (e.g., managed care) may affect government funding for certain programs or clients and the availability of services in remote or rural areas. In addition, a move toward fee-based counseling services challenges career counselors to provide a more diverse range of services than traditional one-to-one counseling. Thus, career counselors must set their practice in the context of the broad environmental-societal system. Awareness of the needs and trends of this system will ensure the compatibility of career counseling services.

One of the most significant trends, which is affecting not only the environmental-societal system but also the social and individual systems, is the growth of technology. Watts (1996b) suggested that computers can be both an opportunity and a possible threat to career practitioners. For example, they may enhance the quality or accessibility of service. However, they can also reduce the amount of human interaction. Thus, Watts (1996b) suggested that the challenge is "to utilize such technologies in ways which supplement and extend human potential rather than acting to restrict or replace it" (p. 269).

Over the last 30 years, computer applications have been incorporated into career counseling (Sampson, Kolodinsky, & Greeno, 1997) as part of the therapeutic system. For example, occupational databases, career assessment programs, and increasingly integrated computer-assisted career counseling programs are common accessories to the career counseling process. Thus, career counselors have had to grapple with the inclusion of computer technology in their work along with the resulting ethical and professional issues.

Sampson et al. (1997) discussed the future trends in relation to computer use, our profession, and the information highway. In particular, they suggested that this technology will open up possibilities for marketing, service delivery, self-help resources, supervision, and case conferencing and research. These possibilities are examples of globalization at work. For example, it will no longer be necessary for the counselor to be in the same room as the client; a supervisor could be located on the other side of the world; and clients could access career information without ever seeing a career professional. However, the down side of this exciting future includes ethical and relationship development issues (Sampson et al., 1997).

Technology fits well into a systems theory perspective. It provides a medium of dialogue not previously available to us. In addition, it provides new language and new information with which we can construct our life and career stories. For example, career narratives may include stories about technology and unemployment, or technology and new opportunities. Technology forges links between the environmental-societal system, the individual, and career counselors. For example, individuals in remote areas can now have access to a career counseling service previously unavailable to them. Thus, technology makes possible the creation of new therapeutic systems.

Technology certainly has a significant role to play in the future. However, career counselors as a profession have an ethical responsibility to monitor its development, anticipate problems, and ensure that safeguards are in place to protect our future consumers. We cannot simply watch technology develop around us and then work out how we can apply it; we must be involved in the whole process.

In addition, technology has significant implications for training those new to the profession and updating the skills of practicing professionals. The rapid pace of technological change mandates that lifelong learning be embraced and promoted by career counselors. In addition, lifelong learning must include learning about technology.

Systems theory also provides for interventions at levels of the system other than that of the individual and raises the possibility that career counselors will become more proactive at the broader systems level. For example, counselors may work with a family or an organization in the belief that interventions anywhere in the system will interact with other elements of the system to bring about change. In addition, they may become advocates for clients with particular needs, such as individuals of low socioeconomic status or minority racial/ ethnic origin. The systems theory construct of feedback loops is relevant here, for an intervention in one part of the system may result in better outcomes for the individual.

A systems theory perspective will assist clients to construct new meanings of their circumstances. For example, it may be helpful for individuals to view their employment circumstances in terms of the social and economic climate of the nation. Career counseling may begin to draw more on techniques and approaches from other counseling fields. In addition, Herr (1992) suggested that counseling may draw on psychoeducational models and structured learning processes. Thus, a systems theory perspective has the capacity to forge links between career counseling and other disciplines.

One area in which career counseling has forged links with another field is that of career counseling in groups. While this is not a new practice, given its capacity to provide effective, cost-efficient service to clients, it is likely to become a growth area in a "user-pays" future in which many individuals may seek career counseling several times in a lifetime. Group counseling also constitutes a therapeutic system that facilitates dialogue between many individuals. It introduces a multiplicity of perspectives, which is important in learning and creating new meaning. In addition, it addresses several issues relevant to career counseling. First, from a multicultural perspective, it has the potential to address the needs of group-oriented cultures. Second, it reduces the cost to individuals, thereby addressing some of the concerns of fee-based services and their accessibility to all individuals. Third, group processes accommodate narrative forms of assessment. Thus, career counseling in a group can be a powerful learning system.

REHEARSAL: A MEANS OF REVIEWING PRACTICE

Career counselors enter the system of influence of the individuals with whom they work. Thus, they need to reflect on the pattern of their own career development and their role as lifelong learners, their practice in relation to the integration of theory and practice, their beliefs and values, and the complexity of the career counseling relationship, as illustrated in Figure 13.1. Such reflection may be done individually or in the context of clinical supervision, a topic discussed further in Chapter 14. The following questions may be used to guide career counselors' personal and professional reflection. Conducting such a review on a regular basis would demonstrate a commitment to lifelong learning.

REFLECTING ON THE PATTERN OF MY OWN CAREER DEVELOPMENT

- What influences operated on my career development as a young person?
- How have I integrated these influences?
- What are the patterns and themes of my career development?
- What is my career narrative?
- What is the place of work in my life?
- What other life roles do I hold, and what are my priorities?
- What conflicts exist between my life roles, and how do I resolve these?
- What values and attitudes do I hold about the following?
    particular types of work, such as certain professions
    the value of education
    individuals of low socioeconomic background
    gay men and lesbians
    individuals of other racial/ethnic groups
    individuals with disabilities
    the impact of technology
    particular work-related issues, such as working mothers, or youth unemployment

DEMONSTRATING THAT I AM A LIFELONG LEARNER

- In what ways do I update my counseling skills?
- In what ways do I update my knowledge of career development theory?
- In what ways do I revisit my career narrative and its influence on my counseling?
- How frequently do I participate in clinical supervision?
- How do I update my knowledge of the changes in the world of work?
- How do I update my knowledge of the use of technology in my work as a career practitioner?
- What learning goals have I achieved recently?
- What are my current learning goals?
- How will I achieve my learning goals?

UNDERSTANDING THE INTEGRATION OF CAREER DEVELOPMENT THEORY AND CAREER COUNSELING PRACTICE

- Do I have an up-to-date working knowledge of career development theory?
- How do I apply this to my work?

- What links am I able to make between career theory and practice that I was once not able to make?
- Am I aware of the integration between career development theories and between theory and career counseling practice?

KNOWING COUNSELING THEORY AND ITS APPLICATION TO CAREER COUNSELING

- What is my background in counseling? What counseling theories inform my work?
- What links am I able to make between counseling theory and career counseling that I was once not able to make?
- What are the implications of this for counseling; for example, what are my beliefs about clients, change, and the role of the counselor?
- What role do I play in career counseling?

MY PERSONAL PRACTICE

- How do I feel about my counseling—for example, bored, excited?
- How do I keep clear boundaries between my own issues, values, and attitudes and those of my client?
- In what ways do I individualize my counseling sessions according to the needs of the clients, or do I follow a fairly standard format?
- Am I aware of the system of influences affecting my clients?
- Do I adopt a narrow or broad focus in my work with clients?
- Are there some clients or issues that I would prefer or not prefer to work with?
- Do I receive supervision to help me clarify my own issues and issues of professional practice?

As evidenced in these questions, career counselors must see themselves as lifelong learners who constantly reflect on their practice and upgrade their knowledge and skills. In a rapidly changing world, not to do so may result in an outdated or narrow range of practices poorly suited to a postmodern world.

A LEAD ROLE? THE DECISION IS OURS!

As career counseling prepares itself to go on the stage of the 21st century, there is ample evidence to suggest a possible script. Recurring throughout this book has been the narrative of change. Reflected in this change is an emerging worldview that poses a significant challenge to traditional career counseling. Career counseling has been offered a lead role by our consumers and by the sociopolitical system. What we do with the offer is up to us as a profession. However, to take the offer implies challenge and change and writing a new script for career counseling. Staying the same is not an option. The lead role is there if we want it. The decision is ours.

14

LIFELONG LEARNING IN SUPERVISORY SYSTEMS

Chapter 13 portrayed career counselors as facilitators of lifelong learning for their consumer groups. However, as emphasized throughout Part Three of this book, there is an increasing need for all individuals to facilitate their own career development through lifelong learning, and in this regard, career counselors are no different. This has long been recognized in the field of counseling, and, significantly, the counseling profession has its own mechanism for lifelong learning in the form of clinical supervision. But although much attention in the literature has been focused on the clinical supervision of counselors (M. Taylor, 1994), much less has been written specifically about the supervision of career counselors, even though it is recognized as vitally important to their ongoing career development.

Nathan and Hill (1992) acknowledged the importance of supervision in the development and support of career counselors and concluded that it is "as essential a requirement for the career counsellor as it is for any other counsellor" (p. 138). In fact, so important is the concept of supervision to the career counseling profession that it is written into the National Career Development Association Professional Standards Committee's (1992) statement on competencies, where knowledge and skills in supervision is identified as one of the ten competencies required by career counselors. In addition to clinical supervision, most career counselors work in organizations and receive administrative or managerial supervision.

It is the purpose of this chapter to focus on clinical supervision. In particular, supervision will be examined as a learning system that facilitates the lifelong career development of career counselors or career development facilitators. While our preferred term is *career development facilitators, career counselor* is the term used in the literature, and therefore both will be used here as appropriate. Specifically, supervision will be defined as a learning system. Elements of the supervisory learning system, including the learning environment, the content of learning, the process of learning and career counselor development, supervision's links with service provision, and the context of supervision, will be discussed. Administrative or managerial supervision will be discussed in relation to the context of career counseling and supervision.

SUPERVISION AS A LEARNING SYSTEM

The discussion on language in previous chapters provides a useful background to this chapter and the use of the term *supervision*. For example, Feltham and Dryden (1994) commented that "unfortunately the term 'supervision' still carries connotations of managerial oversight, control, mistrust and coercion of a worker by an employer"—a significantly different situation from the "professional, consultative, supportive aid for counsellors" that clinical supervision is (p. x). As explained in Chapter 11, language connotes the nature of relationships, and the connotations of the term *supervision* are particularly significant when it should be considered as a means of promoting self-directed lifelong learning in which counselors define their own needs. In addition, such learning occurs within individuals in relation to their own relevant system of influences. However, these characteristics are not reflected in definitions such as that of Bernard and Goodyear (1992), who described supervision as "an intervention that is provided by a senior member of a profession to a junior member or members of that same profession" (p. 4), or that of Remley, Benshoff, and Mowbray (1987), who defined supervision as "regular, ongoing supervision of counseling by another trained and experienced professional" (p. 53).

Concerns about the connotations of the term *supervision* were raised by Kagan (1983), who asked, "Why do none of the approaches include opportunities for the counselor to take the lead in self-criticism, self-analysis . . . (with the supervisor serving as facilitator rather than as authority)?" (p. 71). Kagan's question draws attention to the nature of the relationship in supervision and the need for it to be something other than hierarchical and to be more in keeping with the concept of lifelong learning.

Such concerns extend as well to the use of the terms *supervisor* and *supervisee* to refer to those involved in the supervision process, with *supervisor* connoting "doing to" and *supervisee* connoting "being done to." Clearly, if supervision is to be viewed as a learning system, then appropriate terminology needs to be adopted. Thus, supervisees in the learning process are better described as *counselor/learners* and supervisors as *facilitators of learning*. It should be remembered that the facilitators are also learning as a part of their ongoing involvement in the process; they are also part of the learning system.

The supervisory relationship portrayed in the previous definitions and questioned by Kagan dramatically contrasts with Bordin (1983) and Inskipp and Proctor's (1993) notion of supervision as an "alliance" or Holloway's (1995) concept of a "learning alliance" (p. 6), terms that connote more an image of shared responsibility in a learning system. The definition proposed by Inskipp and Proctor (1993) addressed a number of issues pertinent to conceptualizing supervision as a learning system. These authors defined supervision as

> a working alliance between a supervisor and a counsellor (or counsellors) in which the counsellor can offer an account or recording of her work, reflect on it, receive feedback and where appropriate, guidance. The object of the alliance is to enable the counsellor to gain in ethical competence, confidence and creativity so as to give her best possible service to clients. (p. 313)

This definition places the counselor/learner at the center of a process determined by his or her learning needs and what he or she brings to the process and in this regard is significantly different from other definitions in which the focus is on either the supervisor or the process. In addition, it draws attention to the place of supervision in the broader context of service to clients (thereby reflecting the recursiveness of systems theory thinking) through its links between counselor learning and quality of service.

Quality of service is related to the quality of the therapeutic system, in which connectedness and coconstruction occur between the counselor and the client. Through this process, the counselor becomes aware of his or her own learning needs, and it is on these needs that supervision is based. Thus, the learning needs of counselor/learners reflect recursiveness with the therapeutic system, as demonstrated in the following comment:

> Supervision can help career counsellors to obtain new perspectives, to assess the nature of the client's problem, to discuss the management of difficult cases, to assist in test interpretation, and to deal with feelings in relation to the client. In particular, it can help the counsellor to deal with the pressures of "getting a result." A client's anxiety for a solution is very contagious, and career counsellors often "catch it." (Nathan & Hill, 1992, p. 138)

This comment not only shows the role that supervisors can play as an influence on the therapeutic system but also draws attention to the learning needs that counselor/learners may bring to supervision. Thus, when a supervisory alliance can be described as a "learning alliance" (Holloway, 1995, p. 6), the counselor/learner's needs will be met by learning tasks and teaching strategies provided by the facilitator of the supervision process. Borders (1994) suggested that supervisors can only be effective if they think of "counselors as learners and of themselves as educators who create appropriate learning environments" (p. 5). As a result, the learning needs of the counselor take precedence in the supervisory alliance. Thus, just as Peavy (1992) suggested that "fruitfulness" should be a goal of counseling, so too should it be a goal of supervision. It is important to note here that through the recursiveness of the supervisory system, the facilitator may also become aware of his or her own learning needs.

This discussion raises the issue of the usefulness of definitions in a world where self-reality is the only reality. If, as Littrell, Lee-Bordin, and Lorenz (1979) claimed, the counselor is the "principal designer of his or her learning" (p. 134), supervision is what the individual learner construes it to be. And if learning is defined by the individual in relation to his or her own unique system through language, using language, particularly definitions, that predetermines to some extent the nature of the learning system is not in keeping with constructivist thinking and the concept of lifelong learning.

SUPERVISION AND ITS LINKS WITH SERVICE PROVISION

While the learning needs of the counselor/learner are vitally important in supervision, so too are the quality of service and the care of clients. Feltham and Dryden (1994) commented that "safeguarding clients from potential abuse by counsellors" is a "rather sober ethical dimension" of supervision and that "supervision is dedicated to helping clients by helping their counsellors" (p. x). This concern is reflected in three basic goals of supervision identified by Vargus (1977): (1) ensuring that agencies provide adequate service, (2) helping workers function to the fullest of their capacity, and (3) assisting workers in the attainment of professional independence. The goal of adequate service is made more explicit by several authors who have stressed the need for supervisors to monitor client care (Bernard & Goodyear, 1992; Blocher, 1983; Loganbill, Hardy, & Delworth, 1982) as guided by the ethical code of the profession. For example, ethical behavior related to the nature of the counselor/client relationship, computer-assisted career guidance, information provision, and counselor competencies must all be considered in relation to client care.

ACCOUNTABILITY

As discussed in previous chapters, changes in the world in which we work are increasingly demanding that services be accountable. As early as 1978, Boyd noted that it would be an understatement to say "that the helping professions, and particularly guidance and counseling, are presently in an 'age of accountability'" (p. 16). Indeed, in today's world, where closer ties are being forged between career counseling services and sociopolitical organizations such as governments, an inability to demonstrate accountable practice would be folly.

> Accountability is being demanded by the public that funds these enterprises. . . . The consequence of not being able to satisfy public expectations could be disastrous for the helping professions. Counseling and guidance is most vulnerable because this field has always been forced to fight for federal, state and local dollars and lack of demonstrated effectiveness could reduce or redirect funding, thus changing the support structure of the profession. (Boyd, 1978, p. 16)

While this statement is 20 years old, it accurately reflects the new environment in which career development facilitators work. Thus, clinical supervision provides a mechanism whereby the career counseling profession as a whole can demonstrate its value in a rapidly changing society. Promoting ongoing career development of counselors through lifelong learning in supervision not only is in keeping with today's thinking about individuals as drivers of their own careers but also ensures the provision of proactive services that are responsive to the needs of both consumers and the organizations of the sociopolitical system.

THE CONTENT OF LIFELONG LEARNING

Learning, accountable practice, and service provision are recursively linked, as reflected in Bordin's (1983) conceptualization of the supervisory relationship as a "supervisory working alliance." This alliance is directed toward the achievement of supervisee goals, "including mastery of specific skills, enlargement of the understanding of client concerns and of process issues, awareness of impact of self on the therapeutic process, and initial translation of theory into practice" (L. J. Bradley & Whiting, 1989, p. 460).

Therefore, supervision facilitates not only accountable practices but also learning. In fact, counselors' learning has outcomes for client services because their ongoing professional development facilitates ongoing improved performance in their counseling. In particular, supervision generally facilitates personal, professional, and competency development and thus the ongoing career development of the counselor/learner. In addition, it serves a useful purpose in our rapid-paced society, since it can be used by counselors to prevent burnout. Each of these aspects of counselor development will be examined.

PERSONAL DEVELOPMENT

Counselors need to understand themselves psychologically if they are to be effective in helping others. For example, their reality has been determined through language and culture in relation to their context, and this reality will be different from that of their client. In addition, language is understood differently by individuals. It is essential that career counselors be aware of their reality so that their own "flaws and blocks" do not impede the learning of their clients (Nathan & Hill, 1992, p. 132). In counseling, such "flaws and blocks" could result in misunderstandings between client and counselor and could reduce the potential for empathic communication. Individual or group supervision is a learning process that can assist counselors in becoming aware of these potential impediments to their work.

As discussed in Chapter 13, when counselors enter into a therapeutic system with their client, the permeable boundaries of the two systems come together. The broadening range of client concerns and career counseling practices heightens the need for ongoing personal development since there is a constant need for counselor/learners to process new information. Personal development is therefore critical for counselors so that their awareness of their own issues can be heightened and they can maintain appropriate boundaries between themselves and the client.

PROFESSIONAL DEVELOPMENT

Clinical supervision is a means by which those new to the profession as well as experienced career counselors can clarify their professional role and function throughout their career development. This is an ongoing task, since career counselors continually redefine their roles in response to the needs of a changing society, and it is viewed as an important goal of clinical supervision. For example, Pinkney and Jacobs (1985) found that counselors "ranked both titles and clients that were suggestive of career counseling lower than titles and clients that were suggestive of personal counseling" (p. 454). Therefore, these authors raised questions about how well career counselors are socialized into the profession. As discussed in Chapter 11, concerns have been raised about the training of those new to the profession and their lack of interest in career counseling. These factors significantly affect the quality of career counseling being delivered. The lack of commitment to career counseling is of serious concern, since the sociopolitical agenda and the population at large place increasing demands on career counseling. Clinical supervision is a means by which these concerns may be addressed—for example, by challenging narrowly defined practices and raising awareness of the possible scope of career counseling. In addition, through supervision, counselor/learners may come to recognize the significance of the career counseling role for individuals, groups, and institutions.

COMPETENCY DEVELOPMENT

As early as 1977, Kaslow (1977) commented that "supervision is geared to increasing the supervisee's awareness of his or her role as a practitioner as well as his or her skill, competence and confidence"(p. 306). This is important, since work has shown that the skill level of counselors decreases after their training is completed (Meyer, 1978). Further, Wiley and Ray (1986) found that counselor development is related to supervised rather than unsupervised counseling experience.

Concerns have been expressed that career counseling clients are treated in a routine fashion and that their intake evaluations are less detailed and do not address family dynamics (Gelso et al., 1985). Further, suggestions have been made that career counselors use less empathy, genuineness, and respect for clients with career concerns than for clients with personal-emotional problems (Melnick, 1975). Clinical supervision is a means of addressing this issue and ensuring that counselors perform at their best. To facilitate competency development, Borders and Leddick (1987) suggested assessment of the counselor/learner's skills in introductory supervision sessions. To this end, Engels and Dameron (1990) provided a range of counseling competency checklists, including one that could be used by career counselors in clinical supervision. Competency development is sometimes an overlooked area of supervision, since it is often associated with counselor training. However, as previously suggested, closer ties are being forged between personal and career counseling. There is no point at which a career counselor/learner has learned it all, and it is essential for counselors to continue to develop their competencies in order to keep pace with ever-changing demands.

BURNOUT

Burnout refers "to a progressive loss of idealism, energy, and purpose experienced by people in the helping professions as a result of the conditions of their work" (Edelwich & Brodsky, 1980, p. 14). As discussed in Chapter 10, it is essential that the constantly unfolding world be understood as the backdrop to career counseling activities. This is evidenced in Stoltenberg and Delworth's (1987) claims that burnout occurs in response to work conditions such as understaffing, which in turn is brought about by a worldwide trend of downsizing and increased demand for career counseling services.

There are many other contributing factors to burnout in the helping professions, including the emotional intensity of the work; lack of understanding of the work by other employees including administrators; the nature of the client group; and the quality of the work environment (Savicki & Cooley, 1987; Wade, Cooley, & Savicki, 1986). These factors are becoming more relevant to career counselors as the range of settings in which career services are being provided is increasing, the nature of the client group is diversifying, and accountability is being demanded of career counselors.

Savicki and Cooley (1982) suggested that there is a relationship between supervisory behavior and burnout in the helping professions. Davis, Savicki, Cooley, and Firth (1989) emphasized the importance of this relationship. Cherniss (1980) claimed that "the stress that occurs in human service settings can be mitigated by supportive supervision and interaction with coworkers. Supervisors and coworkers can help staff cope by providing emotional support, technical help, feedback on performance, and organizational power" (p. 23). In a recent study, school counselors cited burnout as a reason for needing supervision (Roberts & Borders, 1994). While further research is needed in the area of clinical supervision and burnout among counselors, there is some evidence of a link between supportive supervision and stress relief (Davis et al., 1989; Savicki & Cooley, 1987).

Savicki and Cooley (1982) claimed that burnout involves physical, cognitive, emotional, personal, and behavioral symptoms. Thus, it occurs within the intrapersonal system of the individual as a response to the influences of the social and environmental-societal systems. The influence of the supervisory system, a subsystem of the social system, can assist in reducing the effects of burnout. As such, burnout, its causes, and the links between supervision and its prevention exemplify recursiveness in the supervision subsystem of the therapeutic system. Directly or indirectly, input into one element of the system may have implications for other elements. For example, the quality of client service may decrease if an organization ceases to provide clinical supervision for its counselors. Similarly, an organization that supports clinical supervision practices for its counselor/learners may have increased productivity and quality of service.

THE PROCESS OF LEARNING AND CAREER COUNSELOR DEVELOPMENT

The previous discussion drew attention to the content of learning in supervision. Through supervision, the counselor/learner

> progressively achieves greater self-awareness, acquires more advanced counseling skills and techniques, and masters theoretical knowledge. These learnings are integrated into a personal and professional identity as a counselor, a growth pro-

cess that is continuous and ongoing across the counselor's professional lifespan. (Borders, 1989, p. 9)

This statement clearly depicts counselors as lifelong learners. In this regard, the definition of Remley et al. (1987) presented earlier in this chapter draws attention to the need for clinical supervision to be regular and ongoing. The lifelong learning facilitated through supervision must become a systematic feature of counseling practice rather than a haphazard or solely needs-based occurrence.

Chapter 3 of the present book focused on theories that have been proposed to account for career development. In general, these models presented a series of stages through which individuals pass as their career develops. During each of these stages, individuals have tasks that they need to achieve. More recently, the concept of recycling and adjusting to changes in career circumstances has been widely accepted, and we believe that this is more in keeping with systems theory thinking. While the theories discussed in Chapter 3 account for career development in general, several models have been proposed to account specifically for counselor development. These models propose stages through which counselors pass and issues that counselors may present in supervision. In essence, they describe the career development and lifelong learning of professional counselors, including career counselors.

STAGES OF DEVELOPMENT

The concept of counselor development came to prominence in the 1980s, when several developmental models were proposed to account for it (Blocher, 1983; Hess, 1986; Loganbill et al., 1982). While there is agreement that counselors pass through a number of stages during their career, there is no agreement on the number of stages, counselors' development after training is not accounted for in most models, and stages of development through which supervisors pass are rarely considered. However, what is clear from the developmental models is that, at different stages, counselor/learners will have different needs and learning goals and, as a result, different expectations of their supervisors. The onus is on the supervisor to be flexible and responsive to the changing learning needs of the counselor/learners and to provide experiences or facilitate processes that can facilitate achievement of their learning goals. Thus, the supervisory relationship and the nature of supervision change over time in response to the learning goals of the counselor/learner.

A CONCEPTUAL MODEL

Most of the developmental models present counselor development in a series of sequential stages, some of which finish at the completion of training. However, the model of Loganbill et al. (1982) is significantly different in that their three stages are cyclic rather than linear, and counselors can pass through stages more than once, each time dealing with issues in greater depth. Because of its lack of emphasis on linearity, their model is more in keeping with systems theory thinking and will be discussed here briefly as an example of a developmental model.

The assumption underlying their model is that "counselor development is continuous and ongoing throughout one's professional lifespan" (Loganbill et al., 1982, p. 17). In its cyclic nature, their model addresses some of the criticisms directed at the developmental models, that they depict progress solely as a forward-moving process and counselor development as ending after training.

The three stages identified by Loganbill et al. (1982) are stagnation, confusion, and integration. Stagnation is characterized by a lack of awareness, such that the supervisee is "frozen in old patterns of thought and behavior" (p. 18). This could be said of traditional approaches to career counseling that are based on the matching approaches. During this stage, the supervisee is not experiencing any emotional drain, since he or she is not working through emotional issues. Consequently, this stage can be regenerative. In contrast, the stage of confusion involves a great emotional drain on the supervisee as he or she experiences instability, disruption, and confusion. The supervisee may feel like a failure or incompetent as his or her "old patterns of thought and behavior" become unstuck and are no longer adequate. For example, the client needs of a career counseling service may change, and a counselor's previous matching approach to counseling may be no longer appropriate so that he or she is forced to learn new ways. While much emotional energy is spent during the stage of confusion, much growth can result. Integration is the stage when a new order has emerged. The counselor/learner has a new conceptual understanding, feels more purposeful, and has a sense of direction that was missing during the stage of confusion. The cyclic nature of this model reflects its relevance to the lifelong learning process of career counselors. In addition, from a systems theory perspective, its cyclic nature is more in keeping with the view of learning as a qualitative rather than an additive process.

The model also identifies eight issues that counselors deal with throughout their development: issues of competence, emotional awareness, autonomy, identity, respect for individual differences, purpose and direction, personal motivation, and professional ethics. Thus, the model provides guidelines for the focus of supervision, since counselor/learners and facilitators of supervision can identify learning goals related to the issues or stages.

COMMENTS ON THE DEVELOPMENTAL MODELS

While the developmental models provide a useful means of tracking a counselor's progress, they are also open to criticism. In particular, most presume that all counselor development will follow the same linear progression (Reising & Daniels, 1983) and do not allow for times at which development plateaus or regresses. Such thinking is not in keeping with a systems theory view of development. In addition, most models do not allow for the concept of recycling through the stages. Nor do they allow for the notion of the counselor and supervisor existing in a relationship and acting on each other recursively. This denies the uniqueness of the supervisee, the supervisor, and the supervisory relationship and can be a danger in supervision (Hawkins & Shohet, 1991). Further, these models overlook the fact that supervisors are also passing through cycles of development (Hess, 1987; Stoltenberg & Delworth, 1987).

It is reasonable to assume that counselor/learners who are receiving regular supervision may spend less time in the stage of stagnation because they and their supervisor are constantly monitoring their development and tailoring learning experiences accordingly. While there is some agreement (Hawkins & Shohet, 1991; Littrell et al., 1979; Usher & Borders, 1993) that supervisees at different stages of development have different supervisory needs, it is important that supervision be driven, not by the developmental models, but by the uniqueness of the supervisee and his or her individual learning needs.

Most developmental models depict counseling supervision as a process of facilitating the progress of counselors through distinct sequential, hierarchical stages (Borders, 1989; Littrell et al., 1979). Each stage requires different supervision interventions, yet the models do not provide advice on the "how" of supervision. Rather, they are a means of conceptualizing counselor/learner development and can be used with a variety of styles of supervision. While a supervisor can use the developmental models to conceptualize the learning needs of the counselor/learner, he or she will also need to select appropriate learning/teaching interventions from the range of supervision practices.

THE LEARNING ENVIRONMENT

Just as constructivist approaches are relevant in counseling (see Chapter 13), they are appropriate in supervision. Thus, a quality supervisory relationship that facilitates learning will be characterized by nonjudgmental acceptance, understanding, trust, and mutual caring. The relationship is the foundation of clinical supervision and ultimately determines whether supervision is effective, regardless of technique.

Given the inherent inequality of the relationship, it is desirable for a supervisor to create a supervisory atmosphere that is conducive to the learning of the supervisee. This is illustrated by Blocher's (1983) concept of supervision as a learning environment . Because he saw supervision as an instructional process, he drew on the psychology of learning and behavior change. He described a developmental learning environment that he conceptualized "in terms of seven basic dynamics involving the interaction of learner and environment" (Blocher, 1983, p. 31): challenge, involvement, support, structure, feedback, innovation, and integration. The model is based on the premise that there is an optimal level of interaction that will contribute to cognitive and professional growth and that the challenge for the facilitator is to fine-tune the learning environment to meet the individual needs of the counselor/learner.

THE SUPERVISORY SYSTEM WITHIN A SYSTEM

Holloway (1992) noted that supervision "exists in the context of the profession's requirements for training, the organization's policies and needs, the supervisee's learning requirements, the supervisor's teaching objectives, and the consumer's need for effective professional service" (pp. 180–181). Further, Hart (1982) commented that both supervisor and supervisee are influenced by the setting but claimed that there was no linear relationship between the influences of the system and the supervisory process. In addition, he claimed that the system could be used as a determinant by supervisors when deciding which model of supervision to use. A number of writers emphasize the importance of the system in which the supervision process takes place (Clarkson & Gilbert, 1991; Loganbill et al., 1982; Shohet & Wilmot, 1991) and the need for the supervisor to be aware of this.

ADMINISTRATIVE SUPERVISION

Within the counseling profession, most counselors receive both administrative and clinical supervision. The difference between administrative or managerial supervision and clinical supervision is clearly spelled out in the Ethical Guidelines for Counseling Supervisors of the Association for Counselor Education and Supervision (ACES; cited in ACES Supervision Interest Group, 1995, p. 270). Specifically:

> Administrative supervision refers to those supervisory activities that increase the efficiency of the delivery of counseling services, whereas clinical supervision includes the supportive and educative activities of the supervisor designed to improve the application of counseling theory and techniques directly to clients. (ACES Supervision Interest Group, 1995, p. 270)

Bimrose and Wilden (1994) have suggested that "the 'managerial' role seeks to ensure that standards are being maintained and that the supervisee is meeting agreed standards and goals both of the profession and of the organisation" (p. 377). Thus, managerial supervision frequently reflects the recursiveness between the organization, the manager, the supervisee, and the client group. For example, organizations may mandate the style of record keeping, referral processes, the type of clients seen, and the type of work undertaken. There can sometimes be conflict between the policy objectives of the organization and the personal and professional needs of the counselor/learner. Reporting processes between counselors and managers generally ensure that the organization's needs are met, while clinical supervision tends to focus more on the personal and professional needs of the counselor that arise from the therapeutic system. A concern in agencies and organizations is that line managers may not always have a counseling background. Therefore, while they understand the need for managerial supervision, they may not understand the nature and purposes of clinical supervision and its differences from managerial supervision. It may not always be easy for counseling professionals to articulate to organizational management the differences between the two forms of supervision (Proctor, 1994).

SUPERVISION FROM A SYSTEMS THEORY PERSPECTIVE

As discussed in Chapter 13, career counselors enter into a therapeutic system with the client and in doing so become one of a system of influences on the client. Similarly, the supervisory relationship becomes a system in its own right, but also a system connected to the therapeutic system. This is reflected in Hawkins and Shohet's (1989) claims that the four elements present in supervision are the supervisee, the supervisor, the work context, and the supervisee's client. The interconnectedness between these elements demands attention to systems theory constructs. For example, an intervention by the supervisor with the counselor may bring about a change in the therapeutic system, which in turn may result in new meaning for the client.

It is widely accepted that supervisors assume different roles—for example, teacher, counselor, or consultant—according to the needs of their supervisees and that their task may also include elements such as support or education. The relationship between the client and the supervisee, the influence of the work context on the supervisee, and the influence of the supervisor on the supervisee are all examples of the interconnectedness of the elements that may be explored in supervision. Bimrose and Wilden (1994) illustrated this by describing the supervisor's role as one of support if the focus is on the supervisee and if his or her need is for encouragement to try new techniques. Where the client is the focus of concern in supervision, the supervisor may take a case study approach.

The supervisory system can consist of two people or a group of people, all of whom become influences on each other in a recursive manner. Exploration of the therapeutic system in supervision may reveal "multiple realities" or "multiple truths" (Richardson, 1993, p. 428) and may identify blocks or points of "stuckness" in the therapeutic system. These in turn may be related to the counselor's family system or work system. Some of these issues may be appropriate to deal with in supervision; others may be left to the counselor to process in an appropriate way—for example, through personal counseling. In any supervisory system, whether individual or group supervision, the dynamics of the supervisory system need to be regularly monitored.

CONCLUSION

Clinical supervision as discussed in this chapter provides continuity between the past, present, and future practices of career counselors. In commenting on career professionals working in university settings, Marginson (1997) claimed that in the future, they will "inevitably need to work harder and better" in an environment that is "more competitive and resource poor" (p. 15). He claimed that "they will also have to retain and enhance professional identity and continue to develop professional skills by sharing with each other, showing solidarity" (p. 15). Clearly, clinical supervision provides an appropriate vehicle for this to occur.

In concluding this chapter and this part, the metaphor of Knowdell (1996) presented in Chapter 10 is again appropriate. At a time of rapid change when the future is clearly determining our practice, it would be unwise not to drive a vehicle appropriate for the terrain and the journey. Supervision is an ideal vehicle for counselor/learners to drive. It facilitates contact, support, and collegiality with similar others—an important consideration, given that career counselors frequently work in isolation from their colleagues. In addition, it assists them to deal with the roadblocks of the past, cope with the rough terrain of the present, and, most important, to chart a course into the future.

REFERENCES

AMES, A., JR. (1960). *The morning notes of Adelbert Ames.* New Brunswick, NJ: Rutgers University Press.

ARBONA, C. (1989). Hispanic employment and the Holland typology of work. *The Career Development Quarterly, 37,* 257–268.

ARBONA, C. (1990). Career counseling research and Hispanics: A review of the literature. Counseling Psychologist, *18,* 300–323.

ARBONA, C. (1995). Theory and research on racial and ethnic minorities: Hispanic Americans. In F. T. L. Leong (Ed.), *Career development and vocational behavior of racial and ethnic minorities* (pp. 37–66). Hillsdale, NJ: Erlbaum.

ARBONA, C. (1996). Career theory and practice in a multicultural context. In M. L. Savickas & W. B. Walsh (Eds.), *Handbook of career counseling theory and practice* (pp. 45–54). Palo Alto, CA: Davies-Black.

ARTHUR, M. B., HALL, D. T., & LAWRENCE, B. S. (Eds.). (1989). *Handbook of career theory.* Cambridge, UK: Cambridge University Press.

ASSOCIATION FOR COUNSELOR EDUCATION AND SUPERVISION INTEREST GROUP. (1995). Ethical guidelines for counseling supervisors. *Counselor Education and Supervision, 34,* 270–276.

ASTIN, H. S. (1984). The meaning of work in women's lives: A sociopsychological model of career choice and work behavior. *Counseling Psychologist, 12,* 117–126.

BACK, A. (1997). Career counselling with Chinese students. In W. Patton & M. McMahon (Eds.), *Career development in practice: A systems theory perspective* (pp. 105–116). Sydney, Australia: New Hobsons Press.

BAILYN, L. (1989). Understanding individual experience at work. In M. B. Arthur, D. T. Hall, & B. S. Lawrence (Eds.), *Handbook of career theory* (pp. 477–489). Cambridge, UK: Cambridge University Press.

BANDURA, A. (1977). Self-efficacy: Toward a unifying theory of behavioral change. *Psychology Review, 84,* 191–215.

BANDURA, A. (1982). The psychology of chance encounters and life paths. *American Psychologist, 37,* 747–755.

BANDURA, A. (1986). *Social foundations of thought and action: A social cognitive theory.* Englewood Cliffs, NJ: Prentice Hall.

BATESON, G. (1972). *Steps to an ecology of mind.* New York: Ballantine.

BATESON, G. (1979). *Mind and nature: A necessary unity.* New York: Dutton.

BATESON, G., JACKSON, D., HALEY, J., & WEAKLAND, J. (1956). Toward a theory of schizophrenia. *Behavioral Science, 1,* 251–264.

BEAVERS, S. (1995, September). *Comprehensive guidance and counselling programs in opera-tion: A new direction for guidance in Australia.* Presented at the 5th National Confer-ence of the Australian Guidance and Counselling Association, Hobart, Australia.

BEDNAR, A. K., CUNNINGHAM, D., DUFFY, T. M., & PERRY, J. D. (1992). Theory into prac-tice: How do we link? In T. M. Duffy & D. H. Jonassen (Eds.), *Constructivism and the technology of instruction: A conversation* (pp. 19–34). Hillsdale, NJ: Erlbaum.

BEITMAN, B. D., GOLDFRIED, M. R., & NORCROSS, J. C. (1989). The movement toward integrating the psychotherapies: An overview. *American Journal of Psychiatry, 146,* 138–147.

BERG, I. K., & DE SHAZER, S. (1993). Making numbers talk: Language in therapy. In S. Friedman (Ed.), *The new language of change* (pp. 5–24). New York: Guilford Press.

BERGER, P., & LUCKMANN, T. (1967). *The social construction of reality.* New York: Doubleday Anchor.

BERNARD, J. M., & GOODYEAR, R. K. (1992). *Fundamentals of clinical supervision.* Boston: Allyn & Bacon.

BETZ, N. E. (1989). Implications of the null environment hypothesis for women's career development and for counseling psychology. *Counseling Psychologist, 19,* 248–253.

BETZ, N. E. (1992). Career assessment: A review of critical issues. In S. D. Brown & R. W. Lent (Eds.), *Handbook of counseling psychology* (2nd ed., pp. 453–484). New York: Wiley-Interscience.

BETZ, N. E. (1993). Toward the integration of multicultural and career counseling. *The Career Development Quarterly, 42,* 53–55.

BETZ, N. E. (1994a). Basic issues and concepts in career counseling for women. In W. B. Walsh & S. H. Osipow (Eds.), *Career counseling for women* (pp. 1–41). Hillsdale, NJ: Erlbaum.

BETZ, N. E. (1994b). Self-concept theory in career development and counseling. *The Ca-reer Development Quarterly, 43,* 32–42.

BETZ, N. E., & CORNING, A. (1993). The inseparability of "career" and "personal" coun-seling. *The Career Development Quarterly, 42,* 137–142.

BETZ, N. E., & FITZGERALD, L. F. (1987). *The career psychology of women.* Orlando, FL: Academic Press.

BETZ, N. E., & FITZGERALD, L. F. (1994). Career development in cultural context. In M. L. Savickas & R. W. Lent (Eds.), *Convergence in career development theories* (pp. 103–117). Palo Alto, CA: CPP.

BETZ, N. E., & HACKETT, G. (1981). The relationship of career related self-efficacy expec-tations to perceive career options in college women and men. *Journal of Counsel-ing Psychology, 28,* 399–410.

BEZANSON, L., & HEIBERT, B. (1996). Career development in Canada: An emerging na-tional strategy. In R. Feller & G. Walz (Eds.), *Career transitions in turbulent times: Exploring work, learning and careers* (pp. 349–362). Greensboro, NC: Educational Resources Information Center, Counseling and Student Services Clearinghouse.

BIMROSE, J., & WILDEN, S. (1994). Supervision in careers guidance: Empowerment of control. *British Journal of Guidance and Counselling, 22,* 373–383.

BINGHAM, R. P., & WARD, C. M. (1994). Career counseling with ethnic minority women. In W. B. Walsh & S. H. Osipow (Eds.), *Career counseling for women* (pp. 165–195). Hillsdale, NJ: Erlbaum.

BINGHAM, R. P., & WARD, C. M. (1996). Practical applications of career counseling with ethnic minority women. In M. L. Savickas & W. B. Walsh (Eds.), *Handbook of career counseling theory and practice* (pp. 291–314). Palo Alto, CA: Davies-Black.

BLAU, P. M., & DUNCAN, O. D. (1967). *The American occupational structure.* New York: Wiley.

BLAU, P. M., GUSTAD, J. W., JESSOR, R., PARNES, H. S., & WILCOCK, R. C. (1956). Occupa-tional choice: A conceptual framework. *Industrial and Labor Relations Review, 9,* 531–543.

BLOCHER, D. (1983). Toward a cognitive developmental approach to counseling super-vision. *Counseling Psychologist, 11,* 27–34.

BLUSTEIN, D. L. (1992). Toward the reinvigoration of the vocational realm of career psychology. *Counseling Psychologist, 20,* 712–723.

BLUSTEIN, D. L. (1994). "Who am I?": The question of self and identity in career development. In M. L. Savickas & R. W. Lent (Eds.), *Convergence in career development theories* (pp. 130–154). Palo Alto, CA: CPP.

BLUSTEIN, D. L. (1997). A context-rich perspective of career exploration across life roles. *The Career Development Quarterly, 45,* 260–274.

BLUSTEIN, D. L., & SPENGLER, P. M. (1995). Personal adjustment: Career counseling and psychotherapy. In W. B. Walsh & S. H. Osipow (Eds.), *Handbook of vocational psychology* (2nd ed., pp. 295–329). Hillsdale, NJ: Erlbaum.

BORDERS, L. D. (1989). Facilitating supervisee growth: Implications of the developmental models of counseling supervision. *Michigan Journal of Counseling and Development, 17,* 9–14.

BORDERS, L. D. (1994, September). *Learning to think like a supervisor.* Paper presented at the Conference of the Queensland Guidance and Counselling Association, Twin Waters, Australia.

BORDERS, L. D. (1996). The Journal of Counseling and Development: On its purpose, function, and goals. *Journal of Counseling and Development, 75,* 3–4.

BORDERS, L. D., & DRURY, S. M. (1992). Comprehensive school counseling programs: A review for policymakers and practitioners. *Journal of Counseling and Development, 70,* 487–498.

BORDERS, L. D., & LEDDICK, G. R. (1987). *Handbook of counseling supervision.* Alexandria, VA: Association for Counselor Education and Supervision.

BORDIN, E. S. (1983). A working alliance based model of supervision. *Counseling Psychologist, 11,* 35–42.

BORDIN, E. S. (1990). Psychodynamic model of career choice and satisfaction. In D. Brown & L. Brooks (Eds.), *Career choice and development: Applying contemporary theories to practice* (2nd ed., pp. 102–144). San Francisco: Jossey-Bass.

BORDIN, E. S. (1994). Intrinsic motivation and the active self: Convergence from a psychodynamic perspective. In M. L. Savickas & R. W. Lent (Eds.), *Convergence in career development theories* (pp. 53–62). Palo Alto, CA: CPP.

BORGEN, F. H. (1991). Megatrends and milestones in vocational behaviour: A 20-year counseling psychology retrospective. *Journal of Vocational Behavior, 39,* 263–290.

BORGEN, F. H. (1995). Leading edges of vocational psychology: Diversity and vitality. In W. B. Walsh & S. H. Osipow (Eds.), *Handbook of vocational psychology* (2nd ed., pp. 427–441). Mahwah, NJ: Erlbaum.

BOROW, H. (1984). Occupational socialization: Acquiring a sense of work. In N. C. Gysbers (Ed.), *Designing careers* (pp. 160–190). San Francisco: Jossey-Bass.

BOROW, H. (1996). Vocational guidance and social activism: A fifty year perspective. In R. Feller & G. Walz (Eds.), *Career transitions in turbulent times: Exploring work, learning and careers* (pp. 3–10). Greensboro, NC: Educational Resources Information Center, Counseling and Student Services Clearinghouse.

BOWEN, M. (1978). *Family therapy in clinical practice.* New York: Aronson.

BOYD, J. D. (1978). *Counselor supervision: Approaches, preparation, practices.* Muncie, IN: Accelerated Development Inc.

BRADLEY, L. J., & WHITING, P. P. (1989). Supervision training: A model. In L. J. Bradley (Ed.), *Counselor supervision: Principles, process and practice* (pp. 447–480). Muncie, IN: Accelerated Development Inc.

BRADLEY, R. W. (1994). Tests and counseling: How did we ever become partners? *Measurement and Evaluation in Counseling and Development, 26,* 224–226.

BRANTLINGER, E. (1992). Unmentionable futures: Postschool planning for low-income teenagers. *School Counselor, 39,* 281–291.

BRATCHER, W. E. (1982). The influence of the family on career selection: A systems perspective. *Personnel and Guidance Journal, 61,* 87–91.

BRONFENBRENNER, U. (1977). Toward an experimental ecology of human development. *American Psychologist, 32,* 513–531.

BRONFENBRENNER, U. (1988). Interacting systems in human development. Research paradigms: Present and future. In N. Bolger, A. Caspi, G. Bowney, & M. Moorehouse (Eds.), *Persons in context: Developmental processes* (pp. 25–49). Cambridge, UK: Cambridge University Press.

BROOKS, L. (1990). Recent developments in theory building. In D. Brown & L. Brooks (Eds.), *Career choice and development: Applying contemporary theories to practice* (2nd ed., pp. 364–393). San Francisco: Jossey-Bass.

BROWN, D. (1987). The status of Holland's theory of vocational choice. *The Career Development Quarterly, 36,* 13–23.

BROWN, D. (1990). Summary, comparison, and critique of the major theories. In D. Brown & L. Brooks (Eds.), *Career choice and development: Applying contemporary theories to practice* (2nd ed., pp. 338–363). San Francisco: Jossey-Bass.

BROWN, D. (1995). A values-based approach to facilitating career transitions. *The Career Development Quarterly, 44,* 4–11.

BROWN, D. (1996a). Brown's values-based, holistic model of career and life-role choices and satisfaction. In D. Brown & L. Brooks (Eds.), *Career choice and development* (3rd ed., pp. 337–372). San Francisco: Jossey-Bass.

BROWN, D. (1996b). Status of career development theories. In D. Brown & L. Brooks (Eds.), *Career choice and development* (3rd ed., pp. 513–525). San Francisco: Jossey-Bass.

BROWN, D., & BROOKS, L. (Eds.). (1990a). *Career choice and development: Applying contemporary theories to practice* (2nd ed.). San Francisco: Jossey-Bass.

BROWN, D., & BROOKS, L. (1990b). Introduction to career development. In D. Brown & L. Brooks (Eds.), *Career choice and development: Applying contemporary theories to practice* (2nd ed., pp. 1–12). San Francisco: Jossey-Bass.

BROWN, D., & BROOKS, L. (1991). *Career counseling techniques.* Needham Heights, MA: Allyn & Bacon.

BROWN, D., & BROOKS, L. (Eds.). (1996a). *Career choice and development* (3rd ed.). San Francisco: Jossey-Bass.

BROWN, D., & BROOKS, L. (1996b). Introduction to theories of career development and choice. In D. Brown & L. Brooks (Eds.), *Career choice and development* (3rd ed., pp. 1–30). San Francisco: Jossey-Bass.

BROWN, D., & CRACE, R. K. (1996). Values in life role choices and outcomes: A conceptual model. *The Career Development Quarterly, 44,* 211–223.

BROWN, M. (1995). The career development of African Americans: Theoretical and empirical issues. In F. T. L. Leong (Ed.), *Career development and vocational behavior of racial and ethnic minorities* (pp. 7–36). Hillsdale, NJ: Erlbaum.

BROWN, S. D., & WATKINS, C. E. (1994). Psychodynamic and personological perspectives on vocational behavior. In M. L. Savickas & R. W. Lent (Eds.), *Convergence in career development theories* (pp. 197–206). Palo Alto, CA: CPP.

BURLEW, L. (1996). Career counseling is not mental health counseling: More myth than fact. In R. Feller & G. Walz (Eds.), *Career transitions in turbulent times: Exploring work, learning and careers* (pp. 371–380). Greensboro, NC: Educational Resources Information Center, Counseling and Student Services Clearinghouse.

BYRNE, E. M., & BEAVERS W. S. (1991). *Shep-Apist research: Curricular choices, Careers Education and Careers Guidance Project Discussion Paper 1.* Unpublished manuscript, University of Queensland, Brisbane, Australia.

CAMPBELL, R. (1969). Vocational ecology: A perspective for the study of careers? *Counseling Psychologist, 1,* 20–23.

CANDY, P., CREBERT, G., & O'LEARY, J. (1991). *Developing lifelong learning through undergraduate education* (National Board of Employment, Education, and Training, Commissioned Rep. No. 28). Canberra: Australian Government Publishing Service.

CANTRIL, H., AMES, A., HASTORF, A., & ITTELSON, W. (1949). Psychology and scientific research: The transactional view in psychological research. *Science, 110,* 517–522.

CAPRA, F. (1975). *The tao of physics.* Berkeley, CA: Shambhala.

CAPRA, F. (1982). *The turning point: Science, society, and the rising culture.* New York: Simon & Schuster.

CHARLAND, W. (1996). Careers in changing times: Learning what comes next. In R. Feller & G. Walz (Eds.), *Career transitions in turbulent times: Exploring work, learning and careers* (pp. 125–134). Greensboro, NC: Educational Resources Information Center, Counseling and Student Services Clearinghouse.

CHARTRAND, J. M. (1991). The evolution of trait and factor career counseling: A person × environment fit approach. *Journal of Counseling and Development, 69,* 518–524.

CHEATHAM, H. E. (1990). Africentricity and career development of African Americans. *The Career Development Quarterly, 38,* 334–346.

CHECKLAND, P. (1979). The shape of the systems movement. *Journal of Applied Systems Analysis, 6,* 129–135.

CHECKLAND, P. (1981). *Systems thinking, systems practice.* New York: Wiley.

CHERNISS, C. (1980). *Staff burnout: Job stress in the human services.* Beverly Hills, CA: Sage.

CHODOROW, N. (1978). *The reproduction of mothering.* Berkeley: University of California Press.

CHUNG, Y. B. (1995). Career decision making of lesbian, gay, and bisexual individuals. *The Career Development Quarterly, 44,* 178–190.

CHUNG, Y. B., & HARMON, L. W. (1994). The career interests and aspirations of gay men: How sex-role orientation is related. *Journal of Vocational Behavior, 45,* 223–239.

CLARKSON, P., & GILBERT, M. (1991). The training of counsellor trainers and supervisors. In W. Dryden & B. Thorne (Eds.), *Training and supervision for counselling in action* (pp. 143–169). Newbury Park, CA: Sage.

COLLETT, I. (1997). Implications of rural location on career development. In W. Patton & M. McMahon (Eds.), *Career development in practice: A systems theory perspective* (pp. 71–82). Sydney, Australia: New Hobsons Press.

COLLIN, A. (1985). The learning circle of a research project on "mid-career change": Through stages to systems thinking. *Journal of Applied Systems Analysis, 12,* 35–53.

COLLIN, A. (1990). Mid-life career change research. In R. A. Young & W. A. Borgen (Eds.), *Methodological approaches to the study of career* (pp. 197–219). New York: Praeger.

COLLIN, A. (1996). New relationships between researchers, theorists and practitioners. In M. L. Savickas & W. B. Walsh (Eds.), *Handbook of career counseling theory and practice* (pp. 377–399). Palo Alto, CA: Davies-Black.

COLLIN, A., & WATTS, A. G. (1996). The death and transfiguration of career—and of career guidance? *British Journal of Guidance and Counseling, 24,* 385–398.

COLLIN, A., & YOUNG, R. A. (1986). New directions for theories of career. *Human Relations, 39,* 837–853.

COLLIN, A., & YOUNG, R. A. (1988). Career development and hermeneutical inquiry Part II: Undertaking hermeneutical research. *Canadian Journal of Counselling, 22,* 191–201.

COOK, E. (1993). The gendered context of life: Implications for women's and men's career life plans. *The Career Development Quarterly, 41,* 227–237.

COOK, E. (1994). Role salience and multiple roles: A gender perspective. *The Career Development Quarterly, 43,* 85–95.

COREY, G. (1991). *Theory and practice of counseling and psychotherapy* (4th ed.). Pacific Grove, CA: Brooks/Cole.

CORNFORD, I., ATHANASOU, J., & PITHERS, R. (1996). Career counsellors and the promotion of lifelong learning. *Australian Journal of Career Development, 5,* 43–46.

CRANACH, M. VON. (1982). The psychological study of goal-directed action: Basic issues. In M. von Cranach & R. Harre (Eds.), *The analysis of action: Recent theoretical and empirical advances* (pp. 35–73). Cambridge, UK: Cambridge University Press.

CRITES, J. O. (1969). *Vocational psychology.* New York: McGraw-Hill.

CRITES, J. O. (1981). *Career counseling: Models, methods, and materials.* New York: McGraw Hill.

CROTEAU, J., & HEDSTROM, S. (1993). Integrating commonality and difference: The key to career counseling with lesbian women and gay men. *The Career Development Quarterly, 41,* 201–209.

CROW, C. (1996). Transitions in turbulent times: A case for education reform. In R. Feller & G. Walz (Eds.), *Career transitions in turbulent times: Exploring work, learning and careers* (pp. 135–142). Greensboro, NC: Educational Resources Information Center, Counseling and Student Services Clearinghouse.

CUNNINGHAM, D. J. (1992). Assessing constructions and constructing assessments: A dialogue. In T. M. Duffy & D. H. Jonassen (Eds.), *Constructivism and the technology of instruction: A conversation* (pp. 35–44). Hillsdale, NJ: Erlbaum.

DAVIDSON, S., & GILBERT, L. (1993). Career counseling is a personal matter. *The Career Development Quarterly, 42,* 149–153.

DAVIS, A. H., SAVICKI, V., COOLEY, E. J., & FIRTH, J. L. (1989). Burnout and counselor expectations of supervision. *Counselor Education and Supervision, 28,* 234–241.

DAWIS, R. V. (1992). The individual differences tradition in counseling psychology. *Journal of Counseling Psychology, 39,* 7–19.

DAWIS, R. V. (1994). The theory of work adjustment as convergent theory. In M. L. Savickas & R. W. Lent (Eds.), *Convergence in career development theories* (pp. 33–43). Palo Alto, CA: CPP.

DAWIS, R. V. (1996). The theory of work adjustment and person-environment correspondence counseling. In D. Brown & L. Brooks (Eds.), *Career choice and development* (3rd ed., pp. 75–120). San Francisco: Jossey-Bass.

DAWIS, R. V., & LOFQUIST, L. H. (1976). Personality style and the process of work adjustment. *Journal of Counseling Psychology, 23,* 55–59.

DAWIS, R. V., & LOFQUIST, L. H. (1984). *A psychological theory of work adjustment: An individual differences model and its application.* Minneapolis: University of Minnesota Press.

DEPARTMENT OF EDUCATION AND SCIENCE. (1989). *Careers education and guidance from 5–16.* London: Her Majesty's Stationery Office.

DEWEY, J., & BENTLEY, A. (1949). *The knowing and the known.* Boston: Beacon.

DIAMANT, L. (Ed.). (1993). *Homosexual issues in the workplace.* New York: Hemisphere.

DIGMAN, J. M. (1990). Personality structure: Emergence of the five-factor model. *Annual Review of Psychology, 41,* 417–440.

ECCLES, J. S. (1994). Understanding women's educational and occupational choices. *Psychology of Women Quarterly, 18,* 585–609.

EDELWICH, J., & BRODSKY, A. (1980). *Burn-out: Stages of disillusionment in the helping professions.* New York: Human Sciences Press.

ELLIOTT, J. E. (1993a). Career development with lesbian and gay clients. *The Career Development Quarterly, 41,* 210–226.

ELLIOTT, J. E. (1993b). Lesbian and gay concerns in career development. In L. Diamant (Ed.), *Homosexual issues in the workplace* (pp. 25–43). New York: Hemisphere.

ELLYARD, P. (1993, July). *Education 2020: Preparing for the 21st century.* Paper presented at the N.S.W. N. S. W. State Guidance Conference of the Australian Guidance and Counselling Association, Sydney, Australia.

ENGELS, D. W., & DAMERON, J. D. (Eds.). (1990). *The professional counselor: Competencies, performance guidelines and assessment.* Alexandria, VA: American Association for Counseling and Development.

ERIKSON, E. H. (1959). Identity and the life cycle. *Psychological Issues, 1,* 50–180.

ETRINGER, B., HILLERBRAND, E., & HETHERINGTON, C. (1990). The influence of sexual orientation on career decision making: A research note. *Journal of Homosexuality, 19,* 103–111.

ETTINGER, J. (1996). Meeting the career development needs of individuals with disabilities. In R. Feller & G. Walz (Eds.), *Career transitions in turbulent times: Exploring work, learning and careers* (pp. 239–244). Greensboro, NC: Educational Resources Information Center, Counseling and Student Services Clearinghouse.

FARMER, H. S. (1984). A shiNew York fresh minted penNew York. *Counseling Psychologist, 12,* 141–144.

FARMER, H. S. (1985). Model of career and achievement motivation for women and men. *Journal of Counseling Psychology, 32,* 363–390.

FARMER, H. S., WARDROP, J. S., ANDERSON, M. Z., & RISINGER, F. (1993, August). *Understanding women's career choices.* Paper presented at the annual meeting of the American Psychological Association, Toronto, Canada.

FASSINGER, R. E. (1985). A causal model of college women's career choice. *Journal of Vocational Behavior, 27*, 123–153.

FASSINGER, R. E. (1990). Causal models of career choice in two samples of college women. *Journal of Vocational Behavior, 36*, 225–248.

FASSINGER, R. E. (Ed.). (1991). Counseling lesbian women and gay men [Special issue]. *Counseling Psychologist, 19*(2).

FASSINGER, R. E. (1995). From invisibility to integration: Lesbian identity in the workplace. *The Career Development Quarterly, 44*, 146–167.

FEATHER, N. T. (1990). *The psychological impact of unemployment.* New York: Springer-Verlag.

FELLER, R. (1996). Redefining "career" during the work revolution. In R. Feller & G. Walz (Eds.), *Career transitions in turbulent times: Exploring work, learning and careers* (pp. 143–154). Greensboro, NC: Educational Resources Information Center, Counseling and Student Services Clearinghouse.

FELLER, R., & WALZ, G. (Eds.). (1996). *Career transitions in turbulent times: Exploring work, learning and careers.* Greensboro, NC: Educational Resources Information Center, Counseling and Student Services Clearinghouse.

FELTHAM, C., & DRYDEN, W. (1994). *Developing counsellor supervision.* Thousand Oaks, CA: Sage.

FITZGERALD, L. F., & BETZ, N. E. (1994). Career development in cultural context: The role of gender, race, class, and sexual orientation. In M. L. Savickas & R. W. Lent (Eds.), *Convergence in career development theories* (pp. 103–117). Palo Alto, CA: CPP.

FITZGERALD, L. F., & CRITES, J. O. (1980). Toward a career psychology of women: What do we know? What do we need to know? *Journal of Counseling Psychology, 27*, 44–62.

FITZGERALD, L. F., FASSINGER, R. E., & BETZ, N. E. (1995). Theoretical advances in the study of women's career development. In W. B. Walsh & S. H. Osipow (Eds.), *Handbook of vocational psychology* (2nd ed., pp. 67–109). Mahwah, NJ: Erlbaum.

FITZGERALD, L. F., & WEITZMAN, L. (1992). Women's career development: Theory and practice from a feminist perspective. In Z. Leibowitz & D. Lea (Eds.), *Adult career development: Concepts, issues and practices* (pp. 125–157). Alexandria, VA: National Career Development Association.

FORD, D. (1987). *Humans as self-constructing living systems.* Hillsdale, NJ: Erlbaum.

FORD, D., & LERNER, R. (1992). *Developmental systems theory: An integrative approach.* Newbury Park, CA: Sage.

FORD, M. (1992). *Motivating humans: Goals, emotions, and personal agency beliefs.* Newbury Park, CA: Sage.

FORD, M., & FORD, D. (Eds.). (1987). *Humans as self-constructing living systems: Putting the framework to work.* Hillsdale, NJ: Erlbaum.

FORREST, L., & MIKOLAITIS, N. (1986). The relational component of identity: An expansion of career development theory. *The Career Development Quarterly, 35*, 76–88.

FOUAD, N. A. (1994). Career assessment with Latinas/Hispanics. *Journal of Career Assessment, 2*, 226–239.

FOUAD, N. A., & ARBONA, C. (1994). Careers in a cultural context. *The Career Development Quarterly, 43*, 96–112.

FOUAD, N. A., & DANCER, L. S. (1992). Cross-cultural structure of interests: Mexico and the United States. *Journal of Vocational Behavior, 40*, 129–143.

FRANKLIN, C., & NURIUS, P. S. (1996). Constructivist therapy: New directions in social work practice. *Families in Society, 77*, 323–324.

FREEMAN, S. (1993). Donald Super: A perspective of career development. *Journal of Career Development, 19*, 255–264.

FRYER, D., & ULLAH, P. (Eds.). (1987). *Unemployed people.* Milton Keynes, UK: Open University Press.

GALLOS, J. V. (1989). Exploring women's development: Implications for career theory, practice and research. In M. B. Arthur, D. T. Hall & B. S. Lawrence (Eds.), *Handbook of career theory* (pp. 110–123). Cambridge, UK: Cambridge University Press.

GELSO, C., & FASSINGER, R. E. (1992). Personality, development, and counseling psychology: Depth, ambivalence, and actualization. *Journal of Counseling Psychology, 39,* 275–298.

GELSO, C., PRINCE, J., CORNFIELD, J., PAYNE, A., ROYALTY, G., & WILEY, M. (1985). Quality of counselors' intake evaluations for clients with problems that are primarily vocational versus personal. *Journal of Counseling Psychology, 32,* 339–347.

GERGEN, K. J. (1993). Foreword. In S. Friedman (Ed.), *The new language of change* (pp. ix–xi). New York: Guilford Press.

GILBERT, L. A. (1984). Comments on the meaning of work in women's lives. *Counseling Psychologist, 12,* 129–130.

GILLIGAN, C. (1977). In a different voice: Women's conceptions of self and morality. *Harvard Educational Review, 47,* 481–517.

GILLIGAN, C. (1979). Woman's place in man's life cycle. *Harvard Educational Review, 49,* 431–445.

GILLIGAN, C. (1982). *In a different voice.* Cambridge, MA: Harvard University Press.

GINZBERG, E. (1972). Toward a theory of occupational choice: A restatement. *Vocational Guidance Quarterly, 20,* 169–176.

GINZBERG, E. (1984). Career development. In D. Brown & L. Brooks (Eds.), *Career choice and development: Applying contemporary theories to practice* (pp. 172–190). San Francisco: Jossey-Bass.

GINZBERG, E., GINSBURG, S. W., AXELRAD, S., & HERMA, J. L. (1951). *Occupational choice: An approach to general theory.* New York: Columbia University Press.

GLEICK, J. (1987). *Chaos: Making of a new science.* New York: Viking Penguin.

GOLDENBERG, I., & GOLDENBERG, H. (1991). *Family therapy: An overview.* Pacific Grove, CA: Brooks/Cole.

GOLDMAN, L. (1990). Qualitative assessment. *Counseling Psychologist, 18,* 205–213.

GOLDMAN, L. (1992). Qualitative assessment: An approach for counselors. *Journal of Counseling and Development, 70,* 616–621.

GOLDMAN, L. (1994). The marriage is over: For most of us. *Measurement and Evaluation in Counseling and Development, 26,* 217–218.

GOTTFREDSON, G. D., HOLLAND, J. L., & OGAWA, D. K. (1982). *Dictionary of the Holland occupational codes.* Palo Alto, CA: CPP.

GOTTFREDSON, L. S. (1981). Circumscription and compromise: A developmental theory of occupational aspirations. *Journal of Counseling Psychology, 28,* 545–579.

GOTTFREDSON, L. S. (1983). Creating and criticizing theory. *Journal of Vocational Behavior, 23,* 203–212.

GOTTFREDSON, L. S. (1986). Special groups and the beneficial use of vocational interest inventories. In W. B. Walsh & S. H. Osipow (Eds.), *Advances in vocational psychology: Assessment of interests* (pp. 127–198). Hillsdale, NJ: Erlbaum.

GOTTFREDSON, L. S. (1996). Gottfredson's theory of circumscription and compromise. In D. Brown & L. Brooks (Eds.), *Career choice and development* (3rd ed., pp. 179–232). San Francisco: Jossey-Bass.

GRANVOLD, D. K. (1996). Constructivist psychotherapy. *Families in Society: The Journal of Contemporary Human Services, 77,* 345–359

GUTEK, B., & LARWOOD, L. (Eds.). (1987). *Women's career development.* Beverly Hills, CA: Sage.

GYSBERS, N. C. (1990). *Comprehensive guidance programs that work.* Ann Arbor, MI: Educational Resources Information Center, Counseling and Personnel Services Clearinghouse.

GYSBERS, N. C. (1996). Beyond career development: Life career development revisited. In R. Feller & G. Walz (Eds.), *Career transitions in turbulent times: Exploring work, learning and careers* (pp. 11–20). Greensboro, NC: Educational Resources Information Center, Counseling and Student Services Clearinghouse.

GYSBERS, N. C., & HENDERSON, P. (1997). Comprehensive guidance programs that work—II. Greensboro, NC: Educational Resources Information Center, Counseling and Student Services Clearinghouse.

GYSBERS, N. C., HEPPNER, M. J., & JOHNSTON, J. A. (1998). *Career counseling. Process, issues and techniques.* Needham Heights, MA: Allyn & Bacon.

GYSBERS, N. C., & MOORE, E. J. (1974). *Career guidance, counseling, and placement: Elements of an illustrative program guide.* Columbia: University of Missouri, Columbia University Press.

HACKETT, G. (1993). Career counseling and psychotherapy: False dichotomies and recommended remedies. *Journal of Career Assessment, 1,* 105–117.

HACKETT, G. (1995). Self-efficacy in career choice and development. In A. Bandura (Ed.), *Self-efficacy in changing societies* (pp. 232–258). Cambridge, UK: Cambridge University Press.

HACKETT, G., & BETZ, N. (1981). A self-efficacy approach to the career development of women. *Journal of Vocational Behavior, 18,* 326–339.

HACKETT, G., BETZ, N. E., CASAS, J. M., & ROCHA-SINGH, I. A. (1992). Gender, ethnicity, and social-cognitive factors predicting the academic achievement of students in engineering. *Journal of Counseling Psychology, 39,* 527–538.

HACKETT, G., & LENT, R. W. (1992). Theoretical advances and current inquiry in career psychology. In S. D. Brown & R. W. Lent (Eds.), *Handbook of counseling psychology* (pp. 419–451). New York.

HACKETT, G., LENT, R. W., & GREENHAUS, J. H. (1991). Advances in vocational theory and research: A 20-year retrospective. *Journal of Vocational Behavior, 38,* 3–38.

HALL, D. T. (Ed.). (1996). *The career is dead—long live the career: A relational approach to careers.* San Francisco: Jossey-Bass.

HANKS, P. (Ed.). (1980). *Collins dictionary of the English language.* Sydney, Australia: Collins.

HANSEN, J. C. (1987). Cross-cultural research on vocational interests. *Measurement and Evaluation in Counseling and Development, 19,* 163–176.

HANSEN, J. C. (1992). Does enough evidence exist to modify Holland's theory to accommodate the individual differences of diverse populations? *Journal of Vocational Behavior, 40,* 188–193.

HANSEN, L. S. (1974). Counseling and career (self) development of women. *Focus on Guidance, 7,* 1–11, 14, 15.

HANSEN, L. S. (1996). ILP: Integrating our lives, shaping our society. In R. Feller & G. Walz (Eds.), *Career transitions in turbulent times: Exploring work, learning and careers* (pp. 21–30). Greensboro, NC: Educational Resources Information Center, Counseling and Student Services Clearinghouse.

HANSEN, L. S. (1997). *Integrative life planning: Critical tasks for career development and changing life patterns.* San Francisco: Jossey-Bass.

HARMON, L. W. (1984). What's new? A response to Astin. *Counseling Psychologist, 12,* 127–128.

HARMON, L. W. (1996). A moving target: The widening gap between theory and practice. In M. L. Savickas & W. B. Walsh. (Eds.), *Handbook of career counseling theory and practice* (pp. 37–44). Palo Alto, CA: Davies-Black.

HARRIS-BOWLSBEY, J. (1996a). Serving all of our people in the 21st century. In R. Feller & G. Walz (Eds.), *Career transitions in turbulent times: Exploring work, learning and careers* (pp. 363–370). Greensboro, NC: Educational Resources Information Center, Counseling and Student Services Clearinghouse.

HARRIS-BOWLSBEY, J. (1996b). Synthesis and antithesis: Perspectives from Herr, Bloch, and Watts. *The Career Development Quarterly, 45,* 54–57.

HART, G. M. (1982). *The process of clinical supervision.* Baltimore: University Park Press.

HASTORF, A. H., & CANTRIL, H. (1954). They saw a game. *Journal of Abnormal and Social Psychology, 49,* 129–134.

HAWKINS, P., & SHOHET, R. (1989). *Supervision in the helping professions.* Milton Keynes, UK: Open University Press.

HAWKINS, P., & SHOHET, R. (1991). Approaches to the supervision of counsellors. In W. Dryden & B. Thorne (Eds.), *Training and supervision for counselling in action* (pp. 99–115). Newbury Park, CA: Sage.

HEALY, C. (1990). Reforming career appraisals to meet the needs of clients in the 1990s. *Counseling Psychologist, 18,* 214–226.

HEPPNER, M., O'BRIEN, K., HINKELMAN, J., & FLORES, L. (1996). Training counseling psychologists in career development: Are we our own worst enemies? *Counseling Psychologist, 24,* 105–125.

HEPPNER, M., O'BRIEN, K., HINKELMAN, J., & HUMPHREY, C. (1994). Shifting the paradigm: The use of creativity in career counseling. *Journal of Career Development, 21,* 77–86.

HERR, E. L. (1992). Emerging trends in career counseling. *International Journal for the Advancement of Counseling, 15,* 255–288.

HERR, E. L. (1996a). Perspectives on ecological context, social policy, and career guidance. *The Career Development Quarterly, 45,* 5–19.

HERR, E. L. (1996b). Toward the convergence of career theory and practice. In M. L. Savickas & W. B. Walsh (Eds.), *Handbook of career counseling theory and practice* (pp. 13–35). Palo Alto, CA: Davies-Black.

HERR, E. L. (1997). Career counselling: A process in process. *British Journal of Guidance and Counselling, 25,* 81–93.

HERR, E. L., & CRAMER, S. H. (1992). *Career guidance and counseling through the lifespan: Systematic approaches* (4th ed.). New York: HarperCollins.

HERRIOTT, P. (1992). *The career management challenge: Balancing individual and organisational needs.* Newbury Park, CA: Sage.

HERSHENSON, D. (1996). Work adjustment: A neglected area in career counseling. *Journal of Counseling and Development, 74,* 442–446.

HESKETH, B. (1985). In search of a conceptual framework for vocational psychology. *Journal of Counseling and Development, 64,* 26–30.

HESKETH, B., & ROUNDS, J. (1995). International cross-cultural approaches to career development. In W. B. Walsh & S. H. Osipow (Eds.), *Handbook of vocational psychology* (2nd ed., pp. 367–390). Mahwah, NJ: Erlbaum.

HESS, A. K. (1986). Growth in supervision: Stages in supervisee and supervisor development. *Clinical Supervisor, 4,* 51–67.

HESS, A. K. (1987). Psychotherapy supervision: Stages, Buber, and a theory of relationship. *Professional Psychology: Research and Practice, 18,* 251–259.

HETHERINGTON, C. (1991). Life planning and career counseling with gay and lesbian students. In N. J. Evans & V. A. Wall (Eds.), *Beyond tolerance: Gays, lesbians and bisexuals on campus* (pp. 131–146). Alexandria, VA: American College Personnel Association.

HETHERINGTON, C., HILLERBRAND, E., & ETRINGER, B. (1989). Career counseling with gay men: Issues and recommendations for research. *Journal of Counseling and Development, 67,* 452–454.

HETHERINGTON, C., & ORZEK, A. (1989). Career counseling and life planning with lesbian women. *Journal of Counseling and Development, 68,* 52–57.

HOLLAND, J. L. (1966). *The psychology of vocational choice.* Waltham, MA: Blaisdell.

HOLLAND, J. L. (1973). *Making vocational choices: A theory of careers.* Englewood Cliffs, NJ: Prentice Hall.

HOLLAND, J. L. (1982, July). *Some implications of career theory for adult development and aging.* Paper presented at the annual meeting of the American Psychological Association, Washington, DC.

HOLLAND, J. L. (1985a). *Making vocational choices: A theory of vocational personalities and work environments.* Englewood Cliffs, NJ: Prentice Hall.

HOLLAND, J. L. (1985b). *Manual for the Vocational Preference Inventory.* Stanford, CA: Stanford University Press.

HOLLAND, J. L. (1985c). *The Self-Directed Search: A guide to educational and vocational planning.* Odessa, FL: Psychological Assessment Resources.

HOLLAND, J. L. (1987). Current status of Holland's theory of careers: Another perspective. *The Career Development Quarterly, 36,* 24–30.

HOLLAND, J. L. (1992). *Making vocational choices* (2nd ed.). Odessa, FL: Psychological Assessment Resources, Inc.

HOLLAND, J. L. (1994). Separate but unequal is better. In M. L. Savickas & R. W. Lent (Eds.), *Convergence in career development theories* (pp. 45–51). Palo Alto, CA: CPP.

HOLLAND, J. L. (1996). Integrating career theory and practice: The current situation and some potential remedies. In M. L. Savickas & W. B. Walsh (Eds.), *Handbook of career counseling theory and practice* (pp. 1–11). Palo Alto, CA: Davies-Black.

HOLLOWAY, E. L. (1992). Supervision: A way of teaching and learning. In S. D. Brown & R. W. Lent (Eds.), *Handbook of counseling psychology* (2nd ed., pp. 177–214). New York: Wiley.

Holloway, E. L. (1995). *Clinical supervision: A systems approach.* Thousand Oaks, CA: Sage.

HOTCHKISS, L., & BOROW, H. (1996). Sociological perspective on work and career development. In D. Brown & L. Brooks (Eds.), *Career choice and development* (3rd ed., pp. 281–336). San Francisco: Jossey-Bass.

HUTTON, D., & SPLETE, H. (1995). Training needs of career development counsellors and facilitators: American and Australian perspectives. *Australian Journal of Career Development, 4,* 43–46.

IMBIMBO, P. (1994). Integrating personal and career counseling: A challenge for counsellors. *Journal of Employment Counseling, 31,* 50–59.

INSKIPP, F., & PROCTOR, B. (1993). *The art, craft and tasks of counselling supervision. Part 1. Making the most of supervision.* Twickenham, UK: Cascade.

ISAACSON, L. E., & BROWN, D. (1993). *Career information, career counseling, and career development* (5th ed.). New York: Allyn & Bacon.

JEPSEN, D. A. (1989). Adolescent career decision processes as coping responses to the social environment. In R. Hanson (Ed.), *Career development: Preparing for the 21st century* (pp. 67–81). Knoxville, TN: Educational Resources Information Center, Counseling and Personnel Services Clearinghouse.

JEPSEN, D. A. (1992). Annual review: Practice and research in career counseling and development. *The Career Development Quarterly, 41,* 98–129.

JEPSEN, D. A. (1996). Relationships between developmental career counseling theory and practice. In M. L. Savickas & W. B. Walsh (Eds.), *Handbook of career counseling theory and practice* (pp. 135–153). Palo Alto, CA: Davies-Black.

JONES, L. (1996). A harsh and challenging world of work: Implications for counselors. *Journal of Counseling and Development, 74,* 453–459.

KAGAN, N. (1983). Classroom to client: Issues in supervision. *Counseling Psychologist, 11,* 69–72.

KAHN, S. (1984). Astin's model of career development: The working lives of women and men. *Counseling Psychologist, 12,* 145–146.

KASLOW, F. W. (1977). *Supervision, consultation and staff training in the helping professions.* San Francisco: Jossey-Bass.

KELLY, G. (1955). *The psychology of personal constructs.* New York: Norton.

KIDD, J. M. (1996). Career planning within work organisations. In A. G. Watts, B. Law, J. Killeen, J. M. Kidd, & R. Hawthorn, *Rethinking careers education and guidance: Theory, policy and practice* (pp. 142–154). London: Routledge.

KNOWDELL, R. (1996). Perspectives shaping career planning in the future. In R. Feller & G. Walz (Eds.), *Career transitions in turbulent times: Exploring work, learning and careers* (pp. 183–192). Greensboro, NC: Educational Resources Information Center, Counseling and Student Services Clearinghouse.

KOLB, D. A. (1984). *Experiential learning.* Englewood Cliffs, NJ: Prentice Hall.

KRAUS, M. A. (1989). Beyond homeostasis: Toward understanding human systems. *Gestalt Review, 3,* 6–10.

KRUMBOLTZ, J. D. (1979). A social learning theory of career decision making. In A. M. Mitchell, G. B. Jones, & J. D. Krumboltz (Eds.), *Social learning and career decision making* (pp. 19–49). Cranston, RI: Carroll Press.

KRUMBOLTZ, J. D. (1993). Integrating career counseling and personal counseling. *The Career Development Quarterly, 42,* 143–148.

KRUMBOLTZ, J. D. (1994). Improving career development from a social learning perspective. In M. L. Savickas & R. W. Lent (Eds.), *Convergence in career development theories* (pp. 9–32). Palo Alto, CA: CPP.

KRUMBOLTZ, J. D. (1996). A learning theory of career counseling. In M. L. Savickas & W. B. Walsh (Eds.), *Handbook of career counseling theory and practice* (pp. 55–80). Palo Alto, CA: Davies-Black.

KRUMBOLTZ, J. D., BLANDO, J. A., KIM, H., & REIKOWSKI, D. J. (1994). Embedding work values in stories. *Journal of Counseling and Development, 73*, 57–62.

KRUMBOLTZ, J. D., MITCHELL, A. M., & JONES, G. B. (1976). A social learning theory of career selection. *Counseling Psychologist, 6*, 71–81.

KRUMBOLTZ, J. D., & NICHOLS, C. W. (1990). Integrating the social learning theory of career decision making. In W. B. Walsh & S. H. Osipow (Eds.), *Career counseling: Contemporary topics in vocational psychology* (pp. 159–192). Hillsdale, NJ: Erlbaum.

KRUMBOLTZ, J. D., & RANIERI, A. (1996). Learn, yearn, and earn. In R. Feller & G. Walz (Eds.), *Career transitions in turbulent times: Exploring work, learning and careers* (pp. 31–38). Greensboro, NC: Educational Resources Information Center, Counseling and Student Services Clearinghouse.

LARWOOD, L., & GUTEK, B. (1987). Working toward a theory of women's career development. In B. Gutek & L. Larwood (Eds.), *Women's career development* (pp. 170–183). Beverly Hills, CA: Sage.

LAW, B. (1996a). A career learning theory. In A. G. Watts, B. Law, J. Killeen, J. M. Kidd, & R. Hawthorn (Eds.), *Rethinking careers education and guidance: theory, policy and practice* (pp. 46–71). London: Routledge.

LAW, B. (1996b). Developing careers programmes in organisations. In A. G. Watts, B. Law, J. Killeen, J. M. Kidd, & R. Hawthorn (Eds.), *Rethinking careers education and guidance: theory, policy and practice* (pp. 307–330). London: Routledge.

LAW, B. (1996c). Recording achievement and action planning. In A. G. Watts, B. Law, J. Killeen, J. M. Kidd, & R. Hawthorn (Eds.), *Rethinking careers education and guidance: theory, policy and practice* (pp. 247–269). London: Routledge.

LENT, R. W. (1996). Career counseling, science and policy: Revitalizing our paradigms and roles. *The Career Development Quarterly, 45*, 58–64.

LENT, R. W., & BROWN, S. D. (1996). Social cognitive approach to career development: An overview. *The Career Development Quarterly, 44*, 310–321.

LENT, R. W., BROWN, S. D., & HACKETT, G. (1994). Toward a unifying sociocognitive theory of career and academic interest, choice, and performance. *Journal of Vocational Behavior, 45*, 79–122.

LENT, R. W., BROWN, S. D., & HACKETT, G. (1996). Career development from a sociocognitive perspective. In D. Brown & L. Brooks (Eds.), *Career choice and development* (3rd ed., pp. 373–422). San Francisco: Jossey-Bass.

LENT, R. W., & HACKETT, G. (1987). Career self-efficacy: Empirical status and future directions. *Journal of Vocational Behavior, 30*, 347–382.

LENT, R. W., & HACKETT, G. (1994). Sociocognitive mechanisms of personal agency in career development: Pantheoretical aspects. In M. L. Savickas & R. W. Lent (Eds.), *Convergence in career development theories* (pp. 77–101). Palo Alto, CA: CPP.

LENT, R. W., & SAVICKAS, M. L. (1994). Postscript: Is convergence a viable agenda for career psychology? In M. L. Savickas & R. W. Lent (Eds.), *Convergence in career development theories* (pp. 259–271). Palo Alto, CA: CPP.

LEONG, F. T. L. (1993). The career counselling process with racial-ethnic minorities. *The Career Development Quarterly, 42*, 26–41.

LEONG, F. T. L. (Ed.). (1995). *Career development and vocational behavior of racial and ethnic minorities*. Hillsdale, NJ: Erlbaum.

LEONG, F. T. L. (1996a). Career interventions and assessment in a multicultural world. In R. Feller & G. Walz (Eds.), *Career transitions in turbulent times: Exploring work, learning and careers* (pp. 275–284). Greensboro, NC: Educational Resources Information Center, Counseling and Student Services Clearinghouse.

LEONG, F. T. L. (1996b). Challenges to career counseling: Boundaries, cultures, and complexity. In M. L. Savickas & W. B. Walsh (Eds.), *Handbook of career counseling theory and practice* (pp. 333–346). Palo Alto, CA: Davies-Black.

LEONG, F. T. L., & BROWN, M. T. (1995). Theoretical issues in cross-cultural career development: Cultural validity and cultural specificity. In W. B. Walsh & S. H. Osipow (Eds.), *Handbook of vocational psychology* (2nd ed., pp. 143–180). Mahwah, NJ: Erlbaum.

LEONG, F. T. L., & SERAFICA, F. C. (1995). Career development of Asian Americans: A research area in need of a good theory. In F. T. L. Leong (Ed.), *Career development and vocational behavior of racial and ethnic minorities* (pp. 67–102). Hillsdale, NJ: Erlbaum.

LERNER, R. M. (1979). A dynamic interactional concept of individual and social relationship development. In R. L. Burgess & T. L. Huston (Eds.), *Social change in developing relationships* (pp. 271–305). New York: Academic Press.

LESTER, J. N. (1996). Turbulence at the (Gallup) polls. In R. Feller & G. Walz (Eds.), *Career transitions in turbulent times: Exploring work, learning and careers* (pp. 193–204). Greensboro, NC: Educational Resources Information Center, Counseling and Student Services Clearinghouse.

LEVINSON, D. J. (1978). *The seasons of a man's life*. New York: Ballantine.

LEWIN, K. (1951). *Field theory in social science*. New York: Harper.

LEWIN, R. (1994). *Complexity: Life at the end of chaos*. New York: Macmillan.

LIMERICK, B. (1991). *Career opportunities for teachers in the Queensland Department of Education*. Brisbane, Australia: Department of Education.

LINCOLN, Y. S., & GUBA, E. G. (1985). *Naturalistic inquiry*. Beverly Hills, CA: Sage.

LITTRELL, J. M., LEE-BORDIN, N., & LORENZ, J. A. (1979). A developmental framework for counseling supervision. *Counselor Education and Supervision, 19*, 119–136.

LOGANBILL, C., HARDY, E., & DELWORTH, U. (1982). Supervision: A conceptual model. *Counseling Psychologist, 10*, 3–42.

LYDDON, W. J. (1989). Root metaphor theory: A philosophical framework for counseling and psychotherapy. *Journal of Counseling and Development, 67*, 442–448.

LYNCH, G. (1997). Therapeutic theory and social context: A social constructionist perspective. *British Journal of Guidance and Counselling, 25*, 5–15.

LYON, R. (1965). Beyond the conventional career: Some speculations. *Journal of Counseling Psychology, 12*, 153–158.

LYONS, N. P. (1983). Two perspectives: On self, relationships, and morality. *Harvard Educational Review, 53*, 124–145.

MAHONEY, M. J., & LYDDON, W. J. (1988). Recent developments in cognitive approaches to counseling and psychotherapy. *Counseling Psychologist, 16*, 190–234.

MAHONEY, M. J., & PATTERSON, K. M. (1992). Changing theories of change: Recent developments in counseling. In S. D. Brown & R. W. Lent (Eds.), *Handbook of counseling psychology* (2nd ed., pp. 665–689). New York: Wiley.

MANUELE-ADKINS, C. (1992). Career counseling is personal counseling. *The Career Development Quarterly, 40*, 313–323.

MARGINSON, S. (1997). Careers in a competitive environment. *Australian Journal of Career Development, 6*, 11–15.

MARSHALL, J. (1989). Re-visioning career concepts: A feminist invitation. In M. B. Arthur, D. T. Hall, & B. S. Lawrence (Eds.), *Handbook of career theory* (pp. 275–291). Cambridge, UK: Cambridge University Press.

MCCOWAN, C., & MCKENZIE, M. (1994). *The guide to career education*. Sydney, Australia: New Hobsons Press.

MCCOWAN, C., & MCKENZIE, M. (1997). *The guide to career education* (2nd ed.). Sydney, Australia: New Hobsons Press.

MCCRAE, R. R., & JOHN, O. P. (1992). An introduction to five factor model and its applications. *Journal of Personality, 60*, 175–215.

MCDANIELS, C., & GYSBERS, N. C. (1992). *Counseling for career development: Theories, resources and practice*. San Francisco: Jossey-Bass.

MCDANIELS, C., & WATTS, G. A. (1994). Introduction. *Journal of Career Development, 20*, 263–264.

McLeod, J. (1996). The emerging narrative approach to counselling and psychotherapy. *British Journal of Guidance and Counselling, 24,* 173–184.

McMahon, M. (1992). Examining the context of adolescent career decision making. *Australian Journal of Career Development, 1,* 13–18.

McMahon, M. (1997a). Training and supervision of career counsellors. In W. Patton & M. McMahon (Eds.), *Career development in practice: A systems theory perspective* (pp. 175–186). Sydney, Australia: New Hobsons Press.

McMahon, M. (1997b). Career education. In W. Patton & M. McMahon (Eds.), *Career development in practice: A systems theory perspective* (pp. 131–146). Sydney, Australia: New Hobsons Press.

McMahon, M., & Patton, W. (1994). Career development as explained by children and adolescents: How can career educators respond? *Australian Journal of Guidance and Counselling, 4,* 81–88.

McMahon, M., & Patton, W. (1995). Development of a systems theory framework of career development. *Australian Journal of Career Development, 4,* 15–20.

McMahon, M., & Patton, W. (1997a). Gender differences in influences on the career development of children and adolescents. *School Counselor, 44,* 368–376.

McMahon, M., & Patton, W. (1997b). School as an influence on the career development of students: Comments by young people and considerations for career educators. *Australian Journal of Career Development, 6,* 23–26.

Meara, N., & Patton, M. (1994). Contributions of the working alliance in the practice of career counseling. *The Career Development Quarterly, 43,* 161–177.

Melnick, R. (1975). Counseling response as a function of problem presentation and type of problem. *Journal of Counseling Psychology, 22,* 108–112.

Meyer, R. J., Jr. (1978). Using self-supervision to maintain counseling skills: A review. *Personnel and Guidance Journal, 57,* 95–98.

Miller, M. J. (1983). The role of happenstance in career choice. *The Vocational Guidance Quarterly, 32,* 16–20.

Miller, M. J. (1985). *Report of the Committee of Review of the Aboriginal and Employment Training Programs.* Canberra: Australian Government Publishing Service.

Miller, M. J., Springer, T., & Wells, D. (1988). Which occupational environments do Black youths prefer? Extending Holland's typology. *School Counselor, 36,* 103–106.

Miller-Tiedeman, A. L. (1988). *Lifecareer: The quantum leap into a process theory of career.* Vista, CA: Lifecareer Foundation.

Miller-Tiedeman, A. L. (1989). *How not to make it and succeed: Life on your own terms.* Vista, CA: Lifecareer Foundation.

Miller-Tiedeman, A. L., & Tiedeman, D. V. (1979). *Personal and common realities in careers: A position exemplified in the young adolescent period.* Los Angeles: University of Southern California, National Institute for the Advancement of Career Education.

Miller-Tiedeman, A. L., & Tiedeman, D. V. (1990). Career decision making: An individualistic perspective. In D. Brown & L. Brooks (Eds.), *Career choice and development: Applying contemporary theories to practice* (2nd ed., pp. 308–338). San Francisco: Jossey-Bass.

Minor, C., & Burtnett, P. (Producers). (1983). *Career development: Linking theory with practice* [Videotape]. Arlington, VA: American Association for Counseling and Development.

Minor, C. W. (1992). Career development theories and models. In D. Montross & C. Shinkman (Eds.), *Career development: Theory and practice* (pp. 7–34). Springfield, IL: Charles C Thomas.

Mirvis, P. H., & Hall, D. T. (1996). New organizational forms and the new career. In D. T. Hall (Ed.), *The career is dead–Long live the career* (pp. 72–100). San Francisco: Jossey-Bass.

Mitchell, A. M., Jones, G. B., & Krumboltz, J. D. (Eds.). (1979). *Social learning theory and career decision making.* Cranston, RI: Carroll Press.

Mitchell, L. K., & Krumboltz, J. D. (1990). Social learning approach to career decision making: Krumboltz's theory. In D. Brown & L. Brooks (Eds.), *Career choice and development: Applying contemporary theories to practice* (2nd ed., pp. 145–196). San Francisco: Jossey-Bass.

MITCHELL, L. K., & KRUMBOLTZ, J. D. (1996). Krumboltz's learning theory of career choice and counseling. In D. Brown & L. Brooks (Eds.), *Career choice and development* (3rd ed., pp. 233–280). San Francisco: Jossey-Bass.

MORGAN, K., & BROWN, L. (1991). Lesbian career development, work behavior, and vocational counseling. *Counseling Psychologist, 19,* 273–291.

NATHAN, R., & HILL, L. (1992). *Career Counselling.* Newbury Park, CA: Sage.

NATIONAL BOARD OF EMPLOYMENT, EDUCATION AND TRAINING. (1991). *Strengthening careers education in schools.* Canberra: Australian Government Publishing Service.

NATIONAL CAREER DEVELOPMENT ASSOCIATION, PROFESSIONAL STANDARDS COMMITTEE. (1992). Career counseling competencies. *The Career Development Quarterly, 40,* 378–386.

NEVILL, D. D. (1997). The development of career development theory. *The Career Development Quarterly, 45,* 288–292.

NICHOLSON, N., & WEST, M. (1989). Transitions, work histories and careers. In M. B. Arthur, D. T. Hall, & B. S. Lawrence (Eds.), *Handbook of career theory* (pp. 181–201). Cambridge, UK: Cambridge University Press.

NIEVA, V. F., & GUTEK, B. A. (1981). *Women and work: A psychological perspective.* New York: Praeger.

O'BRIEN, K. M., & HEPPNER, M. J. (1996). Applying social cognitive career theory to training career counselors. *The Career Development Quarterly, 44,* 367–378.

O'HANLON, W. (1993). Possibility therapy: From iatrogenic injury to iatrogenic healing. In S. Gilligan & R. Price (Eds.), *Therapeutic conversations* (pp. 3–17). New York: Norton.

OSIPOW, S. H. (1968). *Theories of career development.* New York: Appleton-Century-Crofts.

OSIPOW, S. H. (1975). The relevance of theories of career development to special groups: Problems, needed data and implications. In J. S. Picou & R. E. Campbell (Eds.), *Career behavior of special groups* (pp. 9–22). Westerville, OH: Merrill.

OSIPOW, S. H. (1983). *Theories of career development* (2nd ed.). Englewood Cliffs, NJ: Prentice Hall.

OSIPOW, S. H. (1990). Convergence in theories of career choice and development. *Journal of Vocational Behavior, 36,* 122–131.

OSIPOW, S. H. (1994). Moving career theory into the twenty-first century. In M. L. Savickas & R. W. Lent (Eds.), *Convergence in career development theories* (pp. 217–225). Palo Alto, CA: CPP.

OSIPOW, S. H. (1996). Does career theory guide practice or does career practice guide theory? In M. L. Savickas & W. B. Walsh (Eds.), *Handbook of career counseling theory and practice* (pp. 403–410). Palo Alto, CA: Davies-Black.

OSIPOW, S. H., & FITZGERALD, L. F. (1993). Unemployment and mental health. *Applied and Preventative Psychology, 2,* 59–64.

OSIPOW, S. H., & FITZGERALD, L. F. (1996). *Theories of career development* (4th ed.). Boston: Allyn & Bacon.

OSIPOW, S. H., & LITTLEJOHN, E. M. (1995). Toward a multicultural theory of career development: Prospects and dilemmas. In F. T. L. Leong (Ed.), *Career development and vocational behavior of racial and ethnic minorities* (pp. 251–261). Hillsdale, NJ: Erlbaum.

OWEN, I. R. (1991). Using the sixth sense: The place and relevance of language in counselling. *British Journal of Guidance and Counselling, 19,* 307–319.

PARSONS, F. (1909). *Choosing a vocation.* Boston: Houghton Mifflin.

PATTERSON, C. H. (1996). Multicultural counseling: From diversity to universality. *Journal of Counseling and Development, 74,* 227–231.

PATTON, W. (1996). Career guidance with the long term unemployed: A field in need of development. *Australian Journal of Career Development, 5,* 24–27.

PATTON, W. (1997). "Double jeopardy": Dealing with multiple career development issues. In W. Patton & M. McMahon (Eds.), *Career development in practice: A systems theory perspective* (pp. 83–94). Sydney, Australia: New Hobsons Press.

PATTON, W., & MCMAHON, M. (1997). *Career development in practice: A systems theory perspective.* Sydney, Australia: New Hobsons Press.

PAUTLER, A. (1996). The high school transition process. In R. Feller & G. Walz (Eds.), *Career transitions in turbulent times: Exploring work, learning and careers* (pp. 331–338). Greensboro, NC: Educational Resources Information Center, Counseling and Student Services Clearinghouse.

PEAVY, R. V. (1992). A constructivist model of training for career counselors. *Journal of Career Development, 18,* 215–229.

PEAVY, R. V. (1996). Counselling as a culture of healing. *British Journal of Guidance and Counselling, 24,* 141–150.

PENA, E. (1997). Great expectations: The reality of the workplace. *Australian Journal of Career Development, 6,* 32–35.

PEPPER, S. (1942). *World hypotheses.* Berkeley: University of California Press.

PERKINS, D. N. (1992). Technology meets constructivism: Do they make a marriage? In T. M. Duffy & D. H. Jonassen (Eds.), *Constructivism and the technology of instruction: A conversation* (pp. 45–56). Hillsdale, NJ: Erlbaum.

PERUN, P., & BIELBY, D. (1981). Towards a model of female occupational behavior: A human development approach. *Psychology of Women Quarterly, 6,* 234–252.

PETERSON, G. W., SAMPSON, J. P., JR., & REARDON, R. C. (1991). *Career development and services: A cognitive approach.* Pacific Grove, CA: Brooks/Cole.

PETERSON, G. W., SAMPSON, J. P., REARDON, R. C., & LENZ, J. G. (1996). A cognitive information processing approach to career problem solving and decision making. In D. Brown & L. Brooks (Eds.), *Career choice and development* (3rd ed., pp. 423–476). San Francisco: Jossey-Bass.

PHILLIPS, S. D. (1994). Choice and change: Convergence from the decision making perspective. In M. L. Savickas & R. W. Lent (Eds.), *Convergence in career development theories* (pp. 155–163). Palo Alto, CA: CPP.

PHILLIPS, S. D. (1997). Toward an expanded definition of adaptive decision making. *The Career Development Quarterly, 45,* 275–287.

PHIPPS, B. (1995). Career dreams of preadolescent students. *Journal of Career Development, 22,* 19–32.

PINKNEY, J., & JACOBS, D. (1985). New counselors and personal interest in the task of career counseling. *Journal of Counseling Psychology, 32,* 454–457.

PLAS, J. M. (1986). *Systems psychology in the schools.* New York: Pergamon.

PLAS, J. M. (1992). The development of systems thinking: A historical perspective. In M. J. Fine & C. Carlson (Eds.), *The handbook of family school intervention: A systems perspective* (pp. 45–56). Boston: Allyn & Bacon.

POOLE, M. E. (1992). Summary and conclusions: Issues in need of policy formation. In M. E. Poole (Ed.), *Education and work* (pp. 230–238). Melbourne, Australia: Australian Council for Educational Research.

POOLE, M. E., & COONEY, G. (1985). Careers: Adolescent awareness and exploration of possibilities for self. *Journal of Vocational Behavior, 26,* 251–263.

POOLE, M. E., & LANGAN-FOX, J. (1997). *Australian women and their careers: Psychological and contextual influences over the lifecourse.* Melbourne, Australia: Cambridge University Press.

POOLE, M. E., LANGAN-FOX, J., CIAVARELLA, M., & OMODEI, M. (1991). A contextualist model of professional attainment: Results of a longitudinal study of career paths of men and women. *Counseling Psychologist, 19,* 603–624.

POOLE, M. E., & LOW, B. (1985). Career and marriage: Orientations of adolescent girls. *Australian Journal of Education, 29,* 36–46.

POPE, M. (Ed.). (1995). Gay and lesbian career development [Special section]. *The Career Development Quarterly, 44* (2), 146–203.

PRIGOGINE, I. (1980). *From being to becoming: Time and complexity in the physical sciences.* San Francisco: W. H. Freeman.

PROCTOR, B. (1994). Supervision: Competence, confidence, accountability. *British Journal of Guidance and Counselling, 22,* 309–318.

PRYOR, R. G. L. (1985a). Toward a composite theory of career development and choice. *British Journal of Guidance and Counselling, 13,* 225–237.

PRYOR, R. G. L. (1985b). Towards exorcising the self-concept from psychology: Some comments on Gottfredson's circumscription / compromise theory. *Journal of Counseling Psychology, 32,* 154–158.

PRYOR, R. G. L. (1991). Policy challenges confronting careers guidance: Introduction. *British Journal of Guidance and Counselling, 19,* 225–229.

PRYOR, R. G. L. (1993). Returning from the wilderness: Personality in career decision making. *Australian Journal of Career Development, 2,* 13–17.

PSATHAS, G. (1968). Toward a theory of occupational choice for women. *Sociology and Social Research, 52,* 253–268.

RAYNOR, J. O. (1982). Self-possession of attributes, self-evaluation and future orientation: A theory of adult competence motivation. In J. O. Raynor & E. E. Entin (Eds.), *Motivation, career striving and aging* (pp. 207–226). New York: Hemisphere.

REISING, G. N., & DANIELS, M. H. (1983). A study of Hogan's model of counselor development and supervision. *Journal of Counseling Psychology, 30,* 235–244.

REMLEY, T. P., JR., BENSHOFF, J. M., & MOWBRAY, C. A. (1987). A proposed model for peer supervision. *Counselor Education and Supervision, 27,* 53–60.

RICHARDSON, M. S. (1993). Work in people's lives: A location for counseling psychologists. *Journal of Counseling Psychology, 40,* 425–433.

RICHARDSON, M. S. (1996). From career counseling to counseling / psychotherapy and work, jobs, and career. In M. L. Savickas & W. B. Walsh (Eds.), *Handbook of career counseling theory and practice* (pp. 347–360). Palo Alto, CA: Davies-Black.

ROBERTS, E. B., & BORDERS, L. D. (1994). Supervision of school counselors: Administrative program and counseling. *The School Counselor, 41,* 149–157.

ROBERTS, K. (1968). The entry into employment: An approach towards a general theory. *Sociological Review, 16,* 165–184.

ROBERTS, K. (1977). The social conditions, consequences and limitations of career guidance. *British Journal of Guidance and Counselling, 5,* 1–9.

ROE, A. (1956). *The psychology of occupations.* New York: Wiley.

ROE, A. (1957). Early determinants of vocational choice. *Journal of Counseling Psychology, 4,* 212–217.

ROE, A., & LUNNEBORG, P. (1990). Personality development and career choice. In D. Brown & L. Brooks (Eds.), *Career choice and development: Applying contemporary theories to practice* (2nd ed., pp. 68–101). San Francisco: Jossey-Bass.

ROKEACH, M. (1973). *The nature of human values.* New York: Free Press.

ROSE, H. (1986). Women's work: Women's knowledge. In J. Mitchell & A. Oakley (Eds.), *What is feminism?* (pp. 57–81). Oxford, UK: Blackwell.

ROUNDS, J. B., & HESKETH, B. (1994). The theory of work adjustment: Unifying principles and concepts. In M. L. Savickas & R. W. Lent (Eds.), *Convergence in career development theories: Implications for science and practice* (pp. 177–186). Palo Alto, CA: CPP.

ROUNDS, J. B., & TRACEY, T. J. (1990). From trait-and-factor to person-environment fit counseling: Theory and process. In W. B. Walsh & S. H. Osipow (Eds.) *Career counseling: Contemporary topics in vocational psychology* (pp. 1–45). Hillsdale, NJ: Erlbaum.

ROUNDS, J. B., & TRACEY, T. J. (1996). Cross-cultural structural equivalence of RIASEC models and measures. *Journal of Counseling Psychology, 43,* 310–329.

SAMPSON, J. P., JR., KOLODINSKY, R. W., & GREENO, B. P. (1997). Counseling on the information highway: Future possibilities and potential problems. *Journal of Counseling and Development, 75,* 203–212.

SAMPSON, J. P., JR., PETERSON, G. W., LENZ, J. G., & REARDON, R. C. (1992). A cognitive approach to career services: Translating concepts into practice. *The Career Development Quarterly, 41,* 67–74.

SAVICKAS, M. L. (1991). Improving career time perspective. In D. Brown & L. Brooks (Eds.), *Career counseling techniques* (pp. 236–249). Needham Heights, MA: Allyn & Bacon.

SAVICKAS, M. L. (1992). New directions in career assessment. In D. H. Montross & C. J. Shinkman (Eds.), *Career development: Theory and practice* (pp. 336–355). Springfield, IL: Charles C Thomas.

SAVICKAS, M. L. (1993). Career counseling in the postmodern era. *Journal of Cognitive Psychotherapy: An International Quarterly, 7,* 205–215.

SAVICKAS, M. L. (1994). Donald Edwin Super: The career of a planful explorer. *The Career Development Quarterly, 43,* 4–24.

SAVICKAS, M. L. (1995). Current theoretical issues in vocational psychology: Convergence, divergence, and schism. In W. B. Walsh & S. H. Osipow (Eds.), *Handbook of vocational psychology* (pp. 1–34). Mahwah, NJ: Erlbaum.

SAVICKAS, M. L. (1996a). A framework for linking career theory and practice. In M. L. Savickas & W. B. Walsh (Eds.), *Handbook of career counseling theory and practice* (pp. 191–208). Palo Alto, CA: Davies-Black.

SAVICKAS, M. L. (1996b). Public policy and career counseling for the twenty first century [Special section]. *The Career Development Quarterly, 45,* 3–4.

SAVICKAS, M. L. (1997). Career adaptability: An integrative construct for life-span, life-space theory. *The Career Development Quarterly, 45,* 247–259.

SAVICKAS, M. L., & LENT, R. W. (Eds.). (1994). *Convergence in career development theories: Implications for science and practice.* Palo Alto, CA: CPP.

SAVICKAS, M. L., & WALSH, W. B. (Eds.). (1996). *Handbook of career counseling theory and practice.* Palo Alto, CA: Davies-Black.

SAVICKI, V., & COOLEY, E. J. (1982). Implications of burnout research and theory for counselor educators. *Personnel and Guidance Journal, 11,* 47–53.

SAVICKI, V., & COOLEY, E. J. (1987). The relationship of work environment and client contact to burnout in mental health professionals. *Journal of Counseling and Development, 65,* 249–252.

SCHEIN, E. H. (1984). Culture as an environment context for careers. *Journal of Occupational Behavior, 5,* 71–81.

SEARS, S. (1982). A definition of career guidance terms: A National Vocational Guidance Association perspective. *Vocational Guidance Quarterly, 31,* 137–143.

SENGE, P. (1990). *The fifth discipline: The art and practice of the learning organization.* Sydney, Australia: Random House.

SHARF, R. (1992). *Applying career development theory to counseling.* Pacific Grove, CA: Brooks/Cole.

SHARF, R. (1997). *Applying career development theory to counseling* (2nd ed.). Pacific Grove, CA: Brooks/Cole.

SHEARS, M. (1996). Career education state by state. *Australian Journal of Career Development, 5,* 3–11.

SHOHET, R., & WILMOT, J. (1991). The key issue in the supervision of counsellors: The supervisory relationship. In W. Dryden & B. Thorne (Eds.), *Training and supervision for counselling in action* (pp. 87–98). Newbury Park, CA: Sage.

SMITH, E. J. (1983). Issues in racial minorities' career behavior. In W. B. Walsh & S. H. Osipow (Eds.), *Handbook of vocational psychology* (pp. 161–222). Hillsdale, NJ: Erlbaum.

SONNENFELD, J., & KOTTER, J. P. (1982). The maturation of career theories. *Human Relations, 35,* 19–46.

SPOKANE, A. R. (1994). The resolution of incongruence and the dynamics of person-environment fit. In M. L. Savickas & R. W. Lent (Eds.), *Convergence in career development theories* (pp. 119–138). Palo Alto, CA: CPP.

SPOKANE, A. R. (1996). Holland's theory. In D. Brown & L. Brooks (Eds.), *Career choice and development* (3rd ed., pp. 33–74). San Francisco: Jossey-Bass.

SPOKANE, A. R., & GLICKMAN, I. T. (1994). Light, information, inspiration, cooperation: Origins of the clinical science of career intervention. *Journal of Career Development, 20,* 295–304.

STALEY, W. L., & CAREY, A. L. (1997). The role of school counselors in facilitating a quality twenty-first century workforce. *School Counselor, 44,* 377–383.

STEENBARGER, B. N. (1991). All the world is not a stage: Emerging contextualist themes in counseling and development. *Journal of Counseling and Development, 70,* 268–296.

STEENBARGER, B. N., & SMITH, H. B. (1996). Assessing the quality of counseling services: Developing accountable helping systems. *Journal of Counseling and Development, 75,* 145–150.

STOLTENBERG, C. D., & DELWORTH, U. (1987). *Supervising counselors and therapists: A developmental approach.* San Francisco: Jossey-Bass.

STRONG, E. K., JR., & CAMPBELL, D. P. (1981). *Strong-Campbell Interest Inventory.* Stanford, CA: Stanford University Press.

SUBICH, L. M. (1993). How personal is career counseling? [Special section]. *The Career Development Quarterly, 42,* 129–131.

SUBICH, L. M., & TAYLOR, K. M. (1994). Emerging directions of social learning theory. In M. L. Savickas & R. W. Lent (Eds.), *Convergence in career development theories* (pp. 167–176). Palo Alto, CA: CPP.

SUPER, D. E. (1953). A theory of vocational development. *American Psychologist, 8,* 185–190.

SUPER, D. E. (1957). *The psychology of careers.* New York: Harper & Row.

SUPER, D. E. (1980). A life-span, life-space approach to career development. *Journal of Vocational Behavior, 16,* 282–298.

SUPER, D. E. (1990). A life-span, life-space approach to career development. In D. Brown & L. Brooks (Eds.), *Career choice and development: Applying contemporary theories to practice* (2nd ed., pp. 197–261). San Francisco: Jossey-Bass.

SUPER, D. E. (1992). Toward a comprehensive theory of career development. In D. H. Montross & C. J. Shinkman (Eds.), *Career development: Theory and practice* (pp. 35–64). Springfield, IL: Charles C Thomas.

SUPER, D. E. (1994). A life-span, life-space perspective on convergence. In M. L. Savickas & R. W. Lent (Eds.), *Convergence in career development theories* (pp. 63–74). Palo Alto, CA: CPP.

SUPER, D. E., & KNASEL, E. G. (1981). Career development in adulthood: Some theoretical problems and a possible solution. *British Journal of Guidance and Counselling, 9,* 194–201.

SUPER, D. E., & NEVILL, D. D. (1984). Work role salience as a determinant of career maturity in high school students. *Journal of Vocational Behavior, 25,* 30–44.

SUPER, D. E., SAVICKAS, M. L., & SUPER, C. M. (1996). The life-span, life-space approach to careers. In D. Brown & L. Brooks, (Eds.), *Career choice and development* (3rd ed., pp. 121–178). San Francisco: Jossey-Bass.

SWANSON, J. L. (1992). The structure of vocational interests for African American college students. *Journal of Vocational Behavior, 40,* 129–143.

SWANSON, J. L. (1993). Integrating a multicultural perspective into training for career counseling: Programmatic and individual interventions. *The Career Development Quarterly, 42,* 41–49.

TAYLOR, M. (1994). Supervision in counselling and guidance: An introduction. *British Journal of Guidance and Counselling, 22,* 307–308.

TAYLOR, N. B. (1985). How do careers counsellors counsel? *British Journal of Guidance and Counselling, 13,* 166–177.

TAYLOR, R. (1997). Career development, socioeconomic disadvantage and participation in higher education. In W. Patton & M. McMahon (Eds.), *Career development in practice: A systems theory perspective* (pp. 59–70). Sydney, Australia: New Hobsons Press.

THOMAS, R. J. (1989). Blue collar careers: Meaning and choice in a world of constraints. In M. B. Arthur, D. T. Hall, & B. S. Lawrence (Eds.), *Handbook of career theory* (pp. 354–379). Cambridge, UK: Cambridge University Press.

TIEDEMAN, D. V., & O'HARA, R. P. (1963). *Career development: Choice and adjustment.* New York: College Entrance Examination Board.

TYLER, L. (1967). The encounter with poverty: Its effect on vocational psychology. *Rehabilitation Psychology Bulletin, 11,* 61–70.

USHER, C. H., & BORDERS, D. L. (1993). Practicing counselors' preferences for supervisory style and supervisory emphasis. *Counselor Education and Supervision, 33*, 66–79.

VALACH, L. (1990). A theory of goal-directed action in career analysis. In R. A. Young & W. A. Borgen (Eds.), *Methodological approaches to the study of career* (pp. 107–126). Westport, CT: Praeger.

VAN MAANEN, J. (1977). *Organizational career: Some new perspectives*. New York: Wiley.

VARGUS, I. D. (1977). Supervision in social work. In D. J. Karpius & A. Kadushin (Eds.), *Supervision of Applied Training* (p. 153). Westport, CT: Greenwood Press.

VETTER, L. (1973). Career counseling for women. *Counseling Psychologist, 4*, 54–66.

VON BERTALANFFY, L. (1940). Der organismus als psysikalisches system betrachtet. *Die Naturwissenschaften, 28*, 521–531.

VON BERTALANFFY, L. (1968). *General system theory*. New York: George Braziller.

VONDRACEK, F. W. (1990). A developmental-contextual approach to career development research. In R. A. Young & W. A. Borgen (Eds.), *Methodological approaches to the study of career* (pp. 37–56). New York: Praeger.

VONDRACEK, F. W., & FOUAD, N. A. (1994). Developmental-contextualism: An integrative framework for theory and practice. In M. L. Savickas & R. W. Lent (Eds.), *Convergence in career development theories* (pp. 207–214). Palo Alto, CA: CPP.

VONDRACEK, F. W., & KAWASAKI, T. (1995). Toward a comprehensive framework for adult career development theory and intervention. In W. B. Walsh & S. H. Osipow (Eds.), *Handbook of vocational psychology* (2nd ed., pp. 111–141). Mahwah, NJ: Erlbaum.

VONDRACEK, F. W., LERNER, R. M., & SCHULENBERG, J. E. (1983). The concept of development in vocational theory and intervention. *Journal of Vocational Behavior, 23*, 179–202.

VONDRACEK, F. W., LERNER, R. M., & SCHULENBERG, J. E. (1986). *Career development: A life-span developmental approach*. Hillsdale, NJ: Erlbaum.

WADE, D. C., COOLEY, E. J., & SAVICKI, V. (1986). A longitudinal study of burnout. *Children and Youth Services Review, 8*, 161–173.

WALDROP, M. M. (1992). *Complexity: The emerging science at the edge of order and chaos*. New York: Simon & Schuster.

WALSH, W. B., & CHARTRAND, J. M. (1994). Emerging directions of person-environment fit. In M. L. Savickas & R. W. Lent (Eds.), *Convergence in career development theories* (pp. 187–196). Palo Alto, CA: CPP.

WALZ, G., & FELLER, R. (1996). The summing up and a leap to the future. In R. Feller & G. Walz (Eds.), *Career transitions in turbulent times: Exploring work, learning and careers* (pp. 431–434). Greensboro, NC: Educational Resources Information Center, Counseling and Student Services Clearinghouse.

WARNATH, C. F. (1975). Vocational theories: Direction to nowhere. *Personnel and Guidance Journal, 53*, 422–428.

WARNKE, M., KIM, J., KOELTZOW-MILSTER, D., TERRELL, S., DAUSER, P., DIAL, S., HOWIE, J., & THIEL, M. (1993). Career counseling practicum: Transformations in conceptualising career issues. *The Career Development Quarterly, 42*, 180–185.

WARR, P. (1980). The springs of action. In A. Chapman & D. Jones (Eds.), *Models of man* (pp. 161–182). Leicester, UK: British Psychological Society.

WATKINS, C. E. (1994a). On hope, promise, and possibility in counseling psychology, or some simple, but meaningful observations about our speciality. *Counseling Psychologist, 22*, 315–334.

WATKINS, C. E. (1994b). Whole school guidance? *British Journal of Guidance and Counselling, 22*, 143–150.

WATSON, H. J., VALLEE, J. M., & MULFORD, W. R. (1980). *Structured experiences and group development*. Canberra, Australia: Curriculum Development Centre.

WATSON, M. B., STEAD, G. B., & SCHONEGEVEL, C. (1997, July). *Does Holland's career hexagon shape up for disadvantaged students?* Paper presented at the 20th International School Psychology Colloquium, Melbourne, Australia.

WATTS, A. G. (1996a). The changing concept of career: Implications for career counseling. In R. Feller & G. Walz (Eds.), *Career transitions in turbulent times: Exploring work, learning and careers* (pp. 229–236). Greensboro, NC: Educational Resources Information Center, Counseling and Student Services Clearinghouse.

WATTS, A. G. (1996b). Computers in guidance. In A. G. Watts, B. Law, J. Killeen, J. M. Kidd, & R. Hawthorn (Eds.), *Rethinking careers education and guidance: Theory, policy and practice* (pp. 269–283). London: Routledge.

WATTS, A. G. (1996c). Toward a policy for lifelong career development: A transatlantic perspective. *The Career Development Quarterly, 45,* 41–53.

WEINRACH, S. G., & SREBALUS, D. J. (1990). Holland's theory of careers. In D. Brown & L. Brooks (Eds.), *Career choice and development: Applying contemporary theories to practice* (2nd ed., pp. 37–68). San Francisco: Jossey-Bass.

WHITE, B., COX, C., & COOPER, C. (1992). *Women's career development: A study of high fliers.* Oxford, UK: Blackwell.

WHITE, M., & EPSTON, D. (1989). *Literate means to therapeutic ends.* Adelaide, Australia: Dulwich Centre Publications.

WHITE, M., & EPSTON, D. (1990). *Narrative means to therapeutic ends.* New York: Norton.

WHITEHEAD, A. N. (1925). *Science and the modern world.* New York: Macmillan.

WIJERS, G. A., & MEIJERS, F. (1996). Careers guidance in the knowledge society. *British Journal of Guidance and Counselling, 24,* 185–198.

WILEY, M., & RAY, P. (1986). Counseling supervision by developmental level. *Journal of Counseling Psychology, 33,* 439–445.

WILLIAMSON, E. (1939). *How to counsel students: A manual of techniques for clinical counselors.* New York: McGraw-Hill.

WILLIAMSON, E. (1965). *Vocational counseling: Some historical, philosophical, and theoretical perspectives.* New York: McGraw-Hill.

WIRTH-BOND, S., COYNE, A., & ADAMS, M. (1991). A school counseling program that reduces dropout rate. *School Counselor, 39,* 131–137.

WOLFE, D. M., & KOLB, D. A. (1980). Career development, personal growth, and experimental learning. In J. W. Springer (Ed.), *Issues in career and human resource development* (pp. 1–11). Madison, WI: American Society for Training and Development.

YOUNG, R. A. (1983). Career development of adolescents: An ecological perspective. *Journal of Youth and Adolescence, 12,* 401–417.

YOUNG, R. A., & BORGEN, W. A. (Eds.). (1990). *Methodological approaches to the study of career.* New York: Praeger.

YOUNG, R. A., & COLLIN, A. (1988). Career development and hermeneutical inquiry Part 1: The framework of a hermeneutical approach. *Canadian Journal of Counselling, 22,* 153–161.

YOUNG, R. A., & COLLIN, A. (Eds.). (1992). *Interpreting career: Hermeneutical studies of lives in context.* Westport, CT: Praeger.

YOUNG, R. A., & VALACH, L. (1996). Interpretation and action in career counseling. In M. L. Savickas & W. B. Walsh (Eds.), *Handbook of career counseling theory and practice* (pp. 361–376). Palo Alto, CA: Davies-Black.

YOUNG, R. A., VALACH, L., & COLLIN, A. (1996). A contextual explanation of career. In D. Brown & L. Brooks (Eds.), *Career choice and development* (3rd ed., pp. 477–512). San Francisco: Jossey-Bass.

YOUNG, R. A., VALACH, L., DILLABOUGH, J., DOVER, C., & MATTHES, G. (1994). Career research from an action perspective: The self-confrontation procedure. *The Career Development Quarterly, 43,* 185–196.

ZOHAR, D. (1991). *The quantum self: Human nature and consciousness defined by the new physics.* New York: Morrow.

ZUNKER, V. G. (1994). *Career counseling: Applied concepts of life planning* (4th ed.). Pacific Grove, CA: Brooks/Cole.

ZYTOWSKI, D. G. (1969). Toward a theory of career development for women. *Personnel and Guidance Journal, 47,* 660–664.

ZYTOWSKI, D. G., & SWANSON, J. L. (1994). Parsons' contribution to career assessment. *Journal of Career Development, 20,* 303–310.

INDEX

CREDITS

This page constitutes an extension of the copyright page. We have made every effort to trace the ownership of all copyrighted material and to secure permission from copyright holders. In the event of any question arising as to the use of any material, we will be pleased to make the necessary corrections in future printings. Thanks are due to the following authors, publishers, and agents for permission to use the material indicated.

Chapter 2:17: Table 2.1 from "Returning from the wilderness: Personality in career decision making," by R.G.L. Pryor, *Australian Journal of Career Development, 2(3)*, 15. Copyright ©1993 The Australian Council for Educational Research Ltd. Reprinted with permission. **21**: Figure 2.1 from *Holland in Australia: A vocational choice theory in research and practice* (p. xvii), by J.J. Lokan and K.F. Taylor (Eds.). Copyright ©1986 The Australian Council for Educational Research Ltd. Reprinted with permission.

Chapter 3:41: List of 14 Propositions from *Career Choice and Development: Applying Contemporary Theories to Practice, 2nd ed.* by Brown, D., and Brooks, L. (Eds.), pp. 206–208 Copyright ©1990 Jossey-Bass Inc. Publishers. Reprinted with permission. **45**: Figure 3.1 from *Guided Career Exploration*. Copyright ©1979 The Psychological Corporation. All rights reserved. Reprinted with permission. **47**: Figure 3.2 from *Career choice and development: Applying contemporary theories to practice, 2nd edition* by D. Brown and L. Brooks (Eds.), p. 200. Copyright ©1990 Jossey Bass. Reprinted with permission. **54**: Figure 3.3 from "Circumscription and compromise: A developmental theory of occupational aspirations," by L.S. Gottfredson, *Journal of Counseling Psychology Monograph 28(6)*, p. 547. Copyright ©1981 American Psychological Association. Reprinted with permission.

Chapter 4:65: Figure 4.1 from *Career choice and development, 3rd edition*, by D. Brown and L. Brooks (Eds.), p. 387. Copyright ©1993 R.W. Lent, S.D. Brown & G. Hackett. Reprinted with permission. **67**: Figure 4.2 from *Career Development and Services: A Cognitive Approach* by G.W. Peterson, J.P. Sampson, and R.C. Reardon. Copyright ©1991 Brooks/Cole Publishing Company, Pacific Grove, CA 93950, a division of International Thomson Publishing Inc. Reprinted with permission. **69**: Figure 4.3 from *Career Development: A life-span developmental approach* by F.W. Vondracek, R.M. Lerner and J.E. Schulenberg (Eds.), p. 79. Copyright ©1986 L. Erlbaum Associates. Adapted with permission from Lerner, 1984.

Figures 9.1–9.9, 10.1, 12.1, 13.1 from *Career Development in practice: A systems theory perspective* by Patton, W., & McMahon, M. (Eds.), New Hobsons Press, Sydney, Australia. Copyright ©1997 W. Patton & M. McMahon. Reprinted with permission.

TO THE OWNER OF THIS BOOK:

We hope that you have found *Career Development and Systems Theory* useful. So that this book can be improved in a future edition, would you take the time to complete this sheet and return it? Thank you.

School and address: ——————————————————————————

Department: ——————————————————————————

Instructor's name: ——————————————————————————

1. What I like most about this book is: ——————————————————

——————————————————————————————

——————————————————————————————

2. What I like least about this book is: ——————————————————

——————————————————————————————

——————————————————————————————

3. My general reaction to this book is: ——————————————————

——————————————————————————————

4. The name of the course in which I used this book is: ——————————

——————————————————————————————

5. Were all of the chapters of the book assigned for you to read? ——————

   If not, which ones weren't? ——————————————————————

6. In the space below, or on a separate sheet of paper, please write specific suggestions for improving this book and anything else you'd care to share about your experience in using the book.

——————————————————————————————

——————————————————————————————

——————————————————————————————

——————————————————————————————

——————————————————————————————

Optional:

Your name: _____ Date: _____

May Brooks/Cole quote you, either in promotion for *Career Development and Systems Theory* or in future publishing ventures?

Yes: _____ No: _____

Sincerely,

Wendy Patton
Mary McMahon

FOLD HERE

‖‖‖‖

BUSINESS REPLY MAIL

FIRST CLASS   PERMIT NO. 358   PACIFIC GROVE, CA

POSTAGE WILL BE PAID BY ADDRESSEE

ATT: *Wendy Patton, Mary McMahon* _____

**Brooks/Cole Publishing Company
511 Forest Lodge Road
Pacific Grove, California 93950-9968**

‖‖‖‖‖‖‖‖‖‖‖‖‖‖‖‖‖‖‖‖‖‖‖‖‖‖‖‖‖‖‖‖

FOLD HERE